P9-AQF-276

ZAGAT 2014

Los Angeles Restaurants

SENIOR CONSULTING EDITOR
Merrill Shindler

LOCAL EDITORS
Melissa Brandzel, Gillian Ferguson and Grace Jidoun

STAFF EDITOR
Michelle Golden

Published and distributed by
Zagat Survey, LLC
76 Ninth Avenue
New York, NY 10011
T: 212.977.6000
E: feedback@zagat.com
www.zagat.com

ACKNOWLEDGMENTS

We're grateful to our local editors, Merrill Shindler, an ABC radio commentator, food writer, critic and a Zagat editor for more than 25 years; Melissa Brandzel, a freelance writer and cookbook editor; Gillian Ferguson, supervising producer of KCRW's Good Food and freelance food writer; and Grace Jidoun, a freelance food writer. We also sincerely thank the thousands of people who participated in this survey - this guide is really "theirs."

We also thank Stefanie Tuder (editor), Andy Dolan and Toby Nathan, as well as the following members of our staff: Aynsley Karps (editor), Brian Albert, Sean Beachell, Maryanne Bertollo, Reni Chin, Larry Cohn, Nicole Diaz, Kelly Dobkin, Jeff Freier, Alison Gainor, Justin Hartung, Marc Henson, Anna Hyclak, Ryutaro Ishikane, Natalie Lebert, Mike Liao, Vivian Ma, Molly Moker, Polina Paley, Josh Siegel, Albry Smither, Chris Walsh, Art Yagci, Sharon Yates, Anna Zappia and Kyle Zolner.

ABOUT ZAGAT

In 1979, we asked friends to rate and review restaurants purely for fun. The term "user-generated content" had yet to be coined. That hobby grew into Zagat Survey; 34 years later, we have loyal surveyors around the globe and our content now includes nightlife, shopping, tourist attractions, golf and more. Along the way, we evolved from being a print publisher to a digital content provider. We also produce marketing tools for a wide range of corporate clients, and you can find us on Google+ and just about any other social media network.

The reviews in this guide are based on public opinion surveys. The ratings reflect the average scores given by the survey participants who voted on each establishment, while the text is based on quotes from, or paraphrasings of, the surveyors' comments. Ratings and reviews have been updated throughout this edition based on our most recent survey results. Phone numbers, addresses and other factual data were correct to the best of our knowledge when published in this guide.

JOIN IN

To improve our guides, we solicit your comments - positive or negative; it's vital that we hear your opinions. Just contact us at **nina-tim@zagat.com.**

ISBN-13: 978-1-60478-571-5
ISBN-10: 1-60478-571-3
Printed in the
United States of America

Contents

Ratings & Symbols

	Name	Symbols	Cuisine	Zagat Ratings			
				FOOD	DECOR	SERVICE	COST
Area, Address & Contact	Tim & Nina's	◐	*Asian*	▽ 23	9	13	$15

Hollywood | 346 Sunset Blvd. (1st St.) | 213-555-2570 | www.zagat.com

Review, surveyor comments in quotes

"Trend"-spotters hail this "high-concept" production on Sunset offering "fantastic" Asian-deli fare that includes "tantalizing tongue sushi" slathered in "to-die-for hijiki coleslaw"; decor that "hasn't changed since Cecil B. DeMille" was a regular and "reeeal New Yawk-style" service don't seem to deter "agents", "stars" and "working gals" hooked on the "delicious sake-celery soda-tinis."

Ratings **Food, Decor** & **Service** are rated on a 30-point scale.

- 26 - 30 extraordinary to perfection
- 21 - 25 very good to excellent
- 16 - 20 good to very good
- 11 - 15 fair to good
- 0 - 10 poor to fair
- ▽ low response | less reliable

Cost The price of dinner with a drink and tip; lunch is usually 25% to 30% less. For unrated **newcomers,** the price range is as follows:

I	$25 and below	E	$41 to $65
M	$26 to $40	VE	$66 or above

Symbols

- ◐ serves after 11 PM
- Ⓢ closed on Sunday
- Ⓜ closed on Monday
- ⊄ cash only

Maps Index maps show restaurants with the highest Food ratings and other notable places in those areas.

Los Angeles at a Glance

WINNERS:

- **Asanebo** (Food)
- **The Belvedere** (Decor)
- **Mélisse** (Service)
- **Sugarfish by Sushi Nozawa** (Most Popular)
- **Bestia** (No. 1 Newcomer)

SURVEY STATS:

- 1,499 restaurants covered
- 19,694 surveyors
- In our recent Dining Trends Survey, Los Angeles respondents reported that they eat 2.4 dinners out per week, spending an average of $38.62 per person, just under the national average of $40.53.
- When presented with a choice of dining irritants, surveyors selected noise as the most irritating, with 76% of diners saying they avoid restaurants that are too loud.
- Forty-nine percent of Los Angeles surveyors typically make restaurant reservations online, and the same percentage will not wait more than 30 minutes at places that don't take reservations.
- The majority of surveyors (58%) feels that taking pictures of food in a restaurant is ok in moderation, but 33% say it's rude and inappropriate for children to use tablets, iPads and mobile phones at the table.
- Seafood tops the list of cuisines Los Angeles surveyors would like to see more of in their area.

TRENDS: Seafood shacks (**Connie & Ted's, Fishing with Dynamite, Littlefork, Salt Air**); fusion madness (**Alma, Circa, Corazon y Miel, Trois Mec**); small plates still reign (**Bar Amá, Bamboo Izakaya, Paiche, Taberna Arros y Vi**); killer cocktails (**Hinoki & The Bird, MessHall Kitchen, Paiche, Petty Cash**)

HOT NEIGHBORHOODS: Downtown (**Alma, Bar Amá , Bestia, Parish Wine Bar**); Hollywood (**Aventine, Littlefork, Trois Mec**); Little Osaka (**Clusi Batusi, Flores, Tsujita Annex**); South Bay (**Chez Soi, Circa, Fishing with Dynamite, Paiche, Little Sister**); Venice (**Barnyard, Hostaria del Piccolo, Salt Air, Willie Jane**); West Hollywood (**Connie & Ted's, Crossroads Vegan, Fatty's Public House, Hart & the Hunter, RivaBella Ristorante**)

MOST-SEARCHED ON ZAGAT.COM: Bouchon, Boa, The Ivy, Katsuya, Gjelina, Cut, Nobu, Mozza, Bazaar, Piccolo

Los Angeles, CA
September 26, 2013

Merrill Shindler

Key Newcomers

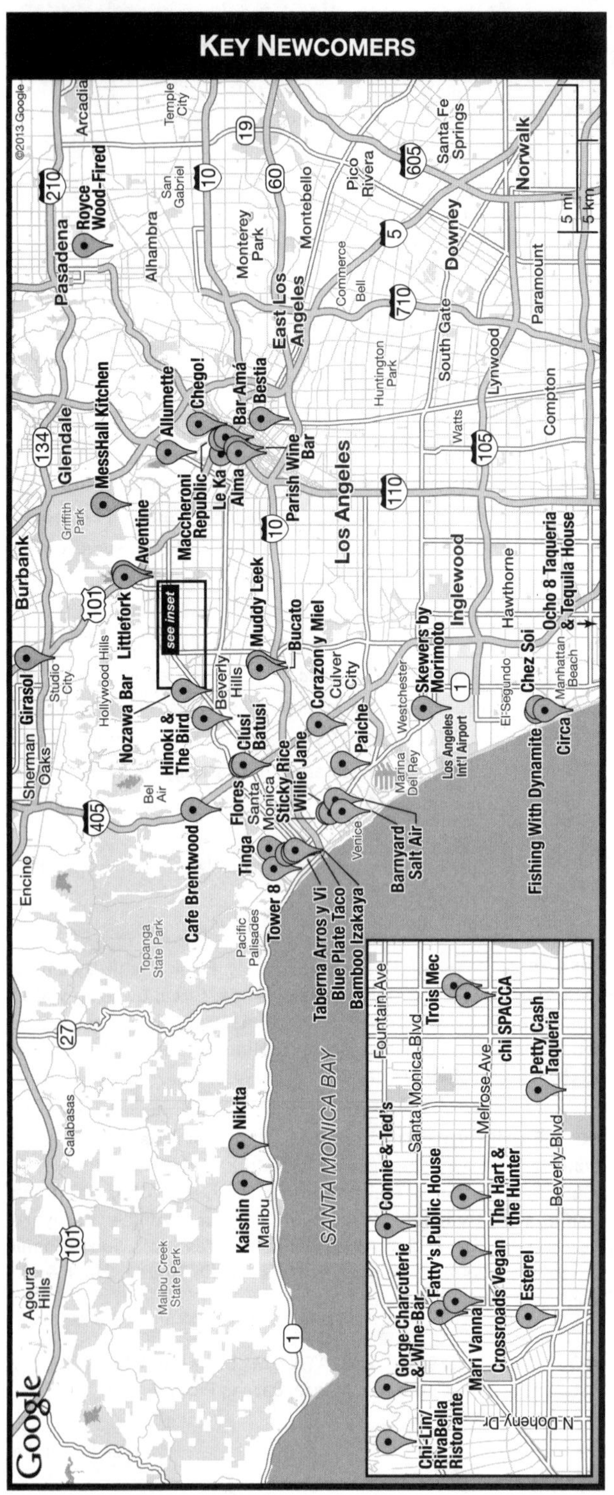

Key Newcomers

Our editors' picks among this year's arrivals. See full list at p. 220.

BIG NAMES

Alma
Bar Amá
Bestia
Chego!
Chez Soi
Chi SPACCA
Circa
Connie & Ted's
Fishing with Dynamite
Hinoki & The Bird
Littlefork
Nozawa Bar
Paiche
Parish Wine Bar
Trois Mec
Willie Jane

EXPENSE ACCOUNT

Esterel
Mari Vanna
Royce Wood-Fired Steakhouse
Tower 8

STRIKING SPACES

Aventine
Chi-Lin
Crossroads Vegan
Hart & the Hunter
Le Ka
Nikita
RivaBella Ristorante

INNOVATORS

Corazon y Miel
Flores
Girasol
Gorge Charcuterie & Wine Bar
Taberna Arros y Vi

NEIGHBORHOOD STARS

Allumette
Bamboo Izakaya
Barnyard
Bucato
Cafe Brentwood
Fatty's Public House
Kaishin
MessHall Kitchen
Muddy Leek
Ocho 8 Taqueria & Tequila House
Salt Air

BARGAIN BITES

Blue Plate Taco
Clusi Batusi
Maccheroni Republic
Petty Cash Taqueria
Skewers by Morimoto
Sticky Rice
Tinga

2014 looks to be the year of LAX's long-planned restaurant upgrade, which means once you're through the rigors of TSA, you can refuel at outposts of local hot spots like **Border Grill, Chaya, Ink Sack, LAMILL Coffee, The Larder** and **Umami Burger** among others. Also in the works: Miami's flashy **Barton G** is headed for La Cienega; the latest incarnation of Nguyen and Thi Tran's pop-up, **Starry Kitchen,** featuring out-there Southeast Asian fare, will open in Chinatown's **Grand Star Jazz Club**; and a branch of Thai street-fooder **Night + Market** is coming to Silver Lake. Walter Manzke is moving ahead with **Republique Restaurant & Bakery,** now planned for the former **Campanile** space. The Sunset Marquis will get **Cavatina,** a modern Med, while Iron Chef Masaharu Morimoto moves into the Hotel Andaz at Sunset. The high-end **Hakkasan** is heading to the MGM Building in Beverly Hills. We'll finally get a Scandinavian restaurant when **Gravlax** opens in Culver City. On Melrose, look for **Gracias Madre,** a Mexican vegan concept from **Café Gratitude.** Downtown's hot streak continues with Josef Centeno's **Orsa & Winston** and a new branch of West LA's venerable **Sushi Zo.** Finally, word is that Nashville institution **Prince's Hot Chicken Shack** is looking for an LA location.

Most Popular

This list is plotted on the map at the back of this book.

1. Sugarfish | *Japanese*
2. Angelini Osteria | *Italian*
3. Mélisse | *American/French*
4. Bazaar by José Andrés | *Spanish*
5. Spago | *Californian*
6. Providence | *American/Seafood*
7. Osteria Mozza | *Italian*
8. In-N-Out Burger | *Burgers*
9. Lawry's The Prime Rib | *Steak*
10. Mastro's Steakhouse | *Steak*
11. Brent's Deli | *Deli*
12. Pizzeria Mozza | *Pizza*
13. Cafe Bizou | *French*
14. Bouchon | *French*
15. Lucques | *Cal./Med.*
16. Ruth's Chris Steak House | *Steak*
17. Palm | *Steak*
18. Chinois on Main | *Asian/French*
19. M.B. Post | *American*
20. Din Tai Fung | *Chinese*
21. Bottega Louie | *Italian*
22. Valentino* | *Italian*
23. Bäco Mercat | *Sandwiches*
24. Drago Centro | *Italian*
25. Umami Burger | *Burgers*
26. A.O.C. | *Cal./French*
27. Joe's | *Californian/French*
28. JiRaffe | *American/French*
29. Hatfield's | *American*
30. Roy's | *Hawaiian*
31. Ink | *American/Eclectic*
32. Gjelina | *American*
33. Morton's | *Steak*
34. Parkway Grill | *Californian*
35. Boa | *Steak*
36. Animal | *American*
37. Father's Office* | *American*
38. Water Grill | *Seafood*
39. Craft | *American*
40. Michael's on Naples | *Italian*
41. Piccolo* | *Italian*
42. Daily Grill | *American*
43. Patina* | *American/Californian*
44. Cut | *Steak*
45. Philippe/Original | *Sandwiches*
46. Arroyo Chop House | *Steak*
47. Border Grill | *Mexican*
48. Cheesecake Factory* | *American*
49. Crustacean | *Asian/Vietnamese*
50. Grill on the Alley* | *American*
51. Il Fornaio | *Italian*
52. Saddle Peak Lodge* | *American*
53. Apple Pan | *American*
54. Tar & Roses* | *Eclectic*
55. Fig & Olive | *Mediterranean*
56. Langer's Deli* | *Deli*
57. Matsuhisa* | *Japanese*
58. Hillstone/Houston's | *American*
59. Ivy | *Californian*
60. Fleming's Prime | *Steak*

Many of the above restaurants are among the Los Angeles area's most expensive, but if popularity were calibrated to price, a number of other restaurants would surely join their ranks. To illustrate this, we have added two pages of Best Buys starting on page 16.

* Indicates a tie with restaurant above

Top Food

29 Asanebo | *Japanese*

28 Sushi Zo | *Japanese*
Hamasaku | *Japanese*
Mélisse | *American/French*
Matsuhisa | *Japanese*
Providence | *American/Seafood*
Angelini Osteria | *Italian*
Urasawa | *Japanese*

27 Gjelina Take Away | *Amer.*
Michael's on Naples | *Italian*
Michael's Pizzeria | *Pizza*
Shiro | *French/Japanese*
Bazaar by José Andrés | *Spanish*
Sushi Masu | *Japanese*
Saam/The Bazaar | *Eclectic*
M.B. Post | *American*
Piccolo | *Italian*
Kiwami | *Japanese*
Hatfield's | *American*
Katsu-ya | *Japanese*
Cut | *Steak*
Lucques | *Cal./Med.*
Pizzeria Mozza | *Pizza*
Leila's | *Californian*
Nanbankan | *Japanese*
Spago | *Californian*
Brandywine | *Continental*
Bashan | *American*
Osteria Mozza* | *Italian*
Babita Mexicuisine | *Mexican*
Animal | *American*
Jitlada | *Thai*
Nobu Malibu | *Japanese*
N/Naka | *Japanese*
Christine | *Med./Pacific Rim*
Mori Sushi | *Japanese*

26 Nobu Los Angeles | *Japanese*
Mistral | *French*
Takao | *Japanese*
Vito's | *Pizza*

Top Decor

28 Belvedere
Mar'sel

27 Sir Winston's
Saddle Peak Lodge
Royce Wood-Fired
Bazaar by José Andrés
Sky Room
WP24
Yamashiro
Cicada
Getty Center

26 Geoffrey's Malibu
Red O
Providence
Crustacean
Penthouse*
Inn of the Seventh Ray
Perch
Mélisse
Culina Modern Italian

Top Service

27 Mélisse
Providence
Urasawa
N/Naka
Belvedere
Shiro
Patina

26 Royce Wood-Fired
Sam's by the Beach
Saam/The Bazaar
Hatfield's
Valentino
Lawry's The Prime Rib
Brandywine
Michael's on Naples
Spago
Rustico
Mistral
Cut
Saddle Peak Lodge

Excludes places with low votes, unless otherwise indicated

TOPS BY CUISINE

AMERICAN (NEW)

28 Mélisse
Providence
27 Gjelina Take Away
M.B. Post
Hatfield's

AMERICAN (TRAD.)

25 Grill on the Alley
Farmshop
Griddle Cafe
Clementine
24 Grill on Hollywood/Westlake

ASIAN/ASIAN FUSION

26 Chinois on Main
25 Crustacean
24 Lukshon
Gina Lee's
23 Spice Table

BAKERIES

25 Porto's Bakery
Bouchon Bakery
Euro Pane
Clementine
24 Joan's on Third Café

BARBECUE

25 Bludso's BBQ
24 Phillips BBQ
Woody's BBQ
23 Johnny Rebs'
Beachwood BBQ

BURGERS

25 Golden State
24 Tommy's
23 In-N-Out Burger
Hole in the Wall
25 Degrees

CALIFORNIAN

27 Lucques
Leila's
Spago
26 Patina
Joe's

CARIBBEAN/CUBAN

25 Porto's Bakery
23 Prado
22 Cha Cha Chicken
Versailles
21 Cha Cha Cha

CHINESE

26 Din Tai Fung
Newport Seafood
25 WP24
Sea Harbour
Elite

CONTINENTAL

27 Brandywine
26 Café 14
25 Dal Rae
24 Sir Winston's
23 Lulu's Cafe

DELIS

26 Bay Cities Deli
Brent's Deli
Langer's Deli
22 Barney Greengrass
Pico Kosher Deli

DIM SUM

25 WP24
Sea Harbour
Elite
21 Bao Dim Sum
Sea Empress

DINERS

23 Cora's Coffee
22 101 Coffee Shop
Uncle Bill's Pancake
21 Nickel Diner
Johnnie's Pastrami

ECLECTIC

27 Saam/The Bazaar
26 Ink
Chez Mélange
25 Depot
Street

FRENCH

28 Mélisse
27 Shiro
26 Mistral
Joe's
Café Beaujolais

GREEK

24 Petros
22 Great Greek
Taverna Tony
Papa Cristo's
Le Petit Greek

INDIAN

26 Addi's Tandoor
24 Bombay Palace
23 Clay Oven
India's Tandoori
22 Nawab of India

ITALIAN

28 Angelini Osteria
27 Michael's on Naples
Piccolo
Osteria Mozza
26 Via Veneto

JAPANESE

29 Asanebo
28 Sushi Zo
Hamasaku
Matsuhisa
Urasawa

KOREAN

25 Park's BBQ
Genwa
24 Soot Bull Jeep
ChoSun Galbee
23 Chego!

MEDITERRANEAN

27 Lucques
Christine
26 Cleo
25 Sam's by the Beach
Tasting Kitchen

MEXICAN

27 Babita
26 El Tepeyac
25 Yuca's
Chichen Itza
24 Alegria on Sunset

MIDDLE EASTERN

26 Raffi's Place
25 Carousel
Carnival
24 Open Sesame
23 Shamshiri Grill

PIZZA

27 Michael's Pizzeria
Pizzeria Mozza
26 Vito's
Mozza to Go
Gjelina

SEAFOOD

28 Providence
26 Water Grill
Son of a Gun
25 Santa Monica Seafood
L&E Oyster Bar

SMALL PLATES

27 Bazaar by José Andrés
M.B. Post
Leila's
26 Cleo
K-Zo

SOUL/SOUTHERN

23 Johnny Rebs'
Les Sisters
Roscoe's
22 Lucille's BBQ
- Willie Jane

SOUTH AMERICAN

25 Picca
24 Mario's Peruvian
Carlitos Gardel
23 Malbec
Mo-Chica

STEAKHOUSES

27 Cut
26 Mastro's Steakhouse
Lawry's Prime Rib
25 Arroyo Chop House
Ruth's Chris

THAI

27 Jitlada
24 Ayara Thai
Sanamluang Cafe
23 Bangkok West
Cholada

VEGETARIAN

23 Café Gratitude
True Food Kitchen
22 Native Foods Café
M Café de Chaya
Veggie Grill

VIETNAMESE

25 Pho So 1
Golden Deli
Crustacean
23 Pho 79
22 Red Medicine

TOPS BY SPECIAL FEATURE

BREAKFAST

25 Julienne
Farmshop
Griddle Cafe
Clementine
24 Milo & Olive

BRUNCH

26 Belvedere
Saddle Peak Lodge
Gjelina
25 Tasting Kitchen
22 Square One Dining

BUSINESS DINING

28 Mélisse
Providence
27 Hatfield's
Cut
Lucques

CRAFT COCKTAILS

27 M.B. Post
26 Rivera
25 Bestia
A.O.C.
- Petty Cash Taqueria

HOTEL DINING

27 Bazaar by José Andrés (SLS)
Saam/The Bazaar (SLS)
Cut (Beverly Wilshire)
26 Belvedere (Peninsula BH)
Cleo (Redbury Hotel)

ICONIC LA

27 Spago
23 Philippe the Original
22 Musso & Frank Grill
21 Pink's Famous Hot Dogs
17 Cole's

LATE DINING

27 Pizzeria Mozza
25 Park's BBQ
24 Pacific Dining Car
23 Dan Tana's
Roscoe's Chicken/Waffles

LOCAVORE/ FARM-TO-TABLE

26 Gjelina
25 Farmshop
Rustic Canyon
24 Tar & Roses
23 Cooks Country

LUNCH

29 Asanebo
28 Matsuhisa
Angelini Osteria
27 Pizzeria Mozza
Spago

NEWCOMERS (RATED)

25 Bestia
24 Royce Wood-Fired
23 Chego!
Hinoki & The Bird
Hole in the Wall

OUTDOOR SEATING

27 Lucques
Spago
26 Belvedere
Saddle Peak Lodge
Joe's

PEOPLE-WATCHING

27 Bazaar by José Andrés
M.B. Post
Nobu Malibu
25 Giorgio Baldi
22 Urth Caffé

POWER SCENES

28 Matsuhisa
Providence
27 Spago
25 Grill on the Alley
24 Wolfgang Puck at Hotel Bel-Air

RAW BARS

26 Water Grill
25 Santa Monica Seafood
L&E Oyster
23 Lobster
- Connie & Ted's

ROMANTIC

28 Mélisse
Providence
27 Michael's on Naples
Bazaar by José Andrés
Piccolo

TRENDY

26 Gjelina
25 Bestia
Bäco Mercat
23 Hinoki & The Bird
- Trois Mec

VIEWS

26 Water Grill (Santa Monica)
Saddle Peak Lodge
Mar'sel
25 Katana
WP24

WINNING BEER LISTS

25 Hot's Kitchen▽
23 Waterloo & City
Black Market Liquor Bar
Father's Office
22 The Misfit

WINNING WINE LISTS

28 Mélisse
27 Bazaar by José Andrés
Saam/The Bazaar
Cut
Lucques

TOPS BY OCCASION

Some best bets in a range of prices and cuisines for these occasions.

ANNIVERSARY

28 Providence
27 Lucques
Spago
26 JiRaffe
25 A.O.C.

BOOZY BRUNCH

27 M.B. Post
25 Bouchon
Raymond
22 Fig
20 Fat Dog

BREAKFAST MEETINGS

24 Maison Giraud
Tavern
22 Barney Greengrass
21 Art's Deli
Nate 'n Al

BRIDAL SHOWERS

28 Mélisse
26 Belvedere
24 Wolfgang Puck at Hotel Bel-Air
23 One Pico
20 Penthouse

FIRST DATE

25 Bestia
A.O.C.
23 Hinoki & The Bird
21 Superba Snack Bar▽
– Fishing with Dynamite

GROUP BIRTHDAY DINNER

27 Pizzeria Mozza
26 Lawry's The Prime Rib
25 Park's BBQ
24 Guelaguetza
23 Bottega Louie

LUNCH WITH YOUR AGENT

28 Providence
26 Sugarfish
25 Craft
Grill on the Alley
22 Musso & Frank Grill

OUTDOOR HAPPY HOUR

26 Drago Centro
25 Street
21 Bar Pintxo
Sunny Spot
17 Perch

POP THE QUESTION

28 Mélisse
26 Patina
Mar'sel
25 Bistro 45
23 Sky Room

POST-WORKOUT

24 Sycamore Kitchen
23 Tender Greens
Café Gratitude
22 M Café de Chaya
21 A Votre Sante

STARGAZING AROUND AWARDS SEASON

28 Matsuhisa
27 Spago
Nobu Malibu
23 Mr. Chow
22 Polo Lounge

TOPS BY LOCATION

BEVERLY BOULEVARD

28 Angelini Osteria
26 Hirozen
25 A.O.C.
24 Jar
23 Susina Bakery & Café

BEVERLY HILLS

28 Matsuhisa
Urasawa
27 Bazaar by José Andrés
Saam/The Bazaar
Cut

BRENTWOOD

26 Takao
Sugarfish
Vincenti
25 Palmeri
Toscana

CHINATOWN

23 Chego!
Philippe the Original
22 Yang Chow
21 Ocean Seafood Restaurant
20 CBS Seafood

DOWNTOWN

26 Sugarfish
Water Grill
Patina
Rivera
Langer's Deli

FAIRFAX

27 Animal
25 Golden State
24 Mendocino Farms
23 Umami Burger
22 Lotería! Grill

HOLLYWOOD

28 Providence
27 Pizzeria Mozza
Osteria Mozza
26 Cleo
25 Stella Barra Pizzeria

LA BREA

24 Cube Cafe
22 Tinga
21 Pink's Famous Hot Dogs
20 Ca'Brea
19 Wirtshaus

LONG BEACH

27 Michael's on Naples
Michael's Pizzeria
25 555 East
24 Café Piccolo
Open Sesame

LOS FELIZ/SILVER LAKE

25 Forage
Yuca's
L&E Oyster Bar
24 Alegria on Sunset
Barbrix

MALIBU

27 Nobu Malibu
24 Malibu Seafood
23 Tra di Noi Ristorante
Mr. Chow
Cholada

MELROSE

27 Hatfield's
24 Carlitos Gardel
Red O
23 Foundry on Melrose
Sweet Lady Jane

PASADENA AREA

27 Shiro
26 Din Tai Fung
Parkway Grill
Café Beaujolais
Maison Akira*

SAN FERNANDO VALL.

29 Asanebo
27 Kiwami
Katsu-ya
Brandywine
Bashan

SAN GABRIEL VALL.

27 Babita Mexicuisine
26 Newport Seafood
25 Dal Rae
Sea Harbour
Golden Deli

SANTA MONICA

28 Mélisse
26 Sugarfish
Chinois on Main
Water Grill
Via Veneto

SOUTH BAY

27 M.B. Post
Christine
26 Addi's Tandoor
Chef Melba's Bistro
Chez Mélange

THIRD STREET

26 Son of a Gun
25 Izaka-ya by Katsu-ya
24 Locanda Veneta
Joan's on Third Cafe
23 Olio Pizzeria & Cafe

VENICE

27 Gjelina Take Away
Piccolo
26 Joe's
Gjelina
25 Ado

WEST HOLLYWOOD

27 Lucques
26 Nobu Los Angeles
Vito's
Mozza to Go
Ink

WEST LA

28 Sushi Zo
Hamasaku
27 Sushi Masu
Nanbankan
Mori Sushi

TOPS BY DESTINATION

A selection of the best bets in a range of prices and cuisines near these points of interest.

DISNEY HALL

26 Sugarfish
Water Grill
Patina
Drago Centro
25 Cicada

DODGER STADIUM

24 Tommy's
23 Philippe the Original
Bottega Louie
22 Yang Chow
Border Grill

DOWNTOWN ARTS DISTRICT/GALLERY ROW

25 Bestia
24 Church & State
23 Wurstküche
21 Nickel Diner
17 Cole's

GRIFFITH PARK

25 Yuca's
22 Little Dom's
Palermo
21 Alcove
18 Fred 62

HOLLYWOOD WALK OF FAME

24 Littlefork∇
Grill on Hollywood
Katsuya
23 25 Degrees
22 Lotería! Grill

LA LIVE/STAPLES CENTER

26 Rivera
25 WP24
Bäco Mercat
24 Katsuya
19 El Cholo

MUSEUM ROW/ MIRACLE MILE

27 Animal
25 Golden State
23 Cooks County
20 Wood Ranch BBQ & Grill
Gumbo Pot

SANTA MONICA PIER

24 Tar & Roses
23 Cora's Coffee Shoppe
22 Blue Plate Oysterette
Ivy at the Shore
16 Blue Plate Taco∇

THIRD ST. PROMENADE

24 Michael's Restaurant
22 Lotería! Grill
Hillstone/Houston's
21 Bar Pintxo
- Taberna Arros y Vi

Best Buys

Top-rated restaurants $25 and under, unless otherwise noted

1. Gjelina Take Away | *Amer.*
2. Michael's Pizzeria | *Pizza*
3. Vito's | *Pizza*
4. Din Tai Fung | *Chinese*
5. Bay Cities Deli | *Deli*
6. Brent's Deli | *Deli*
7. Langer's Deli | *Deli*
8. El Tepeyac | *Mexican*
9. Tsujita LA | *Japanese*
10. Kogi | *Korean/Mexican*
11. Golden State | *Burgers*
12. Porto's Bakery | *Bakery/Cuban*
13. Forage | *Californian*
14. Hakata Ramen | *Japanese*
15. Euro Pane | *Bakery*
16. Yuca's | *Mexican*
17. Pho So 1 | *Vietnamese*
18. Village Pizzeria | *Pizza*
19. Blu Jam | *American/European*
20. Golden Deli | *Vietnamese*
21. Bludso's BBQ | *BBQ*
22. Griddle Cafe | *American*
23. Clementine | *American*
24. Santouka Ramen | *Japanese*
25. Chichen Itza | *Mexican*
26. Carnival | *Lebanese*
27. Alegria on Sunset | *Mexican*
28. Malibu Seafood | *Seafood*
29. Mario's Peruvian | *Peruvian*
30. Artisan Cheese | *Sandwiches*
31. Open Sesame | *Lebanese*
32. Eatalian | *Italian*
33. Tommy's | *Burgers/Hot Dogs*
34. Guelaguetza | *Mexican*
35. Daikokuya | *Japanese*
36. Phillips Bar-B-Que | *BBQ*
37. Ayara Thai | *Thai*
38. Boiling Crab | *Cajun/Seafood*
39. Joan's on Third Cafe | *American*
40. Grub | *American*

BEST BUYS BY NEIGHBORHOOD

BEVERLY HILLS

23 Mulberry Street Pizzeria
22 M Café de Chaya
Urth Caffé
Il Tramezzino
21 Greenleaf Gourmet

BRENTWOOD

23 India's Tandoori
22 Fish Grill
21 A Votre Sante
Lemonade
Barney's Gourmet Burgers

DOWNTOWN

26 Langer's Deli
25 Chichen Itza
24 Tommy's
Mendocino Farms
23 Wurstküche

HOLLYWOOD

25 Village Pizzeria
Griddle Cafe
24 Mario's Peruvian
Grub
23 In-N-Out

LOS FELIZ/SILVER LAKE

25 Forage
Yuca's
24 Alegria on Sunset
22 Tomato Pie
LAMILL Coffee Boutique

PASADENA

25 Euro Pane
23 Luggage Room Pizzeria
Roscoe's Chicken/Waffles
Tender Greens
Umami Burger

SANTA MONICA

26 Bay Cities Deli
23 Huckleberry Café & Bakery
Father's Office
Bangkok West
Sweet Lady Jane

VENICE

- 27 Gjelina Take Away
- 23 Abbot's Pizza Company
- Wurstküche
- 3 Square Cafe + Bakery
- Café Gratitude

WEST HOLLYWOOD

- 26 Vito's
- 24 Mendocino Farms
- 23 Lulu's Cafe
- Joe's Pizza
- Tender Greens

BEST BUYS BY CATEGORY

ALL YOU CAN EAT

- 24 Bombay Palace ($12.95)
- 23 Clay Oven ($9.95)
- India's Tandoori ($7.95)
- 22 Nawab ($10.95)
- Robin's Woodfire ($13.95)

BYO

- 25 Yuca's
- 24 Malibu Seafood
- Boiling Crab
- 23 Chego!
- Lulu's Café

CHEAP DATES

- 26 Tsujita LA
- 24 Malibu Seafood
- Pho Café∇
- 23 Wurstküche
- Nyala Ethiopian

FAMILY-STYLE

- 26 Din Tai Fung
- 25 Carnival
- 24 Boiling Crab
- Woody's BBQ
- 23 Luggage Room Pizzeria

HOMETOWN CLASSICS

- 23 Roscoe's Chicken/Waffles
- Philippe the Original
- Casa Bianca
- 21 Zankou Chicken
- 20 Canter's

KID-FRIENDLY

- 23 Philippe the Original
- Umami Burger
- Mulberry Street Pizzeria
- Ocean Seafood
- 21 Oinkster

NOODLE SHOPS

- 26 Tsujita LA
- 25 Hakata Ramen
- Santouka Ramen
- 24 Daikokuya
- 23 Ramen Jinya

PRIX FIXE LUNCH

- 27 Pizzeria Mozza ($20)
- 26 Sugarfish ($17)
- Joe's ($19)
- 23 Katsuya ($12)
- Restaurant 2117 ($18)

PRIX FIXE DINNER

- 27 Lucques ($45, Sundays only)
- Bashan ($40, Tuesday-Thursday)
- Nanbankan ($23)
- 24 Katsuya ($25)
- 23 Restaurant 2117 ($25)

TAQUERIAS

- 25 Yuca's
- Chichen Itza
- 24 CaCao Mexicatessen
- 22 Lotería! Grill
- Tinga

RESTAURANT DIRECTORY

	FOOD	DECOR	SERVICE	COST

Abbot's Pizza Company *Pizza* 23 | 10 | 18 | $14

Venice | 1407 Abbot Kinney Blvd. (California Ave.) | 310-396-7334 | www.abbotspizzaco.com

"Ex-New Yorkers" sing the praises of the "excellent", "chewy-crust" 'za at this "funky" Venice pizzeria also featuring "idiosyncratic" creations like "delicious" salad-topped and bagel-crusted pies; service nets mixed reviews, and "with precious little seating" in the "utilitarian" setting, many find takeout or delivery "much more tolerable."

Abigaile *American* 19 | 20 | 20 | $43

Hermosa Beach | 1301 Manhattan Ave. (bet. 14th St. & Pier Ave.) | 310-999-3508 | www.abigailerestaurant.com

Craft beer and a "foodie"-friendly American menu featuring pig Pop Tarts come together at this "noisy", artfully graffitied microbrewery in Hermosa Beach that was once a church and rehearsal space for punk band Black Flag; moderate prices, "friendly service" and "magnificent ocean views" seal the deal.

Abricott *Eclectic* ▽ 22 | 18 | 19 | $20

Pasadena | 238 S. Lake Ave. (bet. Cordova St. & Del Mar Blvd.) | 626-796-1613 | www.abricott.com

Internationalists welcome the "surprising" Eclectic menu bringing together Thai, Vietnamese and French (pho, grilled seafood, croque monsieur with frites) at this morning-to-night Pasadena eatery set in an "arty, relaxed" space lined with books; "large servings" for "reasonable prices" are deemed an "unbelievable value" and the mood is "friendly", leading early backers to "hope it stays forever."

Absolutely Phobulous *Vietnamese* 20 | 12 | 18 | $15

West Hollywood | 350 N. La Cienega Blvd. (Oakwood Ave.) | 310-360-3930
Encino | 15928 Ventura Blvd. (bet. Gaviota & Gloria Aves.) | 818-788-3560 ⊠
Tarzana | 18612 Ventura Blvd. (bet. Amigo & Yolanda Aves.) | 818-757-0460 Ⓜ
www.abpho.com

"If you can't make it" to Little Saigon, this "cheap, cheerful" Vietnamese mini-chain "will do", serving up bowls of "straightforward" pho plus "huge, fresh" spring rolls - all deemed "authentic enough"; service gets mixed marks and the "plain" decor is just "one step up from a diner", but "no one cares when slurping up" the soups.

Aburiya Toranoko *Japanese* 22 | 20 | 20 | $43

Downtown | 243 S. San Pedro St. (bet. 2nd & 3rd Sts.) | 213-621-9500 | www.toranokola.com

This "groovy izakaya on the edge of Little Tokyo" caters to Downtown's "loud", "hip and tattooed" with "interesting, tasty" Japanese small plates and sushi; bills can "run high" if you factor in cocktails, but on the whole, it's a lot of "fun."

Adagio Ⓜ *Italian* 22 | 16 | 23 | $39

Woodland Hills | 22841 Ventura Blvd. (Fallbrook Ave.) | 818-225-0533

"Gracious" owner Claudio Gontier "makes it a joy to visit" this Woodland Hills "classic" turning out "consistently good", "uncomplicated" Northern Italian; while a few note the "old standby" could use "some freshening up", its "personal" service coupled with "more-than-fair" tabs have kept neighborhood customers "coming back for years"; P.S. "reservations advised", especially on the weekends.

Addi's Tandoor *Indian* 26 | 18 | 24 | $30

Redondo Beach | 800 Torrance Blvd. (bet. PCH & Prospect Ave.) | 310-540-1616 | www.addistandoor.com

"Fabulous Goan-inspired" Indian cuisine with plenty of "heat" waits at this "neighborhood treasure" in Redondo Beach; "don't let the strip-mall location fool you" - bills can be a little "pricey", the setting is "inviting" and the service is "top-notch" too; P.S. reservations recommended.

Admiral Risty *Seafood* 22 | 20 | 22 | $42

Rancho Palos Verdes | Golden Cove Shopping Ctr. | 31250 Palos Verdes Dr. W. (Hawthorne Blvd.) | 310-377-0050 | www.admiral-risty.com

The "beautiful" ocean views "go on and on" at this '60s "stalwart" in Palos Verdes serving "well-prepared, basic" seafood along with "perfect" martinis in a nautical setting overseen by an "experienced, genuine" crew; so while the "dazzling" sunsets tend to trump the surf 'n' turf, backers point out "it's been there since the beginning of time so they must be doing something right"; P.S. frequent live music at the bar adds to the atmosphere.

Ado *Italian* 25 | 19 | 22 | $57

Venice | 796 Main St. (Abbot Kinney Blvd.) | 310-399-9010 | www.adovenice.com

Casa Ado *Italian*

Marina del Rey | 12 Washington Blvd. (Speedway) | 310-577-2589 | www.casaado.com

Out of an "unassuming little yellow cottage", this Venice "gem" (with a larger outpost in Marina del Rey) delivers "luscious" Italian fare to a "trendy" clientele; though "crowded" tables are a drawback, the candlelit setting is otherwise "romantic" and the "charming" staff "greets you like friends", so it's a "special" (and "expensive") "treat."

A-Frame *Eclectic* 23 | 18 | 20 | $34

Culver City | 12565 W. Washington Blvd. (Neosho Ave.) | 310-398-7700 | www.aframela.com

"The fried chicken alone is worth the price of admission" at this "hip", well-priced Culver City Eclectic from Roy Choi featuring an "inventive", globe-trotting "mash-up" of dishes in an old IHOP; it can be "loud and hectic" and you'll sit "elbow-to-elbow" at "picnic-style communal tables", but for most the "delicious" eats make up for it.

Ago *Italian* 22 | 21 | 21 | $59

West Hollywood | 8478 Melrose Ave. (La Cienega Blvd.) | 323-655-6333 | www.agorestaurant.com

"The people-watching alone" scores points at this West Hollywood "showbiz hangout" co-owned by Robert De Niro, where luminaries "turn heads" on the tiled patio, often overshadowing the "excellent" Tuscan food by Agostino Sciandri; observers say the "accommodating" service is even more so "if you're a known entity" and bills seem "too expensive for what you get", but after brushing shoulders with the A-list in "lovely" environs, most feel they "totally got their money's worth."

	FOOD	DECOR	SERVICE	COST

Agra Cafe *Indian* 22 | 14 | 17 | $20

Silver Lake | Sunset Plaza | 4325 W. Sunset Blvd. (Fountain Ave.) | 323-665-7818 | www.agracafe.com

Tucked in amongst a "liquor store and tae kwon do studio", this "secluded" Silver Laker plates "consistent", "correctly spiced" Indian fare that makes for "bargain" meals; service can vary, but most find it "A-ok" and call the "online ordering" a plus.

Ahi Sushi *Japanese* 23 | 18 | 20 | $32

Studio City | 12915 Ventura Blvd. (Coldwater Canyon Ave.) | 818-981-0277 | www.ahisushi.com

"Inventive and delicious" takes on both its namesake and crudo make this "cozy" Japanese stand out on Studio City's sushi row, as does its premium on "fresh, fresh, fresh" fish; maybe the interior is "nothing special", but "outdoor dining" helps lure a loyal clientele.

AKA Bistro *American* 23 | 23 | 22 | $36

Pasadena | One Colorado | 41 Hugus Alley (De Lacey Ave.) | 626-564-8111 | www.akabistro.com

Set in an "old-school brick courtyard away from the street" in Old Pasadena's One Colorado Plaza, this "easy" New American from Robert Simon (Bistro 45) delivers "high-quality" gastropub grub backed by a "winning wine list" in a "hip", yet "relaxing" setting with a "beautiful" patio; an "eager-to-please" staff and moderate pricing make it a "top choice for the neighborhood."

Akasha *American* 22 | 21 | 21 | $39

Culver City | 9543 Culver Blvd. (Washington Blvd.) | 310-845-1700 | www.akasharestaurant.com

It's now a Culver City "standby", but chef-owner Akasha Richmond's updated "farm-to-table" cuisine is as "consistently exciting" as ever at this "reasonable" New American, known for its "healthy", "organic-driven" menu and "top-notch desserts"; the "airy" space sports concrete floors and high ceilings, so "go early before the noise level deafens" or snag a seat on the patio.

Akbar Cuisine of India *Indian* 22 | 17 | 20 | $28

Marina del Rey | 3115 Washington Blvd. (bet. Stanford & Yale Aves.) | 310-574-0666

Santa Monica | 2627 Wilshire Blvd. (bet. Princeton & 26th Sts.) | 310-586-7469

Hermosa Beach | 1101 Aviation Blvd. (Prospect Ave.) | 310-937-3800

Pasadena | 44 N. Fair Oaks Ave. (Union St.) | 626-577-9916

www.akbarcuisineofindia.com

"Rich, complex flavors" skew to "the spicy side" but can be "adjusted to your liking" at this "stellar" Indian chainlet where "a mix of traditional and modern dishes" and "delicious" naan are set down by "pleasant" servers; the ambiance varies by location, but prices are eminently "reasonable" and regulars insist it "never disappoints."

Alcove ◐ *American* 21 | 21 | 18 | $21

Los Feliz | 1929 Hillhurst Ave. (bet. Finley & Franklin Aves.) | 323-644-0100 | www.alcovecafe.com

Los Feliz hipsters fill up the "amazing sun-drenched patio" at this "adorable" bungalow boasting "tasty" American eats, "jet-fuel" coffee and "indulgent" desserts "so picture-perfect you feel lustful just looking at them"; true, the counter-service line can get a little "chaotic", but it's perennially "popular" so clearly no one minds too much.

Alegria *Nuevo Latino* 23 | 21 | 22 | $31

Long Beach | 115 Pine Ave. (bet. B'way & 1st St.) | 562-436-3388 | www.alegriacocinalatina.com

A "wonderful variety" of Nuevo Latino dishes turns up at this Downtown Long Beacher, where highly "drinkable" sangria fuels the "party atmosphere" amid mosaic-adorned surroundings; flamenco dancers provide "evening entertainment" some nights, so though some gripe that the "food could be better", for a "fun" atmosphere, this "is the place to go."

Alegria on Sunset ☒ *Mexican* 24 | 15 | 21 | $22

Silver Lake | 3510 W. Sunset Blvd. (Golden Gate Ave.) | 323-913-1422 | www.alegriaonsunset.com

It's "like eating in your mother's kitchen (if your mother was Mexican)" at this "cute" neighborhood standby in a "random strip mall in Silver Lake" serving "unique" regional fare like "superb mole" that's "comforting and consistent"; the digs are colorful, and although it's "small and crowded, that doesn't hurt the food"; P.S. there's no alcohol, but don't miss the "amazing" fresh-fruit elixirs muddled with herbs.

Alejo's Italian Restaurant *Italian* 21 | 11 | 19 | $22

Westchester | 8343 Lincoln Blvd. (bet. 83rd & 85th Sts.) | 310-670-6677 | www.alejoswestchester.com

"Garlic, garlic everywhere" "keeps vampires at bay" at this "neighborhood staple" in Westchester doling out "huge portions" of "homey" Italian fare; true, the "stripped-down" setting is "not the greatest", but the mood is "exuberant" and bills are "small", so "good luck getting in."

Alessio Bistro *Italian* 21 | 19 | 20 | $33

West Hills | Platt Vill. | 6428 Platt Ave. (bet. Haynes St. & Victory Blvd.) | 818-710-0270 | www.alessiobistro.com

Bistro Alessio *Italian*

Northridge | 9725 Reseda Blvd. (Superior St.) | 818-709-8393 | www.bistroalessio.com

Tucked away in the "sleepy" North Valley suburbs, this separately owned pair of "neighborhood" Italians are "reliable" venues for "tasty", well-priced fare; there's "more noise and bustle" due to weekend live music at the West Hills locale, but in general both branches offer a "relaxing" vibe, and though service garners mixed reviews, most agree they're "local favorites."

Alfredo's *Mexican* ∇ 26 | 19 | 26 | $19

Lomita | 2372 PCH (Pennsylvania Ave.) | 310-784-0393 | www.alfredosrestaurant.com

This Lomita Mexican "satisfies cravings" with a broad menu of "perfectly cooked" traditional dishes plus some less common Yucatán-influenced specialties; the "atmosphere is a little cold", but prices are "fair" so most insist "you have to try it."

	FOOD	DECOR	SERVICE	COST

All India Cafe *Indian* 21 | 14 | 18 | $22

West LA | Santa Monica Plaza | 12113 Santa Monica Blvd. (Bundy Dr.) | 310-442-5250
Pasadena | 39 S. Fair Oaks Ave. (bet. Colorado Blvd. & Green St.) | 626-440-0309
www.allindiacafe.com

The menu's chock-"full of variety" at this "brightly decorated" Indian chainlet in Pasadena and West LA serving "consistently good" if "not spectacular" cuisine alongside some "interesting" uncommon dishes like Frankie rolls; "friendly" servers and "decent" prices help offset the "slow" pace of things as well as "crowds" and "noise."

NEW **Allumette** S M *American* - | - | - | M

Echo Park | 1320 Echo Park Ave. (bet. Montana St. & Sunset Blvd.) | 213-935-8787 | www.allumettela.com

This moderately priced New American brings one more bit of culinary gentrification to formerly funky Echo Park, with a limited menu (no more than 12–15 dishes per night) of farm-sourced fare; all dark-wood and red accents, the dining room features a small bar that serves drinks with names like Gentleman's Breakfast (made with two brands of scotch).

NEW **Alma** S M *American* ▽ 26 | 15 | 23 | $51

Downtown | 952 S. Broadway (Olympic Blvd.) | 213-244-1422 | www.alma-la.com

"Talented chef" Ari Taymor has anchored his once-roving pop-up at this Downtown "rendezvous", serving "mind-blowing" "seasonal" New American fare (e.g. seaweed-and-tofu beignets) with a focus on small plates; just "don't let the humble decor fool you", as these "moments of brilliance" don't come cheap.

Amalfi *Italian* ▽ 20 | 19 | 19 | $41

La Brea | 143 N. La Brea Ave. (bet. Beverly Blvd. & 1st St.) | 323-938-2504 | www.amalfiristorante.com

"Reliable, if not thrilling" is the word on this La Brea "neighborhood Italian" plying pizzas and pastas (including a noteworthy pumpkin ravioli with short rib) in a cozy setting and also playing host to a lively bar scene and comedy acts next door; even if a few feel it's "nothing to run back for", it's deemed a "solid", midrange choice if you're seeing a show.

Amarone Kitchen & Wine S *Italian* 24 | 15 | 21 | $59

West Hollywood | 8868 W. Sunset Blvd. (San Vicente Blvd.) | 310-652-2233 | www.amaronela.com

Although it's "not much from the outside", inside this "warm, cozy" West Hollywood Italian awaits "exceptional" "bliss"-inducing pastas delivered by a "charming" staff; tabs can be "costly", but the "dark, intimate" setting is made for "dates", and acolytes insist it's "as close to Italy as it gets in LA."

Amici Brentwood *Italian* 21 | 19 | 21 | $44

Brentwood | 2538 San Vicente Blvd. (26th St.) | 310-260-4900 | www.amicibrentwood.com

Trattoria Amici *Italian*

Beverly Hills | Beverly Terrace Hotel | 469 N. Doheny Dr. (Santa Monica Blvd.) | 310-858-0271 | www.tamici.com

(continued)

Trattoria Amici

Glendale | Americana at Brand | 783 Americana Way (bet. Brand Blvd. & Central Ave.) | 818-502-1220 | www.amicila.com

Locals "in the know" like these "warm, welcoming" separately owned trattorias where "accommodating" servers "aim to please" and the "classic Italian" cuisine is "tasty", if "not especially exciting"; the Beverly Terrace Hotel branch has a "sweet" patio, while the Brentwood outpost feels "fancier", and outside tables at the Americana at Brand branch in Glendale provide a prime vantage point for "watching the action go by."

Ammo *Californian* 22 | 18 | 21 | $45

Hollywood | 1155 N. Highland Ave. (Lexington Ave.) | 323-871-2666 | www.ammocafe.com

NEW Ammo at The Hammer M *Californian*

Westwood | Hammer Museum | 10899 Wilshire Blvd. (Westwood Blvd.) | 310-443-7037 | www.hammer.ucla.edu

A "favorite" among "industry" types, this "hip" Hollywood Californian plates "marvelous" "market"-driven fare that "leaves you feeling healthy" in a "chic, well-weathered" setting offering a "good chance at a celebrity sighting"; "special" cocktails and cool playlists are further boosts, and though a few are irked by "too expensive" bills, most put it on their "must-return list"; P.S. the branch at the Hammer Museum features an abridged menu and wine.

Angelini Osteria M *Italian* 28 | 19 | 24 | $55

Beverly Boulevard | 7313 Beverly Blvd. (bet. Fuller Ave. & Poinsettia Pl.) | 323-297-0070 | www.angeliniosteria.com

"Rustic perfection" sums up the menu at this "convivial" Beverly Boulevard trattoria, where "king of authentic Italian" Gino Angelini makes "taste buds sing" with his "mouthwatering" meats, pastas and "not-to-be-missed" whole branzino; yes, the "noisy" quarters are so "cramped" you can "vicariously enjoy what your neighbors are eating", but unfazed fans will gladly pay "high prices" for "a foolproof meal."

Animal *American* 27 | 17 | 22 | $52

Fairfax | 435 N. Fairfax Ave. (Oakwood Ave.) | 323-782-9225 | www.animalrestaurant.com

A "meat lover's dream", this Fairfax New American from celeb chefs Vinny Dotolo and Jon Shook is an "exploration of everything carnivore" where the "superbly prepared" snout-to-tail plates are bound to entice you "out of your comfort zone"; a daily changing menu keeps the "adventure" "addicting", and "excellent" service offsets a "loud", "minimalist" setting.

Antonio's M *Mexican* 20 | 18 | 22 | $28

Melrose | 7470 Melrose Ave. (bet. Gardner & Vista Sts.) | 323-658-9060 | www.antoniosonmelrose.com

While not "discovered by the hipsters yet", this '50s-vintage Melrose "institution" steadily caters to "loyal and happy patrons" with "old-style Mexican" classics in dimly lit digs lined with celeb photos; regulars report "the food is only bested by [owner] Antonio's smile" - and perhaps the 300 tequilas that stock the bar.

FOOD | DECOR | SERVICE | COST

A.O.C. *Californian/French* 25 | 23 | 23 | $54

Beverly Boulevard | 8700 W. Third St. (Hamel Rd.) | 310-859-9859 | www.aocwinebar.com

"Beautiful new digs" with a "gorgeous" courtyard get the "A-OK" from "low-key power" patrons who "never get bored" with this Third Street showcase for star chef Suzanne Goin's "splendid" Cal-French small plates (including "top-notch" cheese and charcuterie), "fantastic wine selection" and "wonderful" brunch; though the full bar is new, the "attentive" service and premium pricing carry over.

Apple Pan ◐ M ≠ *American* 23 | 12 | 20 | $15

West LA | 10801 W. Pico Blvd. (bet. Glendon Ave. & Westwood Blvd.) | 310-475-3585

An "LA original", this "quaint" little spot in West LA has been turning out "wonderful" "classic" hickory burgers, "fabulous" pies and other "simple, but good" grub to a "packed" house since 1947; "it's no frills and nothing fancy" with an "old-school" staff serving at a U-shaped counter, but "grab a stool and be satisfied."

NEW **Ara's Tacos** *Mexican* - | - | - | I

Glendale | 901 W. Glenoaks Blvd. (Highland Ave.) | 818-547-5461

Opened by the Armenian family behind Zankou Chicken, this fast-service Mexican grill in Glendale follows the same family-friendly, inexpensive formula where you order at the counter, find a table and grab the food when you're called; the signature rotisserie chicken makes an appearance in the tacos, and there's also beef, burritos and rice bowls on the brief menu.

Aroma *Italian* 24 | 18 | 22 | $30

Silver Lake | 2903 W. Sunset Blvd. (Perman Ave.) | 323-644-2833 | www.aromaatsunset.com

"The location in a strip mall is a little odd, but the food makes up for it" at this "quaint, charming" Silver Lake "treasure" delivering "delicious", "top-quality" Italian fare from ex-Valentino chef Edin Marroquin; "personal" service and relatively modest pricing make it a "great find."

Aroma Café *E European* 20 | 15 | 18 | $22

West LA | Rancho Park Plaza | 2530 Overland Ave. (Cushdon Ave.) | 310-836-2919 | www.aromacafe-la.com

"Savory", "carb-filled" "cuisine from the Adriatic" lures lovers of Eastern-European fare to this "casual", "reasonably priced" cafe in West LA, where the expat crowd "sits for hours" over "fab desserts" and "addictive" Turkish coffee; those put off by the parking lot views and sometimes "slow" service can check out the mini "Euro market" for grab 'n' go cheeses and other delicacies.

Arroyo Chop House *Steak* 25 | 24 | 24 | $61

Pasadena | 536 S. Arroyo Pkwy. (California Blvd.) | 626-577-7463 | www.arroyochophouse.com

A "top-notch" "special-occasion" spot, this "classic" Pasadena meatery from the Smith Brothers (Parkway Grill) is "comparable to the best" for steaks "so tender you hardly need a knife"; Craftsman-style surrounds with "ambiance to spare" and "generous wine pours" from the "gracious" servers help ease "the sticker shock."

FOOD | DECOR | SERVICE | COST

Artisan Cheese Gallery *Cheese/Sandwiches* — 24 | 14 | 18 | $20

Studio City | 12023 Ventura Blvd. (Laurel Canyon Blvd.) | 818-505-0207 | www.artisancheesegallery.com

"Fantastic" sandwiches and a "bountiful" array of all the "rare" cheeses known to man and mouse "delight" *fromage* fans at this upmarket shop/cafe, a "wonderful find in Studio City"; the "knowledgeable" staff "indulges every customer" with free nibbles, so "be prepared to wait" at the "crowded" counter; P.S. it also serves wine and beer.

Art's Deli *Deli* — 21 | 13 | 20 | $22

Studio City | 12224 Ventura Blvd. (bet. Laurelgrove & Vantage Aves.) | 818-762-1221 | www.artsdeli.com

On the Studio City scene since 1957, this "no-nonsense", family-run deli doles out the obligatory "sky-high" sandwiches that staunch supporters swear are "better than bubbe's"; "old-fashioned" booths and "fast", "snappy" waitresses lend it a bit of "NY style", though critics kvetch it's "a little too pricey for what you get."

Asahi Ramen *Japanese* — 20 | 10 | 18 | $14

West LA | 2027 Sawtelle Blvd. (bet. La Grange & Mississippi Aves.) | 310-479-2231 | www.asahiramen.com

"Excellent", "filling" ramen in "steaming hot broth" "hits the spot" at this "tiny storefront" in Little Osaka, where the "cheap, huge portions" come fast and furious thanks to "lightning service"; just bring cash and "be prepared for a wait", since the line often "spills out onto Sawtelle."

Asaka *Japanese* — 22 | 19 | 20 | $27

Rancho Palos Verdes | Golden Cove Shopping Ctr. | 31208 Palos Verdes Dr. W. (Hawthorne Blvd.) | 310-377-5999

Redondo Beach | 1870 S. Elena Ave. (Catalina Ave.) | 310-373-5999

www.asakausa.com

Handy for locals, these Japanese joints present "fresh", "tasty" sushi and "reasonably priced" rolls that are "good for everyday meals"; though service is uneven and the "mini-mall" decor "ordinary in the extreme", the Rancho Palos Verdes branch ups the ante with "spectacular" ocean views from a "spacious" outdoor deck.

Asakuma *Japanese* — 22 | 16 | 20 | $34

Beverly Hills | 141 S. Robertson Blvd. (bet. Charleville & Wilshire Blvds.) | 310-659-1092

Venice | Hoyt Plaza | 2805 Abbot Kinney Blvd. (Washington Blvd.) | 310-577-7999

West LA | 11769 Santa Monica Blvd. (bet. Granville & Stoner Aves.) | 310-473-8990

www.asakuma.com

Offering a "rare" option for Angelenos, these "wonderful", separately owned Japanese spots focus on delivery to satisfy sushi "cravings"; even if the settings are "not really set up for a dine-in experience", when you're "too lazy to leave your living room" they're "worth the price."

Asanebo *Japanese* — 29 | 18 | 25 | $91

Studio City | 11941 Ventura Blvd. (bet. Carpenter & Radford Aves.) | 818-760-3348 | www.asanebo-restaurant.com

"Amazing", "top-tier omakase" featuring the "freshest fish from around the world" plus other "innovative" dishes make this modest Studio

City Japanese from "master" chef Tetsuya Nakao LA's No. 1 for Food; sure, it's in a "dumpy strip mall" and you might have to "take out a mortgage to indulge", but acolytes insist "you won't regret it."

Auntie Em's Kitchen *American* 22 | 15 | 19 | $18

Eagle Rock | 4616 Eagle Rock Blvd. (Corliss St.) | 323-255-0800 | www.auntieemskitchen.com

"Arty locals line up" for this "funky" inexpensive "Eagle Rock institution" dishing out "creative", locally sourced American "comfort food", including "swell" breakfasts, "phenomenal" sandwiches and "top-notch" cupcakes; the vibe is "friendly and upbeat", but be ready to roll with a "divey-cafe" atmosphere.

NEW Aventine *Italian* - | - | - | M

Hollywood | 1607 N. Cahuenga Blvd. (Selma Ave.) | 323-500-0969 | www.aventinehollywood.com

Hearty trattoria fare is on the menu at this trendy Hollywood Italian, but the setting may be the real star; it features a wood-beamed farmhouse interior and outsized patio with a bar, leather couches and two 80-year-old olive trees entwined with twinkly Christmas lights.

A Votre Sante *Health Food* 21 | 16 | 20 | $25

Brentwood | 13016 San Vicente Blvd. (bet. Avondale Ave. & 26th St.) | 310-451-1813 | www.avotresantela.com

"Those who want to live to 120" - including "San Vicente runners", "bikers" and "yoga maidens" - hit up this veg-friendly Brentwood health-fooder for "generous portions" of "beautiful", "satisfying" fare with "all the right foodie/eco values"; "basic but homey" and "not too fussy" or expensive, it benefits from a "nice attitude" and "neighborhood vibe" that's "hard to beat."

Axe M *Californian* 23 | 18 | 18 | $39

Venice | 1009 Abbot Kinney Blvd. (B'way) | 310-664-9787 | www.axerestaurant.com

Employing "excellent" organic and local ingredients on a "well-edited" menu, this Venice "gem" (pronounced "ah-shay") nails the "clean, vegetarian-conscious" Californian genre in an airy "minimalist" setting with a "charming" garden out back; though a few complain of "attitude" and "uncomfortable" seating, an "eclectic clientele" relies on it, especially for brunch.

Ayara Thai *Thai* 24 | 17 | 22 | $22

Westchester | 6245 W. 87th St. (La Tijera Blvd.) | 310-410-8848 | www.ayarathaicuisine.com

Setting the "local" standard for "what Thai should be", this "family-owned" Westchester "favorite" "near LAX" "consistently" turns out "excellent", "authentic" Siamese that's "sometimes so hot it brings tears to your eyes" ("watch out"); "attentive" service and "reasonable prices" are further reasons "everyone loves" it.

Azeen's Afghani Restaurant *Afghan* ▽ 26 | 20 | 23 | $26

Pasadena | 110 E. Union St. (Arroyo Pkwy.) | 626-683-3310 | www.azeensafghanirestaurant.com

Pasadenans explore the "amazing goodness" of affordable, "home-cooked" Afghan cuisine - including "some of the best kebabs anywhere" - at this "small" "charmer" on the edge of Old Town; "exquisite flavors" and a staff as "welcoming" as "family" keep the faithful "going back" for more.

Babalu *Californian* 18 | 15 | 17 | $26

Santa Monica | 1002 Montana Ave. (10th St.) | 310-395-2500 | www.babalu.info

"Dessert should be your first course" declare sweet tooths at this Santa Monica spot known for "decadent pies" and cakes from the in-house bakery and "satisfying" Cal cuisine spiked with "Caribbean flair"; dissenters dis the "cramped" seating and "erratic" service, but between the "relaxed vibe", tropical decor and sidewalk tables it remains "popular."

Babita Mexicuisine ⊠ M *Mexican* 27 | 14 | 25 | $45

San Gabriel | 1823 S. San Gabriel Blvd. (Norwood Pl.) | 626-288-7265 | www.babita-mexicuisine.com

"Don't judge the decor, judge the wonderful dishes" at this "family-run" San Gabriel destination, a "best-kept secret" where chef-owner Roberto Berrelleza's "inspired" Mexican creations will "set your tongue aquiver"; it's "expensive" given the "modest" venue, but "they really take care of you here."

Baby Blues BBQ *BBQ* 21 | 14 | 18 | $26

West Hollywood | 7953 Santa Monica Blvd. (Hayworth Ave.) | 323-656-1277 | www.babyblueswh.com

Venice | 444 Lincoln Blvd. (Sunset Ave.) | 310-396-7675 | www.babybluesvenice.com

"Chow down" on a "belly-busting meal" of "total man food" at this "legit" Venice BBQ joint and its marginally "fancier" West Hollywood spin-off, "four-napkin" purveyors of "killer", "Fred Flintstone-esque" ribs; they're known for "long waits" and "whistle-stop decor" relieved by "eye-candy" servers, and while the tabs may run "high for a hole-in-the-wall", you'll "roll yourself" out, baby.

Baby's Badass Burgers ⇏ *Burgers* ▽ 24 | 17 | 22 | $16

Location varies; see website | 877-962-2297 | www.babysbadassburgers.com

"Seriously awesome burgers" "plus a cute staff equals dining heaven" at this hot pink-hued food truck, where the 'Burger Babes' shtick - namely the crew of "lively", "pretty" ladies - doesn't overshadow some "of the best" patties in town; flirty menu monikers like She's Smokin', Cougar and The Perfect 10 further a "fun" bite that's "amazing for its price."

Bäco Mercat ⊠ *Sandwiches* 25 | 18 | 21 | $36

Downtown | 408 S. Main St. (Winston St.) | 213-687-8808 | www.bacomercat.com

"Addicting" bäco sandwiches ("the love child of a taco and a pita") and other "complex" Spanish-inspired dishes suit a "sophisticated" "hipster" following at this "delightfully creative" hit from Downtown "pioneer" Josef Centeno (Bar Amá); "solid" service, "reasonable prices" and an "extensive libations list" distract from the "funky" room's "energized" "din."

B.A.D. Sushi *Japanese* 22 | 18 | 21 | $28

West LA | 11617 Santa Monica Blvd. (Federal Ave.) | 310-479-4910

El Segundo | 357 Main St. (bet. Grand & Holly Aves.) | 310-648-8671

(continued)

(continued)

B.A.D. Sushi

NEW **Pasadena** | 29 E. Holly St. (Electric Dr.) | 626-568-1500
www.badsushi.net

"Don't let the name fool you" at this Japanese chainlet, which area devotees deem "anything but bad" (the name stands for 'best and delicious') thanks to the sushi samurais cutting up "creative rolls"; "quick", "friendly service" offsets the nondescript decor, and yen-watchers confirm the prices are pretty "good."

The Baker *Bakery/Sandwiches* ▽ 24 | 15 | 20 | $16

Woodland Hills | 21600 Ventura Blvd. (bet. Baza & De Roja Aves.) | 818-340-1987 | www.thebakerbread.com

"Don't let the plain storefront fool you", this low-key bakery/cafe in a Woodland Hills strip mall is "a go-to" for "excellent" artisanal breads and "yummy" breakfasts and lunch items and "homemade soups" at sensible prices; there's often "a line to get in", but locals insist it's "worth it."

Bamboo Cuisine *Chinese* 23 | 18 | 21 | $26

Sherman Oaks | 14010 Ventura Blvd. (bet. Costello & Murietta Aves.) | 818-788-0202 | www.bamboocuisine.com

"Crowded for a reason", this "relaxed" Sherman Oaks "standby" ranks among "the best Chinese in the Valley" for "solid" chow ferried by "efficient servers" to tables with "lazy Susans" where parties can "share family-style"; between the "dependable quality" and fair prices, the "locals love it" whether to "eat in or take out."

NEW **Bamboo Izakaya** *Japanese* - | - | - | M

Santa Monica | 1541 Ocean Ave. (Colorado Ave.) | 310-566-3860 | www.bambooizakaya.com

This Santa Monica izakaya across from the pier distinguishes itself with stellar views of the ocean; the brightly lit space features lots of polished wood, tile walls and a bar where you can watch chefs labor away at midpriced Japanese small plates made with a multitude of ingredients; P.S. check out the extensive sake list.

Bamboo Restaurant *Caribbean* 21 | 16 | 21 | $26

Culver City | 10835 Venice Blvd. (Westwood Blvd.) | 310-287-0668 | www.bamboorestaurant.net

For "lovers of exotic spices", the "down-home Caribbean food" is "da bomb" at this "casual" Culver City joint, a "neighborhood staple" also favored for its "no-attitude" service; the decor's decidedly "nothing fancy", but a few "yummy" mojitos on the bamboo-bordered patio will "transport you to the islands" ("well, almost").

Bandera *Southwestern* 23 | 22 | 22 | $39

West LA | 11700 Wilshire Blvd. (Barrington Ave.) | 310-477-3524 | www.hillstone.com

Like a "sexy" version of Houston's, this West LA chain spin-off is a "consistent" "winner" for "solid" Southwestern-American fare according to "well-heeled" "grown-ups" who applaud the "attentive" service and "attractive" environs replete with "leather booths", "live jazz" and a "hoppin'" "singles bar"; while it's "not cheap", all that "scenery" draws "crowds like a movie opening."

	FOOD	DECOR	SERVICE	COST

Bangkok West *Thai* | 23 | 20 | 22 | $25

Santa Monica | 606 Santa Monica Blvd. (6th St.) | 310-395-9658 | www.bangkokwestthaicuisine.com

"Upscalish" airs and an "expansive menu" of "wonderful" "standards" take things "up a notch from your typical Thai" at this "reliable" Santa Monican "conveniently located" near The Promenade; the "attentive service" and "white tablecloths" justify tabs that skew "a bit pricier" than its "local" rivals.

NEW **Bank of Venice** ◐ *American* | - | - | - | M

Venice | 80 Windward Ave. (Pacific Ave.) | 310-450-5222 | www.bankofvenicerestaurant.com

Situated in the heart of wild and wacky Venice just a block from the beach, this 1905 building is now home to a gastropub from the owners of Venice Ale House with a bar that's three deep and lots of booths in which to chew on usual suspects like mac 'n' cheese plus a few healthy options like a quinoa and kale bowl; everything is washed down with local beers, at prices fit for starving artists.

Bao Dim Sum House *Chinese* | 21 | 21 | 22 | $28

Beverly Boulevard | 8256 Beverly Blvd. (Sweetzer Ave.) | 323-655-6556 | www.baodimsum.com

"Bao wow!" bay fans of the "melt-in-your-mouth" dumplings and other "tasty" (albeit "not totally authentic") "dim sum classics" at this Beverly Boulevard Chinese, a "rare find" for folks who "don't want to drive to Monterey Park"; the "made-to-order" menu and "contemporary" milieu may explain why it's "spendy" for its kind.

NEW **Bar Amá** *Tex-Mex* | ▽ 23 | 17 | 21 | $38

Downtown | 118 W. Fourth St. (bet. Main & Spring Sts.) | 213-687-8002 | www.bar-ama.com

The family recipes of celebrated chef-owner Josef Centeno (Baco Mercat) yield "delicious takes on Tex-Mex" in a "casual", wood-planked space at this "creative" Downtown newcomer; it's also "elevating" the cantina genre with "innovative" tequila-based cocktails, though some find slightly "pricey" tabs less inspiring.

Bar Bouchon *French* | 23 | 23 | 22 | $44

Beverly Hills | 235 N. Canon Dr. (bet. Dayton Way & Wilshire Blvd.) | 310-271-9910 | www.bouchonbistro.com

This "easily accessible" "cafe version" of Thomas Keller's Beverly Hills bistro upstairs will leave you "dreaming of Paris" with a small-plates lineup of "scrumptious" French dishes and "swell cocktails" served at an "elegant" zinc bar or on a "wonderfully civilized veranda for alfresco dining"; "service is variable", but the bills are low given the chef's pedigree, and "happy-hour prices are excellent."

Barbrix *Italian/Mediterranean* | 24 | 20 | 22 | $40

Silver Lake | 2442 Hyperion Ave. (Tracy St.) | 323-662-2442 | www.barbrix.com

"Small plates are where it's at" for "foodies in Silver Lake" who flock to this "inventive" Med-Italian "gem", which matches its "sensational" bites with a "smart wine list" that won't "break the bank"; the "intimate" space is often "hopping" with a "convivial" crowd, but the service stays "well informed" and there's a bar and "cute patio" for any overflow.

	FOOD	DECOR	SERVICE	COST

Ba Restaurant Ⓜ *French* | - | - | - | M |

Highland Park | 5100 York Blvd. (Ave. 51) | 323-739-6243 | www.restaurantba.com

This Highland Park French brings a touch of European elegance to a working-class neighborhood, with an open kitchen turning out classic, moderately priced Gallic fare and seasonal specials; the husband-and-wife team behind the sun-drenched restaurant goes for a baroque punk-rock vibe, with pastel-pink walls offset by black framework.

Bar Hayama ◐ *Japanese* | 24 | 24 | 23 | $47 |

West LA | 1803 Sawtelle Blvd. (Nebraska Ave.) | 310-235-2000 | www.bar-hayama.com

"Dining by the light" of a "gorgeous" fire pit is a "romantic" *hai* point at this "excellent" West LA Japanese, where chef-owner Toshi Sugiura's "talented" team turns out "fresh", "inventive" sushi and small plates paired with an "interesting sake list" until late; the "knowledgeable staff" and smooth "modern" decor keep the feel "comfortable" "inside or out."

Bar | Kitchen ◐Ⓢ *American* ∇ | 24 | 23 | 21 | $35 |

Downtown | O Hotel | 819 S. Flower St. (bet. 8th & 9th Sts.) | 213-623-9904 | www.barandkitchenla.com

Downtown's boutique O Hotel berths this "charming" bar/eatery in "funky" neo-rustic digs, where "creative" American grub ("wonderful small plates" included) is matched with craft beers, small-production wines and "incredible" custom cocktails; hedgers suggest "it's still coming into its own", "but the scene and food make up for" any misgivings.

Barney Greengrass *Deli* | 22 | 19 | 19 | $33 |

Beverly Hills | Barneys New York | 9570 Wilshire Blvd. (Camden Dr.) | 310-777-5877 | www.barneys.com

"The lox rox" at this "outpost of the legendary NYC" Jewish deli perched atop Barneys, where "agents", "celebs" and "rich wannabes" do lunch over "superior" smoked fish and other posh noshes; out on the "pretty" terrace "overlooking Beverly Hills", no one minds if it's as "pricey" as the threads downstairs.

Barney's Gourmet Hamburgers *Burgers* | 21 | 13 | 18 | $17 |

Brentwood | 11660 San Vicente Blvd. (bet. Barrington & Darlington Aves.) | 310-447-6000
Santa Monica | Brentwood Country Mart | 225 26th St. (bet. Brentwood Terr. & San Vicente Blvd.) | 310-899-0133
Sherman Oaks | Westfield Fashion Square Mall | 14006 Riverside Dr. (Woodman Ave.) | 818-808-0680
www.barneyshamburgers.com

"Variety" brings burger buffs to this SF-based trio, which furnishes "juicy, cooked-to-order" patties "styled a zillion different ways" plus "super" fries (and even noteworthy salads, "but why bother?"); they're "informal joints" and service is uneven, but for an "affordable" feed this is a "good bet"; P.S. the Brentwood Country Mart site is mostly alfresco.

NEW Barnyard *American* | - | - | - | M |

Venice | 1715 Pacific Ave. (Mildred Ave.) | 310-581-1015 | www.barnyardvenice.com

This much-anticipated Venice American, just steps from the boardwalk, offers a reasonably priced menu by Jesse Barber built around "delicious" farm-to-table small plates and tapas; the "lovely" space is more beach house than barn, with hardwood tables and lots of light flowing through the large windows.

Bar Pintxo *Spanish* 21 | 17 | 19 | $35

Santa Monica | 109 Santa Monica Blvd. (Ocean Ave.) | 310-458-2012 | www.barpintxo.com

Ever a "lively" scene, this pint-sized Santa Monica Spaniard from Joe Miller (Joe's) has supporters "squeezed" in to graze on "scrumptious" "traditional tapas", "addictive" sangria and by-the-glass wines courtesy of "personable" staffers; *sí*, it's a "tight space" and the checks run "pricey", but "go with fun in mind" and it's "like you're in Barcelona."

Bar Toscana ⊠ *Italian* 23 | 23 | 23 | $43

Brentwood | 11633 San Vicente Blvd. (Darlington Ave.) | 310-826-0028 | www.bartoscana.com

Milan-style nibbling in sleek digs has "trendy" "locals" touting this "Brentwood watering hole" alongside Toscana, where the "wonderful" *stuzzichini* (small plates) are almost overshadowed by the "meticulously crafted cocktails" and "attractive" waiters "with Italian accents"; given the "upscale pickup scene" featuring "the future housewives of Brentwood", needless to say the tabs "aren't cheap."

Bashan Ⓜ *American* 27 | 19 | 25 | $58

Montrose | 3459 N. Verdugo Rd. (bet. Ocean View & Sunview Blvds.) | 818-541-1532 | www.bashanrestaurant.com

"Each plate arrives like a piece of modern art" at this "upscale" Montrose "gem" from a husband-and-wife team, whose "amazing", market-driven New American meals are "cutting-edge without being too experimental"; given the "attentive staff" and "intimate" atmosphere ("you can actually talk and hear"), most agree it's "well worth the trip."

Bashi *Asian* - | - | - | E

Rancho Palos Verdes | Terranea Resort | 100 Terranea Way (Palos Verdes Dr.) | 310-265-2800 | www.terranea.com

Sitting pretty on the edge of the Pacific in the Terranea Resort in Palos Verdes, this pricey Pan-Asian combines an ocean view with fusiony small plates from the other side of the sea; nab a seat in the wood-heavy dining room or opt to sit alfresco in the heated patio with "million dollar views."

Basix Cafe *Californian/Italian* 19 | 16 | 19 | $24

West Hollywood | 8333 Santa Monica Blvd. (Flores St.) | 323-848-2460 | www.basixcafe.com

Living up to its name, this WeHo "neighborhood joint" "gets the job done" with "well-made", "uncomplicated" Cal-Italian eats (especially for brunch or breakfast) at a "decent" price; despite occasional "service with a snicker", most find it "welcoming" with a "lively, diverse crowd" and "excellent" outdoor people-watching, adding a bit of "Hollywood charm and chatter."

Bay Cities Deli Ⓜ *Deli* 26 | 11 | 16 | $14

Santa Monica | 1517 Lincoln Blvd. (bet. B'way & Colorado Ave.) | 310-395-8279 | www.bcdeli.com

The Godmother sub is the "perfect marriage of bread and meat" declare devotees who "fight the throngs" at this Santa Monica deli "treasure", which doubles as a grocery stocked with "exotic Italian delicacies"; there's "no decor" to speak of and limited outdoor seating, and while the staff is "super-efficient", the line can still be "hell" - but those "sandwiches are heaven"; P.S. "pre-order online to beat the wait."

Bazaar by José Andrés *Spanish* 27 | 27 | 25 | $83

Beverly Hills | SLS at Beverly Hills | 465 S. La Cienega Blvd. (Clifton Way) | 310-246-5555 | www.thebazaar.com

"An experience like no other", this "culinary Disneyland" in the SLS Hotel from José Andrés presents "wild", "whimsical" Spanish-inspired small plates and "fantastic" drinks "that look like they were made in chemistry class" in an "extravagant", "noisy" Philippe Starck-designed setting out of "*Alice in Wonderland*" (complete with a pink patisserie for dessert); "trust the waiters to advise" and then "be prepared to spend hours" and "beaucoup bucks" here.

BCD Tofu House *Korean* 22 | 12 | 15 | $17

Koreatown | 3575 Wilshire Blvd. (Kingsley Dr.) | 213-382-6677 ◐
Koreatown | 869 S. Western Ave. (bet. 8th & 9th Sts.) | 213-380-3807 ◐
Cerritos | 11818 South St. (Pioneer Blvd.) | 562-809-8098
Torrance | 1607 Sepulveda Blvd. (bet. Lockness & Western Ave.) | 310-534-3480
Reseda | 18044 Saticoy St. (bet. Hesperia & Lindley Aves.) | 818-342-3535 ◐
Rowland Heights | Yes Plaza | 1731 Fullerton Rd. (bet. Camino Bello & Colima Rd.) | 626-964-7073 ◐
www.bcdtofu.com

"Warning: the spicy soft tofu is extremely habit-forming" at this "late-night" mini-chain meting out big bowls of "delicious" "piping-hot tofu soup" and other "Seoul-style" comfort food; the decor is nothing to speak of and the staff is often "harried" ("you have to practically trip someone to get the check"), but "cheap" and "satisfying" trump all.

Beachwood BBQ 🅼 *BBQ* 23 | 19 | 22 | $23

Long Beach | 210 E. Third St. (Long Beach Blvd.) | 562-436-4020 | www.beachwoodbbq.com

Smoke lovers give the nod to this Long Beach BBQ joint pairing "expert", "dry-rubbed" meats with "addictive" sides and an "ever-changing" array of "esoteric" microbrews on tap; "affordable" tabs and a "thoughtful" staff give the midcentury-styled interior a "homey" feel, but "get there early", or prepare to wait; P.S. you can see which beers are being served daily through an online 'HopCam.'

Beckers Bakery & Deli 🅼 *Bakery/Deli* ∇ 21 | 11 | 18 | $14

Manhattan Beach | 1025 Manhattan Ave. (11th St.) | 310-372-3214 | www.beckersbakeryanddeli.com

This "pleasant", '40s-era Manhattan Beach bakery and deli, with its "huge", "old-fashioned" sandwiches and "crowd-pleasing" sweets ("note the colorful surfboard cookies"), proves a cupcake "doesn't have to cost four bucks to taste fantastic"; it's a basic counter-service spot, so many opt to "grab something delicious" and "take it down to the beach."

Beer Belly ◐ *Eclectic* 23 | 20 | 18 | $24

Koreatown | 532 S. Western Ave. (bet. 5th & 6th Sts.) | 213-387-2337 | www.beerbellyla.com

"It ain't just beer that rounds off your belly here" - the "offbeat" Eclectic grub (like "crazy good" duck-fat fries) is also "worth adding to your waistline" at this modestly priced gastropub in an "unsuspecting" Koreatown location; as a bonus, the "unique" urban-industrial space with concrete floors, mahogany walls and steel tables is a "cool" place to "hang."

Bel Air Bar + Grill *Californian* 21 | 22 | 22 | $51

Bel-Air | 662 N. Sepulveda Blvd. (bet. Moraga Dr. & Ovada Pl.) | 310-440-5544 | www.belairbarandgrill.com

Bel-Air's "old guard" appreciates the "well-prepared" Californian fare and "attentive service" at this "expensive" Getty-area "standby" owned by Walt Disney's niece; with its multiroom space "tarted up" following an "extensive remodel", it remains "reliable" in an area where options are limited.

Belmont Brewing Co. *American* 20 | 20 | 20 | $26

Long Beach | 25 39th Pl. (Ocean Blvd.) | 562-433-3891 | www.belmontbrewing.com

From its "awesome" "berth by the beach", this "long-running" brewpub (one of SoCal's first) at Long Beach's Belmont Pier pairs "filling" American fare with an "excellent" list of "quality" "house-made" suds; "casual", "friendly" and "reasonably priced", it corners a "young crowd" vying to "soak up the California sun" on the "hard-to-top" patio.

The Belvedere *American* 26 | 28 | 27 | $73

Beverly Hills | Peninsula Beverly Hills | 9882 S. Santa Monica Blvd. (Wilshire Blvd.) | 310-788-2306 | www.peninsula.com

Well-heeled diners "feel pampered" at this "first-class" fixture in the "stunning" Peninsula Beverly Hills where "white-glove" servers set down "sublime" New American meals in a "lovely", "quiet" dining room (and landscaped patio) rated No. 1 for Decor in Los Angeles; the "top-of-the-line" performance extends to breakfast and Sunday brunch, though, of course, you'll "have to pay for this bliss."

Benley Vietnamese Kitchen ☒ *Vietnamese* ▽ 27 | 16 | 22 | $27

Long Beach | 8191 E. Wardlow Rd. (Norwalk Blvd.) | 562-596-8130

Banh vivants savor the "fresh", "exquisite" Vietnamese dishes - "perpetually well prepared and flavorful" - at this low-cost Long Beach "phenomenon" "tucked in an unassuming strip mall"; while the "intimate" digs aren't the "Ritz-Carlton", it's "charming" enough with a "wonderful, efficient" staff.

Berlin Currywurst *German* 21 | 15 | 22 | $14

Silver Lake | 3827 W. Sunset Blvd. (Hyperion Ave.) | 323-663-1989

NEW **Berlin Currywurst: The Beer Garden** ◐ *German*

Hollywood | 1620 N. Cahuenga Blvd. (bet. Hollywood Blvd. & Selma Ave.) | 323-467-7593

www.berlincurrywurst.com

Named for the iconic Teutonic street food, these sausage centrals in Silver Lake and Hollywood furnish "cheap", "authentic wursts" doused with tangy curry sauce; "hospitable" counter folk led by the "real German" owners lend warmth to the stripped-down interiors, and the Hollywood branch boasts ample outdoor seating.

	FOOD	DECOR	SERVICE	COST

Beso 🅂 *Pan-Latin* 18 23 18 $54

Hollywood | 6350 Hollywood Blvd. (Ivar Ave.) | 323-467-7991 | www.besohollywood.com

With a "fabulous" "Hollywood atmosphere" beneath the exposed beams and chandeliers, it's no wonder "pretty people" "pack the bar" of Eva Longoria and chef Todd English's Pan-Latin "hot spot"; though critics call the "expensive" menu "lackluster" and service gets "so-so" marks, most concede "it's a place to be seen, not a foodie haven."

NEW Bestia 🄼 *Italian* 25 24 23 $59

Downtown | 2121 E. Seventh Pl. (Santa Fe Ave.) | 213-514-5724 | www.bestiala.com

Husband-and-wife team Ori Menashe (ex Angelini Osteria) and Genevieve Gergis "are a force to be reckoned with" at this "new fave" in Downtown's Arts District, a "hot" destination for "on-point" "rustic Italian" fare from an open kitchen; "urban-trendy" digs and "cool" servers are more reasons it's "so crowded" and "deafening" - "not that you need to talk with food like this!"; P.S. "reservations are difficult."

BierBeisl ◐ 🅂 *Austrian* 22 17 20 $47

Beverly Hills | 9669 Santa Monica Blvd. (Bedford St.) | 310-271-7274 | www.bierbeisl-la.com

Expect the "best of the wurst" at this "delightful" Beverly Hills boîte from "talented chef-owner" Bernhard Mairinger, home to "fantastic schnitzel", sausage-and-beer pairings and other "stick-to-your-ribs Austrian" fare; "the warmth of the staff" and an "intensely flavored schnapps" selection temper the somewhat "small" confines.

Billingsley's *Steak* 17 13 20 $28

West LA | 11326 W. Pico Blvd. (Corinth Ave.) | 310-477-1426 | www.billingsleysrestaurant.com

Though it's no longer owned by the family of June Cleaver (Barbara Billingsley), this "nostalgic" West LA "institution" from 1946 will still "transport you back to when red Naugahyde was the rage" and "hearty family fare" consisted of steaks, martinis and "all the cheese toast you could muster"; early birds dig the waitresses who "talk your ears off", as well as the "modest" tabs.

Bistro de la Gare 🄼 *French* 20 18 19 $37

South Pasadena | 921 Meridian Ave. (bet. El Centro & Mission Sts.) | 626-799-8828 | www.bistrodelagare.com

This "casual" "little French bistro" next to the South Pas Gold Line is a "world unto itself", turning out a "tight menu" of "well-executed" fare amid "comfortable" old-world surroundings (complete with antique mahogany bar); though the "friendly Frenchmen" sometimes provide uneven service, "moderate" prices enhance the "value."

Bistro 45 🄼 *Californian* 25 23 25 $51

Pasadena | 45 S. Mentor Ave. (bet. Colorado Blvd. & Green St.) | 626-795-2478 | www.bistro45.com

"Winning in every regard", this Californian tucked down a quiet side street in Pasadena offers a "refined" yet "innovative" menu abetted by a "stupendous" wine and beer list and "thoughtful" service; it may be "expensive" for the area, but with "beautiful" restyled art deco surroundings, it's still a "favorite" for "a special night out."

	FOOD	DECOR	SERVICE	COST

Bistro Garden at Coldwater *Continental* 21 25 22 $49

Studio City | 12950 Ventura Blvd. (Van Noord Ave.) | 818-501-0202 | www.bistrogarden.com

An "airy" "winter garden" with light streaming through "gorgeous casement windows" makes for "elegant" dining at this "pricey" Studio City locale, one of the "last bastions" in the Valley for "tasteful" Continental fare with "attentive" service (as well as live piano at dinner); some say the food "comes in second to the ambiance", but an "older crowd" still counts it as a "special place to celebrate."

Bistro Provence ⓢ *French* 23 17 22 $39

Burbank | Lakeside Ctr. | 345 N. Pass Ave. (Oak St.) | 818-840-9050 | www.burbankbistroprovence.com

"One of the hidden treasures in Burbank" muse mavens of this "unassuming" strip-mall bistro specializing in "high-quality", "beautifully prepared" Southern French cooking that's particularly "affordable" for weekday lunches; the "tiny" space leaves almost "no room for decor", but a "personable" crew lends it lots of "warmth."

Black Dog Coffee *Coffeehouse* ▽ 21 14 19 $13

Mid-City | 5657 Wilshire Blvd. (Hauser Blvd.) | 323-933-1976 | www.blackdogcoffee.com

LACMA-goers and local office workers refuel at this "wonderful little" Mid-City coffeehouse dispensing "outstanding daily soups", "packed sandwiches with flair" and "custom hot dogs" - not to mention "great coffee"; set in a simple storefront with "personable" service, it's a "good bet" for "grabbing a quick bite" or "snacks for meetings", and "makes your everyday pickup lunch special."

Black Hogg Ⓜ *American* ▽ 22 18 22 $37

Silver Lake | 2852 W. Sunset Blvd. (Silver Lake Blvd.) | 323-953-2820 | www.blackhogg.com

This "tiny" storefront New American sits on a Silver Lake block where it offers a midpriced menu with roasted marrow bones and other "modern" "meat-centric" eats; the space is cleanly functional, with blond-wood tables, chairs covered with black fabric and lots of mirrors on the wall to give the illusion of space.

Black Market Liquor Bar ◐ *Eclectic* 23 21 21 $36

Studio City | 11915 Ventura Blvd. (Carpenter Ave.) | 818-446-2533 | www.blackmarketliquorbar.com

"Antonia Lofaso's *Top Chef* talents shine" at this late-night gastropub in Studio City, turning out an Eclectic mix of "fantastic" market-driven small plates designed to go with the "innovative" stylings of "stellar mixologists"; the "casual" room's "curved brick ceiling and candlelight help set a romantic atmosphere" and the staff "works as a team", but "be prepared for a loud crowd", a "long wait" and somewhat "pricey" bites.

Blair's *American* 24 20 22 $43

Silver Lake | 2903 Rowena Ave. (bet. Glendale Blvd. & Hyperion Ave.) | 323-660-1882 | www.blairsrestaurant.com

This "lovely" Silver Laker wins hearts with its "phenomenal" short ribs, mac 'n' cheese and other "chilly-evening" New American dishes "prepared with care" and served by a "casual but professional" staff in a "calm" setting warmed up with terra-cotta tones; slightly upscale yet "fairly priced", it's an "unexpected gem" for the neighborhood.

NEW Blaze Fast-Fire'd Pizza *Pizza* — | — | — | I

Torrance | Rolling Hills Plaza | 2625 PCH (Crenshaw Blvd.) | 310-325-9500
Pasadena | 667 E. Colorado Blvd. (Molino Ave.) | 626-440-7358
www.blazepizza.com

At these outposts of a customized pizza chain, patrons stand in line to order from a large selection of pies, which are delivered to the tables in an industrial setting; reasonable prices keep it busy with families.

BLD *American* 21 | 18 | 20 | $34

Beverly Boulevard | 7450 Beverly Blvd. (Vista St.) | 323-930-9744 | www.bldrestaurant.com

"All hail" chef Neal Fraser who "spruces up old staples" in "thoughtful" ways at this "decently priced" New American on Beverly Boulevard, famous for "amazing blueberry ricotta pancakes" at its "dandy", "crowded" brunch (it's "secretly fantastic for lunch and dinner too, without all the chaos"); the staff lends a "pleasant" air to the "bright, open" space, which is a bit "austere" but "cool without being pretentious."

Bloom Cafe *Californian* 23 | 16 | 20 | $19

Mid-City | 5544 W. Pico Blvd. (Sierra Bonita Ave.) | 323-934-6900 | www.bloomcafe.com

"Conscious eaters" say "yes, please!" to the "healthful, delicious twists" on traditional eats at this "cute", all-day Cal-American BYO in Mid-City; with a "laid-back" vibe and "friendly" service, plus colorful digs and "reasonable prices", it's a "darn-good neighborhood cafe."

Blossom *Vietnamese* 21 | 13 | 19 | $18

Downtown | 426 S. Main St. (Winston St.) | 213-623-1973 [S]
Silver Lake | 4019 W. Sunset Blvd. (Sanborn Ave.) | 323-953-8345 [M]
www.blossomrestaurant.com

Pho phans hankering for "healthy" Vietnamese head to this super-"chill" duo in Downtown and Silver Lake for the "dependable" signature soup and other "fresh", "flavorful" Saigon standards, along with a "surprisingly sophisticated" wine list; expect "fast" service and a "funky, modern" vibe in a casual setting - though without "sky-high prices."

Bludso's BBQ [M] *BBQ* 25 | 9 | 19 | $18

NEW Mid-City | 609 N. La Brea Ave. (bet. Clinton St. & Melrose Ave.) | 323-931-2583
Compton | 811 S. Long Beach Blvd. (Alondra Blvd.) | 310-637-1342
www.bludsosbbq.com

"Rib aficionados" are "sold on" the "genuine" Texas barbecue at this low-cost Compton "hole-in-the-wall", where "down-home" flavors earn the "stamp of approval" despite a table-free, window-service setup; those who prefer the "comforts of La Brea" mosey to the offshoot, which comes "complete with mixologists" and plenty of seating.

BlueCow Kitchen & Bar [S] *American* 22 | 20 | 21 | $27

Downtown | Two California Plaza | 350 S. Grand Ave. (4th St.) | 213-621-2249 | www.bluecowkitchen.com

"Farm-fresh bites" are a "welcome" alternative "to the stuffier, more upscale eateries" near the Disney Concert Hall say Downtowners who "nosh" on "gourmet sandwiches" and other "modestly priced" eats at this New American cousin to Mendocino Farms; the patio is "perfect for a quick lunch", and happy hour draws "office drones drowning their sorrows" in craft brews.

Blue Hen *Vietnamese* ▽ 21 | 16 | 18 | $18

Eagle Rock | 1743 Colorado Blvd. (bet. Argus Dr. & La Roda Ave.) | 323-982-9900 | www.eatatbluehen.com

This "no-nonsense" eatery in an Eagle Rock strip mall produces "fresh" twists on Vietnamese classics - using local, organic ingredients in its banh mi and "addictive" spring rolls; maybe it's "not the best", but for an inexpensive, takeout-ready spot, it's just "what you want."

Blue Plate *American* 20 | 15 | 19 | $24

Santa Monica | 1415 Montana Ave. (bet. 14th & 15th Sts.) | 310-260-8877 | www.blueplatesantamonica.com

For a "little of everything", locals visit this Santa Monica "neighborhood haunt", where "simple" American "comfort food" is served by a "friendly" crew in a bright, "beachy" atmosphere; some say the "cramped" digs "can get noisy", but the outdoor seating and mild prices provide regulars with enough "fuel" for area shopping.

Blue Plate Oysterette *Seafood* 22 | 17 | 20 | $37

Santa Monica | 1355 Ocean Ave. (Santa Monica Blvd.) | 310-576-3474 | www.blueplatesantamonica.com

"You'd think you're on the East Coast" at this "little" "Cape Cod-meets-Santa Monica" eatery, a local fave for "excellent" "simply prepared" seafood (including "slurp-worthy" oysters) and wines; other perks are "pleasant" service and "casual", "seafood-shack" digs with water views - mitigating some complaints about pricing that "ain't cheap."

NEW Blue Plate Taco *Mexican* ▽ 16 | 18 | 17 | $29

Santa Monica | Shore Hotel | 1515 Ocean Ave. (B'way) | 310-458-2985 | www.blueplatesantamonica.com

The "ocean view and splashy Shore Hotel" location steps away from the Santa Monica Pier ensure that this airy Mexican sib to Blue Plate and Blue Plate Oysterette stays "packed"; fans applaud the "unique" tacos and a "variety" of other plates, but in such a "Mexican-food-intensive town", some connoisseurs sniff "not up to snuff."

Bluewater Grill *Seafood* 21 | 21 | 21 | $36

NEW Catalina Island | 306 Crescent Ave. (bet. Metropole & Summer Aves.) | Avalon | 310-510-3474 | www.bluewateravalon.com

Redondo Beach | King Harbor Marina | 665 N. Harbor Dr. (Yacht Club Way) | 310-318-3474 | www.bluewatergrill.com

The "delightful" views "enhance" the "good, but not exceptional" fare and "creative sushi" at these "casual" well-priced seafooders whose "old-school" nautically themed settings hook locals and tourists alike; "attentive" service and a "relaxing" mood make them a "dependable" catch.

Blu Jam Café *American/European* 25 | 19 | 22 | $22

Melrose | 7371 Melrose Ave. (bet. Fuller & Martle Aves.) | 323-951-9191

NEW Sherman Oaks | 15045 Ventura Blvd. (Noble Ave.) | 818-906-1955

www.blujamcafe.com

"Popular with weekend brunchers", these Melrose and Valley "gems" deliver "creative" American-European "comfort food" (the "crunchy

French toast is a must-try") with a local-ingredient focus throughout the day; the "super-nice" staff navigates the "cozy" digs well, and though patrons point out "crowds", they generally agree it's "worth the wait."

The Blvd ◐ *Californian* 22 | 23 | 23 | $56

Beverly Hills | Beverly Wilshire | 9500 Wilshire Blvd. (Rodeo Dr.) | 310-385-3901 | www.fourseasons.com

"Glam up to be part of the ladies who lunch" at this "lovely" hotel dining room inside the Beverly Wilshire hosting premium "people-watching" in a "beautiful" art deco setting; service is generally "professional", but many find the Californian menu "pricey for what you get", although drinks at the bar is a less-expensive option.

Boa *Steak* 24 | 25 | 22 | $67

West Hollywood | 9200 Sunset Blvd. (Doheny Dr.) | 310-278-2050
Santa Monica | 101 Santa Monica Blvd. (Ocean Ave.) | 310-899-4466
www.boasteak.com

"Go big or go home" when you wine and dine at this "swanky steakhouse" pair in Santa Monica and WeHo, "a carnivore's playground" where "attentive" servers deliver pricey cuts of "quality beef" to "pretty people" and "trust-fund babies"; both sites are "stunning" and "epitomize" LA "buzz" with "TMZ photogs" standing by, though a few snipe they're more about "scene" than cuisine.

Boiling Crab *Cajun/Seafood* 24 | 16 | 18 | $25

Koreatown | 3377 Wilshire Blvd. (Alexandria Ave.) | 213-389-2722
Alhambra | 33 W. Main St. (bet. 1st St. & Garfield Ave.) | 626-300-5898
Alhambra | 742 W. Valley Blvd. (bet. 7th & 8th Sts.) | 626-576-9368
Rowland Heights | 18902 E. Gale Ave. (Nogales St.) | 626-964-9300
www.theboilingcrab.com

"Wear a bib" and "get your hands dirty" at this midpriced Cajun-seafood chain where diners dig into "spicy", "magically seasoned" crabs, shrimp and crawfish in a casual "seasidey" setting; some gripe about "waits" and merely "ok" service, but to fans, the food "makes up for everything"; P.S. a Westwood branch is coming soon.

Bollywood Cafe *Indian* ▽ 24 | 16 | 21 | $23

Studio City | 11101 Ventura Blvd. (Vineland Ave.) | 818-508-8400
Ventura | 500 E. Main St. (bet. California & Main Sts.) | 805-648-2533 M
Westlake Village | 860 Hampshire Rd. (bet. Lakefield Rd. & Wild Rose St.) | 805-777-7100 S
www.bollywood3.net

Regulars call this Indian chainlet "a cut above" with "authentic" cooking "with the perfect amount of heat" and plenty of vegetarian options; perhaps the modest setting lacks the pizzazz of the real Bollywood, but "courteous service" and "low prices" make up for it and there's always "fast delivery."

Bombay Cafe *Indian* 22 | 15 | 19 | $32

West LA | 12021 W. Pico Blvd. (Bundy Dr.) | 310-473-3388 | www.bombaycafe-la.com

After all these years, this West LA Indian still produces "high-quality", "spicy" "street food" ("no tired steam table here") alongside other traditional dishes, plus cocktails such as ginger margaritas - furnished by a "knowledgeable" staff in a "casual" yellow-and-blue setting; a few knock the "upscale prices", but it's certainly "worth going for a Mumbai fix."

Bombay Palace *Indian* 24 | 22 | 23 | $39

Beverly Hills | 8690 Wilshire Blvd. (bet. Hamel & Willaman Drs.) | 310-659-9944 | www.bombaypalace.com

"Classy and elegant" describes this Beverly Hills Indian, a "tried-and-true" mainstay since 1985 for "celestial", "authentic" fare (including a lunchtime buffet) offered in an upscale space with statues and "dramatic lighting"; allies appreciate the "gracious" servers too, and though some call prices "a little high", "you're paying for the complete package."

Boneyard Bistro ◐ *BBQ* 22 | 16 | 20 | $34

Sherman Oaks | 13539 Ventura Blvd. (Allott Ave.) | 818-906-7427 | www.boneyardbistro.com

"So much more than a BBQ place", this "down-home-meets-Downtown" Sherman Oaks eatery regales diners with both "top-notch" slow-smoked meats and "amazing" Eclectic bistro fare, plus a "dizzying" array of beers; critics call it "pricey" for the genre, but a "knowledgeable" staff and "upscale" environs with a patio help keep it on 'cue.

Border Grill *Mexican* 22 | 19 | 20 | $35

Downtown | Union Bank Tower | 445 S. Figueroa St. (5th St.) | 213-486-5171

Santa Monica | 1445 Fourth St. (bet. B'way & Santa Monica Blvd.) | 310-451-1655

www.bordergrill.com

"The Too Hot Tamales" (celeb chef-owners Susan Feniger and Mary Sue Milliken) maintain their "groove" dishing out "flavorful" "twists" on midrange Mexican fare at these "lively" Downtown and Santa Monica "favorites"; "helpful servers" and "funky", "colorful" digs boost "festive" vibes that suit "large groups" and "happy-hour" habitués.

Bossa Nova Restaurants ◐ *Brazilian* 22 | 16 | 19 | $24

Hollywood | 7181 W. Sunset Blvd. (Formosa Ave.) | 323-436-7999

West Hollywood | 685 N. Robertson Blvd. (Santa Monica Blvd.) | 310-657-5070

West LA | 10982 W. Pico Blvd. (bet. Military & Veteran Aves.) | 310-441-0404

www.bossafood.com

You get "lots of meat" for the money at this "casual" Brazilian trio, where the "massive" menu runs from "tasty" South American standards to steaks and salads; diners cite "slow" (though "friendly") service and "ridiculously packed" digs, but weekend late hours, plus take-out and delivery options, sate night owls and "value"-hunters.

Boss Sushi *Japanese* 24 | 16 | 23 | $39

Beverly Hills | 270 S. La Cienega Blvd. (Gregory Way) | 310-659-5612 | www.bosssushi.com

Carving up "fresh, tasty" fish for relatively little yen (including a "value" lunch menu), this "low-key" Beverly Hills Japanese manned by chef-owner Tom Sagara - the eponymous sushi "Boss" - showcases an array of "imaginative" rolls, served by a "friendly" staff; the modern decor suits the fin fare well, so don't be surprised if you "find yourself coming back."

	FOOD	DECOR	SERVICE	COST

Bottega Louie *Italian* 23 | 23 | 20 | $36

Downtown | 700 S. Grand Ave. (7th St.) | 213-802-1470 | www.bottegalouie.com

"The noise level's just shy of an LAX landing strip", but the "excellent pizzas", pastries and other "quality" Italian fare are "worth it" according to the "well-dressed thirtysomethings" who flock to this "energetic" Downtown eatery/market "looking to score a sophisticated meal at a moderate price"; the "grand" setting's "fresh flowers, high ceilings and white marble" lend a "smart" "New York sensibility", but with no reservations taken, "expect to wait."

The Bottle Inn Ristorante *Italian* 21 | 18 | 22 | $39

Hermosa Beach | 26 22nd St. (22nd Ct.) | 310-376-9595 | www.thebottleinn.com

For "special" nights, "you can't go wrong" with this "hideaway" near the ocean, an "old-fashioned" Hermosa Beach "favorite" known for its "friendly" service and "lovely" classic-Italian cuisine since 1974; coupled with choices from the "superb" wine list, it may not be the cheapest meal, but its "cozy" ambiance works wonders - especially if you dine in the "romantic" wine cellar.

BottleRock *European* 18 | 18 | 19 | $28

Downtown | Met Lofts | 1050 S. Flower St. (11th St.) | 213-747-1100 | www.bottlerockla.com ◐

Culver City | 3847 Main St. (Culver Blvd.) | 310-836-9463 | www.bottlerockculvercity.com

Oenophiles relish these "informal" wine-bar twins, where a "knowledgeable" staff "helps you discover" new bottles while providing affordable, "gourmet" European munchies; that's manna for "couples and singles" alike, who dig the happy hours and modern spaces at the Staples Center-convenient Downtown location (with a full kitchen) and Culver City (best for little bites).

Bouchon *French* 25 | 25 | 24 | $63

Beverly Hills | 235 N. Canon Dr. (bet. Dayton Way & Wilshire Blvd.) | 310-271-9910 | www.bouchonbistro.com

If you can't make it to the Yountville original, Thomas Keller's "civilized" Beverly Hills bistro showcases "terrific" French fare and "kitchen savvy" "worthy of its provenance"; add "professional" service, "magnificent decor" and "a celebrity or two", and it sizes up as "expensive but worth it."

Bouchon Bakery *Bakery* 25 | 21 | 22 | $38

Beverly Hills | 235 N. Canon Dr. (bet. Dayton Way & Wilshire Blvd.) | 310-271-9910 | www.bouchonbakery.com

An "informal glimpse" into Thomas Keller's world, this "fabulous" Beverly Hills French bakery in the Bouchon bistro lobby "wows" with "fantastic" breads, pastries and sandwiches costing relatively little dough; it's a to-go kiosk, so the setting's "casual" (though service is of typical Keller quality), but for fans, it's one of the "best secrets in town."

Bouzy Gastropub at Chez Mélange *American* 22 | 18 | 21 | $30

Redondo Beach | 1611 S. Catalina Ave. (bet. H & I Aves.) | 310-540-1222 | www.chezmelange.com

"Always filled with energy", this "foodie paradise" gastropub in Chez Mélange's front room draws Redondo Beach denizens with "inventive", midpriced New American fare, partnered with "creative cocktails" and microbrews; "friendly" service and a "comfortable", dimly lit setting, plus "top-notch" happy hours, offer a prime venue to "get your booze on."

Bow & Truss ◐ *Spanish* ▽ 18 | 18 | 18 | $32

North Hollywood | 11122 Magnolia Blvd. (bet. Blakeslee Ave. & Lankershim Blvd.) | 818-985-8787 | www.bowandtruss.com

This "nice, local" North Hollywood taverna serves midpriced tapas, tacos and Pan-Latin large plates, plus "terrific cocktails" and artisanal beers; the handsome space is built inside of a former auto body shop, with high-beamed ceilings, bare-brick walls and a dramatic bar, along with a sheltered outdoor patio.

Bowery ◐ *American* 22 | 19 | 21 | $27

Hollywood | 6268 W. Sunset Blvd. (Vine St.) | 323-465-3400 | www.theboweryhollywood.com

A "little slice of New York" in Hollywood, this American near the ArcLight is a popular late-night spot for its "awesome" trademark burger, complemented by a "sophisticated" wine list and intriguing beer selection; its "hip" clientele also likes the "surprisingly good" service and "decent prices", making the small subway-tiled room a "go-to" destination.

Brandywine ☒ *Continental* 27 | 20 | 26 | $66

Woodland Hills | 22757 Ventura Blvd. (Fallbrook Ave.) | 818-225-9114

The Continental fare's as "exquisite" as ever at this "romantic" Woodland Hills "gem", where "gracious" service led by the husband-and-wife owners "allows one to truly dine"; a few modernists call for "updating" the "countryside" decor, but most find it "charming in an old-school way" and willingly pay a premium to "feel special."

Brats Brothers *German* 22 | 14 | 19 | $17

Sherman Oaks | 13355 Ventura Blvd. (bet. Dixie Canyon & Fulton Aves.) | 818-986-4020

NEW **Thousand Oaks** | 2160 Newbury Rd. (Michael Dr.) | 805-716-3242

www.bratsbrothers.com

"It's a party any day of the week" at this Sherman Oaks German joint, where "convivial" patrons clink "giant steins" over "awesome" brats both "regular and exotic" (varieties include elk, alligator and venison); "corny decor", "servers who get the vibe" and live accordion on Saturdays pump up the atmosphere; P.S. there's also a Thousand Oaks spin-off.

Bravo Cucina *Italian/Pizza* 20 | 14 | 17 | $23

Santa Monica | Third St. Promenade | 1319 Third St. Promenade (bet. Arizona Ave. & Santa Monica Blvd.) | 310-394-0374

Bravo Pizzeria ◐ *Italian/Pizza*

Santa Monica | 2400 Main St. (bet. Hollister Ave. & Ocean Park Blvd.) | 310-392-7466

www.bravosantamonica.com

These "reliable" spots on Santa Monica's Third Street Promenade and Main Street offer "solid" Italian fare such as pastas, Gotham-style pizzas and cannoli flown in from New York; providing "quick" service, modest tabs and casual settings with "people-watching"-capable patios, they "do the job" - especially for "big groups."

	FOOD	DECOR	SERVICE	COST

Breadbar *Bakery* 18 15 16 $22

Century City | Westfield Century City Shopping Ctr. | 10250 Santa Monica Blvd. (Ave. of the Stars) | 310-277-3770 | www.breadbar.net

The "carbs are worth it" at this casual Century City American bakery that purveys "comforting" breads, along with "well-prepared" sandwiches and salads; the modern decor and "convenient" location make it suitable for breakfast, lunch or a "bite after shopping", but some snicker at "indifferent" service and "overpriced" eats, noting it's "not worth traveling to."

Brent's Deli *Deli* 26 15 22 $23

Northridge | 19565 Parthenia St. (bet. Corbin & Shirley Aves.) | 818-886-5679
Westlake Village | 2799 Townsgate Rd. (Westlake Blvd.) | 805-557-1882
www.brentsdeli.com

"Come hungry, leave stuffed" after noshing on "huge sandwiches" and other "fabulous", "real-deal" deli fare that's "worthy of NYC status" at this "bustling" Northridge vet and its "more modern" Westlake Village offshoot; conditions are "often crowded", but given the "efficient" service and "good value", "what's not to love?"

The Brentwood ◐ *American* 23 22 23 $51

Brentwood | 148 S. Barrington Ave. (bet. Barrington Pl. & Sunset Blvd.) | 310-476-3511 | www.brentwoodrestaurant.com

"Well-heeled Westsiders" and "industry" folks frequent this "cozy, little" Brentwood watering hole to "soak up worthy libations" with "wonderfully prepared" New American cuisine "served with care and personality"; the "denlike atmosphere" with black leather booths and dim lighting is "perfect for canoodling" – just "make sure your credit card has plenty of room for the tab."

Brewco Manhattan Beach ◐ *American* 19 18 19 $25

Manhattan Beach | 124 Manhattan Beach Blvd. (bet. Manhattan Ave. & Ocean Dr.) | 310-798-2744 | www.brewcomb.com

"Crowded and noisy", this Manhattan Beach sports bar is "a great place to grab a bite after a day at the beach" with an affordable American menu starring a "tasty burger" that's "worth every calorie", plus a wide range of draft beers; there's no outdoor seating, but the interior features a garage-door front, and there are plenty of TVs showing the game.

Brighton Coffee Shop *Diner* 19 11 19 $17

Beverly Hills | 9600 Brighton Way (Camden Dr.) | 310-276-7732 | www.brightoncoffeeshop.com

"What a coffee shop should be", this "refreshingly genuine" Beverly Hills diner has been slinging "solid" American "comfort food" (the tuna and meatloaf sandwiches draw raves) since 1930; nostalgists laud the "old-fashioned" vibe, fostered by servers who "aim to please", a vintage setting and prices that "can't be beat" – there's a reason it's "been there forever."

Brophy Bros. Restaurant & Clam Bar *Seafood* 21 19 20 $29

Ventura | 1559 Spinnaker Dr. (Navigator Dr.) | 805-639-0865 | www.brophybros.com

"The fish hop from the water to your plate" at this "casual" Ventura seafooder, where diners devour "fresh" fare and Bloody Marys while watching "seagulls begging" amid a "happening" harborside atmosphere; "friendly" service, "postcard sunsets" and "cheap" tabs are yours if you can handle the "wait" to get in.

Brother Sushi *Japanese* 25 | 15 | 21 | $40

Woodland Hills | 21418 Ventura Blvd. (bet. Canoga & De Roja Aves.) | 818-992-1284

"Don't blink or you might miss" this "tiny" Japanese in Woodland Hills, "still primo" after all these years for "fantastic" sushi and rolls, proffered in a setting where you "always feel welcome"; belt-tighteners say it's "not cheap", but it's often hopping, as regulars know "you get what you pay for."

Brunello Trattoria *Italian* 22 | 16 | 22 | $32

Culver City | 6001 Washington Blvd. (Hargis St.) | 310-280-3856 | www.brunello-trattoria.com

The "secret" may be out on this "charming" "mom-and-pop" trattoria - nestled in Culver City's art-gallery district - where "delightful" pastas, "fresh" breads and other "tastes-like-Italy" fare regale diners at "reasonable" prices; "warm", "accommodating" servers and a "homey", picture-filled room where it's "easy to chat" round out the setting, making it just the right mix for a "neighborhood" spot.

Bru's Wiffle *American* 22 | 15 | 19 | $18

Santa Monica | 2408 Wilshire Blvd. (bet. Chelsea Ave. & 24th St.) | 310-453-2787 | www.bruswiffle.com

The "amazing" waffles are "made with love" and provide "hearty" "deliciousness" in "many options" - including an "out-of-this-world" selection with fried chicken - at this American breakfast-and-lunch hub in Santa Monica; service is "friendly and efficient", and while the space is "small", so are the tabs.

NEW Bucato *Italian* - | - | - | M

Culver City | 3280 Helms Ave. (Washington Blvd.) | 310-876-0286 | www.bucato.la

Chef Evan Funke (ex Rustic Canyon) is in the kitchen at this moderately priced modern Italian in the Helms Bakery complex; the look is sleek and Milanese with seating both indoors and out, and there's a non-negotiable policy of no cell phones and no photos.

Buddha's Belly *Asian* 20 | 18 | 20 | $26

Beverly Boulevard | 7475 Beverly Blvd. (Gardner St.) | 323-931-8588
Santa Monica | 205 Broadway (2nd St.) | 310-458-2500
www.bbfood.com

"Meditate" on the "love" generated by this "trendy" Pan-Asian duo on Beverly Boulevard and in Santa Monica, which provides "nourishing", "satisfying" eats, plus soju and sake cocktails, in a casual environment that's "full of energy"; "courteous" service and "reasonable prices" are welcome, and while bellyachers carp about "noise" and a "lack of authenticity", overall it "hits the mark."

Buffalo Club *American* 19 | 20 | 20 | $59

Santa Monica | 1520 Olympic Blvd. (bet. 14th & 16th Sts.) | 310-450-8600 | www.thebuffaloclub.com

"Hidden" in an "industrial" section of Santa Monica is this "clublike" American, where a "dark" art deco-style dining room and "enchanting" patio attract LA "bigwigs" for "solid" "comfort-food" and small-plates menus; "welcoming" service also charms, and while a few dismiss "expensive", just-"ok" fare, late hours and a "scene" compensate.

Buffalo Fire Department *American* 22 | 19 | 21 | $23

Torrance | 1261 Cabrillo Ave. (Torrance Blvd.) | 310-320-2332 | www.buffalofiredepartment.com

For "juicy", "over-the-top" patties ("mac 'n' cheese burger, need I say more?") and spicy wings, try this "casual", mildly priced Torrance American from chef-owner and Buffalo, NY, native Michael Shafer of Depot across the street; "spot-on" service and a "vibrant" firehouse decor help spark the "kid-friendly" atmosphere, making it a local "favorite."

Buggy Whip *Seafood/Steak* 19 | 16 | 20 | $40

Westchester | 7420 La Tijera Blvd. (74th St.) | 310-645-7131 | www.buggywhipsteakhouse.com

"Old-school class" lives on at this Westchester "treasure", a circa-1949 chophouse where a "charming" staff delivers "ample" portions of "satisfying" prime rib and seafood, plus "wonderful" Green Goddess dressing, in a "clubby", "dimly lit" setting; though a minority calls it "tired" and "expensive", the "days-gone-by" atmosphere spurs loyalists to "settle into a leather booth" and enjoy.

NEW Bunker Hill Bar & Grill *American* - | - | - | I

Downtown | One Bunker Hill | 601 W. Fifth St. (Grand Ave.) | 213-688-2988

This tree-lined destination offers an unexpected respite from the gridlock of Downtown, in a space with warm wood, modernist dangling lights and an outdoor patio with many overhead umbrellas; it offers lots of craft beers and wines, along with numerous burgers with exotic toppings.

Burger Continental *Mideastern* 18 | 11 | 17 | $19

Pasadena | 535 S. Lake Ave. (California Blvd.) | 626-792-6634 | www.burgercontinentalpasadena.com

"It's not just burgers" being proffered at this Pasadena "institution" known for its "varied", "cheap" menu of Middle Eastern dishes distributed by an "attentive" staff; its Cal-Techie clientele also fancies the "pleasant" covered patio and regular belly dancing, and though some huff about "quantity over quality", it's certainly a "unique" experience.

Burger Lounge *Burgers* - | - | - | I

West Hollywood | 8539 W. Sunset Blvd. (La Cienega Blvd.) | 310-289-9250
Beverly Hills | 281 S. Beverly Dr. (Gregory Way) | 310-385-0898
NEW Brentwood | 11740 San Vicente Blvd. (Gorham Ave.) | 424-248-3789
NEW Santa Monica | 213 Arizona Ave. (2nd St.) | 424-238-8950
www.burgerlounge.com

This grass-fed burger chain with roots in San Diego continues to pop up in trendy 'hoods around LA serving patties alongside salads and other healthier and gluten-free options; the trademark orange-and-chrome setting offers lots of outdoor seats, and inexpensive prices cap things off.

Ca'Brea *Italian* 20 | 20 | 20 | $44

La Brea | 346 S. La Brea Ave. (bet. 3rd & 4th Sts.) | 323-938-2863 | www.cabrearestaurant.com

"Quality still rules" at this "unassuming" La Brea Northern Italian, a local "standby" for "solid", "old-school" standards dispensed by an "attentive" staff in a "cozy" space; a few thrifty types grimace at "pricey" fare, but the fact that it's often "crowded" speaks for itself.

	FOOD	DECOR	SERVICE	COST

CaCao Mexicatessen 🅜 *Mexican* | 24 | 14 | 15 | $21

Eagle Rock | 1576 Colorado Blvd. (Townsend Ave.) | 323-478-2791 | www.cacaodeli.com

No longer Eagle Rock's "best little secret", this taqueria produces "top-notch" Mexican eats ("duck tacos, are you kidding?"), "fantastic" specials and cocktails in a "cute" setting; pricing's "reasonable", and you can also buy spices, grains and its signature hot chocolate at the on-site deli.

Ca' del Sole *Italian* | 22 | 22 | 22 | $42

North Hollywood | 4100 Cahuenga Blvd. (Lankershim Blvd.) | 818-985-4669 | www.cadelsole.com

"Playing home to the heavy-hitters of the Valley media circuit", this "charming" North Hollywood Venetian, modeled after a country inn, blends "beautifully executed" Northern Italian cuisine (and a 700-bottle wine list) with "prompt" service, making it *perfetto* for "business-lunchers"; couple that with a "divine" plant-filled patio with private cabanas, and it's a "great value."

Cafe Angelino *Italian* | ▽ 23 | 15 | 24 | $36

Mid-City | 8735 W. Third St. (bet. George Burns Rd. & Robertson Blvd.) | 310-246-1177 | www.cafeangelino.com

Boasting the cozy "atmosphere of a small kitchen in Italy", this Mid-City "standby" appeals to "neighborhood" types with a "family-friendly" vibe and "wholesome" cooking like pastas and pizzas; prices are low and digs are "comfortable" enough, so consensus is "you can't go wrong."

Café Beaujolais 🅜 *French* | 26 | 19 | 23 | $36

Eagle Rock | 1712 Colorado Blvd. (bet. La Roda Ave. & Mt. Royal Dr.) | 323-255-5111

C'est toujours Paris at this "moderately priced" Eagle Rock bistro, where the "incredible", traditional French fare is served by "dreamy" waiters who are nearly as "authentic" as the food; *bien sûr,* the "convivial", poster-adorned setting adds to the feeling that you're in the City of Light, leading *admirateurs* to say it's "not to be missed."

Cafe Bizou *French* | 22 | 19 | 21 | $33

Santa Monica | Water Gdn. | 2450 Colorado Ave. (26th St.) | 310-453-8500 🅢

Pasadena | 91 N. Raymond Ave. (Holly St.) | 626-792-9923

Sherman Oaks | 14016 Ventura Blvd. (bet. Costello & Murietta Aves.) | 818-788-3536

www.cafebizou.com

"Consistent quality" "brings 'em in" to this "congenial" "local bistro" trio that still "packs a punch" thanks to "well-executed" French fare and "outstanding value" (the $2 corkage for BYO is "one of the few bargains in town"); trendsetters shrug "stable but not exciting", but they're "always crowded" so reservations are advised.

Café Brasil *Brazilian* | 22 | 15 | 17 | $19

Culver City | 11736 W. Washington Blvd. (bet. Kensington Rd. & McLaughlin Ave.) | 310-391-1216

Palms | 10831 Venice Blvd. (Westwood Blvd.) | 310-837-8957

www.cafe-brasil.com

Regulars "leave full" after downing the "tasty" grilled meats, "heavenly" juices and other "inexpensive" staples purveyed at these "cheerful"

Culver City and Palms Brazilians, where the "funky", "beach-shacky" ambiance (complete with outdoor seating) accentuates the "charm"; the "friendly" staff makes the counter-style service manageable, and enthusiasts have no qualms about labeling them a "winner."

NEW Cafe Brentwood *American* - - - M

Brentwood | 150 S. Barrington Ave. (Barrington Pl.) | 310-472-0766 | www.cafebrentwood.com

Chef-restaurateur Bruce Marder (Capo, The Brentwood) is behind this cafe just off Sunset Boulevard serving moderately priced American dishes for breakfast, lunch and dinner; it's built to look like a coffee shop from the '30s, with floor-to-ceiling windows, a long counter and gleaming stainless fixtures.

Cafe Del Rey *Californian/Mediterranean* 23 23 22 $51

Marina del Rey | 4451 Admiralty Way (bet. Bali Way & Vía Regatta) | 310-823-6395 | www.cafedelreymarina.com

An "exception to the rule" concerning typical waterside restaurants, this "high-class" Marina del Rey Cal-Med features "stunning" harbor views that are as "wonderful" as the food - no small feat, considering the scope of the "innovative" menu; moreover, the "romantic" ambiance, "personable" staff and "chichi" crowd assuage tabs some deem "pricey"; P.S. the bar is "excellent" for apps, especially when the fireplace is going.

Cafe Fiore *Italian* 22 21 21 $36

Ventura | 66 S. California St. (bet. Main & Santa Clara Sts.) | 805-653-1266 | www.fiorerestaurant.net

"Delicious" Southern Italian accompanied by a martini lounge with live music sets the scene at this midpriced neighborhood "hangout" in Old Town Ventura, favored by locals for its "intimate", patio-enhanced trattoria decor and concomitant service; savants advise "getting reservations", citing the "noisy", "busy" environs, but that won't stop advocates from itching to "go again."

Cafe Firenze M *Italian* 22 22 20 $38

Moorpark | Mission Bell Plaza | 563 W. Los Angeles Ave. (Leta Yancy Rd.) | 805-532-0048 | www.cafefirenze.net

Locals "love" Fabio Viviani, the former *Top Chef*-er and "face" of this mildly priced Moorpark "gem", which supplies "memorable" Northern Italian food (including pastas and thin-crust pizzas) to a charmed crowd; the "lovely" space - featuring an open kitchen and patio - compensates for what cynics call "variable" service, but an unwavering attribute is FV himself, who'll often "take a moment to greet" starstruck guests.

Café 14 M *Continental* 26 21 24 $50

Agoura Hills | Reyes Adobe Plaza | 30315 Canwood St. (Reyes Adobe Rd.) | 818-991-9560 | www.cafe-14.com

Nestled in an Agoura Hills strip mall just off the 101, this "wonderful little hideaway" delights diners with "sophisticated" Continental cuisine served by a staff that treats you like "royalty"; with its muted, upscale ambiance, "cozy" patio and "neighborhood feel", it's an "extraordinary" dining experience - and it carries price points to match.

Café Gratitude *American* 23 19 21 $25

Hancock Park | 639 N. Larchmont Blvd. (Melrose Ave.) | 323-580-6383

(continued)

Café Gratitude

Venice | 512 Rose Ave. (bet. 5th & Rennie Aves.) | 424-231-8000
www.cafegratitudela.com

There's "vegan magic" in this American chainlet's "innovative" organic cuisine, characterized by "exceptional" green-oriented dishes; a "sweet" staff oversees the modern, airy digs with an "amazing" patio, and if a minority pooh-poohs the "hippie" sensibility, there's still plenty to be "grateful" for - including the sensible prices.

Café Habana ◐ *Cuban/Mexican* 20 | 21 | 17 | $31

Malibu | Malibu Lumber Yard | 3939 Cross Creek Rd. (bet. Civic Center Way & PCH) | 310-317-0300 | www.habana-malibu.com

The "cheese-covered, char-grilled corn" is an "addiction" of "Malibu locals" who "meet and eat" at this "flavorful" Cuban-Mex, an NYC import by impresario Rande Gerber, sporting a "pleasant patio" with a huge Shepard Fairey mural; service is free of the "typical 'tude" and prices are down-to-earth as well, but it's still "TMZ-central for star sightings."

Cafe La Boheme *Californian* 20 | 24 | 21 | $50

West Hollywood | 8400 Santa Monica Blvd. (Orlando Ave.) | 323-848-2360 | www.cafelaboheme.us

With decor that's like "*The Phantom of the Opera* on steroids", this West Hollywood "destination" "shines" for "romantic" gatherings in its "magnificent" space with indoor and outdoor fireplaces; in comparison to the setting, some find the Californian cuisine only "fair", although "friendly" service, "reasonable" prices and a "vibrant happy hour" win over many.

Café Laurent *French* 20 | 16 | 18 | $20

Culver City | 4243 Overland Ave. (Barman Ave.) | 310-558-8622 | www.cafelaurent.com

"Sit on the patio and make believe you're in France" at this Culver City bistro dishing up crêpes, omelets and other "delicious" French fare that's a "favorite" for brunch; the interior's "a bit cramped", but it still works "if you're in the neighborhood."

Cafe Med *Italian* 20 | 19 | 20 | $36

West Hollywood | Sunset Plaza | 8615 W. Sunset Blvd. (Sunset Plaza Dr.) | 310-652-0445 | www.cafemedlosangeles.bicegroup.com

"Pizza and people-watching from the patio facing Sunset" make a winning combo at this "easy, no-attitude" West Hollywood Italian, a "chill-out" spot where "the occasional celebrity can be found just hanging with friends"; it's "reasonable", so even if most go for the "prime location", they're satisfied with the "consistent" cooking too.

Cafe Montana *Californian* 20 | 17 | 20 | $32

Santa Monica | 1534 Montana Ave. (16th St.) | 310-829-3990 | www.cafemontana.net

Attracting "ladies who lunch" since 1984, this "cute", "convivial" locale in Santa Monica succeeds with "spot-on" Cal fare ranging from "nice salads" to "huge", "amazing" desserts for "reasonable" tabs; given the "accommodating" service and a "sunny" setting with glass walls overlooking Montana Avenue, it's a "comfortable neighborhood" stop; P.S. "try the Lithuanian meat dumplings."

	FOOD	DECOR	SERVICE	COST

Café Piccolo *Italian* 24 | 23 | 23 | $37

Long Beach | 3222 E. Broadway (bet. Coronado & Obispo Aves.) | 562-438-1316 | www.cafepiccolo.com

It's all about the "enchanting" "garden atmosphere" at this "romantic" Long Beach oasis featuring fountains, a waterfall and "cozy" fire pits on the patio to complement "scrumptious" Northern Italian food; add in "unbeatable" service and moderate tabs, and it's "popular for dates, special occasions" and simply as a "go-to" "any day of the week."

Café Pierre *French* 24 | 20 | 23 | $47

Manhattan Beach | 317 Manhattan Beach Blvd. (bet. Highland Ave. & Morningside Dr.) | 310-545-5252 | www.cafepierre.com

Bringing "a bit of Paris to Manhattan Beach" for 35 years, this "old neighborhood favorite" by chef-owner Guy Gabriele is still a "solid performer" when it comes to "excellent" French bistro fare with "interesting" touches and "great service"; the "tight, noisy" quarters don't diminish the "quality at a reasonable price."

Cafe Pinot *Californian/French* 24 | 25 | 23 | $52

Downtown | 700 W. Fifth St. (Flower St.) | 213-239-6500 | www.cafepinot.com

Diners "delight" to this "Downtown hideaway" from Joachim Splichal providing "wonderful upscale Cal-French" dishes and "very good" wines that fit the "pre-theater" bill (plus servers are adept in "getting you out in time" for the show); most distinctively, the "tranquil" patio "overlooking the gardens" of the Central Library "adds a magical element" that makes it "worth the price tag."

Café Santorini *Mediterranean* 21 | 21 | 20 | $35

Pasadena | 64 W. Union St. (bet. De Lacey & Fair Oaks Aves.) | 626-564-4200 | www.cafesantorini.com

A "beautiful" rooftop balcony "tucked away from the hustle and bustle" of Old Town Pasadena "adds to the allure" of this "refreshing" Med specializing in "simple", "affordable" seafood, pizza and mezes; service gets mixed marks, but with the iPic Theater just steps away, it's "quite popular on weekend nights" with showgoers.

Cafe Verde *Californian/Pan-Latin* 23 | 16 | 21 | $29

Pasadena | 961 E. Green St. (Mentor Ave.) | 626-356-9811 | www.cafeverdepasadena.com

A "loyal following" "squeezes" into this "unique" sidewalk cafe in Pasadena for "excellent", "creatively prepared" Cal fare, plus some Latin twists at breakfast; while "claustrophobes" would balk at the "cramped" interior (and a "parade of pedestrians bumping your chair" outside), it's still has its "charms", boosted by modest prices and an "attentive" staff.

Caffé Delfini *Italian* 24 | 19 | 22 | $46

Santa Monica | 147 W. Channel Rd. (PCH) | 310-459-8823 | www.caffedelfini.com

Oozing "Italian charm", this upscale, dinner-only "gem" in the Santa Monica Canyon delivers "on-the-money" pasta and seafood with a little "stargazing" on the side; diners differ over whether the simple candelit room is "cozy" or "crammed", but loyalists just "love" it.

	FOOD	DECOR	SERVICE	COST

Caffe Luxxe *Coffeehouse* 21 17 19 $12

Brentwood | 11975 San Vicente Blvd. (bet. Montana & Saltiar Aves.) | 310-394-2222
Santa Monica | Brentwood Country Mart | 225 26th St. (bet. Brentwood Terr. & San Vicente Blvd.) | 310-394-2222
Santa Monica | 925 Montana Ave. (bet. 9th Ct. & 10th St.) | 310-394-2222
www.caffeluxxe.com

"No need to go to Italy", the "espresso jockeys" at these Euro-style coffeehouses know how to fashion "strong, rich" caffeinated creations (with "artistic foam toppings") at equally rich prices; there are "great pastries" and sandwiches too, and while you may not nab a spot to "work on your screenplay", "it's all about" the "top-notch" java here.

Caffe Opera *American/Eclectic* ▽ 21 21 22 $32

Monrovia | 402 S. Myrtle Ave. (Lime Ave.) | 626-305-0094

This "tasty" American-Eclectic strikes the right chord with Monrovia locals, bringing a meaty menu - including coffee bean-crusted rib-eye - to Old Town business-lunchers and others for a "surprisingly low price"; strong service and a "relaxing", "date"-friendly dining room with big windows overlooking the main drag are additional high notes.

Caffe Pinguini Ⓜ *Italian* ▽ 21 19 20 $43

Playa del Rey | 6935 Pacific Ave. (Culver Blvd.) | 310-306-0117 | www.caffepinguini.com

Both a "trusted neighborhood fixture" and "seaside escape", this "fairly priced" Playa del Rey Italian offering "delicious" fare and "classy" service provides a "romantic" prelude to a "walk on the beach"; given its "quiet trattoria ambiance" enhanced by Roman-style frescoes and a heated patio, guests wonder how it's "continued to stay a well-kept secret."

Caffe Roma ◐ *Italian* 22 20 20 $39

Beverly Hills | 350 N. Canon Dr. (Brighton Way) | 310-274-7834 | www.cafferomabeverlyhills.com

Beverly Hills' "old guard" are livin' "la dolce vita" at this "*tutto Italiano*" cafe by Agostino Sciandri (Ago) where the "extraordinary people-watching" often upstages the "reliable" food ("rocking" salads and pizzas) at moderate to high prices; "happy hour is beyond happy", and nighttime touches like silent black-and-white flicks, live music and DJ sets amp up the "amazing scene."

Caioti Pizza Cafe *Pizza* ▽ 21 9 15 $22

Studio City | 4346 Tujunga Ave. (bet. Moorpark & Woodbridge Sts.) | 818-761-3588 | www.caiotipizzacafe.com

Seekers of the "original" California pizza feed their fancy at this Studio City cafe from Spago's first pizza chef, the late Ed LaDou, that still turns out a "variety" of "awesome" pies and famous salads in casual quarters; a few critics "expect more" given the pedigree, and service is hit-or-miss, but it's an economical choice that many "wish" were in their neighborhood; P.S. no alcohol, no BYO.

Canal Club *Californian/Eclectic* ▽ 20 21 20 $36

Venice | 2025 Pacific Ave. (Venice Blvd.) | 310-823-3878 | www.canalclubvenice.com

Done up in "dark, sexy" style by local artists, this "hoppin'" Cal-Eclectic bro to James' Beach offers a diverse (some say "random")

dinner menu of grilled meats and "especially tasty" sushi to go with its "Venice vibe"; a "well-stocked bar", "no-stress happy hour" and staff that "adds to the fun" are a boon for "young eaters and drinkers" who say it's "all good."

C & O Cucina *Italian* 21 | 18 | 21 | $27

Marina del Rey | 3016 Washington Blvd. (bet. Abbot Kinney Blvd. & PCH) | 310-301-7278 | www.cocucina.com

C & O Trattoria *Italian*

Marina del Rey | 31 Washington Blvd. (bet. Pacific Ave. & Speedway) | 310-823-9491 | www.cotrattoria.com

"An endless supply" of "scrumptious" garlic knots "just keeps on coming" at this "kitschy" midpriced Italian duo in Marina del Rey, where "gargantuan" helpings of "familiar, well-prepared" pastas are set down by "friendly" opera-singing waiters; "rousing renditions of *That's Amore* occur hourly" and the "pitchers of wine" keep flowing, so even if it's "totally a madhouse" with perpetual "waits", most still find it all a lot of "fun."

Canelé 🅜 *Mediterranean* 23 | 16 | 20 | $38

Atwater Village | 3219 Glendale Blvd. (bet. Brunswick & Edenhurst Aves.) | 323-666-7133 | www.canele-la.com

Chef/co-owner Corina Weibel (ex Lucques) "lets the ingredients shine" in her "terrific", "fresh-from-the-farmer's-market" Med fare at this "homey" Atwater Villager with moderate prices, "attentive" service and an "intimate", "bohemian" feel; "beautifully prepared" brunches and "lovely" canelé pastries as a takeaway after dinner are added allures, so while it does get "busy", it's "just what you'd want in a neighborhood bistro."

Canter's ◐ *Deli* 20 | 12 | 17 | $22

Fairfax | 419 N. Fairfax Ave. (bet. Oakwood & Rosewood Aves.) | 323-651-2030 | www.cantersdeli.com

"Eat like there's no tomorrow" at this 24/7 Fairfax "nostalgia nosh", an "old Hollywood" "icon" famed for "generous" deli sandwiches from a "crazily immense menu" served by "spunky", "been-there-forever" waitresses; even if it's "faded from its days of glory", "everyone has to try it once"; P.S. "don't forget the bakery" or nightly live music in the Kibitz Room lounge.

The Capital Grille *Steak* 22 | 23 | 24 | $68

Beverly Hills | Beverly Ctr. | 8614 Beverly Blvd. (La Cienega Blvd.) | 310-358-0650 | www.thecapitalgrille.com

It's "hard to believe this is a chain" declare devotees of this "solid" "upscale chophouse" in the Beverly Center, where the prime cuts are "cooked to perfection" and paired with "spot-on" service from "a caring staff"; "gargantuan portions" and a "handsome setting" trimmed with "warm woods" help justify the "high" price tag.

Capo 🅢🅜 *Italian* 26 | 23 | 23 | $82

Santa Monica | 1810 Ocean Ave. (Vicente Terr.) | 310-394-5550 | www.caporestaurant.com

An "intimate" locale for "tremendous" dining, this Santa Monica Italian restaurant by Bruce Marder is dubbed the "*capo di tutti capi*" for its "exquisitely grilled meats" and other "superlative" fare backed by an "amazing" wine selection and "solid" service; its "Tuscan-villa" decor with an "open hearth" provides the "romance" factor big-time, but even ardent supporters are less than enamored with the "astronomical prices."

Carlitos Gardel *Argentinean/Steak* 24 | 20 | 25 | $49

Melrose | 7963 Melrose Ave. (bet. Edinburgh & Hayworth Aves.) | 323-655-0891 | www.carlitosgardel.com

It feels like the "Buenos Aires of the '50s" at this "charming" Melrose Argentinean "attracting expats" and locals alike with "mouthwatering" grass-fed steaks "as big as the table" and other upscale "*comida excelente*"; with its "dark, romantic" digs, carefully curated wine cellar and "top-notch" service overseen by a "dedicated family", it's a "real" find - "all that's missing is the tango."

Carnival *Lebanese* 25 | 11 | 19 | $23

Sherman Oaks | 4356 Woodman Ave. (bet. Moorpark St. & Ventura Blvd.) | 818-784-3469 | www.carnivalrest.com

"Heavenly" hummus, "great kebabs" and "fabulous fluffy rice" star at this "real-deal" Lebanese restaurant in Sherman Oaks that's frequently "as busy as a Beirut market", but "worth the wait"; it's also a "great value", despite sometimes "so-so service" and a "no-atmosphere" storefront setting.

Carousel Ⓜ *Mideastern* 25 | 17 | 22 | $32

East Hollywood | High Plaza | 5112 Hollywood Blvd. (bet. Normandie Ave. & Winona Blvd.) | 323-660-8060

Glendale | 304 N. Brand Blvd. (California Ave.) | 818-246-7775

www.carouselrestaurant.com

"Prepare to eat" and then "roll out" of this "authentic" Middle Eastern duo doling out "huge" platters of Lebanese-Armenian fare "for vegetarians and meat lovers" alike (one "tasty" meze platter "could be dinner on its own"); East Hollywood is a "no-frills, but friendly" setup, while weekend belly dancers in Glendale create a "wonderfully exotic atmosphere", and the occasional Kardashian sighting is icing on the cake.

NEW Carson House ◐ Ⓢ *American* - | - | - | M

Beverly Hills | 8635 Wilshire Blvd. (Carson Rd.) | 310-289-2800 | www.carsonhousebh.com

Just around the corner from La Cienega's Restaurant Row, this mid-priced Beverly Hills New American specializes in edgy small plates, flatbread pizzas and creative cocktails; the handsome space has lots of windows looking out onto busy Wilshire, as well as a private room off to one side.

Casa Bianca ◐ Ⓢ Ⓜ ⊄ *Pizza* 23 | 13 | 17 | $19

Eagle Rock | 1650 Colorado Blvd. (Vincent Ave.) | 323-256-9617 | www.casabiancapizza.com

"Thin-crust heaven" awaits those who brave the "lines" at this cash-only Eagle Rock pizza "icon" famed for its "sweet homemade sausage" ("the only topping you need") and "classic" 1950s setting reminiscent of "an Italian grandma's dining room" but with "smiling" waitresses; critics call the "buzz" "overrated", but diehards deem it "the best", thanks in part to the "great prices."

	FOOD	DECOR	SERVICE	COST

Casa Vega ◐ *Mexican* 19 | 17 | 19 | $26

Sherman Oaks | 13301 Ventura Blvd. (Fulton Ave.) | 818-788-4868 | www.casavega.com

A "very-happy happy hour" complete with "knock-your-socks-off margaritas" keeps Valleyites (and "celebs") coming to this "dark", "moody" "'50s throwback" in Sherman Oaks serving "solid" "gringo Mex" grub; yes, there's often a "ridiculous wait" to get in, but it's one of the few locals open till 1 AM, so "have another margarita and get over it."

NEW **Cast** *Californian* - | - | - | E

Santa Monica | Viceroy Santa Monica | 1819 Ocean Ave. (Pico Blvd.) | 310-260-7511 | www.viceroyhotelsandresorts.com

Replacing the more-formal Whist, this remodeled dining room at The Viceroy is open to the sea breezes, with walls that slide away, communal tables and mosaics on the walls; the pricey menu is rustic Californian, built around what's fresh at the nearby farmer's market.

Catch *Seafood* 22 | 25 | 23 | $52

Santa Monica | Hotel Casa del Mar | 1910 Ocean Way (bet. Bay St. & Pico Blvd.) | 310-581-7714 | www.hotelcasadelmar.com

For "elegant" dining with "outstanding" ocean views, Santa Monicans surface at this "high-class" Californian inside the Hotel Casa del Mar plying "excellent" local seafood in modern, leather-appointed digs; "splendid service" plus live music filtering in from the "happening" lounge add up to a "a thoroughly wonderful experience" - "with prices to match."

Caulfield's *American* 23 | 21 | 22 | $54

Beverly Hills | Thompson Beverly Hills | 9360 Wilshire Blvd. (Crescent Dr.) | 310-388-6860 | www.caulfieldsbeverlyhills.com

Bicoastal chef Stephen Kalt (ex Le Cirque in NYC) now oversees an "interesting", Mediterranean-influenced grill menu at this New American in Beverly Hills' "high-end" Thompson Hotel; Pullman booths, a mural of blacklisted writers and a name saluting the *Catcher in the Rye* hero drive home the midcentury theme - if only the prices were as nostalgic.

CBS Seafood *Seafood* 20 | 10 | 13 | $21

Chinatown | 700 N. Spring St. (Ord St.) | 213-617-2323

The carts keep on rolling at this "authentic Hong Kong-style" dim sum palace in Chinatown, where you can sample a "good variety" of "standard" morsels and seafood dishes on the cheap; it's "not the fanciest" place, to say the least, and the service score speaks for itself, but the fare is "solid" and an "extensive" to-go menu is a bonus.

Cecconi's *Italian* 22 | 24 | 22 | $60

West Hollywood | 8764 Melrose Ave. (Robertson Blvd.) | 310-432-2000 | www.cecconiswesthollywood.com

A "gorgeous crowd" convenes at this "posh" WeHo Italian - a "London transplant" in the former Morton's space - decked out in blue leather with patterned floors and chandeliers lending a "Rome-in-the-mid-'60s feel"; the "expensive" Venetian cuisine and "endearing" staff are equally "fabulous", and if you "go for brunch on the patio, you'll feel like a movie star."

FOOD | DECOR | SERVICE | COST

Celestino *Italian* 25 | 20 | 24 | $43

Pasadena | 141 S. Lake Ave. (bet. Cordova & Green Sts.) | 626-795-4006 | www.celestinopasadena.com

One of Pasadena's more "sophisticated" Italians, this "wonderful local" from the Drago Brothers delivers "amazing fresh pastas" and other "dependably delicious" fare at the "right price"; expect "charming" service from "actual Italian waiters" and "noisy", "informal" digs with a patio providing a quieter atmosphere.

Cha Cha Cha *Caribbean* 21 | 19 | 19 | $25

Silver Lake | 656 N. Virgil Ave. (Melrose Ave.) | 323-664-7723 | www.theoriginalchachacha.com

This "funky", "colorful" "Silver Lake icon" still satisfies that "Caribbean urge" after 27 years with "tasty" platters of "spicy" jerk chicken and "delish" sangria in a pleasantly "tacky" setting; some bemoan the "so-so service", but "the value is good" - it's so "filling", you "won't be able to cha cha cha out the door."

Cha Cha Chicken *Caribbean* 22 | 17 | 18 | $16

Santa Monica | 1906 Ocean Ave. (Pico Blvd.) | 310-581-1684 | www.chachachicken.com

"Spicy" Caribbean staples like jerk chicken are accompanied by "amazing fruit juices" at this "funky" open-air "shack" in Santa Monica that "looks like an island-style cabana with mismatched tables and chairs" and "vibrant, colorful" decor; it's counter service only, but food arrives "quickly" and BYO abets the "bang-for-the-buck" prices.

Chadaka *Thai* ▽ 21 | 20 | 20 | $29

Burbank | 310 N. San Fernando Blvd. (bet. Magnolia Blvd. & Palm Ave.) | 818-848-8520 | www.chadaka.com

"Small and chic", this "upscale" Burbank Thai has locals "hopelessly addicted" to well-priced staples like pad Thai, chicken satay and yellow curry; reports on service are mixed, and diehards declare it "isn't the most authentic", but a "unique" wine list and full bar make it a "best-kept secret" for a "fancy-pants" meal that won't break the bank.

Chakra *Indian* ▽ 23 | 23 | 22 | $35

Beverly Hills | 151 S. Doheny Dr. (bet. Charleville & Wilshire Blvds.) | 310-246-3999 | www.chakracuisine.com

Diners find "toothsome", "well-prepared" subcontinental cuisine and a "lovely" atmosphere with a full bar at this "upscale" Indian in Beverly Hills appealing to "vegetarians and carnivores" alike; a few find it "too expensive" for the genre, although the "divine lunch buffet" is a less costly option.

Chan Dara *Thai* 22 | 17 | 20 | $30

Hancock Park | 310 N. Larchmont Blvd. (bet. Beverly Blvd. & Rosewood Ave.) | 323-467-1052

West LA | 11940 W. Pico Blvd. (Westgate Ave.) | 310-479-4461 www.chandararestaurants.com

Chan Darae *Thai*

Hollywood | 1511 N. Cahuenga Blvd. (Sunset Blvd.) | 323-464-8585 | www.chan-darae.com

The "smokin' hot waitresses" almost upstage the "tasty" fare at these independently owned Thais offering "lots to choose from" in a menu that "runs a fine line between authentic and accessible"; although it's sometimes "a scene" with a "higher-end" atmosphere, tabs are still easy on the wallet.

Chaya Brasserie *Asian/French* 23 | 23 | 22 | $49

West Hollywood | 8741 Alden Dr. (bet. George Burns Rd. & Robertson Blvd.) | 310-859-8833 | www.thechaya.com

"Still going strong", this "timeless" West Hollywood Asian-French pulls a "beautiful" crowd with "consistently innovative" dishes, "excellent" service and a "lovely" "Zen"-like interior that feels "trendy, but isn't a hassle to get into"; it's "not cheap", but consensus is "you can wear a blindfold and still pick something good to eat."

Chaya Downtown *Asian/French* 23 | 24 | 22 | $50

Downtown | City Nat'l Plaza | 525 South Flower Street (bet. 5th & 6th Sts.) | 213-236-9577 | www.thechaya.com

This "classy" Downtown eatery in the Chaya empire is a "favorite" for business lunches and pre-theater dining thanks to its "creative, delicious" Asian-French fusion fare and "terrific cocktails" served by a "brisk, professional" staff in a "stylish", "sophisticated" setting; some say prices are "best suited for an expense account", or try a seat at the "happening" bar for nibbles and drinks at happy hour.

Chaya Venice *Asian/French* 23 | 22 | 21 | $45

Venice | 110 Navy Street (Main St.) | 310-396-1179 | www.thechaya.com

"After all these years", this perpetually "packed" Venice canteen is still hot, attracting lots of "pretty people" with "wonderfully fresh" sushi and "consistently delicious" Asian-French fare served by a "sophisticated" staff; there's also a "cool bar scene" - just "go early if you value your eardrums", and take advantage of the "epic" happy hour.

Checkers Downtown *Californian* 22 | 23 | 21 | $50

Downtown | Hilton Checkers | 535 S. Grand Ave. (bet. 5th & 6th Sts.) | 213-891-0519 | www.hiltoncheckers.com

The place to go for a "civilized business breakfast meeting" or pre-theater dining, this "quiet" Californian in the Hilton Checkers Downtown serves all "the usual suspects" with "excellent" execution; while it's expensive, the setting's "refined" and service is "thoughtful", so most are "never disappointed."

Cheebo *Italian* 21 | 17 | 19 | $28

Hollywood | 7533 W. Sunset Blvd. (Sierra Bonita Ave.) | 323-850-7070 | www.cheebo.com

A "neighborhood" crowd counts on this "buzzy" Hollywood joint featuring a "wide-ranging", "healthy", mostly organic Italian menu and "tasty" pizza sold by the slab; some say it's "pricier than you might think", but with an unpretentious bright-orange setting and affable service, it's "always busy"; it also works well for takeout.

Cheesecake Factory *American* 18 | 17 | 18 | $28

Fairfax | The Grove | 189 The Grove Dr. (bet. Beverly Blvd. & 3rd St.) | 323-634-0511

Beverly Hills | 364 N. Beverly Dr. (bet. Brighton & Dayton Ways) | 310-278-7270

Marina del Rey | 4142 Via Marina (Panay Way) | 310-306-3344

(continued)

Cheesecake Factory

Redondo Beach | 605 N. Harbor Dr. (Portofino Way) | 310-376-0466
Arcadia | 400 S. Baldwin Ave. (Huntington Dr.) | 626-447-2800
Pasadena | 2 W. Colorado Blvd. (Fair Oaks Ave.) | 626-584-6000
Sherman Oaks | Sherman Oaks Galleria | 15301 Ventura Blvd. (Sepulveda Blvd.) | 818-906-0700
Woodland Hills | 6324 Canoga Ave. (bet. Trillium Dr. & Victory Blvd.) | 818-883-9900
Thousand Oaks | Thousand Oaks Mall | 442 W. Hillcrest Dr. (McCloud Ave.) | 805-371-9705
www.thecheesecakefactory.com

There's "always something for everyone" on the "massive menu" at this "popular, noisy" chain famed for its "gigantic, shareable" helpings of American grub; it can feel a tad "corporate" and "lines are expected" at peak hours, but most find it "reliable" for the price, and "you can't beat the selection of cheesecake" either "if you still have room for dessert."

Chef Melba's Bistro Ⓜ *Californian* 26 | 16 | 23 | $44

Hermosa Beach | 1501 Hermosa Ave. (15th St.) | 310-376-2084 | www.chefmelbasbistro.com

A "small place with big taste", this Hermosa Beach bistro is a "top pick" thanks to the "delicious", "lovingly prepared" Cal cuisine cooked up by chef Melba herself in an open kitchen; the mood is "warm and welcoming" too, but "the best part is the shockingly affordable price."

NEW **Chego!** Ⓜ *Korean/Mexican* 23 | 12 | 15 | $15

Chinatown | Far East Plaza | 727 N. Broadway (Alpine St.) | 323-380-8680 | www.eatchego.com

Kogi truck creator Roy Choi has moved his inexpensive Korean-Mex eatery from the Westside to a busy mall in Chinatown, adjacent to a bunch of dim sum parlors, offering his "clever", mega-spicy rice bowls in a purposely nondescript setting; you order from a counter, then grab a seat and feast - either inside the restaurant or outside on the mall.

Cheval Bistro Ⓜ *French* 23 | 22 | 22 | $45

Pasadena | 41 S. De Lacey Ave. (Fraser Alley) | 626-577-4141 | www.chevalbistro.com

It's like "Paris in Pasadena" at this Old Town French from the Smith Brothers, earning a "thumbs-up" for its "enjoyable" menu elevated by specialty cocktails and an "epic" wine list in a "quiet" space whose centerpiece is a 100-year-old mahogany bar; midrange pricing is a plus, and although a few find fault with "inconsistent" food and service, most leave "satisfied."

Chez Jay ◐ *Steak* 20 | 17 | 20 | $33

Santa Monica | 1657 Ocean Ave. (Colorado Ave.) | 310-395-1741 | www.chezjays.com

"An oldie but goodie", this circa-1959 Santa Monica "dive" is a "sentimental favorite" for "decent" steaks that "won't break the bank" helped along by "stiff drinks" in a "kitschy" setting with red-checkered tablecloths and sawdust on the floor; most "don't go for the food", but "if you want to experience a little bit of Hollywood history by the beach, then this is the place."

	FOOD	DECOR	SERVICE	COST

Chez Mélange *Eclectic* 26 | 21 | 25 | $44

Redondo Beach | 1611 S. Catalina Ave. (bet. H & I Aves.) | 310-540-1222 | www.chezmelange.com

"As reliable as ever", this Redondo Beach "local favorite" continues to be "ahead of the curve" with an "imaginative" Eclectic menu that "shines with local, seasonal ingredients" and an "A+ wine list"; with "gracious" service and a "lovely" setting, most find it a "delightful experience that pleases the palate but doesn't hurt the wallet"; P.S. the Trust the Chef prix fixe dinners are "a bargain and delicious."

NEW Chez Mimi M *French* ∇ 19 | 16 | 18 | $60

Pacific Palisades | 548 Palisades Dr. (Sunset Blvd.) | 310-393-0558

"A favorite throughout the years" for "competently prepared classic French food" and weekend brunch, this bistro is already "popular" in its "new neighborhood" in Pacific Palisades; the ambiance is "lovely" and "you can hear the people at your table", and fans of "fine dining" say it's "nice to have it back."

NEW Chez Soi *Californian* - | - | - | M

Manhattan Beach | Metlox Plaza | 451 Manhattan Beach Blvd. (bet. Morningside & Valley Drs.) | 310-802-1212 | www.chezsoirestaurant.com

Chef Mark Gold and restaurateur Thierry Perez (ex Fraîche) head south to the stylish Metlox Plaza in groovy Manhattan Beach for this snappy, medium-priced Californian; the homey setting is dominated by a long bar and tall windows that look out at the plaza.

Chichen Itza *Mexican* 25 | 11 | 19 | $17

Downtown | Mercado La Paloma | 3655 S. Grand Ave. (bet. 35th & 37th Sts.) | 213-741-1075 | www.chichenitzarestaurant.com

"*Que sabroso!*" say fans of the "startlingly unique" Yucatecán cuisine like cochinita pibil and other "amazing", "authentic" items that "have legitimate wow factor" at this "no-frills" Mexican in Downtown's Mercado La Paloma; it's counter service only, but the staff is "helpful" with recommendations, and it's one of the "best bets around USC for sure."

Chi Dynasty *Chinese* 20 | 19 | 19 | $28

Los Feliz | Los Feliz Plaza | 1813 Hillhurst Ave. (bet. Melbourne & Russell Aves.) | 323-667-3388

Glendale | The Americana at Brand | 769 Americana Way (Central Ave.) | 818-500-9888

Studio City | 12229 Ventura Blvd. (Laurel Canyon Blvd.) | 818-753-5300 www.chidynasty.com

Locals "love the Chinese chicken salad" and other "fresh, flavorful" (if "inauthentic") eats at this chainlet manned by a "pleasant" staff; the menu is a "tad pricier than your average take-out" joint, but the ambiance is a step up too, with a "dark", contemporary look that "makes you want to drink mai tais all night."

NEW Chi-Lin *Chinese* - | - | - | E

West Hollywood | Sunset Medical Tower | 9201 Sunset Blvd. (Doheny Rd.) | 310-278-2068 | www.innovativedining.com

At this glossy West Hollywooder adjacent to sibling restaurant RivaBella, culinary and film legend Cecile Tang offers a pricey menu of her 'New Chinese' takes on classic Hong Kong dishes, served in a striking space dominated by shades of red and black with hundreds of Chinese lanterns hanging from the ceiling.

Chin Chin *Asian* | 19 | 16 | 18 | $26

West Hollywood | Sunset Plaza | 8618 W. Sunset Blvd. (Sunset Plaza Dr.) | 310-652-1818
Beverly Hills | 206 S. Beverly Dr. (Charleville Blvd.) | 310-248-5252
Brentwood | San Vincente Plaza | 11740 San Vicente Blvd. (Gorham Ave.) | 310-826-2525
Studio City | 12215 Ventura Blvd. (Laurel Canyon Blvd.) | 818-985-9090
www.chinchin.com

It's all about the "addictive" Chinese chicken salad at this 1980s-era chainlet offering Asian fare that's "not terribly genuine, but still damn tasty" (chocolate-dipped fortune cookies, anyone?) and "well priced" too; even if decor "needs a face-lift", "generous portions" and a "courteous" staff make for a pleasantly "predictable" experience; it's also "good for takeout."

Chinois on Main *Asian/French* | 26 | 20 | 24 | $65

Santa Monica | 2709 Main St. (Hill St.) | 310-392-9025 | www.wolfgangpuck.com

A "pioneer of Asian-French fusion fare", this "pricey" Wolfgang Puck flagship in Santa Monica "still delivers the goods" "after all these years", in the form of "marvelous" "old standards" such as "lobster and catfish to die for", backed by a winning wine list and "superb" service; opinions are divided on the "distinctly '80s" teal interior ("beautiful" vs. "dated"), but most agree this "classic" has "withstood the test of time."

NEW chi SPACCA *Italian* | - | - | - | M

Hollywood | 6610 Melrose Ave. (Highland Ave.) | 323-297-1133 | www.chispacca.com

From the superstar team of Nancy Silverton, Mario Batali and Joe Bastianich comes this midpriced Italian eatery adjacent to their Osteria Mozza on Melrose featuring a meat-heavy menu that includes house-cured items, pâtés and hearty mains; the warm setting evokes Tuscany with its worn wood tables, open kitchen and shelves full of wine bottles on display.

Cholada *Thai* | 23 | 11 | 18 | $23

Malibu | 18763 PCH (Old Malibu Rd.) | 310-317-0025
Thousand Oaks | 1774 E. Thousand Oaks Blvd. (Zuniga Ridge Pl.) | 805-557-0899 M
www.choladathaicuisine.com

"Soak in the salty sea breeze" at this "funky" Thai "beach shack" nestled on PCH in Malibu, where "wonderfully authentic" "mouthwatering" fare makes a "true believer" out of many; the bills are low, so the only downside is that "service is so efficient, you may be out the door in 30 minutes"; P.S. the Thousand Oaks location is less of a charmer.

ChoSun Galbee *Korean* | 24 | 20 | 19 | $37

Koreatown | 3330 W. Olympic Blvd. (Manhattan Pl.) | 323-734-3330 | www.chosungalbee.com

This "upscale", "elegant" Korean "impresses" guests with "tender, flavorful" grill-your-own meats of "excellent quality" and "good wines" in a "lovely" modern milieu that's "rare for K-town"; service is "attentive" and a patio is a plus, so the only drawback is the "premium pricing."

	FOOD	DECOR	SERVICE	COST

Christine *Mediterranean/Pacific Rim* | 27 | 19 | 24 | $45

Torrance | Hillside Vill. | 24530 Hawthorne Blvd. (Via Valmonte) | 310-373-1952 | www.restaurantchristine.com

Chef-owner Christine Brown "makes magic in the kitchen" in the form of "creative", "steady" Mediterranean-Pacific Rim cuisine at her "neighborhood place" nestled in an "unassuming" Torrance strip mall; "excellent" service (though a few find it "too quick" for comfort), a "warm, inviting" vibe in the space evoking a Tuscan villa and "reasonable" prices all make it a "solid" choice for "special occasions."

Church & State *French* | 24 | 20 | 20 | $48

Downtown | 1850 Industrial St. (Mateo St.) | 213-405-1434 | www.churchandstatebistro.com

Expect "pitch-perfect" French fare at this "boisterous" bistro where a resident "cocktail wizard", "unusual wines" and "perfect steak frites" draw Downtown's "hipster chic" contingent; service is "friendly" and the "inspiring" digs in the circa-1925 former Nabisco factory are often "noisy without being overwhelming", filled with the sounds of diners "enjoying each other's company."

The Churchill ◐ *American* | ▽ 15 | 18 | 15 | $39

West Hollywood | Orlando Hotel | 8384 W. Third St. (Orlando Ave.) | 323-655-8384 | www.the-churchill.com

It "looks like a pub" but "feels like a club" at this "sceney" two-story WeHo gastropub that's "ridiculously packed at night" with "young professionals chitchatting and networking" who ignore the "unapologetically slow" service and slightly high tabs; some say the food's "tasty" enough, but the consensus is it's more about the "swell" cocktails and "excellent" beer selection than the "mediocre" eats.

Cicada Ⓜ *Californian/Italian* | 25 | 27 | 24 | $58

Downtown | 617 S. Olive St. (bet. 6th & 7th Sts.) | 213-488-9488 | www.cicadarestaurant.com

For a dining event that "feels like you're in a movie", this "fabulous" Cal-Italian in Downtown's historic James Oviatt Building flaunts its art deco ambiance with 30-ft. gold-leaf ceilings and swing bands on Sundays; although it's "not inexpensive" and hours are limited, well-heeled theatergoers who appreciate "superb meals" and "attentive service" say it's "always a good time."

NEW Circa ◐Ⓜ *Eclectic* | - | - | - | M

Manhattan Beach | 903 Manhattan Ave. (9th St.) | 310-374-4422 | www.circamb.com

The Zislis Group is behind this modernist Eclectic in Manhattan Beach helmed by famously edgy chef Octavio Becerra (ex Palate Food + Wine), who's created a moderately priced menu of small dishes, along with an extensive cocktail list; all is served in a room dominated by brick walls and wooden tables that lend the space a casual air.

City Tavern *American* | 19 | 19 | 18 | $28

Culver City | 9739 Culver Blvd. (Duquesne Ave.) | 310-838-9739 | www.citytavernculvercity.com

"If you love beer" you'll certainly appreciate the self-serve taps at the tables (a "fun gimmick") and the selection of ever-changing local brews at this rustic-chic Culver City tavern; a "limited menu" of "inventive", well-priced American comfort food pleases, but service is erratic and some find the "frat-boy" crowd a little hard to handle.

Clay Oven *Indian* | 23 | 17 | 20 | $26

Sherman Oaks | 14611 Ventura Blvd. (Cedros Ave.) | 818-995-1777 | www.myindiancuisine.com

The "sumptuous" lunch buffet is the "best deal" at this Sherman Oaks Indian offering "solid", "well-prepared" fare in a selection that "changes daily"; although reviews on service are mixed, prices are reasonable and the patio is a plus.

Clementine ☒ *American* | 25 | 13 | 16 | $20

Century City | 1751 Ensley Ave. (Santa Monica Blvd.) | 310-552-1080 | www.clementineonline.com

"Simply adorable", this "tiny, little" Century City cafe is a find for "delish" sandwiches and salads, plus "wonderful" "artisan-style" pastries and breads; counter service is "kind", but the vibe is "hectic" thanks to "scarce" parking and "cramped", "crowded" quarters, so many prefer takeout; P.S "don't miss" the special grilled cheese menu in April.

Cleo *Mediterranean* | 26 | 25 | 22 | $50

Hollywood | Redbury Hotel | 1717 Vine St. (Hollywood Blvd.) | 323-962-1711 | www.cleorestaurant.com

"A see-and-be-seen scene" permeates this "terminally hip", "gorgeous" destination in Sam Nazarian's Redbury Hotel, where "expertly prepared" Mediterranean small plates, a "solid wine list" and "fun" cocktails "raise the bar" for Hollywood nightlife; a "knowledgeable" staff is a plus, but the bill adds up quickly and the partylike atmosphere makes it "incredibly loud."

Cliff's Edge *Californian/Italian* | 21 | 26 | 20 | $40

Silver Lake | 3626 W. Sunset Blvd. (Edgecliffe Dr.) | 323-666-6116 | www.cliffsedgecafe.com

"Lingering alfresco is what it's all about" at this Silver Lake charmer - a "surprising oasis" in an "unassuming strip mall" - boasting a "magical" patio shaded by trees that works for brunch or "when you have a date you want to impress"; it's not inexpensive, but service is solid and the Cal-Italian menu (kale salad, Cornish hen) is "enjoyable" too.

NEW Clusi Batusi ☒ *Pizza* | - | - | - | I

West LA | 2047 Sawtelle Blvd. (Mississippi Ave.) | 310-477-7707 | www.clusibatusi.com

In the middle of West LA's thriving Little Osaka, this affordable we-do-it-your-way quick-service pizzeria features dozens of topping options and a 1,200-degree oven that cooks pies in under a minute; sit inside at the plain-Jane red-and-white storefront, or grab a seat at a handful of sidewalk tables.

Coast *Californian/Seafood* | 22 | 24 | 22 | $44

Santa Monica | Shutters on the Beach | 1 Pico Blvd. (Ocean Ave.) | 310-587-1707 | www.coastsantamonica.com

"As close as you can get to the beach" without being sand-bound, this "expensive" Santa Monica Californian at Shutters Hotel regales diners with "wonderful" ocean views from its waterside patio; some say the "competent" seafood may not match the ambiance, but service is "excellent" and to most it's a "class act."

	FOOD	DECOR	SERVICE	COST

Coco Laurent *French* | - | - | - | M |

Downtown | 707 S. Grand Ave. (7th St.) | 213-623-0008 | www.cocolaurent.com

Add one more destination eatery to Downtown's busy Restaurant Row, a moderately priced French bistro that brings a touch of Gallic elegance to the area, complete with a delicatessen next door that offers small bites for those on the run; built on the ground floor of a historic structure, the 300-seat space boasts a soaring ceiling, handmade chandeliers and hand-carved crown molding.

Cole's ◐ *Sandwiches* | 17 | 18 | 15 | $20 |

Downtown | 118 E. Sixth St. (bet. Los Angeles & Main Sts.) | 213-622-4090 | www.colesfrenchdip.com

A dose of "old-fashioned goodness", this circa-1908 Downtown "classic" "feels like a trip back in time" with "fair" French dips made with beef and lamb served in an "atmospheric" setting; critics claim it's "expensive" and "used to be better", so its biggest asset may be the hidden speakeasy in back - The Varnish - known for its crafty mixologists, "designer" cocktails and "hipster" crowd.

Comme Ça *French* | 23 | 21 | 21 | $50 |

West Hollywood | 8479 Melrose Ave. (bet. Croft Ave. & La Cienega Blvd.) | 323-782-1104 | www.commecarestaurant.com

Feel transported to "Paris in a flash" at this "beloved" West Hollywood brasserie from David Myers, where "Oscar winners and wannabes" tuck into "fabulous", "authentic" eats and "wonderful cheeses" plus a "phenomenal" burger in a "swank" setting; with "creative cocktails" and a "good-looking" staff, it makes for a "delightful", if "pricey", experience - now if only they could "turn down the volume."

Congregation Ale House *American* ▽ | 18 | 18 | 17 | $18 |

Long Beach | 201 E. Broadway (Long Beach Blvd.) | 562-432-2337 ◐
Pasadena | 300 S. Raymond Ave. (Del Mar Blvd.) | 626-402-2337 ◐
Azusa | 619 N. Azusa Ave. (bet. Foothill Blvd. & 6th St.) | 626-334-2337
www.congregationalehouse.com

This gastropub chainlet set in "cathedrallike sanctuaries" is a "beer-lover's heaven" with a "varied" brew selection backed by cheap, "yummy" sausages and other American eats; service can be slow, but waitresses in "little school uniforms" make up for it.

NEW Connie & Ted's *Seafood* | - | - | - | M |

West Hollywood | 8171 Santa Monica Blvd. (Havenhurst Dr.) | 323-848-2722 | www.connieandteds.com

Popular from day one, this casual seafooder in West Hollywood from Michael Cimarusti (Providence) features a medium-priced menu served in a room that looks lifted from the Maine shoreline; it sports bright-orange seats, polished wood tables and an open kitchen and raw bar with everything on display.

Cooks County *Californian* | 23 | 18 | 22 | $44 |

Beverly Boulevard | 8009 Beverly Blvd. (bet. Edinburgh & Laurel Aves.) | 323-653-8009 | www.cookscountyrestaurant.com

"Creative" "farm-to-table" "comfort food" at "reasonable prices" is the "lure" at this casual Californian on Beverly Boulevard, with "top-notch" service as a bonus; a "neighborhood" crowd packs into what some describe as "tight" quarters, which can get "loud, loud, loud" at peak times, but many insist the fare is "worth the din."

Cook's Tortas *Mexican* ∇ 23 | 13 | 18 | $13

Monterey Park | 1944 S. Atlantic Blvd. (bet. Brightwood St. & Floral Dr.) | 323-278-3536 | www.cookstortas.com

"The definition of a hidden gem", this Monterey Park Mexican sandwich shop purveys "the platonic ideal of tortas" crafted with "flavorful" meats and "fresh" "homemade" bread, in "imaginative" combinations; "long lines" can be the norm in the deli-style space, but "fast, friendly" service keeps the crowds moving and prices won't break the bank; P.S. don't forget the agua frescas!

Coral Tree Café *Sandwiches* 19 | 15 | 16 | $18

Brentwood | 11645 San Vicente Blvd. (Darlington Ave.) | 310-979-8733
Encino | 17499 Ventura Blvd. (Encino Ave.) | 818-789-8733

Coral Tree Express *Sandwiches*

Century City | Westfield Century City Shopping Ctr. | 10250 Santa Monica Blvd. (Ave. of the Stars) | 310-553-8733
www.coraltreecafe.com

Neighborhood types rely on these "comfy" cafes for "healthy" "dependable" sandwiches, salads and pastries crafted from organic ingredients, and "decent coffee"; decor is a "mixed bag", but free WiFi helps, and most find "friendliness trumps its few flaws."

Cora's Coffee Shoppe *Diner* 23 | 16 | 18 | $23

Santa Monica | 1802 Ocean Ave. (Pacific Terr.) | 310-451-9562 | www.corascoffee.com

Locals love this "cool breakfast spot" in Santa Monica slinging "gourmet coffee-shop" grub "geared for foodies" and offered till 3 PM daily; service is "efficient", and it boasts a "cute" covered patio, but it's often "so crowded" that it's "tough to get a seat."

NEW **Corazon y Miel** M *Pan-Latin* - | - | - | M

Bell | 6626 Atlantic Ave. (Gage Ave.) | 323-560-1776 | www.corazonymiel.com

This cozy Pan-Latin in Bell offers interesting, well-priced dishes inspired by Mexico and South America like braised oxtail and a burger topped with jalapeño relish; the setting features old brick walls decorated with original art.

Corkbar *Eclectic* 21 | 22 | 21 | $37

Downtown | 403 W. 12th St. (Grand Ave.) | 213-746-0050 | www.corkbar.com

A "fantastic" selection of nearly 70 wines by the glass paired with "solid" Eclectic nibbles (like fish tacos and grilled cheese) makes this "minimalist" Downtown bar a "cool" hangout after work or before a game at Staples Center; "wonderful" happy-hour deals draw "noisy" crowds, so snag a seat near the outdoor fire pit for more elbow room.

Corner Door ◐ *American* - | - | - | M

Culver City | 12477 W. Washington Blvd. (Wasatch Ave.) | 310-313-5810 | www.thecornerdoorla.com

The door is indeed in the corner of this Culver City New American offering a moderately priced menu of farm-to-table pub fare and creative cocktails (plus beer and wine); the spacious bare-brick and polished wood-lined interior and brightly lit bar are a welcome addition to the burgeoning Westside Restaurant Row.

The Counter *Burgers* 19 | 13 | 17 | $19

Mid-Wilshire | 5779 Wilshire Blvd. (Curson Ave.) | 323-932-8900
West Hollywood | 7919 Sunset Blvd. (Hayworth Ave.) | 323-436-3844
Century City | Century City Center Shopping Ctr. | 10250 Santa Monica Blvd. (bet. Ave. of the Stars & Century Park) | 310-282-8888
Marina del Rey | 4786 Admiralty Way (Fiji Way) | 310-827-8600
Santa Monica | 2901 Ocean Park Blvd. (bet. 29th & 30th Sts.) | 310-399-8383
El Segundo | 700 S. Allied Way (Hughes Way) | 310-524-9967
Hermosa Beach | 719 Pier Ave. (PCH) | 310-374-1511
North Hollywood | 10123 Riverside Dr. (Talofa Ave.) | 818-509-1881
Studio City | 12117 Ventura Blvd. (Laurel Canyon Blvd.) | 818-980-0004
Westlake Village | 30990 Russell Ranch Rd. (Lindero Canyon Rd.) | 818-889-0080
www.thecounterburger.com
Additional locations throughout the Los Angeles area

"Create your own masterpiece" from "quality" patties and a "veritable plethora" of "gourmet" toppings at this "custom burger" chain, where the "happy" staffers also serve up "habit-forming" fries, thick shakes and "interesting" craft brews; critics counter they're "stark", "clamorous" and "pricey", but the "casual" approach that's "fun for kids" is "a hit."

Coyote Cantina *Southwestern* 21 | 19 | 20 | $26

Redondo Beach | King Harbor Marina | 531 N. PCH (Beryl St.) | 310-376-1066 | www.coyotecantina.net

Serving "exotic taste treats" (Mexican lasagna, anyone?), this affordable Southwestern on King Harbor Marina in Redondo Beach is a "nice change" from the "everyday" with its "freshly prepared", "dependable eats" and "strong" margaritas; service get the "ok" from diners and the coyote-themed room, graced with art by Markus Pierson, is "pleasant" - just be "prepared to rub elbows with the person next to you", because it's "always packed."

Craft ☒ *American* 25 | 26 | 24 | $71

Century City | 10100 Constellation Blvd. (bet. Ave. of the Stars & Century Park) | 310-279-4180 | www.craftrestaurant.com

Celeb chef Tom Colicchio's Century City New American showcases "amazingly fresh", "highest-quality" local, seasonal fare served family-style by an "impeccable" staff; the "sophisticated" glass-encased space is often full of "industry types" at lunch, and while it may require an "expense account" or "two trips to the ATM", to many it's "what an upscale restaurant is all about"; P.S. you can order from the more affordable Craftbar menu at the bar or on the patio.

Craig's *American* 22 | 23 | 23 | $58

West Hollywood | 8826 Melrose Ave. (La Peer Dr.) | 310-276-1900 | www.craigs.la

Owner Craig Susser "could not be more gracious" at his pricey West Hollywood American, a "celeb scene" where the menu covers "pretty much everything", from "fantastic" vegan offerings to "generous cuts of steak"; exposed brick and leather banquettes are features of

	FOOD	DECOR	SERVICE	COST

the "old-school" digs where "you can actually hear the conversation at the table."

Crazy Fish *Japanese* 21 | 12 | 16 | $28

Beverly Hills | 9105 W. Olympic Blvd. (Doheny Dr.) | 310-550-8547

"Monster-size" "fried, battered and cream-cheesed" sushi rolls "for the masses" turn up at this Beverly Hills Japanese boasting solid "bang for the buck"; the service and setting are strictly "no frills", but it's still often "crowded" and "waits" are the norm.

NEW **Creation Grill** *Mediterranean* - | - | - | I

Santa Monica | 2901 Ocean Park Blvd. (bet. 29th & 30th Sts.) | 310-396-2400 | www.creationgrill.com

The cooking is from the eastern edge of the Mediterranean at this easy-on-the-wallet Santa Monica Airport-adjacent cafe with a menu of kebabs, wraps and salads, served in a snappy space with bare brick walls and dark ceiling tiles; the breakfast menu leans more toward America, with lots of overstuffed omelets.

NEW **Crossroads Vegan** *Vegan* - | - | - | M

West Hollywood | 8284 Melrose Ave. (Sweetzer Ave.) | 323-782-9245 | www.crossroadskitchen.com

This upscale vegan from chef Tal Ronnen brings meatless meals to trendy Melrose Avenue; the strikingly elegant room boasts hand-crafted chandeliers and an antique glasswork bar, while the creative cuisine is similarly refined and backed by wines and cocktails.

Crustacean *Asian/Vietnamese* 25 | 26 | 22 | $63

Beverly Hills | 9646 Little Santa Monica Blvd. (Bedford Dr.) | 310-205-8990 | www.houseofan.com

Seafood lovers find "crab bliss" at this "divine" Beverly Hills Vietnamese, a longtime purveyor of "glorious" shellfish and other "excellent" eats ("oh, those garlic noodles!"); it's "like dining in another world" in the "stunning" space with "fish swimming under your feet" in an "elaborate" sub-floor aquarium, and "lovely service" completes the picture - just remember to "bring a full wallet."

Cube Cafe ◐ S M *Italian* 24 | 18 | 22 | $41

La Brea | 615 N. La Brea Ave. (Clinton St.) | 323-939-1148 | www.eatatcube.com

"A foodie favorite", this "adorable, little" La Brea Italian packs a big punch with "imaginative" small plates, "outstanding pastas" and "well-chosen" cheeses and salumi all at "reasonable" prices; add in an "unpretentious" atmosphere and "knowledgeable" service, and it's "satisfying" all around.

Culina Modern Italian *Italian* 23 | 26 | 25 | $64

Beverly Hills | Four Seasons Beverly Hills | 300 S. Doheny Dr. (Burton Way) | 310-860-4000 | www.culinarestaurant.com

"Lovely" "on all counts", this "Italian stunner" in the Four Seasons Beverly Hills Hotel offers "delicious" high-end fare (including a "very special" crudo bar), an extensive wine list and "attentive" service to the "Hollywood elite" in a "stylish, sexy" setting with a fire-lit patio; though it's "quite expensive", many deem it a "fabulous" venue for a "special occasion."

	FOOD	DECOR	SERVICE	COST

Cut 🅂 *Steak* — 27 | 25 | 26 | $100

Beverly Hills | Beverly Wilshire | 9500 Wilshire Blvd. (Rodeo Dr.) | 310-276-8500 | www.wolfgangpuck.com

"A cut above" is how carnivores describe Wolfgang Puck's "top"-tier Beverly Hills steakhouse where they feast on "world-class" meats; "celebrity sightings are highly likely" in the "contemporary", "glistening" space designed by Richard Meier (architect of the Getty Center) and the staff treats you "like a million bucks" - and though your bill may seem to approach that level, most insist "you won't regret it."

Cuvée *Californian* — 21 | 17 | 18 | $21

West Hollywood | 145 S. Robertson Blvd. (bet. Alden Dr. & 3rd St.) | 310-271-4333

Century City | 2000 Ave. of the Stars (Constellation Blvd.) | 310-277-3303 🅂

www.mycuvee.com

When you need a "quick, healthy bite" these "reliable" Cal cafes in Century City and West Hollywood do the trick with an "enormous selection" of "beautifully prepared" sandwiches, salads and smoothies; prices are "fair" for the location and service is "fast and friendly", plus there's outdoor seating for those who want to linger.

Daikokuya *Japanese* — 24 | 12 | 16 | $15

Little Tokyo | 327 E. First St. (bet. Central Ave. & Judge John Aiso St.) | 213-626-1680 ◐ ₡

Hacienda Heights | 15827 E. Gale Ave. (Hacienda Blvd.) | 626-968-0810

NEW **West LA** | 2208 Sawtelle Blvd. (Olympic Blvd.) | 310-575-4999

Arcadia | 1220 S. Golden W. Ave. (Duarte Rd.) | 626-254-0127 ₡

Monterey Park | 111 N. Atlantic Blvd. (Garvey Ave.) | 626-570-1930 ◐

www.daikoku-ten.com

"Warm, bouncy noodles" and "rich", "flavorful broth" "make all the difference" for the "superior ramen" at this affordable chainlet of Japanese "greasy spoons"; there's "minimal service, little capacity and long lines", but "is it worth it? - absolutely."

Daily Grill *American* — 19 | 18 | 20 | $32

Downtown | Pegasus Apartments | 612 S. Flower St. (6th St.) | 213-622-4500

Brentwood | Madison Brentwood | 11677 San Vicente Blvd. (bet. Barrington & Darlington Aves.) | 310-442-0044

Santa Monica | Yahoo! Ctr. | 2501 Colorado Ave. (bet. Cloverfield Blvd. & 26th St.) | 310-309-2170 🅂

LAX | LA Int'l Airport, Terminal TBIT | 380 World Way (Center Way) | 310-215-5180

Burbank | Burbank Marriott | 2500 Hollywood Way (Thornton Ave.) | 818-840-6464 ◐

Studio City | Studio City Plaza Shopping Ctr. | 12050 Ventura Blvd. (Laurel Canyon Blvd.) | 818-769-6336

www.dailygrill.com

Known for a "varied menu" of "reliable comfort food" "that fills you up without emptying the wallet", this midpriced American chain is staffed by a "competent" crew that helps foster a "comfortable", "relaxed" atmosphere in otherwise unremarkable settings; a few find it "nothing special", but most consider it a "good fall-back" for a "business lunch", "casual dinner" or "before getting on a long flight" at the airport-adjacent locations.

Dal Rae *Continental* 25 | 20 | 25 | $53

Pico Rivera | 9023 E. Washington Blvd. (Rosemead Blvd.) | 562-949-2444 | www.dalrae.com

"Dress to the nines" and "step back in time" for a trip to this "expensive" Pico Rivera "icon" delivering "top-shelf", "old-school" Continental fare; service is "outstanding" in the dim wood-and-leather setting with a piano bar, making it "one of the last of its kind."

Dan Tana's ◐ *Italian* 23 | 20 | 22 | $60

West Hollywood | 9071 Santa Monica Blvd. (Doheny Dr.) | 310-275-9444 | www.dantanasrestaurant.com

An "iconic" "showbiz hangout", this late-night West Hollywood Italian proffers "reliable", "old-school" fare in a "clubby", "Rat Pack" setting; it's "expensive", and some caution "unless you are someone special", "be prepared to wait", but others insist it's "worth it" to "pretend you're doing studio deals" while spotting "celebrities."

Da Pasquale ⊠ *Italian* 24 | 17 | 23 | $38

Beverly Hills | 9749 Little Santa Monica Blvd. (bet. Linden & Roxbury Drs.) | 310-859-3884 | www.dapasqualecaffe.com

This "charming" Beverly Hills "mom-and-pop" Italian is a standby for "simple", "unpretentious" fare like "homemade pastas" and "hearty", "rustic" mains; "good-value" pricing, "quaint", "cozy" surroundings and a "welcoming" staff further the "warm" mood.

NEW Del Frisco's Grille *Steak* - | - | - | M

Santa Monica | 1551 Ocean Ave. (Colorado Ave.) | 310-395-7333 | www.delfriscosgrille.com

This nationwide New American chain is a casual sibling of the famed Del Frisco's Double Eagle Steakhouse, serving a family-friendly menu of burgers, steaks and bites like cheesesteak egg rolls in a bright, sun-splashed room across from the Santa Monica Pier; there's also a sizable outdoor patio from which to watch the beach people parade by.

Delmonico's Steak & Lobster House *Seafood* 23 | 21 | 23 | $50

Encino | 16358 Ventura Blvd. (Noeline Ave.) | 818-986-0777 | www.delmonicossteakandlobsterhouse.com

An "old standby", this Encino seafooder delivers "reliable" surf 'n' turf and an "excellent brunch" in a mahogany-trimmed room with private booths ("a nice touch"); it's "a bit pricey" and a minority is "underwhelmed" by the food, but service is "polite" and it remains a "special-occasion" mainstay nonetheless.

Delphine *American* 21 | 21 | 22 | $44

Hollywood | W Hollywood Hotel | 6250 Hollywood Blvd. (Vine St.) | 323-798-1355 | www.restaurantdelphine.com

This "sleek, chic" bistro in the W Hollywood Hotel is a find for "artful" New American dishes and "drinks with a kick" "served with just the right amount of attitude"; its proximity to the Pantages ("right across the street") also makes it a "cool" change of pace for theatergoers, even if some call it "underwhelming, except for prices."

	FOOD	DECOR	SERVICE	COST

The Depot ☒ *Eclectic* 25 | 21 | 24 | $41

Torrance | 1250 Cabrillo Ave. (Torrance Blvd.) | 310-787-7501 | www.depotrestaurant.com

"Witty" chef-owner Michael Shafer "entertains the palate" with "imaginative", "exceptional" Eclectic cuisine at this "tried-and-true" Torrance "favorite"; it's "a little high-priced" for the area, but pays off with an "attractive", inviting" setting in an old train depot and "gracious" service that makes it well suited to "special celebrations."

The Derby *Steak* 23 | 23 | 24 | $43

Arcadia | 233 E. Huntington Dr. (bet. Gateway Dr. & 2nd Ave.) | 626-447-2430 | www.thederbyarcadia.com

"Place your bets on this winner" cheer fans of this Arcadia steakhouse near Santa Anita Park that's been a "top-of-the-line" "post-race tradition" since 1938 for "classic" chops and seafood; "attentive service" and a "charming" "old-school" atmosphere with equestrian mementos make it "memorable", and "you may even see a famous jockey or two."

Dinah's Family Restaurant *Diner* 18 | 11 | 19 | $17

Westchester | 6521 S. Sepulveda Blvd. (Centinela Ave.) | 310-645-0456 | www.dinahsrestaurant.com

"It ain't fancy" but this "old-fashioned" diner from 1959 with "retro" red-vinyl booths is "the place to go" for "tender, juicy" fried chicken and "breakfast all day" including "endless" varieties of pancakes; tabs are cheap, "waitresses call you 'hon'" and proximity to LAX makes it a "must-stop" before the airport for many.

Din Tai Fung *Chinese* 26 | 16 | 18 | $22

Arcadia | 1088 S. Baldwin Ave. (Arcadia Ave.) | 626-446-8588
Arcadia | 1108 S. Baldwin Ave. (bet. Arcadia Ave. & Duarte Rd.) | 626-574-7068
www.dintaifungusa.com

"Fung-tastic" proclaim connoisseurs of the "sublime" handmade soup dumplings at this affordable Chinese duo in Arcadia (a Glendale location is in the works) dishing out "little morsels of heaven" along with other Taiwanese delicacies; while the staff is "helpful", fans warn of "long lines" and a "crowded, hectic" scene - still, most agree it's "worth the wait" and the "trek."

Dish *American* 20 | 16 | 19 | $23

La Cañada Flintridge | 734 Foothill Blvd. (Hobbs Dr.) | 818-790-5355 | www.dishbreakfastlunchanddinner.com

La Cañada Flintridge locals "cozy up" at this "homey", "kid-friendly" American serving "approachable" all-day fare at "modest" rates in a "pleasant", "countrylike" setting; the staff is "well intentioned", but regulars report "slow" service during peak hours.

Divino *Italian* 24 | 19 | 23 | $43

Brentwood | 11714 Barrington Ct. (Barrington Ave.) | 310-472-0886 | www.divinobrentwood.com

A "best-kept secret" in Brentwood, this "neighborhood" "trattoria" "consistently delivers" "outstanding" Italian eats and "warm, personal service" in "inviting", "elegant" environs; it's a bit "expensive" and you have to have a high tolerance for "sardinelike" seating at peak hours, though most agree it gets "better every year."

	FOOD	DECOR	SERVICE	COST

Dominick's ◐ *Italian* 20 | 21 | 20 | $40

West Hollywood | 8715 Beverly Blvd. (bet. Robertson & San Vicente Blvds.) | 310-652-2335 | www.dominicksrestaurant.com

An "upbeat" young crowd convenes on the "wonderful, Tuscan-style patio" of this longtime West Hollywood Italian also lauded for its "strong drinks" and "inexpensive" red-sauce fare that's a "throwback to the old days"; late hours are a perk, but for many the real draw is the $15 three-course Sunday night dinner - "one of the best deals in town."

Doughboys *American* 23 | 15 | 18 | $20

Third Street | 8136 W. Third St. (bet. Crescent Heights Blvd. & La Jolla Ave.) | 323-852-1020 | www.doughboyscafe.com

"Famous for its red-velvet cake", this casual Third Street American eatery and bakery is also beloved for its "inventive" breakfast items ("who else has PB&J pancakes?") and other "stick-to-your-ribs", "hangover"-curing fare served all day; some say service is "not the best", but prices are low and "the food makes up for it"; P.S. watch out for "crazy lines at brunch."

NEW **The Doughroom** M *Italian* - | - | - | M

Palms | 3409 Overland Ave. (Woodbine St.) | 424-258-6194 | www.thedoughroom.com

Located in the restaurant-lacking Palms section of West LA, this quirky midpriced Italian gastropub offers a wide selection of pizzas, comfort dishes and unexpected twists on traditional fare (e.g. corned beef gnocchi hash); the space has bare-brick walls, an open-beam ceiling and a long bar at which to bend an elbow over artisanal brews and wines.

Drago Centro *Italian* 26 | 26 | 24 | $60

Downtown | City Nat'l Plaza | 525 S. Flower St. (bet. 5th & 6th Sts.) | 213-228-8998 | www.dragocentro.com

"For that special Downtown date night", fans tout Celestino Drago's "elegant" Italian offering "authentic", "sumptuous" cuisine, backed by an "extensive wine list" and served by an "attentive" staff in a "modern, open dining room" with a "sophisticated" ambiance; for those who may balk at the "extravagant prices", the "out-of-this-world" all-day happy hour is a "true steal."

Dr. Hogly Wogly's BBQ *BBQ* 22 | 8 | 19 | $22

Van Nuys | 8136 Sepulveda Blvd. (Sepulveda Pl.) | 818-780-6701 | www.hoglywogly.com

"Get extra napkins" for the "epic portions" of "juicy, meaty", "irresistible" BBQ at this "oldie but goodie" in Van Nuys offering solid "bang for the buck"; parking is tough and "there's no decor" to speak of, "but you go for the 'cue and don't worry about the rest."

Duck House *Chinese* 22 | 17 | 17 | $32

Monterey Park | 501 S. Atlantic Blvd. (Harding Ave.) | 626-284-3227 | www.duckshouse.com

"Tender" Peking duck is "served just the way it's done in China", carved tableside with "super-crispy skin" and "thin, tortillalike" pancakes at this Monterey Park one-dish wonder also offering "traditional" banquet-style fare; reasonable tabs and comfortable environs make it "excellent for groups"; P.S. duck must be ordered in advance, so call ahead.

	FOOD	DECOR	SERVICE	COST

Duke's *Pacific Rim* 17 22 19 $34

Malibu | 21150 PCH (Las Flores Canyon Rd.) | 310-317-0777 | www.dukesmalibu.com

"A view of ocean waves crashing just outside" makes you feel "like you're in Hawaii" at this "laid-back" surfer-themed Malibu spot boasting a "barefoot bar" (toes in the sand encouraged) and a "nice '50s vibe"; the Pacific Rim menu includes "well-prepared fish plates", and while some find the fare "average" and the service "slow", for most, the scenery "makes up for any downsides"; P.S. there are Tahitian dancers and live Hawaiian music on weekends.

Du-par's ◐ *Diner* 17 13 17 $19

Fairfax | Farmers Mkt. | 6333 W. Third St. (Fairfax Ave.) | 323-933-8446
Studio City | Studio City Plaza Shopping Ctr. | 12036 Ventura Blvd. (Ventura Pl.) | 818-766-4437
www.dupars.com

"Trek down memory lane" at this chainlet of "classic coffee shops" where "the menu, the ambiance and the waitresses" all "bring you back to the '50s"; it's "nothing fancy, but always reliable" with "yummy" pancakes, pies and other affordable grub served late into the night, though some loyalists lament it's "not what it used to be."

Duplex on Third ◐ *American* - - - M

West Hollywood | 8722 W. Third St. (bet. George Burns Rd. & Robertson Blvd.) | 310-276-6223 | www.duplexonthird.com

Situated directly across from Cedars-Sinai in West Hollywood, this midpriced New American has a sprawling three-squares farm-to-table menu with something for everyone, plus a mixology-based bar where medicos kick back after a long shift; the two-story space in a century-old residence has been rebuilt to look like a home once again, with sofas and armchairs in the lounge, bookcases and patchwork rugs in the dining room and a cute patio in the back.

Dusty's *American/French* 22 20 20 $27

Silver Lake | 3200 W. Sunset Blvd. (Descanso Dr.) | 323-906-1018

Hipsters "shake off the grogginess after a late night out" at this "neighborhood" American-French bistro boasting a "laid-back" feel that's "perfect for Silver Lake"; baskets of fresh breads and homemade jams at brunch are appreciated and service is "super-sweet", but some "wish they were more adventurous" with the dinner menu.

Eatalian ⊠ *Italian* 24 15 19 $24

Gardena | 15500 S. Broadway (Redondo Beach Blvd.) | 310-532-8880 | www.eataliancafe.com

"Move over, Mario" say enthusiasts of this "fabulous" "diamond-in-the-rough" Gardena Italian, where the "thin-crust" pizzas, "fresh pastas" and "otherworldly" gelato "transport" you to Italy at "bargain prices"; perhaps the "industrial" space is "not conducive to leisurely dining", but the eating alone is "worth the trip"; P.S. it serves beer and wine.

Eat.Drink.Americano ◐ M *American* - - - M

Downtown | 923 E. Third St. (bet. Garey St. & Santa Fe Ave.) | 213-620-0781 | www.eatdrinkamericano.com

This Arts District gastropub offers a multicultural menu of midpriced plates ranging from steak tartare with mustard ice cream to soft-shell crab with pickled seaweed, plus plenty of craft beers; the exposed-brick and wood interior comes complete with a zinc bar, vintage bottle dryer and a dazzling assortment of oddball sconces and chandeliers.

Eat Well Cafe *American* 20 | 14 | 19 | $16

West Hollywood | 8252 Santa Monica Blvd. (Harper Ave.) | 323-656-1383
Glendale | 1013 S. Brand Blvd. (bet. Acacia Ave. & Chevy Chase Dr.) | 818-243-5928

It's all about "breakfast" at these "bright" retro diners in Glendale and WeHo dishing out "no-frills", "homestyle" American grub at "super-cheap" rates; service can sometimes be "nonexistant", but it's generally a "fun place to connect with friends over a burger."

E. Baldi *Italian* 23 | 18 | 19 | $64

Beverly Hills | 375 N. Canon Dr. (bet. Brighton & Dayton Ways) | 310-248-2633 | www.ebaldi.com

"Studio execs", "agents with their newly minted starlets" and other "heavy-hitters" come to dine at this Beverly Hills Northern Italian from Giorgio Baldi's son, Edoardo, known for "sophisticated, superb" cuisine set down in a "tight", "noisy" setting; the bills are "enormous", and you can expect "lots of attitude" given the "see-and-be-seen" scene.

Echigo *Japanese* 26 | 10 | 20 | $52

West LA | 12217 Santa Monica Blvd. (Amherst Ave.) | 310-820-9787

"Purists" praise this "traditional" West LA Japanese specializing in simple, "ultrafresh", "tender" fish "harmoniously" paired with "warm, vinegary rice" at prices that are moderate for the genre; just overlook the strip-mall decor, grab a seat at the bar and "go for the omakase"; P.S. the lunch set is one of the "best deals in town."

888 Seafood *Chinese/Seafood* 23 | 18 | 19 | $30

Rosemead | 8450 Valley Blvd. (Delta St.) | 626-573-1888

"Dim sum on weekends is the main event" at this Rosemead Chinese where a "wonderful selection" of "well-prepared" seafood dumplings, buns and other "delights" are circulated on rolling carts in a pleasant, "not-too-fancy" dining room; the "place can get mobbed" (and fills up for wedding banquets), but it's good for groups and "family dining", and the cost is "fair."

800 Degrees Pizzeria *Pizza* 23 | 17 | 19 | $15

Westwood | 10889 Lindbrook Dr. (bet. Glendon Ave. & Westwood Blvd.) | 424-239-5010 | www.800degreespizza.com

"Fabulous" "custom-built pizzas" with "inspired" toppings lead to "lines out the door" for this "high-concept, assembly line"-style parlor in Westwood from the Umami Burger folks; "it can be difficult to get a table" in the spare setting, but bills are "budget-friendly" and "the pies make up for it"; P.S. new locations are in the works.

El Cholo Cafe *Mexican* 19 | 19 | 20 | $26

Mid-City | 1121 S. Western Ave. (11th St.) | 323-734-2773
Santa Monica | 1025 Wilshire Blvd. (11th St.) | 310-899-1106
www.elcholo.com

El Cholo Downtown *Mexican*

Downtown | 1037 S. Flower St. (bet. 11th St. & Olympic Blvd.) | 213-746-7750 | www.elcholo.com

(continued)

(continued)

El Cholo Pasadena *Mexican*

Pasadena | Paseo Colorado | 260 E. Colorado Blvd. (bet. Los Robles & Marengo Aves.) | 626-795-5800 | www.elcholopasadena.com

An "LA original", this Mid-City mainstay from 1923 and its offshoots "haven't changed much over the years" with "straightforward" "Cali-Mex" grub (with standout green-corn tamales) that's either "decent" or "delicious" "depending on how many margaritas you drink"; although some say it's "living on its long history", the "old-world" decor is "charming", costumed servers "pleasant" and, on the whole, "it just oozes fun."

El Coyote Cafe *Mexican* 16 | 16 | 19 | $21

Beverly Boulevard | 7312 Beverly Blvd. (bet. Fuller Ave. & Poinsettia Pl.) | 323-939-2255 | www.elcoyotecafe.com

With over-the-top decor that's "right out of an old Carmen Miranda movie", this "LA institution" on Beverly Boulevard still offers a "festive atmosphere after 80 years in business"; the Mexican "comfort food" is "nothing special", but it's "nice for the price" and served by a "staff as cool as a margarita."

Elf Café *Mediterranean/Vegetarian* ▽ 25 | 19 | 22 | $26

Echo Park | 2135 W. Sunset Blvd. (Alvarado St.) | 213-484-6829 | www.elfcafe.com

"Vegetarians rejoice" over the "well-crafted", "soul-soothing" dishes at this "hipster" Echo Park Mediterranean offering a variety of "savory" vegan choices for a moderate price; it packs "lots of tables in a small space" ("reservations are a must"), but the nonetheless "charming" locale remains a "pure joy" for many.

Elite Restaurant *Chinese* 25 | 15 | 16 | $26

Monterey Park | 700 S. Atlantic Blvd. (El Portal Pl.) | 626-282-9998 | www.elitechineserestaurant.com

"Dim sum is all the rage" - served "hot to the table, not from carts" - at this "upscale Cantonese-style" Monterey Park Chinese featuring a "super" menu for the "adventurous eater"; just prepare for a wait on weekends, and a likely "rushed" meal in the "standard-issue" environs.

El Pollo Inka *Peruvian* 21 | 14 | 19 | $18

Lawndale | Lawndale Plaza | 15400 Hawthorne Blvd. (154th St.) | 310-676-6665

Gardena | Gateway Plaza | 1425 W. Artesia Blvd. (bet. Dalton & Normandie Aves.) | 310-516-7378

Hermosa Beach | 1100 PCH (Aviation Blvd.) | 310-372-1433

Torrance | 23705 Hawthorne Blvd. (bet. 236th & 238th Sts.) | 310-373-0062

www.elpolloinka.com

"Terrific" rotisserie chicken with "out-of-this-world" green sauce makes for a "zesty" combo at this "quick" Peruvian mini-chain serving "high-quality" fare in "not fancy, but upbeat" settings; it's a "real value for the money", and weekend entertainment at some locales is a bonus.

El Rocoto *Peruvian* ▽ 23 | 17 | 21 | $20

Cerritos | Cerritos Promenade | 11433 South St. (Gridley Rd.) | 562-924-1919

Gardena | 1356 W. Artesia Blvd. (Normandie Ave.) | 310-768-8768

www.elrocoto.com

Locals "love" the "excellent Peruvian" at this "wonderful neighborhood" duo in Cerritos and Gardena proffering "tasty" specialties and sauces with a "kick"; "reasonable prices", strong service and simple but "pleasant" decor round out the "solid" meal.

El Tepeyac *Mexican* 26 | 13 | 22 | $15

Boyle Heights | 812 N. Evergreen Ave. (bet. Blanchard & Winter Sts.) | 323-267-8668 | www.manuelseltepeyac.com

This "homey", "heartwarming" East LA Mexican "landmark" from 1955 is where diners endure "long lines" for "delicious", "gargantuan" Hollenbeck burritos (a "true eating challenge"), "top" guacamole and other "real home-cooked" dishes that make it one of the city's "best buys"; while some may be "put off by the location", fans insist "it has never been a problem."

Emle's *Californian/Mediterranean* ▽ 23 | 15 | 23 | $21

Northridge | 9250 Reseda Blvd. (bet. Dearborn & Prairie Sts.) | 818-772-2203 | www.emlesrestaurant.com

"What a find" say fans of this Cal-Med in Northridge, known for its "nice range" of food, "decadent" French toast and "terrific" early-bird specials, all in portions that are nothing short of "redonkulous"; the decor is plain, but it "isn't expensive" and the staff "treats you like relatives."

Engine Co. No. 28 *American* 20 | 22 | 21 | $38

Downtown | 644 S. Figueroa St. (bet. 7th St. & Wilshire Blvd.) | 213-624-6996 | www.engineco.com

Housed in a restored "vintage" fire station Downtown, this "cozy but upscale" American offers "reliable" "gourmet comfort food" in a "charming" atmosphere; though service can "fluctuate" and some feel it's "overpriced", others say it's just right for a "business lunch" or "pre-concert" dinner, made extra-convenient with a free shuttle to the Music and Staples Centers.

Enoteca Drago *Italian* 22 | 20 | 22 | $48

Beverly Hills | 410 N. Canon Dr. (Brighton Way) | 310-786-8236 | www.celestinodrago.com

Celestino Drago (Il Pastaio, Drago) attracts an atypical Beverly Hills crowd to his "elegant", "old world-style" Italian providing an "interesting wine list" and "enjoyable" large and small plates "better than mama ever made"; it's "less hectic" than others and dishes are "served with a smile", though some claim it's "nothing extraordinary" for the price.

Enzo & Angela ⊠ *Italian* 21 | 16 | 23 | $39

West LA | Brentwood Place Shopping Ctr. | 11701 Wilshire Blvd. (Barrington Ave.) | 310-477-3880 | www.enzoandangela.com

Servers treat you "as if you're their long-lost cousin" at this "visit to Italy" in West LA presenting a "remarkable" roster of "unusual dishes as well as the standards", all "prepared from the heart"; some are put off by the "expensive" specials, though fans call the food and service "first class."

NEW Esterel *French* - | - | - | E

West Hollywood | Sofitel LA | 8555 Beverly Blvd. (La Cienega Blvd.) | 310-278-5444 | www.sofitel.com

This pricey West Hollywood French in the Sofitel LA serves the sort of serious French cooking that's nearly vanished from Los Angeles; it features a spacious outdoor patio and an elegant interior marked by space dividers resembling Dalí-esque tree branches and the sort of oversized booths that you can lose yourself in.

	FOOD	DECOR	SERVICE	COST
Euro Pane *Bakery*	25	14	16	$15

Pasadena | 345 E. Colorado Blvd. (Euclid Ave.) | 626-844-8804
Pasadena | 950 E. Colorado Blvd. (Mentor Ave.) | 626-577-1828
"Delectable pastries" ("try the fleur de sel macarons"), "glorious bread" and a signature egg salad sandwich are "invariably first-rate" at this "cute neighborhood bakery" and cafe duo offering "a little bit of Paris in Pasadena"; "lines can be long", service "slow" and seating tight, so "be ready to sit in close quarters" if you can score a table.

Eveleigh *American/European* 20 | 24 | 19 | $47

West Hollywood | 8752 W. Sunset Blvd. (Sherbourne Dr.) | 424-239-1630 | www.theeveleigh.com
It feels like a *"A Midsummer Night's Dream"* on the rustic, covered patio of this New American-European that will "transport you far away" from the Sunset Strip; small and large plates of "imaginative", "wholesome" cuisine and "terrific" cocktails are served with "no pretensions", and if a few find the food "unspectacular", the view adds a "dramatic" touch.

Fab Hot Dogs *Hot Dogs* 22 | 10 | 18 | $11

NEW **Westwood** | 920 Broxton Ave. (Le Conte Ave.) | 818-794-0333 ◐
Reseda | Loehmann's Plaza | 19417 Victory Blvd. (Tampa Ave.) | 818-344-4336
www.fabhotdogs.com
"Fab-tastic!" rave reviewers of this chainlet that elevates the basic frank "into another category", offering a "huge variety" of "delish dogs", sausages and burgers, recommended with "spicy relish", "tots and a drink on the side"; "there's no decor to speak of", but the "fair" prices, "friendly staff and quick service make it a pleasure."

Fabiolus Cucina Italiana *Italian* 21 | 17 | 22 | $27

Hollywood | 6270 Sunset Blvd. (bet. El Centro Ave. & Vine St.) | 323-467-2882 | www.fabiolus.org
The staff always makes you "feel special" and the "homemade pastas" and Northern Italian entrees are an "excellent value" at this "Hollywood favorite" for chowing down in the "ArcLight area"; it provides a "quieter start to the evening" than many, and guests also give props to its "good work in the community for the homeless."

Factor's Famous Deli *Deli* 19 | 14 | 19 | $23

Pico-Robertson | 9420 W. Pico Blvd. (bet. Beverly & Rexford Drs.) | 310-278-9175 | www.factorsdeli.com
"Order the lox and eggs with a bagel and be in heaven" at this Pico-Robertson "classic" supplying the "whole panoply of deli food", from "good-size sandwiches" to "delicious soups"; there's "helpful" service and "rarely a wait for a table", though some would like to see the place "spruced up."

Falafel King *Mideastern* 18 | 8 | 14 | $13

Santa Monica | Third St. Promenade | 1315 Third St. Promenade (bet. Arizona Ave. & Santa Monica Blvd.) | 310-587-2551
Westwood | 1010 Broxton Ave. (bet. Kinross & Weyburn Aves.) | 310-208-4444
Loyalists of this "real-deal" Middle Eastern duo in Westwood and Santa Monica "can't get enough" of the falafel, shawarma and "killer" fried potatoes, with "just the right balance of ingredients overflowing your

pita"; despite some claims that it's sliding into "mediocrity", most feel the "cheap eats" still "hit the mark."

Falafel Palace *Mediterranean/Mideastern* ∇ 22 | 10 | 19 | $13

Northridge | 9255 Reseda Blvd. (bet. Lassen & Plummer Sts.) | 818-993-0734 | www.falafelpalacenorthridge.com

An "always satisfying" "falafel shack" near Cal State Northridge, this little "joint" turns out "tasty" Med-Middle Eastern fare that stirs up "cravings"; sure, it's a "hole-in-the-wall", but customers agree "there's a reason it's been there forever."

Farfalla Trattoria *Italian* 22 | 18 | 20 | $34

Los Feliz | 1978 Hillhurst Ave. (Finley Ave.) | 323-661-7365 | www.farfallatrattoria.com

Encino | Encino Mktpl. | 16403 Ventura Blvd. (Hayvenhurst Ave.) | 818-380-0200 | www.farfallaencino.com

Westlake Village | The Promenade at Westlake | 160 Promenade Way (Thousand Oaks Blvd.) | 805-497-2355 | www.farfallawestlakevillage.com

Vinoteca Farfalla ◐ *Italian*

Glendale | 1968 Hillhurst Ave. (Finley Ave.) | 323-661-8070 | www.vinotecafarfalla.com

"Consistently satisfying", these "neighborhood Italians" offer "healthy portions" of "dependable" basics, like "tasty" homemade pastas, at "reasonable prices for the quality"; it's staffed by "friendly, well-meaning folk" (though some caution "be prepared to wait"), and the "wonderful" atmosphere can make for a "romantic dine"; P.S. the Glendale branch is primarily a wine bar.

Farm of Beverly Hills *American* 18 | 17 | 17 | $30

Downtown | LA Live | 800 W. Olympic Blvd. (Figueroa St.) | 213-747-4555

Beverly Hills | 439 N. Beverly Dr. (Santa Monica Blvd.) | 310-273-5578 www.thefarmofbeverlyhills.com

The "home cooking" "meets expectations for the price" and desserts "steal the show" at these "decent" Americans; service varies and the brunch crowds can make it "difficult to get in", but otherwise it's "good for families", with "cute" "farmhouse decor" and "pleasant" patios.

Farmshop *American* 25 | 18 | 22 | $45

Santa Monica | Brentwood Country Mart | 225 26th St. (bet. Brentwood Terr. & San Vicente Blvd.) | 310-566-2400 | www.farmshopla.com

Jeff Cerciello (ex Yountville's French Laundry) has "done it right" at his Cal-American "gem" in the Brentwood Country Mart that's "wonderful all times of the day" for "fantastic" fare made with "farm-fresh ingredients"; the "casual", "homey" room is usually "jammed" with "pretty people", and while some grouse about "paying through the nose", others deem it a "good value"; P.S. the "attached gourmet shop is great fun for foodies."

Farm Stand *Eclectic* 22 | 16 | 19 | $27

El Segundo | 422 Main St. (bet. Holly & Pine Aves.) | 310-640-3276 | www.farmstand.us

"Down-home" yet "unique" Eclectic dishes with a Mediterranean touch arrive at an "easy pace" at this "hidden" nook in El Segundo offering a number of "vegetarian and vegan options"; "understated" with "good bang for the buck", it's "very popular with locals."

FOOD | DECOR | SERVICE | COST

Far Niente *Italian* 24 | 19 | 22 | $40

Glendale | 204½ N. Brand Blvd. (Wilson Ave.) | 818-242-3835 | www.farnienteristorante.net

"Superior food continues to reign" at this "classy" Northern Italian in Glendale inspired by flavors of the Cinque Terre, a "friendly place to bring an out-of-towner" or dine before heading to the Alex Theater next door; the room is "comfortable" and the prices "fair", so while service can be a bit inconsistent, it's "popular" for a reason.

Fat Cow [S] [M] *American* 18 | 17 | 17 | $31

Fairfax | The Grove | 189 The Grove Dr. (bet. Beverly Blvd. & 3rd St.) | 323-965-1020 | www.thefatcowla.com

While some assert "pizzas are a high point" at Gordon Ramsay's "casual" New American gastropub at The Grove, others say "there are no bad items on the menu"; the space sports a rustic look featuring exposed brick, vintage mirrors and bare bulbs, and though a few gripe about "slow" service, its "great location" makes it an easy date-night pick.

Fat Dog ◐ *American* 20 | 17 | 21 | $24

West Hollywood | 801 N. Fairfax Ave. (Waring Ave.) | 323-951-0030
Montrose | 2265 Honolulu Ave. (Ocean View Blvd.) | 818-236-4810
www.thefatdogla.com

"Dolled-up", "innovative bar eats" "prepared amazingly well" and "delightful brews on tap" are the stars at these "friendly", late-night Americans in West Hollywood and Montrose; Montrose is "primarily a bar scene" with "dark" narrow digs, but WeHo's canine-inspired decor and Fido-friendly patio make it a "hip little place to hang out", and a "good happy hour" appeals to wallet-watchers.

Father's Office ◐ *American* 23 | 16 | 15 | $25

Culver City | Helms Bldg. | 3229 Helms Ave. (bet. Venice & Washington Blvds.) | 310-736-2224
Santa Monica | 1018 Montana Ave. (bet. 10th & 11th Sts.) | 310-736-2224
www.fathersoffice.com

"It's all about the burger" at this "dark, crowded" American gastropub duo in Santa Monica and Culver City famed for its "decadent" blue-cheese patties and "world-class selection of beers on tap"; no menu substitutions (or ketchup) are allowed, and "you're on your own to find a table" so "get there early" or prepare to wait.

NEW **Fatty's Public House** ◐ *American* - | - | - | M

West Hollywood | 829 N. La Cienega Blvd. (bet. Waring & Willoughby Aves.) | 310-854-0756 | www.fattysla.com

This casual WeHo watering hole set in the former home of silent film star Fatty Arbuckle serves midpriced gastropub grub with plenty of brews and craft cocktails; you enter the lively space by passing under a mural of Old Hollywood stars, which opens into a high-ceilinged, woodsy room dominated by a long bar.

Feast from the East *Asian* 22 | 10 | 18 | $15

West LA | 1949 Westwood Blvd. (bet. La Grange & Missouri Aves.) | 310-475-0400 | www.ffte.com

For over 30 years, customers have been returning to this "terrific" West LA Asian for "the best Chinese chicken salad this side of Hong Kong" (with dressing that's "practically an industry unto itself") and sesame wings that "run a close second"; it's not so much "a place for dining" due to the lack of atmosphere, but a hit for "fast", "inexpensive" takeout.

Federal Bar *American* 19 | 19 | 18 | $25

NEW **Long Beach** | 102 Pine Ave. (bet. B'way & Ocean Blvd.) | 562-435-2000
North Hollywood | 5303 Lankershim Blvd. (Weddington St.) | 818-980-2555
www.thefederalbar.com

Set in converted old banks done up in "sophisticated" Prohibition style, this "boisterous" NoHo bar and its new Long Branch sibling attract a "young, hip" crowd with a "huge selection of beer and wine" and American pub grub "kicked up a notch"; "unpretentious" service, a "comfy" vibe and "reasonable" prices are further pluses, and at the original location, DJs and burlesque shows add to the nightly "revelry."

Fig *American/French* 22 | 22 | 22 | $48

Santa Monica | Fairmont Miramar Hotel & Bungalows | 101 Wilshire Blvd. (Ocean Ave.) | 310-319-3111 | www.figsantamonica.com

"Creative, but not over-the-top" New American dishes are "packed with flavor" using "selections from the local farmer's market" at this "warm-weather favorite" with "intelligent" service at Santa Monica's "pretty" Fairmont Miramar Hotel; early-goers tout the "Fig at Five" happy hour as a "tremendous" bargain, and the "attractive poolside setting" has a "definite hideaway feel", encouraging you to "relax and enjoy."

Fig & Olive *Mediterranean* 22 | 25 | 21 | $56

West Hollywood | 8490 Melrose Pl. (La Cienega Blvd.) | 310-360-9100 | www.figandolive.com

This "gorgeous", "vibrant" West Hollywood entry "does everything right", as evidenced by the "phenomenal" Med cuisine, the "knowledgeable" staff and the "über-trendy" crowds "packed to the rafters" of the "modern", "airy" space; a few insist it's "overpriced" and "overrated", but most agree it's "utterly satisfying."

NEW **Figaro** *French* - | - | - | M

Downtown | 618 S. Broadway (bet. 6th & 7th Sts.) | 213-622-2116 | www.figarobistrot.com

The venerable Figaro Bistrot in Los Feliz has spawned this massive Downtown restaurant that feels like a bit of Paris with a moderately priced menu of bistro classics; the 17,000-sq.-ft. space is spread over two levels and includes a sprawling dark-wood bar, numerous booths and both a boulangerie and patissierie, *bien sûr.*

Figaro Bistrot *French* 22 | 23 | 19 | $34

Los Feliz | 1802 N. Vermont Ave. (Melbourne Ave.) | 323-662-1587 | www.figarobistrot.com

Maybe the "closest thing to a visit to Paris" in Los Feliz - from the "sidewalk dining" to the vintage decor to the "authentic wait for service" - this "truly French" bistro is a "best-kept secret" for savoring the "classics" in a "wonderful atmosphere"; some swear by the "to-die-for" pastries ("breakfast is the best bet"), while others advise everything's "plentiful for the price" at happy hour.

	FOOD	DECOR	SERVICE	COST

FigOly *Californian/Italian* | - | - | - | E |

Downtown | Luxe City Center Hotel | 1020 S. Figueroa St. (Olympic Ave.) | 213-743-7600 | www.figoly.com

Named for its intersection (Figueroa and Olympic), this Downtown Cal-Italian in the Luxe City Center Hotel serves pricey pastas, house-made charcuterie and wood-fired mains; the dining room - decked out with a chrome chandelier and floor-to-ceiling wine cellar - opens via a glass stairway to an expansive patio, making it an upscale destination before an event at nearby Staples Center or Nokia Theater.

Firefly ◐ *American* | 20 | 23 | 18 | $40 |

Studio City | 11720 Ventura Blvd. (Carpenter Ave.) | 818-762-1833 | www.fireflystudiocity.com

Still a Studio City "scene" after more than a decade, this "gorgeous" New American has "ambiance" to spare, with a fire-lit patio, curtained cabanas and an "inviting bar" (open until 2 AM); though some find the Med-influenced fare merely "decent" and the service just "fine", it's "always packed" nonetheless, so reservations are a must.

Firefly Bistro 🅼 *American* ▽ | 19 | 19 | 19 | $37 |

South Pasadena | 1009 El Centro St. (bet. Diamond & Meridian Aves.) | 626-441-2443 | www.eatatfirefly.com

The "pleasing" menu "changes with the seasons" at this midpriced New American in South Pasadena, a "tented venue" that delights with an "outdoor feel" and frequent live music (Wednesday-Thursday and during Sunday brunch); an "attentive (but not intrusive)" staff adds to the "breezy" mood.

Firenze Osteria *Italian* | 22 | 20 | 21 | $45 |

North Hollywood | 4212 Lankershim Blvd. (Valley Spring Ln.) | 818-760-7081 | www.firenzeosteria.com

Locals feel "lucky" to have this trattoria from *Top Chef* contestant Fabio Viviani in North Hollywood, providing "generous portions" of "gourmet yet approachable" Italian in an "energetic" setting with "ok" service; less satisfied surveyors feel it's "overpriced" and wish they could "turn down the noise."

First & Hope 🅼 *American* | 17 | 21 | 16 | $48 |

Downtown | 710 W. First St. (Hope St.) | 213-617-8555 | www.firstandhope.com

An "easy walk to Disney Hall and the Music Center", this "swellegant" Downtown American with an "attractive" atmosphere for "pre-show dinner and drinks" stirs up mixed reviews, with some calling it "surprisingly good" and "offbeat", and others citing a costly, "too-cute" menu that changes but "never succeeds"; on the plus side, "they'll get you out before curtain" and the occasional live piano is "entertaining."

Fishbar ◐ *Seafood* ▽ | 22 | 17 | 21 | $31 |

Manhattan Beach | 3801 Highland Ave. (bet. 38th & 39th Sts.) | 310-796-0200 | www.fishbarmb.com

Customers give "kudos" to this "local hangout" in Manhattan Beach offering "simple but delicious" seafood (mesquite-grilled skewers, the "best clam chowder") from "plenty of fresh fish options" while it "rocks" a "casual" "sports-bar atmosphere"; the staff does a "wonderful job", prices are "amazingly fair" and weekend breakfast boasts a "fabulous" Bloody Mary ("you can't go wrong with shrimp, bacon and asparagus in your drink"), so it's a "welcome surprise."

Fish Grill *Seafood* 22 | 14 | 18 | $20

Beverly Boulevard | 7226 Beverly Blvd. (bet. Alta Vista Blvd. & Formosa Ave.) | 323-937-7162

Pico-Robertson | 9618 W. Pico Blvd. (Beverwil Dr.) | 310-860-1182

Brentwood | 12013 Wilshire Blvd. (bet. Bundy Dr. & Saltair Ave.) | 310-479-1800

Malibu | 22935 PCH (Malibu Pier) | 310-456-8585

www.fishgrill.com

"Nothing but the freshest", "wonderful kosher seafood" comes "fast" and "flavorful" off the grill at this "deli-style" mini-chain offering "unexpected" delights (like "awesome" fish tacos) for a "bargain"; even if the locales lend themselves to "takeout", the Malibu patio is a "hot spot by the pier" ("who knew?"); P.S. closed Friday after 2:30 PM and Saturday, and there's no alcohol or shellfish.

NEW Fishing with Dynamite *Seafood* - | - | - | M

Manhattan Beach | 1148 Manhattan Ave. (12th St.) | 310-893-6299 | www.eatfwd.com

Seafood icon David LeFevre follows his adjacent M.B. Post with this moderately priced oyster house, a compact spot with a bleached wood raw bar, and a mix of old-school and new-school dishes on the menu - spanning from New England clam chowder to miso black cod; there are also plenty of oysters to slurp fresh from the shell.

555 East *Steak* 25 | 23 | 24 | $52

Long Beach | 555 E. Ocean Blvd. (bet. Atlantic & Linden Aves.) | 562-437-0626 | www.555east.com

"Steaks and ambiance" come together in "winning" fashion at this Long Beach bastion of "old-time elegance" proffering "remarkable" cuts in a "classic", "über-masculine" space replete with wood, brass and marble; factor in an "awesome" wine list and servers who "go out of their way to please", and reviewers "highly recommended" it as a "place to celebrate and splurge."

Five Guys *Burgers* 16 | 11 | 16 | $12

Mid-Wilshire | 5550 Wilshire Blvd. (Burnside Ave.) | 323-939-2360

Carson | Southbay Pavilion | 20700 Avalon Blvd. (Del Amo Blvd.) | 310-515-7700

Cerritos | Cerritos Promenade | 11461 South St. (Gridley Rd.) | 562-809-0055

Culver City | Westfield Culver City | 6000 Sepulveda Blvd. (Slauson Ave.) | 310-391-0603

NEW Torrance | 23228 Hawthorne Blvd. (Lomita Blvd.) | 310-378-4035

Studio City | 12930 Ventura Blvd. (Coldwater Canyon Ave.) | 818-817-2318

www.fiveguys.com

Fans throw a "high five" to this East Coast fast-food transplant turning out burgers that "taste like something you'd grill on a summer day in the backyard" served with "lots of toppings", "jazzed-up fries" and "free peanuts while you wait" ("a nice touch"); detractors "don't get all the hype", although "quick" service and "not-that-expensive" tabs keep them perpetually "busy."

FOOD DECOR SERVICE COST

Fleming's Prime Steakhouse & Wine Bar *Steak* 23 21 22 $61

Downtown | LA Live | 800 W. Olympic Blvd. (Figueroa St.) | 213-745-9911
NEW Beverly Hills | 252 N. Beverly Dr. (Dayton Way) | 310 278-8710
El Segundo | Atrium Ct. | 2301 Rosecrans Ave. (Douglas St.) | 310-643-6911
Woodland Hills | 6373 Topanga Canyon Blvd. (Victory Blvd.) | 818-346-1005
www.flemingssteakhouse.com

Carnivores call this steakhouse chain a "genuine top-tier" choice for "flavorful" cuts, a "terrific" wine list and "tremendous" service provided in "plush" surroundings; it works for "business or pleasure" among a "jovial crowd", and while it's certainly "expensive", you "can't beat the price" for happy hour - "if you can find a place at the bar."

Float *American*

Pasadena | Burlington Arcade | 380 S. Lake Ave. (bet. Del Mar Blvd. & San Pasqual St.) | 626-844-3488

There are more than floats at this retro Pasadena storefront where coffees and teas accompany ice cream from Fosselman's in Alhambra, bread from the Brooklyn Bagel Bakery and a wall of sodas from Galco's, along with oversized sandwiches; all are served in a space fronted by elegantly curved glass windows, and a smattering of tables provide seating both in and outside.

NEW Flores *American*

West LA | 2024 Sawtelle Blvd. (bet. La Grange & Mississippi Aves.) | 424-273-6469 | www.floreslosangeles.com

The former Sawtelle Kitchen has been transformed into this stylish farm-to-table New American with a midpriced menu from the husband-and-wife team of Angela Hernandez and Rob Lawson; the glowing space has soft lighting, lots of polished wood and a distinctive circular central counter surrounded by tall wooden stools.

Flore Vegan Cuisine *Vegan* ∇ 20 15 18 $20

Silver Lake | 3818 W. Sunset Blvd. (bet. Hyperion & Lucille Aves.) | 323-953-0611 | www.florevegan.com

"A vegan lover's dream" where both "your body and wallet will be happy", this Silver Laker "satisfies" with its "delicious", "imaginative and varied" dishes proffered by a "friendly" crew; the "quaint" space with flea-market stylings is on the "spare" side, but comfortable enough to stay for the "well-made" desserts.

Fogo de Chão *Brazilian/Steak* 23 21 22 $67

Beverly Hills | 133 N. La Cienega Blvd. (bet. Clifton Way & Wilshire Blvd.) | 310-289-7755 | www.fogodechao.com

A "festival of meat" awaits at this "traditional" Brazilian steakhouse chain in Beverly Hills, where "endless" skewers of meats "come at you from left and right", and there's also an "impressive", "exotic" salad bar; yes, the cost is "substantial", but the "all-you-can-eat aspect makes it an unparalleled experience" - just "bring a grizzly bear's appetite."

Food *American* 22 14 20 $18

Rancho Park | 10571 W. Pico Blvd. (Prosser Ave.) | 310-441-7770 | www.food-la.com

Grab "soul-satisfying breakfasts and lunches" "among the locals" - and even "spot a celeb once in a while" - at this "inviting" contemporary American cafe that's "strong on sandwiches, pastries" and "personable" service in Rancho Park; there's limited indoor and outdoor seating, but the "lovely" deli case provides tempting take-out options.

Food + Lab *Californian* 21 | 16 | 16 | $18

Silver Lake | 3206 W. Sunset Blvd. (Descanso Dr.) | 323-661-2666
West Hollywood | 7253 Santa Monica Blvd. (Poinsettia Dr.) | 323-851-7120
www.foodlabcatering.com

Admirers "absolutely love" these West Hollywood and Silver Lake cafes whose Austrian-influenced Californian fare includes "high-quality" sandwiches, salads and "perfectly cooked" omelets; they're small and "cool" with some outdoor seating, though they're "not the cheapest" and a few find the service "too laid-back."

Forage ⊠ Ⓜ *Californian* 25 | 15 | 18 | $19

Silver Lake | 3823 W. Sunset Blvd. (bet. Hyperion & Lucille Aves.) | 323-663-6885 | www.foragela.com

"Amazingly fresh" ingredients from "local sources" go into the "rotating menu" of "savory" dishes (with vegan options) and appealing desserts at this "tiny" Silver Lake Californian that's a "lifesaver in the neighborhood", even if it is "a little pricey"; "order at the counter" and then "hope that there'll be an empty table somewhere, indoors or outside" - or simply take your meal to go.

Ford's Filling Station *American* 20 | 18 | 19 | $38

Culver City | 9531 Culver Blvd. (bet. Cardiff & Watseka Aves.) | 310-202-1470 | www.fordsfillingstation.net

"Drop by for drinks and a nibble" at this "cool", "loud" Culver City gastropub from Harrison's son, Ben, featuring an "inventive" American menu focusing on "glorified bar food" like housemade charcuterie and an "outstanding burger" backed by "terrific cocktails" and beers; service earns mixed marks and some call it "pricey for what you get", but the "rustic" space is "always busy" with a "young, vibrant crowd" nonetheless.

Formosa Cafe ◐ *Asian* 14 | 20 | 16 | $29

West Hollywood | 7156 Santa Monica Blvd. (Formosa Ave.) | 323-850-9050

This "vintage" WeHo Asian from the 1930s is "a slice of LA history" and still has the aura of an "old movie-star hangout", complete with signed photos on the walls from its famous former clientele; the menu isn't highly regarded, but most go for the drinks, the "cool" ambiance and the "nostalgia" factor.

Foundry on Melrose *American* 23 | 19 | 21 | $47

Melrose | 7465 Melrose Ave. (bet. Gardner & Vista Sts.) | 323-651-0915 | www.thefoundryonmelrose.com

Grilled cheese "fit for foodies" leads the lineup at this "feel-good" Melrose New American where chef-owner Eric Greenspan turns out "bold, fun" fare in a space with live blues and jazz in the lounge up front and a patio in back; at press time the dining room and menu were undergoing a spruce-up.

Freddy Smalls Bar & Kitchen ◐ ⊠ *American* ∇ 23 | 19 | 21 | $33

West LA | 11520 W. Pico Blvd. (Gateway Blvd.) | 310-479-3000 | www.freddysmalls.com

"Crowds of Westside hipsters" cram into this "fantastic" West LA American from Jeff Weinstein (The Counter), where the white subway tiles and vintage decor make it "feel like NY"; expect "swell cocktails", "adventurous", well-priced small plates and a "noisy" scene.

Fred 62 ◐ *Diner* 18 | 17 | 17 | $20

Los Feliz | 1850 N. Vermont Ave. (Russell Ave.) | 323-667-0062 | www.fred62.com

"Plenty casual", this round-the-clock, "nifty neighborhood joint" with "retro decor" in Los Feliz offers a "wide selection" of "modern" takes on diner staples to satisfy "late-night cravings" and "breakfast-sandwich" needs; a few call the food "hit-or-miss", but the "super-chill" service and "reasonable" tabs go over well with an "interesting cross-section of people", including the "tight-jeans and liberal-arts-degree" set.

Frida *Mexican* 19 | 18 | 18 | $33

Melrose | 7217 Melrose Ave. (Formosa Ave.) | 323-549-4666
Beverly Hills | 236 S. Beverly Dr. (bet. Charleville Blvd. & Gregory Way) | 310-278-7666
Santa Monica | Brentwood Country Mart | 225 26th St. (bet. Brentwood Terr. & San Vicente Blvd.) | 310-395-9666
Glendale | Americana at Brand | 750 Americana Way (bet. Brand Blvd. & Central Ave.) | 818-551-1666
www.fridarestaurant.com

"Refreshing", "higher-end" Mex dishes are served with "style" at this "gourmet" mini-chain with a "contemporary" touch; there's a "lively" "after-work" scene in Beverly Hills and Glendale, while the taquerias on Melrose and in the Brentwood Country Mart are best for on-the-go bites.

Fritto Misto *Italian* 22 | 14 | 20 | $24

Santa Monica | 601 Colorado Ave. (6th St.) | 310-458-2829
Hermosa Beach | 316 Pier Ave. (bet. Monterey Blvd. & Sunset Dr.) | 310-318-6098

"Create-your-own-pasta" plates "hit the spot" (and fit your "budget") at these "family-friendly" Hermosa Beach and Santa Monica Italians where "customization never tasted so good" - and the various options accommodate even the "most complicated diets"; the spaces are "simple and clean" (decorated with tabletops made from wine crates) and the service "helpful", but "expect a long wait" on weekend nights.

Fromin's Deli *Deli* 16 | 11 | 17 | $20

Santa Monica | 1832 Wilshire Blvd. (bet. 18th & 19th Sts.) | 310-829-5443 | www.frominsdeli.com

Guests flash back to "grandma's kitchen" at this slightly "frumpy" but "reliable" deli in Santa Monica dishing up "old-fashioned, stick-to-your-ribs" faves like potato pancakes and corned beef sandwiches set down by a "no-nonsense" staff; some say it's "second-tier" and "more expensive" than it should be, though dinner specials help keep the bill in check.

Frysmith Ⓢ Ⓜ *American* 23 | 17 | 21 | $9

Location varies; see website | 818-371-6814 | www.eatfrysmith.com

Tater connoisseurs are "mildly stalking" this truck for "crisp", "gourmet fries" covered with "outstanding toppings" ("delicious" kimchi, "amazing" rajas) that add up to a "whole meal"; "you may hate yourself a little" afterward, but "it's worth every minute of penance at the gym."

	FOOD	DECOR	SERVICE	COST

Fuego at the Maya *Mexican/Pan-Latin* ▽ 22 | 27 | 24 | $35

Long Beach | Hotel Maya | 700 Queensway Dr. (Harbor Plaza) | 562-481-3910 | www.fuegolongbeach.com

Boasting a "beautiful deck" looking out to the waterfront and Downtown Long Beach, this "exquisitely decorated" Mexican-Pan-Latin at the Hotel Maya is "great for apps" and other "scrumptious" seafood-focused fare, as well as an "incredible selection of tequila"; Sunday brunch is a "blast" too, so while a few find the prices "steep for what you get", night or day it's the place to "impress a date."

Fundamental LA Ⓜ *Sandwiches* 22 | 16 | 19 | $20

Westwood | 1303 Westwood Blvd. (bet. Rochester & Wellworth Aves.) | 310-444-7581 | www.fundamental-la.com

"Delicious", "interesting" sandwiches, small plates and housemade vanilla cream soda make this small, seasonal eatery a "godsend" to Westwood foodies; though "its facade is so nondescript you'll likely miss it", the interior is "modern" and "friendly", and most agree it's worth seeking out for the "excellent" grub.

Gaby's Mediterranean ◐ *Mediterranean* 20 | 10 | 17 | $17

Palms | 10445 Venice Blvd. (Motor Ave.) | 310-559-1808

Gaby's Express *Mediterranean*

NEW **West Hollywood** | 8873 Sunset Blvd. (Clark St.) | 310-854-1172

Culver City | 12219 Jefferson Blvd. (bet. Centinela Ave. & Randall St.) | 310-306-9058

Culver City | 2901 La Cienega (Washington Blvd.) | 310-202-8122

Marina del Rey | 3216 Washington Blvd. (Lincoln Blvd.) | 310-823-7299

www.gabysexpress.com

"Get your hummus on" at this "solid" Med chain that proves "healthy doesn't have to be boring" with "fresh", "tasty" eats like kebabs topped with an "addictive" garlic sauce, plus a "wide variety" of meze; sure, some of the locations "could use a makeover", but it's "quick", "affordable" and "convenient" for eat-in or takeout, and "cops love it" too.

Gale's Restaurant Ⓜ *Italian* 22 | 16 | 22 | $33

Pasadena | 452 S. Fair Oaks Ave. (Bellevue Dr.) | 626-432-6705 | www.galesrestaurant.com

The "warm" staff greets you "like a long-lost friend" at this "informal, family-friendly" Italian in Pasadena prized for its "lovingly prepared" "traditional" fare; "fair prices" and a "jovial" (some say "loud") atmosphere mean most "can't wait to go back."

Galletto Bar & Grill ◐ *Brazilian/Italian* ▽ 24 | 19 | 20 | $38

Westlake Village | Westlake Plaza | 982 Westlake Blvd. (bet. Agoura & Townsgate Rds.) | 805-449-4300 | www.gallettobarandgrill.com

Live music and lots of caipirinhas create a festive scene at this upscale-casual Westlake Villager offering an "extensive" Brazilian-Italian menu of steaks and pastas; critics call the food and service only "ok" for the price, although many agree it's still an appealing "change of pace."

The Galley *Seafood/Steak* 19 | 19 | 21 | $40

Santa Monica | 2442 Main St. (bet. Hollister Ave. & Ocean Park Blvd.) | 310-452-1934 | www.thegalleyrestaurant.net

"An oldie but a goodie", this "one-of-a-kind" Santa Monica surf 'n' turfer with a "kitschy", nautical-themed setting opened in 1934 and is "still full of character (and characters)"; most find the fare merely "decent", but the drinks are "stiff" and there's "tons of charm" in the "warm" atmosphere, while the happy-hour pricing is "very reasonable" too.

Gaucho Grill *Argentinean/Steak* 21 19 21 $28

Brentwood | 11754 San Vicente Blvd. (Gorham Ave.) | 310-447-7898 | www.gauchobrentwood.com
Long Beach | 200 Pine Ave. (B'way) | 562-590-5000 | www.gauchogrillusa.com

"If you like meat" and "don't want to spend a bundle", head to these "easy" Argentinean grills in Brentwood and Long Beach for "large portions" of "reliable" steaks, chicken and fish dressed up with chimichurri sauce; they're "nothing too fancy", but "comfortable" enough, and wallet-watchers insist the "lunch specials alone make it worth a visit."

Genwa *Korean* 25 22 25 $37

Hancock Park | 5115 Wilshire Blvd. (Orange Dr.) | 323-549-0760
NEW **Beverly Hills** | 170 N. La Cienega Blvd. (Clifton Way) | 310-854-0046
www.genwakoreanbbq.com

"Korean BBQ novices and pros" alike get "grilling suggestions" galore from the "friendly" staff at these "superb" spots in Beverly Hills and K-town where the meat quality is "outstanding" and the "variety of side dishes" is "really over the top"; plus, thanks to "excellent ventilation" in the contempo settings, you'll leave with "no smoky smell on your clothes."

Geoffrey's Malibu *Californian* 22 26 22 $60

Malibu | 27400 PCH (Escondido Beach Rd.) | 310-457-1519 | www.geoffreysmalibu.com

A "romantic" cliffside setting "overlooking the Pacific" is the hook at this "expensive" Malibu Californian also appreciated for its "solid" fare that's "kind of old-school" but "prepared beautifully" (think baked Brie, steamed lobster); service is generally "excellent" too, and "you can't beat brunch on a beautiful day."

Getty Center, Restaurant at the M *Californian* 23 27 24 $44

Brentwood | Getty Ctr. | 1200 Getty Center Dr. (Sepulveda Blvd.) | 310-440-6810 | www.getty.edu

The "magnificent views" "fit right in with the elegant architecture" at this "lovely" restaurant atop the Getty Center serving "ambitious", "farm-fresh" fare that "always surprises"; an "attentive" staff helps foster a "serene" mood, and most agree it's a "wonderful way to end a trip to the museum"; P.S. dinner served only on Saturdays.

Gina Lee's Bistro M *Asian/Californian* 24 16 24 $40

Redondo Beach | Riviera Plaza | 211 Palos Verdes Blvd. (bet. Catalina Ave. & PCH) | 310-375-4462

"Creative", "beautifully presented" Cal-Asian dishes shine at this Redondo Beach "strip-mall treasure" by owners Gina and Scott Lee, who "take food seriously" and "really care" about their customers; the "fairly priced" wine list also impresses, and while the "loud" digs "could be better", most call it a "delightful dining experience" nonetheless; P.S. "go for the bento box."

	FOOD	DECOR	SERVICE	COST

Gingergrass *Vietnamese* | 22 | 16 | 19 | $25

Silver Lake | 2396 Glendale Blvd. (Brier Ave.) | 323-644-1600 | www.gingergrass.com

"Tasty" noodle bowls and other "California-ized" Vietnamese dishes win a following for their "simple, clean flavors" at this Silver Lake locale with "fantastic" prices; service is "prompt", and while the "crowded" room doesn't stand out, "you're there for the food, not the scenery."

Gin Sushi *Japanese* | ∇ 22 | 16 | 17 | $25

Pasadena | 3589 E. Colorado Blvd. (Lotus Ave.) | 626-440-9611 | www.ginsushi.com

"Excellent sushi" and "surprisingly affordable" prices make a "rare" combo at this Japanese where the chef himself is a "Pasadena institution"; it's nothing "fancy" but regulars say they "always enjoy" it.

Giorgio Baldi M *Italian* | 25 | 18 | 20 | $81

Santa Monica | 114 W. Channel Rd. (PCH) | 310-573-1660 | www.giorgiobaldi.us

Expect "star sightings galore" at this "iconic" ultra-"expensive" Santa Monica Italian famed for its "out-of-this-world" handmade pastas; on the downside is a "dark", "crowded" dining room and sometimes "snobby" service ("if you are not a celeb, forget it").

Giovanni Ristorante *Italian* | 21 | 15 | 20 | $34

Woodland Hills | Gateway Plaza | 21801 Ventura Blvd. (Don Pio Dr.) | 818-884-0243 | www.giovanniristorante.com

"Well-prepared", "generous" plates of "homestyle" Italian food come with "family"-oriented hospitality and "fair" prices at this Woodland Hills staple; while some say the "simple" decor lacks "charm", others find the "friendly owner" keeps it a "warm neigborhood place."

NEW **Girasol** *American* | - | - | - | M

Studio City | 11334 Moorpark St. (Bakman Ave.) | 818-924-2323 | www.girasolrestaurant.com

Chef CJ Jacobson of *Top Chef* finds a home in Studio City at this reasonably priced New American with a menu that draws inspiration from the seasons, as well as the chef's stint at Copenhagen's Noma; the sleek, contemporary space is dominated by grays and browns, with a distinctive swirly paint job on the walls, flamelike designs on the ceiling and seating at tables and banquettes.

Gjelina ◐ *American* | 26 | 21 | 18 | $46

Venice | 1429 Abbot Kinney Blvd. (bet. California & Milwood Aves.) | 310-450-1429 | www.gjelina.com

"A must" on the "hipster" "farm-to-table" circuit, this "fabulous" Abbot Kinney American features "delicious, unique" pizzas and other "shareable" "ultrafresh" plates in a "loud", "sceney" setting; while service can be "spotty" and the "waits" are a "pain", most "can't wait to go back"; P.S. "try to get a seat on the patio."

Gjelina Take Away *American* | 27 | 15 | 19 | $25

Venice | 1429 Abbot Kinney Blvd. (bet. California & Milwood Aves.) | 310-450-1429 | www.gjelina.com

"You'll never forget the pork belly sandwich" say those who swear by this all-day Venice take-out spin-off of Gjelina offering the same "tremendous" seasonal American food (including "excellent pizzas") without the need for "month-in-advance" reservations; it's "a little expensive for lunch every day" and service can be "slow", but reviewers recommend it "if you don't mind sitting on milk crates."

Gladstone's *Seafood* 17 | 20 | 17 | $42

Long Beach | 330 S. Pine Ave. (Shoreline Dr.) | 562-432-8588 | www.gladstoneslongbeach.com

Gladstones Malibu *Seafood*

Pacific Palisades | 17300 PCH (Sunset Blvd.) | 310-454-3474 | www.gladstones.com

"Fabulous" water views and "large portions" of "basic seafood" "draw people in" to these separately owned Pacific Palisades and Long Beach fixtures; although sometimes "slow service", "cramped" quarters and "high prices" have some labeling them "tourist traps", it's still "tough to top" the "beautiful beach" atmosphere.

Go Burger *Burgers* 20 | 16 | 18 | $22

Hollywood | 6290 Sunset Blvd. (Vine St.) | 323-327-9355 | www.goburger.com

An "inspired" menu of "flavorful" burgers, "duck fat fries and spiked shakes" makes this BLT offshoot with a "happening" Hollywood atmosphere "one of the better" upscale patty-slingers around; a "diligent" staff keeps up the pace, so despite costs for the "convenient" location, it's filled with "locals day and night."

Golden Deli *Vietnamese* 25 | 11 | 15 | $15

San Gabriel | Las Tunas Plaza | 815 W. Las Tunas Dr. (Mission Dr.) | 626-308-0803 | www.thegoldendeli.com

"Wildly popular for a reason", this San Gabriel Vietnamese has been setting the "standard" since 1981, delivering "fool-proof delicious" dishes, particularly the "don't-miss" egg rolls and "rich, piping-hot" bowls of pho; it's "not fancy" but "friendly" - just expect to wait on a "line out the door."

Golden State M *Burgers* 25 | 13 | 21 | $19

Fairfax | 426 N. Fairfax Ave. (bet. Oakwood & Rosewood Aves.) | 323-782-8331 | www.thegoldenstatecafe.com

Go for the "revelatory", "amazingly made" burgers and "keep the pig-out ball rolling" with sweet potato fries and Coke floats at this "tiny" storefront on Fairfax where the "cool owners and staff" also "know their beer"; despite "standing in line" for counter service and "waiting for tables to open up", diehards declared it the "hands-down best" around; P.S. Let's Be Frank hot dogs are on the menu too.

NEW **Goldie's** *Californian* - | - | - | M

Third Street | 8422 W. Third St. (La Cienega Blvd.) | 323-677-2470 | www.goldiesla.com

Opened by the same Australian team responsible for the trendy Eveleigh on the Sunset Strip, this somewhat upscale New American near the Beverly Center features a stylish indoor-outdoor space with a garage door that goes up and down depending on the temps; the daily changing menu is made up of seasonal small dishes and only a handful of entrees, and augmented by an ample cocktail selection.

	FOOD	DECOR	SERVICE	COST

Gonpachi *Japanese* — 19 | 23 | 18 | $40

Torrance | Miyako Hybrid Hotel | 21381 S. Western Ave. (213th St.) | 310-320-6700 | www.gonpachi.us

Diners encounter a "slice of Japan in Torrance" at this "refreshing" hotel locale serving "delicious" soba noodles and sushi in a "beautiful", "hip" setting; "helpful" servers enhance it as an "asset" to the area, even if it can get "expensive" for dinner (lunch and brunch are more "reasonable").

Good Girl Dinette Ⓜ *Vietnamese* — ∇ 22 | 18 | 20 | $20

Highland Park | 110 N. Ave. 56 (Figueroa St.) | 323-257-8980 | www.goodgirlfoods.com

The "unique fusion" of Vietnamese and American "comfort food with a kick" gets a "thumbs-up" at this Highland Park "local" with "the charm of a small diner"; though it's not "traditional" or speedy enough for some, it's a "cheap" go-to for the "hipster" set.

The Gorbals ◐ ⊠ *Eclectic* — 20 | 15 | 18 | $38

Downtown | Alexandria Hotel | 501 S. Spring St. (5th St.) | 213-488-3408 | www.thegorbalsla.com

Top Chef winner Ilan Hall offers "original" "Scottish-Jewish" small plates with "a sense of humor" and "spot-on" cocktails at this "hip" Downtown Eclectic set in "wildly weird" "basement-chic" digs in an old hotel; factor in "laid-back" service and pricing and it's a perfect "conversation starter" and "date spot for the semi-adventurous."

Gordon Biersch ◐ *Pub Food* — 18 | 19 | 19 | $26

Burbank | 145 S. San Fernando Blvd. (Angeleno Ave.) | 818-569-5240 | www.gordonbiersch.com

"Stick to the beer" and the "easy stuff" ("excellent garlic fries") at this American brewpub in Burbank serving "bar grub at its chain-iest" in a "comfortable" atmosphere that works for "happy hour" with a "large group" or just "watching sports"; there's "friendly" service too, though the operation feels too "generic" to some.

Gordon Ramsay ◐ *Californian/French* — 23 | 23 | 22 | $84

West Hollywood | London West Hollywood | 1020 N. San Vicente Blvd. (Sunset Blvd.) | 310-358-7788 | www.thelondonwesthollywood.com

"Exceptional" Californian-French cuisine and "fantastic" wine pairings make for an "outstanding meal" at this "destination" in the London West Hollywood (where Ramsay acts as a consultant); the "serene" setting may not be "something to get excited about", and a few pooh-pooh "small portions" and "fussy" leanings, but most agree the "beautiful" service supports the highly "expensive" tabs.

NEW Gorge Charcuterie & Wine Bar ◐ ⊠ *French* — - | - | - | M

West Hollywood | 8917 W. Sunset Blvd. (bet. Clark St. & Hilldale Ave.) | 310-657-6328 | www.gorgela.com

This casual WeHo storefront serves midpriced Gallic fare and housemade charcuterie - along with plenty of *vin* - courtesy of former *Top Chef*-testant Elia Aboumrad and Le Cirque veteran Uyen Nguyen; the narrow space goes for a vintage vibe with pressed-tin ceilings, olive-green walls and distressed wooden chairs.

	FOOD	DECOR	SERVICE	COST

Gottsui ◐ *Japanese* ▽ 21 | 17 | 17 | $24

West LA | 2119 Sawtelle Blvd. (bet. Mississippi Ave. & Olympic Blvd.) | 310-478-0521

Lovers of Japanese "street food" dig this "great new place" in West LA specializing in "delicious" okonomiyaki (savory grilled pancakes) and yakisoba (Japanese fried noodles) in a minimalist black-and-white setting; "be prepared to wait" and pay slightly "high" prices for the "small" savories, but it's "easier than going to Toyko."

Granville Cafe *American* 21 | 20 | 20 | $24

Burbank | 121 N. San Fernando Blvd. (bet. Olive & Orange Grove Aves.) | 818-848-4726

Glendale | Americana Way | 807 Americana Way (Harvard St.) | 818-550-0472

www.granvillecafe.com

"For a night out" or an "amazing" breakfast, these "upscale" yet casual twins in Burbank and Glendale - lauded for "moderate" prices - serve up "solid" (some say "generic") American "comfort food" to diners of all ages in a homey, bistro-style environment; the "energetic" staff "treats everyone like family", and for voyeurs, the patios offer "great people-watching" too.

Great Greek *Greek* 22 | 19 | 22 | $30

Sherman Oaks | 13362 Ventura Blvd. (bet. Dixie Canyon & Nagle Aves.) | 818-905-5250 | www.greatgreek.com

"*Opa!*" shout fans of this "boisterous" Sherman Oaks taverna "straight out of *Never on Sunday*", which plates "abundant" portions of "authentic" Greek delicacies in a "party atmosphere" ("be prepared to join a line dance"); philosophical types find the photo-bedecked digs "crazy loud", but with "no shortage of hospitality" and fair prices, it's "as close to Athens as you'll get" in SoCal.

Greenblatt's Deli & Fine Wines ◐ *Deli* 19 | 12 | 17 | $25

Hollywood | 8017 W. Sunset Blvd. (Laurel Ave.) | 323-656-0606 | www.greenblattsdeli.com

"You can't go wrong" with a "generous" pastrami sandwich and a "nice bottle of red" at this Hollywood deli and "impressive" attached wine shop; kvetchers lament "slow" service amid the "old-school", two-floor setting, though late hours (till 2 AM) can be a godsend.

Greenleaf Gourmet Chopshop ☒ *American* 21 | 15 | 18 | $15

Beverly Hills | 9671 Wilshire Blvd. (Bedford Dr.) | 310-246-0756

Century City | 1888 Century Park E. (Santa Monica Blvd.) | 424-239-8700

www.greenleafchopshop.com

Pleasing "even non-vegetarians", these Beverly Hills and Century City saladeers let customers build their own leafy creations, in addition to spinning out other "fresh", "healthy" American eats and juices; pleasant service and modern settings make them "welcome" for lunch, though a few tree-shruggers gripe "who knew greens could cost that much?"

Green Street Restaurant *American* 21 | 16 | 19 | $25

Pasadena | 146 Shoppers Ln. (Cordova St.) | 626-577-7170 | www.greenstreetrestaurant.com

Pasadena families and "ladies who lunch" frequent this casual American "mainstay" for its "generous" portions of "comfort-food" standards, including a "still-tops" Dianne salad and "delish" zucchini bread; quibblers sniff at "spotty" service and a "plain" interior, but a "delightful" patio and "fair prices" entrench it as a "local institution."

Green Street Tavern *Californian* 23 | 19 | 22 | $37

Pasadena | 69 W. Green St. (De Lacey Ave.) | 626-229-9961 | www.greenstreettavern.net

"Tucked away on Green Street" is this "charming" Pasadena "treasure", which offers "sophisticated", "reasonably priced" Californian cuisine with an "eclectic" European flair - plus a "glorious" wine list - in a "cozy" yet "urbane" atmosphere; coupled with its "warm hospitality" and brunch menu, fans wish it could remain a "best-kept secret."

Griddle Cafe *American* 25 | 14 | 20 | $19

Hollywood | 7916 W. Sunset Blvd. (bet. Fairfax & Hayworth Aves.) | 323-874-0377 | www.thegriddlecafe.com

"Hubcap-sized" pancakes in myriad "over-the-top" combinations and other "amazing" treats "drive lines of locals and tourists" to this "gold standard" of American breakfast spots, right in the heart of Hollywood; the "hip", "urban" space, enhanced by a "gorgeous" staff, is often "extremely busy" (particularly on weekends), so regulars suggest "arriving early" to avoid a "long wait."

The Grilled Cheese Truck *Sandwiches* 24 | 15 | 20 | $10

Location varies; see website | 323-522-3418 | www.thegrilledcheesetruck.com

It "ain't your mother's grilled cheese" at this "top-tier" truck turning out "incredible, gourmet" sammies in "novel" combos like the "genius" mac and rib accompanied by shots of tomato soup and tater tots to perpetual "lines" of followers; sure, some say you can "make them at home for half the price", but it works for a "comfort-food fix" on the run.

NEW **Grill 'Em All** *Burgers* ▽ 19 | 13 | 20 | $16

Alhambra | Alhambra Renaissance Ctr. | 19 E. Main St. (Garfield Ave.) | 626-284-2874

This winner of the 2010 *Great Food Truck Race* finally goes brick-and-mortar in Downtown Alhambra, serving gloriously sloppy burgers with names like The Dee Snider, The Waste 'Em All and The Behemoth; the space is dominated by heavy-metal band posters, with a long counter, sundry booths and an art piece on one wall that reads, "Death to False Burgers."

The Grill on Hollywood *American* 24 | 24 | 25 | $52

Hollywood | Hollywood & Highland Ctr. | 6801 Hollywood Blvd. (Highland Ave.) | 323-856-5530

The Grill on the Alley Westlake *American*

Thousand Oaks | Promenade at Westlake | 120 Promenade Way (Thousand Oaks Blvd.) | 805-418-1760

www.thegrill.com

These Hollywood and Westlake follow-ups to The Grill on the Alley provide "delish" steaks and other American classics in traditional surroundings; tabs "on the pricey side" have some saving them "for a special event" or "a date", though their happy hour proffers "quality" bites at "bargain" rates.

	FOOD	DECOR	SERVICE	COST

The Grill on the Alley *American* 25 | 23 | 25 | $61

Beverly Hills | 9560 Dayton Way (bet. Camden & Rodeo Drs.) | 310-276-0615 | www.thegrill.com

"See and be seen" feasting on "outstanding" steaks, chops and seafood alongside "the power brokers of Hollywood" at this "iconic" Beverly Hills "magnet" for the "entertainment biz"; the "old-school steakhouse" setting offers "a real sanctuary" for "wheelin' 'n' dealin'" over lunch, and given waiters who "treat everyone like royalty", there's "no need to be famous here."

Grissini Ristorante Italiano ☒ *Italian* 21 | 19 | 21 | $36

Agoura Hills | Agoura Hills Town Ctr. | 30125 Agoura Rd. (bet. Agoura Ct. & Reyes Adobe Rd.) | 818-735-9711 | www.grissiniristoranteitaliano.com

With countless variations of "mix-and-match" pastas enthralling diners, this "authentic", shopping center-located Italian "gem" in Agoura Hills is "always a delight", offering pizzas and other "delicious" fare in a candlelit, frescoed setting; the "charming" owner wins over fans as well, and though some say meals can get "a bit pricey", most have a "memorable" experience.

Grub *American* 24 | 19 | 22 | $20

Hollywood | 911 N. Seward St. (bet. Romaine St. & Willoughby Ave.) | 323-461-3663 | www.grub-la.com

"They really have something special" cooking inside this "charming" former bungalow on a residential block in Hollywood, where former *Top Chef* contestant Betty Fraser cooks up "quirky" yet "homey" American eats - including a grilled-cheese-and-tomato-soup combo that may "transport you to mother's kitchen" - at modest prices; grubsters also dig the "excellent" brunch, "personable" staff and "lovely" patio, which make the experience like "hanging out at a friend's house."

Guelaguetza *Mexican* 24 | 18 | 21 | $24

Koreatown | 3014 W. Olympic Blvd. (Normandie Ave.) | 213-427-0608 | www.ilovemole.com

The black mole's "to die for" at this "definitive" Mexican spot in Koreatown, where families dig into "big", "value"-oriented portions of "authentic, honest" Oaxacan cuisine; a staff that "likes to help" and "quirky", traditional decor accented with live music create an ambiance that's "full of life."

Guido's *Italian* 21 | 20 | 22 | $43

West LA | 11980 Santa Monica Blvd. (Ohio Ave.) | 310-820-6649 | www.guidosla.com

"Take a walk down memory lane" at this "dependable" Italian, where the "impeccable", tux-clad waiters "fuss over you" like in "the good old days"; the "traditional" cuisine - served in an "intimate" (some say "dated") West LA location featuring red booths and a fireplace - entices locals, though some warn of "sticker shock" come tab time.

Gulfstream *American/Seafood* 22 | 21 | 22 | $40

Century City | Westfield Century City Shopping Ctr. | 10250 Santa Monica Blvd. (Ave. of the Stars) | 310-553-3636 | www.hillstone.com

Surveyors deem this "fishy sibling of Houston's" "another success story" from the Hillstone group, with "fresh", "honest" American seafood luring businessfolk to its upscale Century City outpost; a "knowledgeable" staff, "slick" setting and prices that are "reasonable" for the quality keep these spots "busy", despite some complaints about "noise" and "waits."

Gumbo Pot *Cajun* 20 | 9 | 15 | $16

Fairfax | Farmers Mkt. | 6333 W. Third St. (Fairfax Ave.) | 323-933-0358 | www.thegumbopotla.com

This "super-casual" stall in the Fairfax Farmers Market is the "real deal", churning out gumbo, beignets and other "classic Cajun" treats that are so good, "you think you're in the Big Easy"; sure, critics fret over chow that's "nothing memorable" while citing "passable" outside seating, but for a "quick", inexpensive bite, it "hits the spot."

Gus's BBQ *BBQ* 19 | 17 | 20 | $27

South Pasadena | 808 Fair Oaks Ave. (bet. Hope & Mission Sts.) | 626-799-3251 | www.gussbbq.com

"Cholesterol and calories be damned" say 'cueheads of this "friendly" South Pasadena joint, a mainstay since 1946 for "solid" BBQ staples such as pulled pork and beer-braised brisket, along with "rich sauces"; the "spiffy" nostalgic-meets-modern space makes for a "lively", family-oriented atmosphere, and while rib-sticklers sniff "it's not Texas or Memphis", with such moderate prices, "it'll do."

Gusto M *Italian* ▽ 23 | 15 | 19 | $52

Third Street | 8432 W. Third St. (bet. La Cienega Blvd. & Orlando Ave.) | 323-782-1778 | www.gusto-la.com

"Superlative" pastas, pizzas and other midpriced seasonal fare make this "small, rustic" Italian on Third Street "stand out", as does the "personal attention" from ever-present chef-owner Vic Casanova; just prepare for noise "and be ready to squish in."

Gyu-Kaku *Japanese* 20 | 17 | 18 | $32

Beverly Hills | 163 N. La Cienega Blvd. (Clifton Way) | 310-659-5760
West LA | 10925 W. Pico Blvd. (bet. Veteran Ave. & Westwood Blvd.) | 310-234-8641
Torrance | Crossroads Shopping Ctr. | 24631 Crenshaw Blvd. (Skypark Dr.) | 310-325-1437
Pasadena | 70 W. Green St. (De Lacey Ave.) | 626-405-4842
Canoga Park | Westfield Topanga Ctr. | 6600 Topanga Canyon Blvd. (bet. Vanowen St. & Victory Blvd.) | 818-888-4030
Sherman Oaks | 14457 Ventura Blvd. (bet. Tyrone Ave. & Van Nuys Blvd.) | 818-501-5400
www.gyu-kaku.com

The "novelty" of "DIY" tabletop grilling intrigues adventurers at this "festive" Japanese yakiniku chain, where families, friends and first dates cook their own "scrumptious" meats in an Asian-themed setting; meanwhile, some grumble about the "hit-or-miss" staff serving "small", "pricey" portions, though "bargains" may be found during regular happy hours.

Hakata Ramen Shinsengumi ◐ *Japanese* 25 | 15 | 20 | $15

Gardena | 2015 W. Redondo Beach Blvd. (Gramercy Pl.) | 310-329-1335 | www.shinsengumigroup.com

"Outstanding" ramen awaits at this inexpensive Japanese "dive" in Gardena, where servers help you "customize" your noodles before they're "cooked to perfection"; pundits cite the "casual" atmosphere where you may have to "yell across the table" to be heard and say to "expect a wait", but overall, it "feels like Tokyo."

Hal's Bar & Grill ◐ *American* 20 | 20 | 20 | $37

Venice | 1349 Abbot Kinney Blvd. (California Ave.) | 310-396-3105 | www.halsbarandgrill.com

The "quintessential" Venice "hangout", this longtime neighborhood "institution" is "solid as always" with its "top-notch" turkey burgers and other "tasty" midpriced Americana, "generous pours" on drinks and "happening" bar scene filled with the "local literati"; add in live jazz and "great art" covering the walls, and even if it's "deafening when crowded", most find it always "comes through."

Hamasaku ⊠ *Japanese* 28 | 18 | 25 | $66

West LA | 11043 Santa Monica Blvd. (bet. Bentley & Camden Aves.) | 310-479-7636 | www.hamasakula.com

The "incredible", "innovative" rolls are named for celebs at this "high-class" West LA Japanese from Michael Ovitz also featuring "clever" small plates; an "impeccable" staff treats everyone - from plebs to Hollywood luminaries - "like a VIP" in the serene space, but know "your wallet will take a hit."

Hama Sushi *Japanese* 23 | 16 | 20 | $38

Venice | 213 Windward Ave. (Main St.) | 310-396-8783 | www.hamasushi.com

"Traditional", "inventive" rolls, "no-nonsense" sushi and other Japanese classics "keep 'em coming back" to this longtime Venice "hole-in-the-wall", a popular "local hang" that attracts ichthyophiles for its "friendly" "group vibe" and "reasonable" prices, including happy-hour deals; a patio's also on hand for those seeking more subdued dining.

Hamburger Hamlet *Diner* 18 | 16 | 18 | $24

Pasadena | 214 S. Lake Ave. (bet. Cordova St. & Del Mar Blvd.) | 626-449-8520

Sherman Oaks | 4419 Van Nuys Blvd. (Moorpark St.) | 818-784-1183

www.hamburgerhamlet.com

For "a bit of old LA", try these "classic" diners in Pasadena and Sherman Oaks, a "standby" for "moderately priced" Americana; some, however, say it's "not what it was", finding the dark-wood setting "outdated" and the service "adequate", though for nostalgia it remains "tried-and-true."

Hannosuke ⊭ *Japanese* - | - | - | I

Mar Vista | Mitsuwa Mktpl. | 3760 S. Centinela Ave. (Venice Blvd.) | 310-397-4676 | www.hannosuke.com

The busy Mitsuwa Marketplace in Mar Vista hosts the first American outpost of this hugely popular Tokyo tempura specialist, which offers just two options, both wallet-friendly: tempura (fried fish and vegetables over rice) or eel donburi; local foodies and Japanese expats alike queue up for a taste of the freshly fried treat.

Harold & Belle's *Creole* ▽ 24 | 17 | 18 | $34

Mid-City | 2920 W. Jefferson Blvd. (bet. 9th & 10th Aves.) | 323-735-3376 | www.haroldandbellesrestaurant.com

You'd "have to drive to Louisiana to do better" than the "home cookin'" - think étouffée and gumbo - of this "old-school" Creole in Mid-City, where locals enjoy "humongous" portions and authentic "Southern hospitality" in a warm, comfortable space; regular jazz nights add luster, though some point to prices that are "steep" for what you get.

NEW The Hart & the Hunter *American* ∇ 23 | 21 | 23 | $57

West Hollywood | Palihotel | 7950 Melrose Ave. (Doheny Dr.) | 323-424-3055 | www.thehartandthehunter.com

"Unique and expertly prepared" American plates "inspired by the South" have this WeHo newcomer in the Palihotel packing a "too-hip" crowd into its "really cool", "tile-clad" quarters; "friendly" staffers provide smooth service, though some still "wish they took reservations."

Hatfield's *American* 27 | 25 | 26 | $75

Melrose | 6703 Melrose Ave. (Citrus Ave.) | 323-935-2977 | www.hatfieldsrestaurant.com

"Simply sublime", this "elegant", expensive Melrose New American from husband-and-wife team Quinn and Karen Hatfield serves "carefully crafted", "locally sourced" fare (including a "wonderful" tasting menu) and desserts that strike a "high note of creativity"; it's "an oasis of calm" with the staff "moving seamlessly about" an "understated" modern dining room - in sum, "an all-around wonderful experience."

Haven Gastropub ◐ *American* ∇ 19 | 17 | 18 | $25

Pasadena | 42 S. De Lacey Ave. (Mc Cormick Alley) | 626-768-9555 | www.havengastropub.com

"Fab" "calorie-unfriendly menus" of "innovative pub-style" fare and a rotating selection of "obscure" craft beers endear Pasadena patrons to this midrange gastropub with a modern feel; service is solid and it's open late, however, it's "always packed" and some say the "college-campus" crowd can get "noisy" and "spoil your appetite."

Hide Sushi Ⓜ ⊄ *Japanese* 24 | 12 | 20 | $32

West LA | 2040 Sawtelle Blvd. (bet. La Grange & Mississippi Aves.) | 310-477-7242 | www.hidesushi.com

You won't find "exotic or fancy rolls" at this Japanese "hole-in-the-wall" in West LA, which slices up "generous" cuts of "straightforward", "quality" sushi at "bargain" prices; the "sweet" staff moves things along, but surveyors say the "tiny", "bare-bones" space can get "crowded" - a trade-off when you want "the real thing"; P.S. cash only.

Hillstone/Houston's *American* 22 | 20 | 20 | $40

Manhattan Beach | 1550 Rosecrans Ave. (bet. Aviation & Sepulveda Blvds.) | 310-643-7211

Pasadena | 320 S. Arroyo Pkwy. (Del Mar Blvd.) | 626-577-6001

Santa Monica | 202 Wilshire Blvd. (2nd St.) | 310-576-7558

www.hillstone.com

"As non-chainy as the chains get", this "grown-up" franchise "gets everything right" with midpriced American eats (like "tender" ribs and "delish" spinach-artichoke dip) in "clubby" digs with a "top-rate" bar scene; "rapid service" is a plus, but rezzies "are a must if you don't like to wait."

NEW Hinoki & The Bird Ⓢ Ⓜ *Japanese* 23 | 26 | 23 | $78

Century City | The Century | 10 Century Dr. (Ave. of the Stars) | 310-552-1200 | www.hinokiandthebird.com

"Refined, but not precious" sums up the "inventive" Japanese cuisine at this "pricey" Century City entry from David Myers dispensing small and large plates in a "beautiful" rustic room scented with hinoki wood (it "smells like a wonderful sauna"); with interesting seasonal cocktails, the "bar area is a scene" too.

Hirosuke *Japanese* 22 | 14 | 20 | $34

Encino | Plaza de Oro | 17237 Ventura Blvd. (bet. Amestoy & Louise Aves.) | 818-788-7548

"Dependable" sushi and "excellent" specialty rolls may be had at this Encino Japanese, a local fixture for its "fresh", "reasonably priced" fare and accommodating service; the casual setting is often "busy" with regulars, who like its "consistency" – no small feat for a neighborhood spot.

Hirozen ⊠ *Japanese* 26 | 14 | 21 | $44

Beverly Boulevard | 8385 Beverly Blvd. (bet. Kings Rd. & Orlando Ave.) | West Hollywood | 323-653-0470 | www.hirozen.com

Sushiphiles bow to the "wide variety of unusual", "exceptional" fish and "standout" cooked items at this "small" earth-toned Beverly Boulevard Japanese that "remains a favorite" after 25 years; just remember, costs for such "glorious" bites can "mount quickly."

Holdren's Steaks & Seafood *Seafood/Steak* ▽ 24 | 21 | 24 | $49

Thousand Oaks | 1714 Newbury Rd. (bet. Giant Oak Ave. & Kelly Rd.) | 805-498-1314 | www.holdrens.com

"Reasonably priced" steaks and "specials every day but Saturday" mean you'll find a wait "even on a weeknight" at this "dark", saloon-inspired spot in Thousand Oaks; generally "attentive" service is a plus, though critics call it "cramped and noisy" with "hit-or-miss" cooking, adding they just don't "understand the fuss."

NEW Hole in the Wall Burger Joint *Burgers* 23 | 9 | 16 | $14

Santa Monica | 2200 Colorado Ave. (Cloverfield Blvd.) | 310-449-0147 | www.holeinthewallburgerjoint.com

"Build your own burger" at this "fun little dive" in Santa Monica boasting "juicy" grass-fed Angus patties that are "cooked to order at a very reasonable price" and served on "special pretzel bread"; sure, it's "literally a hole-in-the-wall", but "you don't go here for the decor."

Home *Eclectic* 20 | 19 | 18 | $22

Los Feliz | 1760 Hillhurst Ave. (Kingswell Ave.) | 323-665-4663 | www.homelosfeliz.com

Silver Lake | 2500 Riverside Dr. (Fletcher Dr.) | 323-665-0211 | www.homesilverlake.com

It "feels like mama's cooking" at these "two-of-a-kind" "faves" with a "hipster vibe" in Los Feliz and Silver Lake, where an "engaged" staff serves up "huge quantities" of "homey" Eclectic "comfort food" from an "affordable" menu; just be sure to "get there early" if you'd like a "romantic" booth on the "fabulous" patio, or the "wait can be interminable."

Homeboy Diner ⊠ *Sandwiches* ▽ 22 | 16 | 20 | $18

Downtown | Los Angeles City Hall | 200 N. Spring St. (1st St.) | 213-542-6190 | www.homeboy-industries.org

Homegirl Café ⊠ M *American/Mexican*

Chinatown | 130 W. Bruno St. (Alameda St.) | 213-617-0380 | www.homegirlcafe.org

Pegged as the "best-tasting gang-abatement program ever", the bright Homeboy Diner stand inside City Hall offers "quality" soups, salads and sandwiches, while Chinatown's Homegirl Café augments the menu with tacos and other American-Mex fare - some of it sourced through the organization's own gardens - as part of a project supporting at-risk youth; it all adds up to a "fast", low-cost lunch and service is "genuine as you can get", so fans say "keep it going" and fuel the "success stories."

Honda-Ya ◐ *Japanese* 21 | 18 | 18 | $29

Little Tokyo | Little Tokyo Shopping Ctr. | 333 S. Alameda St. (3rd St.) | 213-625-1184
City of Industry | 17200 Railroad St. (Azusa Ave.) | 626-964-6777
www.izakayahondaya.com

"Mix and match all night long" from the menu "like a phone book" at these izakayas in Little Tokyo and the City of Industry, where the "well-priced" "pub-style plates", yakitori skewers and sushi come with plenty of sake, beer and "old-school" atmosphere; the staff aptly handles the "busy" scene, plus it's "open late, a rarity" for these parts; P.S. sit on the floor in the tatami rooms "if you're feeling adventurous."

Hop Li *Chinese/Seafood* 20 | 12 | 17 | $23

Chinatown | 526 Alpine St. (Yale St.) | 213-680-3939
Pico-Robertson | 10974 W. Pico Blvd. (Veteran Ave.) | 310-441-3708
West LA | 11901 Santa Monica Blvd. (Armacost Ave.) | 310-268-2463
www.hoplirestaurant.com

"Multigenerational families chow down with gusto" at these Cantonese "standbys" proffering a "lengthy" menu of "classic seafood" dishes and other "tasty", "typical" fare; while service and decor "won't win any prizes" and some find the eats "uninspired", supporters say the "reasonable" tabs and "bargain" lunches "continue to please."

NEW Horse Thief BBQ *BBQ* - | - | - | I

Downtown | Grand Central Mkt. | 324 S. Hill St. (bet. 3rd & 4th Sts.) | 213-625-0341 | www.horsethiefbbq.com

Among the expanding culinary options at Downtown's venerable Grand Central Market, this low-priced BBQ window serves up brisket, ribs, chicken, pulled pork and the like, which can be eaten at outdoor tables across from the fabled Angels Flight funicular.

Hostaria del Piccolo *Italian* 24 | 21 | 24 | $39

Santa Monica | 606 Broadway (6th St.) | 310-393-6633
NEW Venice | 512 Rose Ave. (Rennie Ave.) | 310-392-8822
www.hostariadelpiccolo.com

"Light", "creative" Italian cuisine is yours at this Santa Monica and Venice duo known for its "divine" pizzas and other "fab" eats that "meet every dietary restriction" (vegetarian, gluten-free, dairy-free); with a "personable" staff and moderate bills it makes for a "perfect night out" "without being too much of a scene."

Hot's Kitchen *Eclectic* ▽ 25 | 18 | 20 | $29

Hermosa Beach | 844 Hermosa Ave. (8th St.) | 310-318-2939 | www.hotskitchen.com

A "wild assortment" of "excellent tacos", "seriously awesome burgers" and seasonal beers mean "it's hard to make a decision" at this midpriced open-air Eclectic near the Hermosa Beach pier; although it's "noisy" and "service is mixed", locals still "dig it."

	FOOD	DECOR	SERVICE	COST

House Café *Eclectic* — 20 | 17 | 19 | $34

Beverly Boulevard | 8114 Beverly Blvd. (bet. Crescent Heights Blvd. & Kilkea Dr.) | 323-655-5553 | www.housecafe.com

One of the "best-kept secrets" on Beverly Boulevard, this "small", "informal" bistro by Bruce Marder (Capo) "fares well" among "bigger names in the neighborhood" by offering "tasty", thoughtfully sourced Eclectic food, including breakfast all day, to please "unstuffy people"; "quality" service and specials provide added "value for the money."

Huckleberry Café & Bakery *American* — 23 | 15 | 15 | $22

Santa Monica | 1014 Wilshire Blvd. (10th Ct.) | 310-451-2311 | www.huckleberrycafe.com

"It's all about brunch" at this organic-minded Santa Monica cafe known for whimsical American specialties like green eggs and ham ("as delicious as Dr. Seuss imagined") and "spectacular" pastries that "taste like home, but better"; "modest prices" are a plus, but expect a "crowded, frenetic" scene at peak hours.

Hudson House ● *American* — 21 | 18 | 18 | $28

Redondo Beach | 514 N. PCH (Beryl St.) | 310-798-9183 | www.hudsonhousebar.com

"Quirky, delicious" dishes like the signature pretzel-bun burger and "an impressive array of beers and ales" keep this "lively", "inviting" gastropub in Redondo Beach "hopping" with a "mix of locals in sandals and hipsters in skinny jeans"; factor in "good-value" prices (especially at happy hour), and "the only downside is the noise."

Hugo's *Californian* — 21 | 15 | 19 | $26

West Hollywood | 8401 Santa Monica Blvd. (Kings Rd.) | 323-654-3993
Studio City | 12851 Riverside Dr. (Coldwater Canyon Ave.) | 818-761-8985
Agoura Hills | Whizin Market Sq. | 5046 Cornell Rd. (bet. Agoura Rd. & Roadside Dr.) | 818-707-0300
www.hugosrestaurant.com

"Organic before it was trendy", these "popular" all-day sibs "cheerfully accommodate every conceivable weirdo dietary restriction" with "fresh", "flavorful" Cal-New American cuisine that "will make you feel healthier than a yoga class"; service can be "scatterbrained" and some "don't get the raves", but the "casual" quarters are often "an absolute zoo", especially during brunch.

Hummus Bar & Grill ● *Mideastern* — 21 | 13 | 18 | $23

Tarzana | 18743 Ventura Blvd. (Burbank Blvd.) | 818-344-6606 | www.hummusbargrill.com

You get "a lot of food for the price" at this Tarzana Middle Eastern doing justice to its namesake with "yummy hummus" joined by "perfectly spiced skewers", "warm bread" and "fresh salads"; "efficient" service and a "crowded", basic setting are in keeping with the "low cost."

Hungry Cat *Seafood* — 23 | 19 | 21 | $50

Hollywood | 1535 N. Vine St. (bet. Selma Ave. & Sunset Blvd.) | 323-462-2155
Santa Monica | 100 W. Channel Rd. (PCH) | 310-459-3337
www.thehungrycat.com

"Interesting", "fresh" seafood, including "glistening" raw-bar selections, plus "sublime burgers" by chef-owner David Lentz are "the cat's meow" at these "hip" "foodie" destinations in LA and Santa Barbara also famed for "exquisite cocktails" made with fresh juices, all served in "minimal" digs; "crowded" conditions, "maddening" acoustics and "moderately high" bills are drawbacks, but on the whole, most find eating here "one of the best decisions you can make."

Il Buco Cucina Italiana *Italian* 21 | 19 | 21 | $41

West Hollywood | 107 N. Robertson Blvd. (bet. Clifton Way & Wilshire Blvd.) | 310-657-1345

"Robust", "ingredient-driven" Italian cuisine is the focus of Giacomino Drago's West Hollywood "hideaway" that's been revitalized with a new chef behind the stove and a sleek, modern aesthetic; those who appreciate "fine service" and "relaxed, intimate dining" for a "mid-range" sum say it "shows promise."

Il Cielo *Italian* 23 | 26 | 23 | $59

Beverly Hills | 9018 Burton Way (bet. Almont & Wetherly Drs.) | 310-276-9990 | www.ilcielo.com

"Wedding proposals are a common sight" at this "gorgeous" Beverly Hills Italian that's "the definition of lovely" with a "twinkle-lit" garden and a "top-notch", "conventional" Northern Italian menu; a few find service "needs to be better" for the prices, but for a "special summer evening", it's hard to beat.

Il Fornaio *Italian* 20 | 19 | 19 | $37

Beverly Hills | 301 N. Beverly Dr. (Dayton Way) | 310-550-8330
Manhattan Beach | Manhattan Gateway Shopping Ctr. | 1800 Rosecrans Ave. (bet. Aviation Blvd. & Redondo Ave.) | 310-725-9555
Pasadena | One Colorado | 24 W. Union St. (bet. De Lacey & Fair Oaks Aves.) | 626-683-9797
www.ilfornaio.com

"True to its name, the bread is marvelous" at this "trustworthy" Italian chain also proffering "affordable" pizzas and pastas, plus monthly regional menus that "keep things interesting" in "pleasant", "business-casual" settings; "considerate" service adds to the "consistent" experience, and even if some find it all a little "run of the mill", it's certainly "serviceable", "especially for lunch."

Il Forno *Italian* 22 | 17 | 21 | $32

Santa Monica | 2901 Ocean Park Blvd. (bet. 29th & 30th Sts.) | 310-450-1241 | www.ilfornocaffe.com

"Delicious, unpretentious" Northern Italian cuisine is the forte of this "well-kept secret" in Santa Monica where both the "accommodating" staff and "simple" recipes come "straight from The Boot"; add in "affordable" prices and an "easy", "no-attitude" atmosphere and it's exactly "what a neighborhood trattoria should be."

Il Forno Caldo *Italian* 21 | 17 | 19 | $33

Beverly Hills | 9705 S. Santa Monica Blvd. (Roxbury Dr.) | 310-777-0040 | www.ilfornocaldo.com

"Cute, cozy and pretty inexpensive for Beverly Hills" sums up this Italian "sleeper" favored by locals for its "good, basic" eats proffered by a "pleasant" staff; with a "quiet", "old-fashioned" setting, it's "nothing fancy", but regulars have "no complaints" and say you always "feel you've gotten your money's worth."

	FOOD	DECOR	SERVICE	COST

Il Grano ☒ *Italian* 25 | 21 | 23 | $59

West LA | 11359 Santa Monica Blvd. (Purdue Ave.) | 310-477-7886 | www.ilgrano.com

"Everything is spot-on" at this "upscale" "undiscovered gem" in West LA, where chef-owner Salvatore Marino crafts "extraordinary" Italian highlighting "superb" seafood (like "great crudo") and other "fresh" ingredients (he "literally feeds patrons from his own garden"); the "low-key" atmosphere is "special without being stuffy", so in the whole it comes "highly recommended for an elegant evening"; P.S. the all-tomato menu in summer "should not be missed."

Il Moro *Italian* 21 | 22 | 22 | $46

West LA | 11400 W. Olympic Blvd. (Purdue Ave.) | 310-575-3530 | www.ilmoro.com

"Ask for a table outside and you'll feel like you left West LA" proclaim proponents of this "elegant" "business-lunch" "favorite" "hidden in an office tower", but boasting a "lovely garden" for "well-prepared" Italian cuisine and mains; "capable" service is another plus, and while critics complain of "expensive" prices, others cheer the happy hour with complimentary apps.

Il Pastaio *Italian* 26 | 18 | 21 | $47

Beverly Hills | 400 N. Canon Dr. (Brighton Way) | 310-205-5444 | www.giacominodrago.com

An "elite clientele" comes in "droves" to this "vibrant" Drago Brother Italian that's "Beverly Hills at its most Beverly Hillsish" with a "see-and-be-seen" crowd tucking into "exquisite" "homemade pastas" and other "fabulous" fare on the patio; indeed, it's "on the expensive side", but after a few visits the "staff knows you by name" and the "jam-packed" setting means "you might actually rub elbows with an A-lister."

Il Piccolino ☒ *Italian* 23 | 19 | 22 | $58

West Hollywood | 350 N. Robertson Blvd. (Rosewood Ave.) | 310-659-2220 | www.ilpiccolinorestaurant.com

"Industry heavyweights" favor this "buzzy" West Hollywood spot known for "exemplary" Italian (including exceptional Dover sole and roast chicken) and "real drinks" served in a "charming", "private" garden patio setting; service is "first-rate", although a few mere mortals feel "blown away" by the bills.

NEW Il Piccolo Ritrovo *Italian* ▽ 26 | 23 | 27 | $36

Brentwood | 140 Barrington Pl. (Sunset Blvd.) | 310-472-4939

Pacific Palisades | 15415 W. Sunset Blvd. (Via De La Paz) | 310-454-2243

www.piccoloritrovo.com

This buzzy, casual Italian duo in Brentwood and the Palisades spotlights "authentic pizzas" ("just like Naples") and a range of other affordable entrees; the cheery yellow spaces with outdoor seating fill up fast, so "don't forget a reservation", or opt for takeout.

Il Tiramisù Ristorante & Bar ◐Ⓜ *Italian* 22 | 19 | 23 | $37

Sherman Oaks | 13705 Ventura Blvd. (Woodman Ave.) | 818-986-2640 | www.il-tiramisu.com

Father-and-son owners Ivo and Peter "make you feel at home" at this "neighborhood jewel" in Sherman Oaks presenting "showstopping" Northern Italian fare in a "quaint" setting decorated with white tablecloths and terra-cotta floors; prices are "reasonable" for the area, and the "monthly wine dinners are a real bargain."

Il Tramezzino *Italian* 22 | 13 | 19 | $21

Beverly Hills | 454 N. Canon Dr. (Santa Monica Blvd.) | 310-273-0501
Studio City | 13031 Ventura Blvd. (bet. Coldwater Canyon & Ethel Aves.) | 818-784-2244
Tarzana | Brown Center Shopping Ctr. | 18636 Ventura Blvd. (Yolanda Ave.) | 818-996-8726
www.iltram.com

"Wonderful" soups, salads and panini make for "quick", "healthy" eating at this "casual" Italian chainlet that's "reasonably priced" too; "friendly waiters" provide "smooth", "swift" service in a "down-to-earth" setting with "delightful" outdoor dining, although many "sandwich lovers" "take it to go."

India's Tandoori *Indian* 23 | 17 | 21 | $21

Mid-Wilshire | 5468 Wilshire Blvd. (bet. Cochran & Dunsmuir Aves.) | 323-936-2050 | www.indiastandoori.net
Brentwood | Granville Plaza | 11819 Wilshire Blvd. (bet. Granville & Westgate Aves.) | 310-268-9100 | www.indias-tandoori.com

"Curry, curry, curry!" cry patrons "thrilled with the prices" and the "tasty" grub at this set of Indians known for its "large portions", "great value" and noteworthy lunch buffet; although most "have no problem" with the service or modest decor, many rely on them for takeout.

Industriel Urban Farm Cuisine *French* ∇ 20 | 19 | 19 | $41

Downtown | 609 S. Grand Ave. (bet. 6th St. & Wilshire Blvd.) | 213-488-8020 | www.industrielfarm.com

"Innovative" farm-to-table fare lands in Downtown via this "hip", "nicely priced" spot employing "amazingly fresh ingredients" in its Provençal-inspired dishes; the "funky" space is full of "old-fashioned charm", and "service with a smile" caps things off.

Ink *American/Eclectic* 26 | 21 | 23 | $65

West Hollywood | 8360 Melrose Ave. (Kings Rd.) | 323-651-5866 | www.mvink.com

"Enjoy the ride" at "rock-star chef" Michael Voltaggio's "innovative" New American-Eclectic in West Hollywood where the "edgy", "excellent" cuisine has fans "obsessing about the next time they can eat here"; with a "well-informed" staff and a "cool" "minimalist" setting, the "only complaint is that reservations are tough to come by."

Ink Sack *Sandwiches* - | - | - | I

West Hollywood | 8360 Melrose Ave. (King St.) | 323-655-7225 | www.mvink.com

This microscopic sandwich shop next door to Michael Voltaggio's Ink features his take on grab-and-go eats like spicy tuna albacore with Sriracha mayo and banh mi with pork three ways and housemade chips; with just a couple of stools, most take out.

Inn of the Seventh Ray *Californian* 20 | 26 | 20 | $44

Topanga | 128 Old Topanga Canyon Rd. (Topanga Canyon Blvd.) | 310-455-1311 | www.innoftheseventhray.com

A "magical", "bucolic" setting "beside a trickling stream" sets the stage at this "rustic", mostly outdoor Californian in Topanga Canyon, a "bohemian" haunt since 1975; even if some find the service and "pricey" fare "uneven", it's still a "special" experience, and many "love the brunch."

In-N-Out Burger ◐ *Burgers* — 23 | 12 | 20 | $9

Hollywood | 7009 W. Sunset Blvd. (Orange Dr.)
Culver City | 13425 W. Washington Blvd. (bet. Glencoe & Walnut Aves.)
Palms | 9245 W. Venice Blvd. (Canfield Ave.)
Westwood | 922 Gayley Ave. (Levering Ave.)
Westchester | 9149 S. Sepulveda Blvd. (bet. 92nd St. & Westchester Pkwy.)
North Hollywood | 5864 Lankershim Blvd. (bet. Califa & Emelita Sts.)
Sherman Oaks | 4444 Van Nuys Blvd. (Moorpark St.)
Studio City | 3640 Cahuenga Blvd. (Fredonia Dr.)
Van Nuys | 7930 Van Nuys Blvd. (bet. Blythe & Michaels Sts.)
Woodland Hills | 19920 Ventura Blvd. (bet. Oakdale & Penfield Aves.)
800-786-1000 | www.in-n-out.com
Additional locations throughout the Los Angeles area

"A true California institution", this "classic" chain delivers "the ultimate fast-food burger" that's "always fresh" and "flavorful" along with "thick shakes" in "bright" vintage settings staffed by a "smiling", "efficient" crew; yes, the "lines can get a little ridiculous" at peak hours, but you still "can't beat it" - especially the prices; P.S. "get your order 'animal style' and you won't be disappointed."

Iroha ◐ *Japanese* — 24 | 18 | 21 | $44

Studio City | 12953 Ventura Blvd. (bet. Coldwater Canyon & Ethel Aves.) | 818-990-9559

"Superlative", "innovative" sushi plus a "quaint" setting that's "like being in a little tucked away house in Japan" makes this Studio City charmer the ultimate "date-night spot"; service is "fast and friendly", and when "you dream up a roll, they'll execute it with ease", although if you "sit at the bar the chefs will tell you what's best."

Itzik Hagadol *Israeli* — 20 | 12 | 18 | $27

Encino | 17201 Ventura Blvd. (Louise Ave.) | 818-784-4080 | www.itzikhagadol.com

"Straight from Tel Aviv", this Encino offshoot of an Israeli grill shop delivers an "authentic eating experience" via "tasty skewers", an "amazing array" of salads and "puffy, warm laffa bread", all at "affordable" prices; "curt" service and minimal decor don't seem to deter the crowds - it's always "jumping" and "you won't leave hungry" either.

The Ivy *Californian* — 22 | 23 | 21 | $60

West Hollywood | 113 N. Robertson Blvd. (bet. Alden Dr. & Beverly Blvd.) | 310-274-8303 | www.theivyrestaurant.com

"It's a scene" replete with paparazzi and "looky-loo" "stargazing" at this "jumpin'" WeHo expense-accounter, where the "lovely" farmhouse setting features "fresh flowers" and a popular patio; many maintain the "people-watching" trumps the eats, but the Cal cuisine's "still delicious", particularly the "outstanding" desserts.

Ivy at the Shore *Californian* — 22 | 22 | 22 | $62

Santa Monica | 1535 Ocean Ave. (Colorado Ave.) | 310-393-3113 | www.theivyrestaurant.com

"A little more relaxed than its West Hollywood sister", this Santa Monica Californian is a "haven for the well-heeled, expense-account and upcale-tourist sets" with "simple" fare served in a "pleasant" seaside setting; some say service can be "arrogant", and it certainly isn't cheap, but the "star sightings will make everything else meaningless."

Izaka-ya by Katsu-ya *Japanese* 25 | 17 | 20 | $41

Third Street | 8420 W. Third St. (bet. La Cienega Blvd. & Orlando Ave.) | 323-782-9536

Manhattan Beach | 1133 Highland Ave. (Center Pl.) | 310-796-1888

www.katsu-yagroup.com

Boasting "all the deliciousness of Katsuya" "without the pretense", these Third Street and Manhattan Beach izakayas offer "inspired modern Japanese" bar food and "revelatory" sushi plus signatures like spicy tuna and crispy rice from chef-owner Katsuya Uechi; acoustics can be "loud enough to wake the fish on your plate" and service can be "rushed", but with relatively "low" pricing, it "won't disappoint."

Jack's on Montana *Californian* 20 | 17 | 20 | $26
(fka 17th Street Cafe)

Santa Monica | 1610 Montana Ave. (bet. 16th & 17th Sts.) | 310-453-2771 | www.jacks-on-montana.com

"When promenading on Montana", Santa Monicans turn to this "neighborhood fixture" for Cal fare like "delicious" salads served in a "light, airy" room that manages to feel both "restful" and "upbeat", rounded out by "lovely" service and "people-watching"; though some dub the food "standard, not special", most are pleased by the "positive difference" the new owners are making, "keeping the favorites and adding new creative dishes", all for "decent" prices.

NEW **Jackson's Food + Drink** *American* ▽ 17 | 17 | 18 | $38

El Segundo | 2041 Rosecrans Ave. (Nash St.) | 310-606-5500 | www.jacksonsfoodanddrink.com

After closing down in Hermosa Beach several years ago, local chef Scott Cooper is back with this "popular" New American tavern in El Segundo; expect an eclectic, "reasonably priced" menu of modern comfort food served in a rustic space with a large outdoor patio; P.S. don't miss the "great happy hour."

Jaipur Cuisine of India *Indian* 22 | 16 | 20 | $25

West LA | 10916 W. Pico Blvd. (bet. Veteran Ave. & Westwood Blvd.) | 310-470-4994 | www.jaipurcuisineofindia.com

"Zingy", "well-seasoned" Indian - offered à la carte or in an "amazing lunch buffet" - makes this long-standing West LA eatery the "spot of choice" for many; the setting is modest and "service varies", but it's often "crowded" nonetheless.

James' Beach *American* 20 | 19 | 20 | $38

Venice | 60 N. Venice Blvd. (Pacific Ave.) | 310-823-5396 | www.jamesbeach.com

"Awesome" fish tacos are the highlight at this "beachy", "casual" canteen in Venice, where the "clever" American menu and "well-mixed cocktails" offer "good value for the money"; it's often quite the "scene", with a "cool" crowd "packed like sardines", but outdoor seating eases the crush, as does a "super-friendly" staff.

	FOOD	DECOR	SERVICE	COST

Jar *American* 24 | 22 | 23 | $59

Beverly Boulevard | 8225 Beverly Blvd. (Harper Ave.) | West Hollywood | 323-655-6566 | www.thejar.com

Devotees "dream about the pot roast" ("perfect on a blustery day") and "top-end" steaks at chef-owner Suzanne Tracht's "sleek, modern" Beverly Boulevard American offering "delicious", "haute" takes on "comfort food" evoking "the way dining used to be"; the decor is "like you just stepped into *Mad Men*" and service is "thoughtful", so most don't mind the "splurge"-worthy tabs.

Javan *Persian* 22 | 16 | 18 | $26

West LA | 11500 Santa Monica Blvd. (Butler Ave.) | 310-207-5555 | www.javanrestaurant.com

"The kebabs are some kind of wonderful" at this West LA Persian also presenting "flavorful" stews on "crispy rice" and other "brilliant" items that "won't break your wallet"; service is "attentive", "if occasionally harried" and the atmosphere is "vibrant", so "what's not to like?"

Jer-ne *American* ∇ 18 | 23 | 20 | $60

Marina del Rey | The Ritz-Carlton Marina del Rey | 4375 Admiralty Way (Via Regatta) | 310-574-4333 | www.ritzcarlton.com

"Eat on the terrace and enjoy the view of the harbor" at this luxurious "special-occasion" New American nestled in the Marina del Rey Ritz-Carlton; opinions on the menu with Cal and Spanish touches are mixed, but "fine cocktails and wine" plus "accommodating" service mean that for some, "the only disappointment is the bill."

Jerry's Famous Deli ◐ *Deli* 15 | 13 | 15 | $24

Marina del Rey | 13181 Mindanao Way (Marina Expwy.) | 310-821-6626
Encino | 16650 Ventura Blvd. (Petit Ave.) | 818-906-1800
Woodland Hills | Gateway Plaza | 21857 Ventura Blvd. (Don Pio Dr.) | 818-340-0810
www.jerrysfamousdeli.com

There's "something for everyone" at this SoCal chain that's an "old standby for Jewish deli food" with "gigantic" sandwiches and "huge bowls of matzo-ball soup" served in "typical" "NYC"-style digs; critics call it "ordinary" with almost "too much food", although it "hits the spot" late at night.

Jinky's *Diner* 20 | 13 | 18 | $19

Santa Monica | 1447 Second St. (bet. B'way & Santa Monica Blvd.) | 310-917-3311
Sherman Oaks | 14120 Ventura Blvd. (Stansbury Ave.) | 818-981-2250
Studio City | 4000 Colfax Ave. (Ventura Blvd.) | 818-308-8418
Agoura Hills | 29001 Canwood St. (bet. Derry Ave. & Kanan Rd.) | 818-575-4216
NEW **Thousand Oaks** | Oakbrook Plaza | 1724 E. Avenida de los Arboles (Moorpark Frwy.) | 805-493-8809
www.jinkys.com

Early birds go bonkers for the "big bountiful breakfasts" from a "huge menu" at this "popular", "kid-friendly" Southwestern-American mini-chain that's "everything a neighborhood coffee shop should be"; it also doubles as a "lunch spot" with "homey" digs, "bang-for-the-buck" tabs and a staff that "aims to please."

	FOOD	DECOR	SERVICE	COST

JiRaffe ☒ *American/French* — 26 | 21 | 24 | $59

Santa Monica | 502 Santa Monica Blvd. (5th St.) | 310-917-6671 | www.jirafferestaurant.com

"Ideal for anniversaries or impressing someone new", this "lovely" Santa Monica restaurant is "always a favorite" for Raphael Lunetta's "outstanding", "inventive" market-driven French-New American cuisine; the staff "really seems to care" too, making the "pricey" bills easier to swallow; P.S. Monday night's prix fixe is a "bargain."

Jitlada *Thai* — 27 | 12 | 15 | $31

East Hollywood | 5233½ W. Sunset Blvd. (bet. Harvard Blvd. & Kingsley Dr.) | 323-667-9809 | www.jitladala.com

"Completely fearless in pushing the envelope in spiciness", this Southern Thai "favorite" in an East Hollywood strip mall "entertains the most adventurous foodie" with Jazz Singsanong's "robust menu" full of "vibrant" flavors ("the mussels are a must"); "tight" digs, "long" waits and "flaky, but sweet, service" are no matter to connoisseurs who call it one of the "best in the U.S."

Joan's on Third Cafe *American* — 24 | 17 | 17 | $24

Third Street | 8350 W. Third St. (bet. Fairfax Ave. & La Cienega Blvd.) | 323-655-2285 | www.joansonthird.com

A "dizzying selection" of "delicious", "sophisticated" salads, sandwiches and desserts awaits at this "wildly popular" "eat-in/take-out", "gourmet" American bakery on Third Street, a "favorite splurge" for picnics; the "bright, open" space with "casual outdoor seating" is "always packed with celebs and beautiful people", who don't mind the "lines and limited seating", nor the somewhat "slow" counter service.

Jody Maroni's *Hot Dogs* — 20 | 9 | 16 | $11

Venice | 2011 Ocean Front Walk (Speedway) | 310-822-5639
Universal City | Universal CityWalk | 1000 Universal Studios Blvd. (Coral Dr.) | 818-622-5639
www.jodymaroni.com

"They know their links" at these sausage stands serving up "tasty", inexpensive dogs and wursts that come "loaded with onions and peppers"; there's no indoor seating, but the Venice original provides a "ringside seat at the boardwalk", and you can even order delivery from the beach.

Joe's 🄼 *Californian/French* — 26 | 21 | 24 | $55

Venice | 1023 Abbot Kinney Blvd. (bet. B'way & Westminster Aves.) | 310-399-5811 | www.joesrestaurant.com

"An oldie but goodie on Abbot Kinney", this "longtime favorite" from Joe Miller puts out "outstanding", "original" Cal-French cuisine crafted from "fresh, local ingredients" in "elegant", "comfortable" digs; although it's not cheap, the weekday lunch special is "a steal."

Joe's Pizza *Pizza* — 23 | 10 | 17 | $12

Hollywood | 6504 Hollywood Blvd. (Wilcox Ave.) | 323-467-9500 ◐
West Hollywood | 8539 W. Sunset Blvd. (Alta Loma Rd.) | 310-358-0900 ◐

(continued)

(continued)

Joe's Pizza

NEW **Century City** | Westfield Century City Shopping Ctr. | 10250 Santa Monica Blvd. (Ave. of the Stars) | 310-286-9988
Santa Monica | 111 Broadway (Ocean Ave.) | 310-395-9222 ◐
NEW **Sherman Oaks** | Westfield Fashion Square Mall | 14006 Riverside Dr. (Woodman Ave.) | 818-990-7755
www.joespizza.it

"As close as you can get to real NYC pizza", these "no-frills", independently operated outlets around LA offer delicious, "crispy-crust" slices and pies that fans find "every bit as good" as their Big Apple counterparts; they're open "late", service is speedy and delivery is a plus, so in all, "you can't beat it."

Johnnie's Pastrami ◐ *Diner* — 21 | 11 | 18 | $16

Culver City | 4017 Sepulveda Blvd. (Washington Pl.) | 310-397-6654 | www.johnniespastrami.com

"Legendary" is the "fat, juicy pastrami sandwich" - "packed with meat" and "worth every penny" - at this "longtime Culver City landmark" dating back to the '50s with little jukeboxes at each booth and "old-school service" by "worldly waitresses"; there's little in the way of frills, but it's a "rare" "late-night guilty pleasure."

Johnny Rebs' *BBQ* — 23 | 20 | 23 | $23

Bellflower | 16639 Bellflower Blvd. (Flower St.) | 562-866-6455
Long Beach | 4663 Long Beach Blvd. (bet. 46th & 47th Sts.) | 562-423-7327
www.johnnyrebs.com

"When you need a rib fix", try these Southern BBQ joints in Bellflower and Long Beach dishing out "down-home" "roadhouse grub", from "nicely smoked" meats slathered in "tangy" sauce to "honest" plates of biscuits and gravy, plus country breakfasts offered every day; "prices are competitive", while the "super-relaxed", "shotgun-shack" atmosphere with peanut shells on the floor is made "warm" and "friendly" by a "cheerful" staff.

John O'Groats *American* — 20 | 14 | 19 | $21

Rancho Park | 10516 W. Pico Blvd. (bet. Beverly Glen Blvd. & Overland Ave.) | 310-204-0692
Encino | 16120 Ventura Blvd. (Woodley Ave.) | 818-501-2366
www.ogroatsrestaurant.com

"Join the breakfast crowd" at these "neighborhood favorites" in Encino and Rancho Park known for "simple", "old-fashioned" Americana ("thick bacon" and "oh those biscuits") with a handful of "healthy" items thrown into the mix; "affable" service and moderate tabs mean it's "filled with regulars" and especially "jammed" on weekends, although "dinner is less crowded."

Josie M *American* — 26 | 23 | 25 | $65

Santa Monica | 2424 Pico Blvd. (25th St.) | 310-581-9888 | www.josierestaurant.com

"A culinary oasis off the beaten path", this Santa Monica New American "does it right" with "deft and delicious", "market-inspired" cuisine from Josie Le Balch set down in a "refined" setting; yes, it's "expensive", but a "first-rate" staff provides "impeccable" service and it's a "rare find" - a place to go "when you want to be a grown-up."

	FOOD	DECOR	SERVICE	COST

JR's BBQ ⓢ *BBQ* 23 | 11 | 18 | $20

Culver City | 3055 S. La Cienega Blvd. (Blackwelder St.) | 310-837-6838 | www.jrs-bbq.com

The "smells are tantalizing" at this Culver City BBQer run by a "terrific" mother-and-son team and turning out "authentic" eats like brisket and mac 'n' cheese; "don't look for atmosphere", but the vibe's "friendly" and prices are a pittance; P.S. the housemade BBQ sauce is also for sale.

Julienne ⓢ *French* 25 | 22 | 21 | $27

San Marino | 2651 Mission St. (bet. El Molino & Los Robles Aves.) | 626-441-2299 | www.juliennetogo.com

"It's not just for ladies who lunch" insist fans of this bistro in San Marino that draws a "crowd" with "splendid breakfasts" and other "top-quality" French-American cuisine capped by "divine" desserts in a "lovely" indoor-outdoor space; an "exceptionally friendly" staff complements the "charming" setting, but to escape the "waits", many opt for takeout from the adjoining cafe/market; P.S. the rosemary currant bread is "a legend."

Kabuki *Japanese* 21 | 18 | 19 | $27

Hollywood | 1545 N. Vine St. (bet. Selma Ave. & Sunset Blvd.) | 323-464-6003

Westchester | Howard Hughes Ctr. | 6081 Center Dr. W. (Sepulveda Blvd.) | 310-641-5524

Pasadena | 3539 E. Foothill Blvd. (bet. Halstead St. & Rosemead Blvd.) | 626-351-8963

Pasadena | 88 W. Colorado Blvd. (bet. De Lacey & Pasadena Aves.) | 626-568-9310

Burbank | 201 N. San Fernando Blvd. (Orange Grove Ave.) | 818-843-7999

Woodland Hills | 20940 Ventura Blvd. (bet. Paralta & Serrania Aves.) | 818-704-8700

www.kabukirestaurants.com

"Nothing extraordinary, but always reliable" is the word on this "bargain" Japanese sushi chain churning out "respectable" renditions of "the standard hits and a few surprises" with "Westernized" twists and "great deals" at happy hour; even though they're usually "bustling", "service is fast but not rushed" and they're "kid-friendly" too.

NEW Kaishin *Chinese* - | - | - | M

Malibu | 23715 Malibu Rd. (Webb Way) | 310-317-9777 | www.kaishinmalibu.com

This moderately priced Chinese located right next door to celeb-heavy Malibu Colony offers straightforward Cantonese dishes; you can dine in at its handsome shopping-mall location or opt for delivery.

NEW Kal's Bistro Ⓜ *Mediterranean* - | - | - | M

Pasadena | 43 E. Union St. (Raymond Ave.) | 626-440-0107 | www.kalsbistro.com

This medium-priced Mediterranean on a quiet block just off Colorado Boulevard in Old Pasadena serves Med fare made with Cal touches such as flat-iron steaks, fish and chicken Milanese; the setting offers old-school elegance in a beer-and-pizza part of town, with lots of dark wood and hanging chandeliers.

	FOOD	DECOR	SERVICE	COST

Katana ◐ *Japanese* 25 | 26 | 23 | $60

West Hollywood | 8439 W. Sunset Blvd. (bet. La Cienega Blvd. & Sweetzer Ave.) | 323-650-8585 | www.katanarobata.com

"Beautiful people" dig the "see-and-be-seen" "scene" at this Sunset Strip Japanese where you can "grab a seat on the patio and watch the action" while nibbling on "fab", "diverse" sushi and yakitori that "never disappoint"; sure, it's "getting up in years", but service from the "actor/model" staff is solid and "it's still a reliable option to wow out-of-town guests."

Kate Mantilini *American* 20 | 19 | 20 | $36

Beverly Hills | 9101 Wilshire Blvd. (Doheny Dr.) | 310-278-3699 ◐
Woodland Hills | 5921 Owensmouth Ave. (bet. Califa & Oxnard Sts.) | 818-348-1095
www.katemantilinirestaurant.com

A "glamorous" take on the coffee shop, this Beverly Hills comfort-fooder delivers a "solid" "all-American" bill of fare and "great martinis" to "industry types" and "lots of head-swivelers looking for stars", from morning till late; the newer Woodland Hills outpost is equally "reliable" with "fine" service, although many insist both are "pricey for what you get."

Katsu-ya *Japanese* 27 | 15 | 20 | $44

Encino | 16542 Ventura Blvd. (Hayvenhurst Ave.) | 818-788-2396
NEW **Northridge** | 9709 Reseda Blvd. (Superior St.) | 818-678-1700
Studio City | 11680 Ventura Blvd. (Colfax Ave.) | 818-985-6976
www.katsu-yagroup.com

A "trailblazer for modern sushi", chef-owner Katsuya Uechi's Studio City "original" and its Encino and Northridge offshoots are famed for "exquisite" "rock-star" sushi and "innovative chalkboard specials" ("the spicy tuna on crispy rice continues to be a revelation"); sure, "you'll have to wait", service can be "rushed" and the settings could "use a face-lift", but even so, most find it's one of the "best for the price" and the food surpasses any "hassle."

Katsuya *Japanese* 24 | 24 | 21 | $57

Downtown | LA Live | 800 W. Olympic Blvd. (Figueroa St.) | 213-747-9797
Hollywood | 6300 Hollywood Blvd. (Vine St.) | 323-871-8777 ◐
Brentwood | 11777 San Vicente Blvd. (bet. Gorham & Montana Aves.) | 310-207-8744
Glendale | Americana at Brand | 702 Americana Way (bet. Brand Blvd. & Central Ave.) | 818-244-5900
www.sbe.com

For sushi with a "side of glam", try these "see-and-be-seen" Japanese "hot spots" delivering "amazing" raw fare, "fun drinks" and "kicked-up", "not-so-authentic" dishes like baked crab rolls and spicy tuna on crispy rice ("a must"); it's "not for purists", service is sometimes "lacking" and tabs are a "splurge", but "where else are you going to go pre-clubbing?"

Kay 'n Dave's *Mexican* 18 | 15 | 19 | $23

Culver City | 9341 Culver Blvd. (Canfield Ave.) | 310-558-8100
Pacific Palisades | 15246 W. Sunset Blvd. (Antioch St.) | 310-459-8118
Santa Monica | 262 26th St. (bet. Georgina Ave. & San Vicente Blvd.) | 310-260-1355
www.kayndaves.com

"Wholesome Mexican" with a "healthy" bent is the thing at these "economically priced" cantinas where "you can gorge or go minimal" in a "casual, laid-back" setting; purists pan the "bland" eats, although it's "great for kids and families" and a "reliable" bet for takeout.

Kendall's Brasserie *French* 19 | 20 | 21 | $49

Downtown | Dorothy Chandler Pavilion | 135 N. Grand Ave. (bet. 1st & Temple Sts.) | 213-972-7322 | www.patinagroup.com

"Concertgoers" rely on this "busy" Patina group bistro Downtown for its efficient servers who handle the pre-performance rush "without fuss or confusion"; critics claim that the "pricey", "traditional" French menu could use a "change up", but most maintain that "convenience" and its "charming" "Parisian" atmosphere more than compensate.

Killer Cafe *American* - | - | - | M

Marina del Rey | 4213 Admiralty Way (Promenade Way) | 310-578-2250 | www.killershrimp.com

This harborside breakfast-and-brunch sibling of Killer Shrimp in Marina del Ray offers crustacean-heavy omelets, Benedicts, Bloodys and more on its midpriced American menu; snag a seat at the expansive waterfront patio or fill up on the wallet-friendly portions indoors, while million-dollar sailboats drift by the floor-to-ceiling windows.

Killer Shrimp ◐ *Seafood* 21 | 17 | 19 | $27

Marina del Rey | 4211 Admiralty Way (Promenade Way) | 310-578-2293 | www.killershrimp.com

"Totally killer" exclaim fans of the "spicy", "satsfying" peel 'n' eat shrimp headlining the menu at this "lively" Marina seafooder; service gets mixed reviews and frequent happy hours in the "ample" bar area keep "noise levels high", but water views from the deck are a plus, so most are "thankful" that it's "on the map" again.

Kincaid's *Seafood/Steak* 22 | 24 | 21 | $41

Redondo Beach | Redondo Beach Pier | 500 Fishermans Wharf (Torrance Blvd.) | 310-318-6080 | www.kincaids.com

"Beautiful" ocean views are the main motivation for dining at this upmarket Redondo surf 'n' turfer prized by "romantics" for date night as well as "locals" with out-of-town guests; the menu is deemed somewhat "hit-or-miss" and service is likewise "sporadic", but the "great happy hour" makes it a "terrific" bet near the pier for drinks and apps.

King's Burgers *Burgers* ▽ 25 | 13 | 20 | $26

Northridge | 9345 Reseda Blvd. (Plummer St.) | 818-885-6456

"Who would've thunk a divey-looking burger joint would have such amazing sushi?" ask admirers of this offbeat Northridge "classic" turning out "high-quality" fish at a small counter in back; tabs are "a bit pricey" for "a place that looks like an old Carl's Jr.", but it's a "local favorite" and "a must" for intrepid eaters nonetheless; P.S. the patties are "alright" too, but the raw stuff is the main draw.

King's Fish House *Seafood* 21 | 18 | 21 | $35

Long Beach | 100 W. Broadway Ave. (bet. Pacific & Pine Aves.) | 562-432-7463

Calabasas | Commons at Calabasas | 4798 Commons Way (Calabasas Rd.) | 818-225-1979

www.kingsfishhouse.com

A "fine assortment of fresh fish" – including oysters and sushi – is the hook at these SoCal seafood houses set in "comfy", "casual" digs with "pleasant" patio seating; they're "reasonably priced" and happily "accommodate" kids, so many consider them "good for the whole family" and "buzzy" enough for just grown-ups.

Kings Road Cafe *American* 17 | 12 | 16 | $21

West Hollywood | 8361 Beverly Blvd. (Kings Rd.) | 323-655-9044 | www.kingsroadcafe.com

"Feel the LA buzz" at this WeHo hangout drawing "loyal regulars" and industry "wannabes talking loudly on their cell phones" for a "so-so" all-day American menu bested by the "tastiest coffee in town" roasted in-house and poured by "serious" baristas; acoustics inside get "noisy", but sidewalk tables provide relief - either way, "plan for a wait on the weekends."

Kiriko M *Japanese* 26 | 16 | 21 | $70

West LA | 11301 W. Olympic Blvd. (Sawtelle Blvd.) | 310-478-7769 | www.kirikosushi.com

"Seriously inventive" chef Ken Namba helms this West LA Japanese "gem", slicing up "fantastic" sushi, plus omakase options, in an "understated" space; "friendly" service heightens the experience, and though it's not cheap, it's "practically unrivaled" in the area.

NEW **Kitchen by Perfecto Rocher** *Spanish* - | - | - | M

Hermosa Beach | 1200 Hermosa Ave. (Pier Ave.) | no phone

The trendy Downtown Hermosa Beach sushi bar Rok is now also home to this moderately priced Spanish eatery from former Lazy Ox chef Perfecto Rocher; with two concepts under a single roof, this might just be the only spot in town where you can order spicy tuna on crispy rice and paella at the same meal; P.S. currently weekends only, so call ahead.

Kitchen 24 ◐ *American* 19 | 19 | 18 | $21

Hollywood | 1608 N. Cahuenga Blvd. (bet. Hollywood Blvd. & Selma Ave.) | 323-465-2424

West Hollywood | 8575 Santa Monica Blvd. (bet. Knoll & Westmount Drs.) | 424-777-0959

www.kitchen24.info

"Open whenever you need it", this 24/7 duo in WeHo and Hollywood's Cahuenga Corridor turns out "elevated" American "diner food" - like cocktails and disco fries - for "hipsters" galore, especially after the bars close; the "good-looking staff" and "modern" digs are appealing, but the "club-volume" music isn't for everyone, though, and a few say it's best for "hanging out" "if the quality of food is not your number one priority."

Kiwami *Japanese* 27 | 20 | 24 | $53

Studio City | 11920 Ventura Blvd. (Carpenter Ave.) | 818-763-3910 | www.katsu-yagroup.com

An "upscale version" of sibling Katsu-ya, this Studio City "jewel" impresses guests with "sublime" sushi, sashimi and "beautifully prepared" small plates; the vibe is "cool" without being "trendy", and though bills can be "painfully high" - especially for the hard-to-reserve private omakase with Katsuya himself - it's regarded as one of "the best" in town; P.S. check out the "great deals" at happy hour.

FOOD | DECOR | SERVICE | COST

Kogi Korean BBQ-to-Go *Korean/Mexican* 26 | 15 | 20 | $10

Location varies; see website | 323-315-0253 | www.kogibbq.com

Redefining the "roach coach" and jump-starting the food-truck craze, Roy Choi's "brilliant" Korean-Mex truck continues to be a magnet for "addicts" who "track Twitter" and "drive miles" to chase down their "fix" of "transcendental" tacos and "crave-worthy" kimchi quesadillas doled out by a "cool" crew; though the "hoopla" has "died down" a wee bit, it's still "a must-try for any dedicated foodie"; P.S. chef Choi's chow also shows up at the Alibi Room, A-Frame, Chego! and Sunny Spot.

Koi *Japanese* 24 | 25 | 22 | $65

West Hollywood | 730 N. La Cienega Blvd. (bet. Melrose Pl. & Waring Ave.) | 310-659-9449 | www.koirestaurant.com

"Showbiz sushi" could be the nickname of this "architecturally gorgeous" WeHo Japanese where "fresh fish" and other "tasty little morsels" are presented amid a "glam" scene rife with a "parade of erstwhile actresses showing up to gain attention"; critics call it "snooty" and "overpriced", but if you're into the "Hollywood" thing, you have to "go at least once."

K-Zo *Japanese* 26 | 19 | 22 | $49

Culver City | 9240 Culver Blvd. (Washington Blvd.) | 310-202-8890 | www.k-zo.com

"Easily rivaling the big names", this "under-the-radar" "jewel" in Culver City turns out "exquisite", "perfectly proportioned" sushi and "innovative" Japanese tapas courtesy of "gifted" chef Keizo Ishiba; it's "expensive", but service is "attentive", and many find the "delectable" omakase well worth the "splurge."

Label's Table *Sandwiches* 22 | 8 | 18 | $18

Century City | 9226 W. Pico Blvd. (bet. Cardiff Ave. & Glenvilla Dr.) | 310-276-0388

Woodland Hills | 23311 Mulholland Dr. (bet. Calabasas & Valmar Rds.) | 818-222-1044

www.labelstabledeli.com

"Pastrami from heaven and rye bread to match" lure locals to these long-standing delis in Century City and Woodland Hills serving "a great variety" of sandwiches for not a lot of dough; "stark" settings with communal tables are part of the shtick.

La Botte *Italian* 22 | 20 | 20 | $62

Santa Monica | 620 Santa Monica Blvd. (7th St.) | 310-576-3072 | www.labottesantamonica.com

Known for its impressive vino list (La Botte translates to wine cask), this "expensive" Santa Monica Italian spotlights "authentic" Northern-style "dishes you wouldn't ordinarily see" (house-cured duck breast, homemade quail sausage) in upscale surrounds; uneven service can be a drawback.

La Bottega Marino *Italian* 21 | 12 | 19 | $25

West LA | 11363 Santa Monica Blvd. (Purdue Ave.) | 310-477-7777 | www.labottegausa.com

"One of the best-kept secrets" in town, this family-run trattoria/deli from Mario and Salvatore Marino (Il Grano) in West LA is held dear for "old-fashioned" Italian served in a way-"casual" setting; service can be "spotty", but the bills are low, so many rely on it for takeout.

	FOOD	DECOR	SERVICE	COST

La Bruschetta Ristorante *Italian* | 23 | 20 | 24 | $44

Westwood | 1621 Westwood Blvd. (bet. Massachusetts & Ohio Aves.) | 310-477-1052 | www.lbwestwood.com

A "local favorite", this "inviting" Westwood Italian is esteemed for "consistently good, traditional" fare and "stellar service" led by "welcoming" chef-owner Angelo Peloni, who seems to "know all his patrons"; prices are "affordable" and the "quiet, civilized" ambiance makes it "easy to hear tablemates", making it a "rare and wonderful option in LA."

La Crêperie Café *French* | 23 | 22 | 21 | $24

Long Beach | 4911 E. Second St. (bet. Argonne & St. Joseph Aves.) | 562-434-8499 | www.lacreperiecafe.net

Francophiles fawn over this "very bohemian" Long Beach cafe offering a "wonderful assortment" of "delicious", "proper" sweet and savory crêpes as well as other affordable French fare like the "must-have" garlic fries; it can get "pretty packed" and "noisy", but sidewalk seating is a plus, "and the prices aren't bad either."

La Dijonaise Café et Boulangerie *French* | 19 | 15 | 17 | $22

Culver City | Helms Bldg. | 8703 Washington Blvd. (Hutchison Ave.) | 310-287-2770 | www.ladijonaise.com

This "cute cafe" in Culver City's Helms Bakery complex is a find for "basic", "low-cost" French fare and pastries ("oh those Napoleons!") in "large, pleasantly airy" digs with a patio; a few detect a little "attitude" amongst staffers, but otherwise it's a "reliable" "neighborhood" option.

La Dolce Vita ☒ *Italian* | 24 | 21 | 24 | $55

Beverly Hills | 9785 Little Santa Monica Blvd. (Wilshire Blvd.) | 310-278-1845 | www.ladolcevitabeverlyhills.com

"Reminiscent of an earlier LA era", this "old-school" Beverly Hills Italian proffers traditional steaks and pastas in an "intimate" "tryst"-worthy setting anchored by dark-red circular leather booths; opinions on service are mixed ("perfect" vs. "unfriendly"), and some complain about pricing, but most agree it's still a "classy" package.

Lago d'Argento Pizzeria ◐ *Italian* | - | - | - | I

Silver Lake | 2611 N. Hyperion Ave. (Evans St.) | 323-300-5500 | www.pizzerialago.com

Pizza rules at this zany Silver Lake Italian from the team behind the nightlife-y Barbarella and Bugatta, with an inexpensive, kid-friendly menu of pies, plus salads and pasta sides for the table; the cartoonish room is full of chalkboard walls with 'Bread' and 'Oil' writ large, a graphic reminder of what you're eating at the big red booths.

La Grande Orange Café *Californian* | 20 | 20 | 19 | $32

Pasadena | 260 S. Raymond Ave. (bet. Del Mar Blvd. & Green St.) | 626-356-4444 | www.lgostationcafe.com

The restored Del Mar train depot in Pasadena makes the "unique" setting for this "vibrant", "crowded" Californian serving "enormous", well-priced portions to families, happy-hour hounds and locals taking advantage of "neighborhood night" deals and the patio; the less-impressed say it's "overrated" and draws "too many kids", but it's a "reliable" bet for most; P.S. the deviled eggs and red-velvet cake are favorites.

	FOOD	DECOR	SERVICE	COST

L.A. Market *American/Californian* ∇ 19 | 18 | 19 | $39

Downtown | JW Marriott at LA Live | 900 W. Olympic Blvd. (Figueroa St.) | 213-765-8600 | www.lalivemarriott.com

"Great before a game", this Cal-American by chef Kerry Simon in the atrium lobby of Downtown's JW Marriott at LA Live doles out "creative", midpriced takes on American fare, from "gourmet" burgers to more substantial entrees and Hostess cupcakes for dessert; the smart, "mod" decor and "lively" atmosphere work well for "large groups", although underwhelmed critics call it "average in every way."

LAMILL Coffee Boutique *Californian/Coffeehouse* 22 | 21 | 18 | $23

Silver Lake | 1636 Silver Lake Blvd. (bet. Berkeley Ave. & Effie St.) | 323-663-4441 | www.lamillcoffee.com

"Obsessive" caffeine lovers hail this Silver Lake lounge - aka the "PhD of coffeehouses" - for its "attentively brewed" java and "innovative", all-day Californian menu served in a "hipster-chic" setting; critics contend it's all a bit "silly" with "expensive" tabs and a "snooty" staff, but defenders insist "it's a splurge that's worth it", adding that there's always the hope of "seeing Jake Gyllenhaal" drink an $8 hand drip.

Lamonica's NY Pizza ◐ *Pizza* 23 | 9 | 15 | $12

Westwood | 1066 Gayley Ave. (bet. Kinross & Weyburn Aves.) | 310-208-8671 | www.lamonicasnypizza.com

"A slice of NY near UCLA", this inexpensive Westwood pizzeria has been vending "true", "tasty" Gotham-style pies with dough flown in from Brooklyn for more than 30 years; naysayers complain about stale decor, saying the "hole-in-the-wall" digs done up like a subway station need an update, but "New Yawkers feel right at home."

L&E Oyster Bar ☒ *Seafood* 25 | 19 | 22 | $47

Silver Lake | 1637 Silver Lake Blvd. (bet. Berkeley Ave. & Effie St.) | 323-660-2255 | www.leoysterbar.com

Showing due "respect for the mollusk", this "excellent" Silver Lake spot specializes in raw, steamed, fried and grilled variations on the oyster plus a "small" mostly seafood menu and an "enticing" wine and cocktail list; the bi-level digs are done up in vintage style with tufted booths, and there's outdoor seating in pleasant weather.

Langer's Deli ☒ *Deli* 26 | 12 | 20 | $22

Downtown | 704 S. Alvarado St. (7th St.) | 213-483-8050 | www.langersdeli.com

"The best deli west of the Hudson River" according to fans, this Downtown "time warp" has been a source for "superb" hand-sliced pastrami on "fabulous Jewish rye" since 1947; it's "no frills" with "fast" service and "limited" hours, but the food "lives up to the hype", especially the No. 19 sandwich; P.S. call ahead for curbside pickup.

La Paella ☒ *Spanish* 22 | 18 | 23 | $43

Beverly Hills | 476 S. San Vicente Blvd. (bet. Drexel Ave. & 5th St.) | 323-951-0745 | www.usalapaella.com

A bit of "Spain" awaits in the form of "authentic" paellas, "terrific tapas" and sangria at this "quaint", midpriced Beverly Hills "hideaway"; "charming" surroundings and a "gracious" staff further the "charm" - "for a romantic night, you can't do better."

FOOD | DECOR | SERVICE | COST

La Parolaccia Osteria Italiana *Italian* 24 | 18 | 23 | $31

Long Beach | 2945 E. Broadway (Orizaba Ave.) | 562-438-1235
Claremont | 201 N. Indian Hill (2nd St.) | 909-624-1516
www.laparolacciausa.com

"*Delizioso*" Neapolitan pizza, "standout" pastas and other "traditional", moderately priced Italiana are on offer at this "lively" duo in Long Beach and Claremont; "engaging" staffers set a "friendly" tone and the "comfortable" vibe is pure "neighborhood trattoria", so though even if some aren't "overly impressed", defenders declare they're "never disappointed."

La Pergola *Italian* 25 | 20 | 24 | $40

Sherman Oaks | 15005 Ventura Blvd. (bet. Lemona & Noble Aves.) | 818-905-8402 | www.lapergolaristorante.net

"Vegetables from the back garden" go into "wonderful" pastas and other "well-priced" Italian dishes at this perennial "favorite" in Sherman Oaks tended by what some call the "nicest staff in town"; antique pottery and other "authentic Tuscan" touches add to the "warm", "charming" atmosphere, so many consider it the "Valley's best-kept secret"; P.S. "don't miss the stuffed zucchini flowers in season."

Larchmont Bungalow *American* 19 | 17 | 15 | $23

Hancock Park | 107 N. Larchmont Blvd. (bet. Beverly Blvd. & 1st St.) | 323-461-1528 | www.larchmontbungalow.com

"Very cozy", this "cute" converted home in the heart of Larchmont Village proffers an all-day American menu with "yummy" savories, "sinful" desserts and a notable breakfast with red-and-blue velvet pancakes that are "a decadent treat"; critics complain that it's a touch "overpriced" and "service can be slow", but it usually fits the bill for a "casual" bite.

NEW Larder at Burton Way *American* - | - | - | I

Beverly Hills | 8500 Burton Way (Le Doux Rd.) | 310-278-8060 | www.larderatburtonway.com

The team of Suzanne Goin and Carolyne Styne from A.O.C. and Tavern now have a small chain of dine-in/grab-and-go cafes, including this flagship just south of the Beverly Center; it offers seasonal New American meals for breakfast, lunch and dinner, plus pastries to-go and a wine bar, all in an airy, casual space with a long counter packed with breads, prepared dishes, cheeses and charcuterie.

Larder at Maple Drive *American* 20 | 19 | 20 | $55

Beverly Hills | 345 N. Maple Dr. (3rd St.) | 310-248-3779 | www.thelarderattavern.com

Suzanne Goin and Caroline Styne (A.O.C., Lucques) are behind this casual daytime New American in the courtyard of a technology-heavy office complex in the Beverly Hills Business District featuring pastries, scones and egg dishes at breakfast with sandwiches, chopped salads and other seasonal fare at lunch; order at the counter, and then "while away" an afternoon at the outdoor tables under umbrellas.

Larry's *American* ▽ 23 | 18 | 17 | $30

Venice | 24 Windward Ave. (Speedway) | 310-399-2700 | www.larrysvenice.com

"The essence of what a gastropub should be", this boardwalk-adjacent Venice hang from the folks behind Waterloo & City is a "great place to grab a drink, a bite and unwind" with lots of "tasty", "creative" small plates, burgers and heartier fare meeting up with an "excellent selection of craft beers" on tap; with moderate prices and a "comfortable" patio, many call it a "welcome addition" to the area; P.S. it's named for local artist Larry Bell and displays some of his work.

Larsen's Steakhouse *Steak* 24 24 24 $59

Encino | Encino Pl. | 16101 Ventura Blvd. (Woodley Ave.) | 818-386-9500 | www.larsensteakhouse.com

Locals "love" having this Encino chophouse "just down the street" with "excellent" steaks and "accommodating" service, which saves them from driving over the hill for a "special evening"; "live piano music is a real plus" in the "dark" wood-and-stone surroundings, so though it's "a bit pricey", consensus is it's "worth it."

La Sandia Mexican Kitchen & Tequila Bar *Mexican* ∇ 21 23 22 $30

Santa Monica | Santa Monica Pl. | 395 Santa Monica Pl. (3rd St. Promenade) | 310-393-3300 | www.richardsandoval.com

With a "magical", "soaring" space, this "cool" Santa Monica Mexican from the Richard Sandoval empire puts a "modern twist" on traditional standards while complementing them with an extensive menu of tequilas; "amazing" service, modest prices and a hopping happy hour complete the picture.

La Scala Ⓢ *Italian* 21 18 21 $40

Beverly Hills | 434 N. Canon Dr. (bet. Brighton Way & Santa Monica Blvd.) | 310-275-0579

La Scala Presto Ⓢ *Italian*

Brentwood | 11740 San Vicente Blvd. (Gorham Ave.) | 310-826-6100 www.lascalabeverlyhills.com

The chopped salad is "legendary" ("everyone orders it in some fashion or another") at these "charming" Italians in Beverly Hills and Brentwood also luring "ladies who lunch" with other "reliable", "nothing-complicated" fare; expect "civilized" settings, "cordial" service and moderate prices; P.S. it's "great for takeaway" too.

La Serenata de Garibaldi *Mexican* 23 17 21 $29

Boyle Heights | 1842 E. First St. (bet. Boyle Ave. & State St.) | 323-265-2887

La Serenata Gourmet *Mexican*

West LA | 10924 W. Pico Blvd. (bet. Veteran Ave. & Westwood Blvd.) | 310-441-9667

www.laserenataonline.com

The "amazing", "inspired" Mexican dishes go "way beyond standard south-of-the-border fare" at this "classy" pair that's "especially good for seafood"; both locales boast an "upscale" ambiance and "friendly" service, but the "warm, pretty" hacienda-style setting at the Boyle Heights original is a "festive" favorite for "rehearsal dinners and parties."

Laurel Hardware ◐ *American* ∇ 19 23 17 $44

West Hollywood | 7984 Santa Monica Blvd. (bet. Edinburgh & Laurel Aves.) | 323-656-6070 | www.laurelhardware.com

Very "sceney", this "hip" WeHo hardware store-turned-restaurant features a midpriced farm-to-table New American menu and an "innovative" cocktail list; those who find the acoustics "unbearably loud" retreat to the "lovely", "quiet" backyard patio shaded by olive trees.

La Vecchia Cucina *Italian* 24 | 18 | 23 | $40

Santa Monica | 2654 Main St. (bet. Hill St. & Ocean Park Blvd.) | 310-399-7979 | www.lavecchiacucina.com

Locals "love the vibe" at this Santa Monica neighborhood "find" where all of the "bustle", "noise" and "garlic aroma emanating throughout" give it the feel of a "real Italian cafe"; expect "top-notch" standards and pizzas proffered by a "helpful" crew, while affordable prices - including a "fab happy hour" - also explain why it's "always a pleasure."

Lawry's Carvery *American* 22 | 14 | 17 | $23

Downtown | LA Live | 1011 S. Figueroa St. (bet. Chick Hearn Ct. & Olympic Blvd.) | 213-222-2212 | www.lawrysonline.com

"Lawry's lite" in Downtown's LA Live offers "mouthwatering" sandwiches made with the chain's signature prime rib plus salads and other items served up "quick", fast-food style; it's a convenient option before a game or concert, and "interesting people-watching" from the sidewalk patio helps make up for the "noisy", "food-court" setting.

Lawry's The Prime Rib *Steak* 26 | 23 | 26 | $61

Beverly Hills | 100 N. La Cienega Blvd. (bet. Clifton Way & Wilshire Blvd.) | 310-652-2827 | www.lawrysonline.com

"Prime rib is elevated to art" at this Beverly Hills "institution", going strong since 1938, where "top-notch", uniformed servers "are still twirling the salad bowls" and "hand-carving" beef from silver carts; it's a "classy, old-style hangout" that's "not cheap", but most agree it's "worth it when the occasion arises."

Lazy Ox Canteen ◐ *Eclectic* 24 | 16 | 20 | $41

Little Tokyo | 241 S. San Pedro St. (bet. 2nd & 3rd Sts.) | 213-626-5299 | www.lazyoxcanteen.com

Dubbed a "foodie paradise", this "exhilarating" little spot in Little Tokyo "wows" with an ever-"evolving" Eclectic menu featuring "amazing" "out-of-the-box" small plates based on "unique" seasonal ingredients and "all things pig", plus a "great burger"; prices are "moderate", servers are "informed" and the vibe is "cool", even if the "ear-splitting" music could "scare off anyone over 28."

Le Chêne *French* ∇ 24 | 23 | 23 | $56

Saugus | 12625 Sierra Hwy. (bet. Sierra Vallejo Rd. & Steele Ave.) | 661-251-4315 | www.lechene.com

You might need a "GPS" to find this "out-of-the-way" Saugus spot featuring "exquisite" classic French fare and game served by a "fantastic" staff in a "romantic setting" that resembles a "country estate" (complete with "beautiful" grounds); though a few find the food and decor "could use a refresh", most say it still fits the bill for "special occasions."

Leila's Ⓜ *Californian* 27 | 20 | 25 | $53

Oak Park | Oak Park Plaza | 706 Lindero Canyon Rd. (Kanan Rd.) | 818-707-6939 | www.leilasrestaurant.com

"A local gem" in an Oak Park shopping center, this "little-known" Californian is "worthy of a spot" alongside the big guns thanks to its "terrific" "original" small and large plates plus a "well-crafted" wine list; the service is "attentive" and the earth-toned setting is "comfortable" enough, making it a "wonderful", "pricey" experience that is "worth seeking out."

NEW Le Ka *Continental* - | - | - | E

Downtown | The Plaza | 800 W. Sixth St. (Flower St.) | 213-688-3000 | www.lekarestaurant.com

This upscale Continental from the owners of the Pan-Asian Wokcano chain serves a pricey menu featuring Californian ingredients and a craft cocktail list, plus local wine and beer; the stylish space - with high ceilings, a covered fire pit and commanding windows overlooking both towers of Downtown - is popular with suits by day and a Staples/Nokia crowd at night.

Lemonade *Californian* 21 | 13 | 16 | $18

Downtown | MOCA | 250 S. Grand Ave. (bet. 2nd & 3rd Sts.) | 213-628-0200
Downtown | Ronald Tutor Student Campus Ctr. | 3607 Trousdale Pkwy. (34th St.) | 213-821-3482
Downtown | 505 S. Flower St. (bet. 5th & 6th Sts.) | 213-488-0299
West Hollywood | 9001 Beverly Blvd. (Almont Dr.) | 310-247-2500
Brentwood | 145 S. Barrington Ave. (Barrington Pl.) | 310-471-9700
Venice | 1661 Abbot Kinney Blvd. (Venice Blvd.) | 310-452-6200
www.lemonadela.com

"Needless to say, the lemonades are terrific" at this "budget"-priced SoCal chainlet also vending a "huge selection" of "fresh, healthy" salads, soups and other "inspired" Californian-casual fare plus "fab" desserts, all dished out cafeteria-style; the "cool, contemporary" digs have a "relaxed" vibe, however, lunch can draw "quite a crowd."

Lemon Moon *Californian/Mediterranean* 20 | 14 | 17 | $21

West LA | Westside Media Ctr. | 12200 W. Olympic Blvd. (bet. Bundy Dr. & Centinela Ave.) | 310-442-9191 | www.lemonmoon.com

"Delicious cafeteria food, who knew?" ask incredulous fans of this "posh" West LA counter-service spot from Josiah Citrin and Raphael Lunetta turning out "tasty" Cal-Med sandwiches and "salads galore"; the "casual" industrial setup is spare, but includes "lovely" outdoor seating and fair prices, so most only "wish they were open for dinner."

NEW Lenny's Deli *Deli* - | - | - | I

West LA | 2379 Westwood Blvd. (Pico Blvd.) | 310-475-5771 | www.lensdeli.com

What used to be the legendary Junior's in West LA has been reborn as Lenny's, a modernized version of an old-school deli, still serving a vast selection of sandwiches, soups and pastries, but now in a space that's been considerably gussied up with new carpets, new booths and more.

Le Pain Quotidien *Bakery* 18 | 15 | 16 | $21

West Hollywood | 8607 Melrose Ave. (Westbourne Dr.) | 310-854-3700
Beverly Hills | 320 S. Robertson Blvd. (bet. Burton Way & 3rd St.) | 310-858-7270
Beverly Hills | 9630 S. Santa Monica Blvd. (bet. Bedford & Camden Drs.) | 310-859-1100
Brentwood | Brentwood Vill. | 11702 Barrington Ct. (Barrington Ave.) | 310-476-0969

(continued)

(continued)

Le Pain Quotidien

Brentwood | Brentwood Town Ctr. | 13050 San Vicente Blvd. (26th St.) | 310-393-8909
Santa Monica | 316 Santa Monica Blvd. (bet. 2nd & 4th Sts.) | 310-393-6800
Westwood | 1055 Broxton Ave. (bet. Kinross & Weyburn Aves.) | 310-824-7900
Manhattan Beach | Metlox Plaza | 451 Manhattan Beach Blvd. (bet. Morningside & Valley Drs.) | 310-546-6411
Pasadena | 88 W. Colorado Blvd. (De Lacey Ave.) | 626-396-0814
Studio City | 13045 Ventura Blvd. (bet. Coldwater Canyon & Ethel Aves.) | 818-986-1929
www.lepainquotidien.com
Additional locations throughout the Los Angeles area

"Amazing bread" is at the center of this well-priced Belgian bakery chain offering mostly organic "fresh, healthy" daytime fare, from "lovely" open-faced sandwiches and "sweet little salads" to "quality" pastries; service tends to be "a bit European", but the "inviting" atmosphere redeems with a "charming", "rustic" space perfect for a meeting or a post-exercise bite.

Le Petit Bistro ◐ *French* — 24 | 21 | 23 | $41

West Hollywood | 631 N. La Cienega Blvd. (Melrose Ave.) | 310-289-9797 | www.lepetitbistro.us

"When there's no time to jet to Paris for the weekend", this WeHo bistro offers "considerable charm" in its "delicious", "bargain"-priced French fare, "pleasant" service and relatively "understated" setting; no wonder it's a "favorite" for "date night" and "still going strong" after close to 20 years.

Le Petit Cafe ☒ *French* — 24 | 18 | 21 | $38

Santa Monica | 2842 Colorado Ave. (bet. Stewart & Yale Sts.) | 310-829-6792 | www.lepetitcafebonjour.com

"*Petite* in size, *grande* in fare", this *très* "adorable" Santa Monica bistro charms locals with "down-home" traditional French cuisine served in a "lovely" space adorned with Provençal pastels; some say "they squeeze you in like sardines" and service can be "spotty", but "reasonable prices" compensate.

Le Petit Greek *Greek* — 22 | 17 | 22 | $36

Hancock Park | 127 N. Larchmont Blvd. (bet. Beverly Blvd. & 1st St.) | 323-464-5160 | www.lepetitgreek.com

"Wonderful", "classic" Greek fare at a "fair value" keeps regulars coming back to this family-run Hancock Park Hellenic manned by a "pleasant" crew; inside is pretty, but it's especially "lovely to sit outside in the summer" at the tables overlooking Larchmont Boulevard.

Le Petit Restaurant *French* — 23 | 20 | 22 | $39

Sherman Oaks | 13360 Ventura Blvd. (bet. Dixie Canyon & Nagle Aves.) | 818-501-7999 | www.lepetitrestaurant.net

A "lovely" "secret in the Valley", this Sherman Oaks bistro is "always a delight" thanks to its "*delicieux*", "affordable" French standards ferried by a "warm" staff; add in an "unpretentious, comfortable" Parisian-style setting and you really "can't go wrong" here; P.S. look for lobster specials on Monday and Tuesday nights.

	FOOD	DECOR	SERVICE	COST

Le Sanglier French Restaurant Ⓜ *French* 24 23 23 $62

Tarzana | 5522 Crebs Ave. (Ventura Blvd.) | 818-345-0470 | www.lesanglierrestaurant.com

Recalling a time when "French food was king and the 405 moved at the speed limit", this circa-1970 Tarzana standby serves "traditional" Gallic fare in a "dark, romantic" "country-style" setting; true, it's "expensive" and critics contend "it should be better for the money you spend", but "it's a gem for people living in the San Fernando Valley."

Les Sisters Southern Kitchen Ⓜ *Southern* 23 8 19 $19

Chatsworth | 21818 Devonshire St. (bet. Jordan & Vassar Aves.) | 818-998-0755 | www.lessisters.com

Devotees "dream of the collard greens" at this Chatsworth Southern specializing in "down-home classics" ("all the stuff you know you shouldn't be eating") like "stupendous po' boys" and BBQ plus some "scrumptious" Cajun-Creole items that "remind you of New Orleans"; there's no alcohol, no BYO and the setting is "not much to look at", but prices are low and the mood's so "inviting" that "eating here is like visiting those Louisiana relatives you didn't know you had."

Let's Be Frank Ⓜ *Hot Dogs* 17 9 18 $10

Culver City | Helms Ave. (National Blvd.) | 888-233-7265 | www.letsbefrankdogs.com

"I'll be frank, I love the dogs!" proclaims a fan of the "superior-quality" links crafted from all-natural meats and "gourmet" condiments at this red trailer parked daytimes Wednesday–Sunday at Culver City's Helms Bakery Complex, and most Thursday nights outside Silverlake Wine; critics growl that they're "overhyped", but most are won over by the "decent" prices.

Limani Taverna *Greek* ▽ 18 17 20 $43

San Pedro | 301 W. Sixth St. (Centre St.) | 310-833-3033

In a sprawling San Pedro space, this cozy Greek serves classic, moderately priced Athenian cuisine like lamb, seafood and gyros, all washed down with retsina and cries of '*Opa!*'; the Hellenic banquet-hall aesthetic is pure fun, even more so with the live entertainment on weekends.

Literati Cafe *Californian/Eclectic* 18 17 17 $24

West LA | 12081 Wilshire Blvd. (Bundy Dr.) | 310-231-7484 | www.literaticafe.com

"Venture capitalists and screenwriters" "fueled by lattes" fill up this "neighborhood destination", an "atmospheric" West LA cafe serving "simple" Cal-Eclectic fare, pastries and "huge cups of coffee" in a high-ceilinged space adorned with photos of authors; folks find it "a great place to stop for a quick bite."

Little Bear ◐ *Belgian* ▽ 22 19 21 $34

Downtown | Joe's Downtown Mkt. | 1855 Industrial St. (bet. Mateo & Mill Sts.) | 213-622-8100 | www.littlebearla.com

This Downtown gastropub from Andre Guerrero and Ryan Sweeney "hidden" away in the Industrial District sets itself apart with a "focus on Belgian" beers, with almost 20 rotating taps of obscure brews; the menu mixes of-the-moment LA fare like a burger made with grass-fed beef, Stilton cheese and truffle oil with "interesting" staples of the Lowcountry, such as gougères and carbonnade de flamande.

	FOOD	DECOR	SERVICE	COST

NEW Little Beast ⊠ M *American* | - | - | - | M |

Eagle Rock | 1496 Colorado Blvd. (Loleta Ave.) | 323-341-5899 | www.littlebeastrestaurant.com

Taking its moniker from the nickname of the owners' 10-year-old daughter, this moderately priced Eagle Rock New American features locally minded fare plus beer and wine and a kids' menu, of course; located in a 1911 bungalow, the quaint space has well-worn wooden floors and a compact bar, with extra seating on the patio.

Little Dom's *Italian* | 22 | 20 | 20 | $37 |

Los Feliz | 2128 Hillhurst Ave. (Avocado St.) | 323-661-0055

Deli at Little Dom's *Italian*

Los Feliz | 2128 Hillhurst Ave. (Avocado St.) | 323-661-0088

www.littledoms.com

This "hipster heaven" in Los Feliz is "always packed" thanks to "freakin'-good" thin-crust pizzas and other Italiana offered in a "cozy, romantic" setting with a bar scene by night and a "deliciously decadent" breakfast in the morn; the setting with an attached deli is like a "flashback to 1956 Mulberry Street", but while "service is usually solid", some say they could lose the "attitude."

Little Door ◐ *French/Mediterranean* | 23 | 24 | 21 | $60 |

Third Street | 8164 W. Third St. (bet. Crescent Heights Blvd. & La Jolla Ave.) | 323-951-1210 | www.thelittledoor.com

Fans heart this Third Street charmer with a candlelit "country-house" interior and a "magical garden" deemed "one of the most romantic" in LA; the service is "gracious" and the French-Med menu is "quite good", although bills are "on the pricey side", even for such an "enchanting" experience.

NEW Littlefork *Seafood* | ▽ 24 | 19 | 21 | $54 |

Hollywood | 1600 Wilcox Ave. (Selma Ave.) | 323-465-3675 | www.littleforkla.com

Chef Jason Travi (ex Fraîche) resurfaces in Hollywood at this dinner-only seafooder serving up a taste of New England in the form of "wonderful" chowder, clam cakes and malt vinegar pork rinds, plus "creative cocktails"; the understated room has mod plastic seats, outsized wood-paneled walls and a small bar.

NEW Little Sister *Asian/European* | - | - | - | M |

Manhattan Beach | 1131 Manhattan Ave. (bet. Center Pl. & Manhattan Beach Blvd.) | 310-545-2096 | www.littlesistermb.com

At this sibling of nearby Abigaile, chef Tin Vuong offers a midpriced menu of Asian dishes with European touches (think red-braised pork belly with roasted wild mushrooms and leek fondue) plus craft beers and wines; the stylish Manhattan Beach storefront looks more Singaporean shophouse than South Bay.

Livello *Eclectic* | 23 | 21 | 20 | $45 |

Beverly Hills | L'Ermitage Beverly Hills | 9291 Burton Way (bet. Foothill Rd. & Maple Dr.) | 310-385-5302 | www.lermitagebh.com

The Beverly Hills L'Ermitage Hotel is home to this new stunner serving an "ambitious", expensive Eclectic menu showcasing a mix of Italian, European and Asian dishes; it's all served in a strikingly "beautiful" indoor-outdoor space that features a dramatic fountain and a fireplace.

	FOOD	DECOR	SERVICE	COST

The Lobster *Seafood* | 23 | 24 | 22 | $57

Santa Monica | 1602 Ocean Ave. (Colorado Ave.) | 310-458-9294 | www.thelobster.com

With a "fabulous" location at the Santa Monica Pier, this seafood mainstay offers "stunning views" of the Pacific plus "terrific" lobster "prepared a zillion ways" and other "market-fresh" dishes; "expensive" tabs and a "loud, crowded" space are drawbacks, but the "wow" factor is high, especially for a "special occasion."

Locanda del Lago *Italian* | 23 | 22 | 23 | $43

Santa Monica | 231 Arizona Ave. (2nd St.) | 310-451-3525 | www.lagosantamonica.com

A "welcoming" "escape" from the "tourist hot zone" of Santa Monica's Third Street Promenade, this expensive Northern Italian specializes in "amazing", "authentic" dishes of the Lake Como region served along an "extensive" wine list; add in a "cozy atmosphere" and "down-home Italian hospitality" and it's an "all-around wonderful experience."

Locanda Positano *Italian* | 25 | 19 | 24 | $53

Marina del Rey | 4059 Lincoln Blvd. (Washington Blvd.) | 310-526-3887 | www.locandapositano.com

This "little jewel" in Marina del Rey "practically defines the term charming" with "exquisite, authentic" Italian cuisine and "fine wines" delivered by "swoon-worthy" accented waiters in a "tiny", "romantic" space; indeed, it's "pricey", but cheaper than "a trip to Italy."

Locanda Veneta *Italian* | 24 | 19 | 23 | $51

Third Street | 8638 W. Third St. (Willaman Dr.) | 310-274-1893 | www.locandaveneta.net

Ever "inviting", this 25-year-old Third Street Italian is "still tops" for fans when it comes to "fantastic" Venetian fare like noteworthy calamari and risotto dishes; the "romantic" setting can be "cramped" and tabs daunting, but the "amazing food and service" enhanced with a "celeb sighting" or two make it one of the city's "little gems."

L'Opera *Italian* | 23 | 23 | 23 | $52

Long Beach | Historic Clock Tower | 101 Pine Ave. (bet. Alta Way & 1st St.) | 562-491-0066 | www.lopera.com

For a "special-occasion" spot or a "high-end business lunch", Long Beachers tout this Northern Italian for its "excellent" homemade pastas and other "rich" Italiana served by a "spot-on" crew; it's all set in the "wonderful" Historic Clock Tower building from 1902 making for a "truly memorable" setting that justifies the upmarket tabs; P.S. there's also live opera singers on Friday and Saturday evenings.

Los Balcones del Peru *Peruvian* | ∇ 20 | 14 | 19 | $26

Hollywood | 1360 N. Vine St. (De Longpre Ave.) | 323-871-9600

"Legit Peruvian" cuisine is served up in a "convenient" Hollywood locale near The ArcLight at this unassuming spot specializing in ceviche, lomo saltado and other well-priced fare; "caring" service and a "neighborhood feel" make up for ambiance that's otherwise "lacking."

Lotería! Grill *Mexican* | 22 | 14 | 16 | $23

Fairfax | Farmers Mkt. | 6333 W. Third St. (Fairfax Ave.) | 323-930-2211

(continued)

(continued)

Lotería! Grill

Hollywood | 6627 Hollywood Blvd. (Cherokee Ave.) | 323-465-2500
Santa Monica | 1251 Third St. Promenade (bet. Arizona Ave. & Wilshire Blvd.) | 310-393-2700
Studio City | Laurel Promenade | 12050 Ventura Blvd. (Laurel Canyon Blvd.) | 818-508-5300
Westlake Village | The Promenade at Westlake | 180 Promenade Way (Thousand Oaks Blvd.) | 805-379-1800
www.loteriagrill.com

"Bright and lively" describes both the scene and the eats at Jimmy Shaw's "colorful" chain of "well-priced" Mexicanos - born as a stand in the Farmers Market - crafting "surprising, delicious" spins on regional specialties; the staff is "friendly" across the board, but only the full-service sit-down branches offer "strong margaritas" and full tequila bars.

NEW Louie's Old School American ◐ M *American* | - | - | - | M |

Mar Vista | 3817 Grand View Blvd. (Pacific Ave.) | 310-915-5300 | www.louiesofmarvista.com

Set in a former butcher shop (named Louie's), this moderately priced American in steadily gentrifying Mar Vista offers the dishes of yesteryear and classic cocktails in a petite storefront setting.

Louise's Trattoria *Californian/Italian* | 19 | 17 | 20 | $26 |

Hancock Park | 232 N. Larchmont Blvd. (bet. Beverly Blvd. & 1st St.) | 323-962-9510
Los Feliz | 4500 Los Feliz Blvd. (Hillhurst Ave.) | 323-667-0777
Santa Monica | 1008 Montana Ave. (10th St.) | 310-394-8888
Santa Monica | 264 26th St. (bet. Georgina Ave. & San Vicente Blvd.) | 310-451-5001
West LA | 10645 W. Pico Blvd. (bet. Manning & Pelham Aves.) | 310-475-6084
Pasadena | 2-8 E. Colorado Blvd. (Fair Oaks Ave.) | 626-568-3030
www.louises.com

"Reliable, but not exciting" Cal-Italian fare gets a lift from the "addictive" complimentary focaccia at this "comfortable" SoCal chain offering just "enough choices to keep your interest" and "friendly" service; critics who are "not terribly impressed" claim "nothing stands out" except for the budget-friendly bills.

Lucille's Smokehouse Bar-B-Que *BBQ* | 22 | 19 | 20 | $28 |

Cerritos | 11338 South St. (bet. Gridley Rd. & Hibbing St.) | 562-916-7427
Culver City | Westfield Culver City | 6000 Sepulveda Blvd. (Slauson Ave.) | 310-390-1227
Long Beach | 4828 E. Second St. (bet. Park & St. Joseph Aves.) | 562-434-7427
Long Beach | Long Beach Towne Ctr. | 7411 Carson St. (Nectar Ave.) | 562-938-7427
Torrance | Del Amo Fashion Ctr. | 21420 Hawthorne Blvd. (bet. Carson St. & Del Amo Circle) | 310-370-7427
www.lucillesbbq.com

"Come hungry" to this "down-home" BBQ chain, a meat-eater's "heaven" that entices with "messy", "generous" portions of "tasty" 'cue and "cute" Southern-themed rooms filled with the "sweet smell of barbecue sauce and smoke"; critics beef about "overpriced tabs", but it's "plenty filling", with "friendly" service to boot.

Lucques *Californian/Mediterranean* 27 | 25 | 25 | $66

West Hollywood | 8474 Melrose Ave. (La Cienega Blvd.) | 323-655-6277 | www.lucques.com

"Always a delight", Suzanne Goin's West Hollywood mainstay continues to be a "foodie haven" thanks to her "smart" market-driven Cal-Med cuisine, boosted by a "lengthy wine list" and an "elegant" but "easy vibe"; set in an "old carriage house" with an "ivy-lined courtyard", it's "pleasurable" all around and "well worth the cost" - plus the "value" prix fixe Sunday Supper is still a "big hit."

LudoTruck *Eclectic* 24 | 15 | 19 | $13

Location varies; see website | 213-289-9816 | www.ludotruck.com

"Mind-blowing" fried chicken is the main attraction at this truck by Burgundy-born chef Ludo Lefebvre (Trois Mec), where the *Provençal pepittes* are accompanied by honey-lavender biscuits and "spicy, kickin' slaw"; perhaps it's a little "expensive" for "glorified chicken nuggets" and the "waits" can be trying, but most "love it anyway."

Luggage Room Pizzeria *Pizza* 23 | 16 | 17 | $25

Pasadena | 260 S. Raymond Ave. (bet. Del Mar Blvd. & Green St.) | 626-356-4440 | www.theluggageroom.com

Set in the luggage room of Pasadena's historic (circa 1934) Del Mar Train Station, this "casual" offshoot of the neighboring La Grande Orange offers a "limited" lineup of "boutique" thin-crust pizzas with "unexpected toppings" capped off with gelato for dessert; service can be "uneven" and it "gets a bit loud when it's packed", but most don't seem to mind.

Lukshon *Asian* 24 | 23 | 22 | $48

Culver City | Helms Bldg. | 3239 Helms Ave. (bet. Venice & Washington Blvds.) | 310-202-6808 | www.lukshon.com

Sang Yoon (Father's Office) does Southeast Asian at his "gem" in Culver City's Helms Building that turns out a "clever menu" of "spicy" small plates in a "sleek" setting of teak and stainless metal; a "pleasant patio", "attentive service" and "unusual" drinks help take the edge off tabs that "can add up quickly."

Lulu's Cafe *American* 23 | 17 | 23 | $22

West Hollywood | 7149 Beverly Blvd. (Detroit St.) | 323-938-6095

This busy corner cafe in West Hollywood is a "good choice" for "well-prepared" American comfort food with a few surprises (think ahi tuna burgers and breakfast pasta) served morning to night at a "reasonable" cost; the small interior can be "noisy", so those in the know nab a seat on the sidewalk and try to ignore the traffic.

Luna Park *American* 19 | 16 | 19 | $34

La Brea | 672 S. La Brea Ave. (bet. Carling Way & Wilshire Blvd.) | 323-934-2110 | www.lunaparkla.com

Specialty cocktails, fondue and make-your-own s'mores ("a must") are the signatures of this "funky" La Brea American serving a well-priced menu that's "strong on comfort food"; "attentive service" and "dark", semi-private booths make it an "excellent date-night sort of place."

	FOOD	DECOR	SERVICE	COST

Lure Fish House *Seafood* 24 | 23 | 24 | $32

Camarillo | 259 W. Ventura Blvd. (Las Posas Rd.) | 805-388-5556 | www.lurefishhouse.com

"Definitely a keeper" declare fans of this well-priced Camarillo seafooder featuring "a wide array" of "fresh", locally caught fin fare that's "well prepared and pleasantly served" with local wines and fruity cocktails; the modern-nautical space with an oyster bar and patio has an "inviting ambiance" – just prepare for "mobs on Saturday night" since they don't take reservations; P.S. happy hour is also popular.

NEW Maccheroni Republic Ⓢ *Italian* - | - | - | M

Downtown | 332 S. Broadway (bet. 3rd & 4th Sts.) | 213-346-9725

Jean-Louis De Mori, former owner of Locanda Veneta, and his longtime chef-partner, Antonio Tomassi, head Downtown with this ultracasual BYO Italian that's heavy on pasta and even heavier on authenticity; served in a space decked out with gleaming white tiles, weathered wooden cabinets and shelves packed with cups, books and bottles of sauces, it's a new restaurant that looks as if it's been around forever.

Madeo *Italian* 26 | 20 | 24 | $72

West Hollywood | 8897 Beverly Blvd. (Swall Dr.) | 310-859-4903

"If you can get past the paparazzi", this "clubby", "celeb-loaded" Northern Italian in West Hollywood offers "excellent" "old-school" dishes (the Bolognese is a highlight) at "eye-popping" prices; many surveyors suggest there's "major attitude if you're not a heavy hitter", but it still "packs them in" each night nonetheless.

Maison Akira Ⓜ *French/Japanese* 26 | 22 | 25 | $59

Pasadena | 713 E. Green St. (bet. El Molino & Oak Knoll Aves.) | 626-796-9501 | www.maisonakira.com

Akira Hirose is still at "the top of his game" at this Pasadena "classic" where "intriguing" French-Japanese dishes that are "uniformly superb" and "worth every penny" are served by a "professional" team; the "quiet, intimate" atmosphere's "a little staid" (and "lost in the 1980s") for some, although it remains "great for special occasions or if you're going to the nearby Pasadena Playhouse."

Maison Giraud *French* 24 | 17 | 18 | $46

Pacific Palisades | 1032 Swarthmore Ave. (Monument St.) | 310-459-7562 | www.maison-giraud.com

The menu is classic French at this Palisades staple, an all-day bakery and restaurant from chef Alain Giraud purveying "buttery, flaky croissants", "wonderful pastries", "approachable" entrees and a "genius" chocolate soufflé for dessert in a sun-dappled space with floor-to-ceiling windows; a few fuss over service that's too "leisurely", "noisy" acoustics and "pricey" bills, but "all is forgiven because of chef Giraud's menu."

M.A.K.E. *Vegan* ∇ 15 | 16 | 18 | $30

Santa Monica | 395 Santa Monica Pl. (B'way) | 310-394-7046 | www.matthewkenneycuisine.com

Raw-food guru Matthew Kenney is behind this restaurant and culinary school at Santa Monica Place with a bright, modern feel, communal tables and a "passionate" staff; although opinions are split on the "healthful" vegan cuisine ("interesting" vs. "overpriced"), enthusiasts insist they'll "definitely be back."

	FOOD	DECOR	SERVICE	COST

Malbec *Argentinean/Steak* 23 | 20 | 22 | $37

Pasadena | 1001 E. Green St. (Catalina Ave.) | 626-683-0550
Toluca Lake | 10151 Riverside Dr. (bet. Forman & Talofa Aves.) | 818-762-4860
www.malbeccuisine.com

"Excellent cuts of meat" await at this Argentinean duo known for its "generous portions" at "fair prices" and "long list of red wines" (including plenty of Malbecs, natch); the "dark", "romantic" settings and "attentive service" earn plaudits, although the "busy" weekends are "too noisy" for some.

Malibu Seafood *Seafood* 24 | 14 | 17 | $21

Malibu | 25653 PCH (bet. Corral Canyon & Malibu Canyon Rds.) | 310-456-3430 | www.malibuseafood.com

"Bring your own wine and tablecloth" and "take in the ocean breezes" at this "no-frills" seafood shack on the PCH in Malibu serving up affordable, "fresh, cooked-to-order" fare on three patios with "killer" views; it gets "crowded", but a "seriously organized ordering system" keeps the "long lines" moving; P.S. the "tasty clam chowder and excellent fish 'n' chips are easy pleasers."

Malo *Mexican* 19 | 18 | 17 | $27

Silver Lake | 4326 W. Sunset Blvd. (bet. Bates & Fountain Aves.) | 323-664-1011 | www.malorestaurant.com

"*Muy bueno*" say late-night "hipsters" of this dark, "trendy" Silver Lake Mexican known as much for its "cool vibe" as its unusual "chewy chips", "fabulous" salsa flights and "creative" tacos that may be "a bit gringo" but are "decent" nonetheless; "fantastic margaritas" from the attached tequila bar take the edge off servers "with attitude"; P.S. happy hour is also popular.

Mama D's *Italian* 23 | 13 | 23 | $27

Manhattan Beach | 1125 Manhattan Ave. (bet. Center Pl. & Manhattan Beach Blvd.) | 310-546-1492 | www.mamadsrestaurant.com

"Homey" describes this "archetypal family-friendly Italian" in Manhattan Beach moving "cheap and voluminous" platters of "home cooking" plus "irresistible" garlic bread while you wait; despite the fact that you'll be "packed in like sardines" at traditional red-checkered tables, it's nonetheless "popular" with "locals" who "go back again and again."

Mama Terano *Italian* ▽ 22 | 12 | 23 | $30

Rolling Hills Estates | 815 Deep Valley Dr. (Silver Spur Rd.) | Rolling Hills | 310-377-5757 | www.mamaterano.com

Robert Bell (Chez Mélange, Bouzy) relies on "grandmama's recipes from the old world" at this Rolling Hills Estates Italian putting out "delicious" pastas, flatbread pizzas and the like for "unusually reasonable" sums; service is "attentive", and it's often "crowded like a neighborhood bistro should be."

Mandarette *Chinese* 19 | 17 | 19 | $28

Beverly Boulevard | 8386 Beverly Blvd. (bet. Kings Rd. & Orlando Ave.) | West Hollywood | 323-655-6115 | www.mandarettecafe.com

"Dependable" for nearly 30 years, this Beverly Boulevard Sichuan features a "well-balanced" menu incorporating "interesting twists" on

Chinese standards, as well as "healthy" options; combined with "efficient" service and a red-hued setting, it "hits the spot."

Manna *Korean* ∇ 17 | 12 | 16 | $26

Downtown | Little Tokyo Shopping Ctr. | 333 S. Alameda St. (3rd St.) | 323-733-8516 | www.mannabbq.com

"All-you-can-eat deliciousness" is yours at this "loud, smoky" Korean BBQ joint Downtown, where diners "stuff themselves to the gills" with midpriced galbi and other sear-it-yourself meats plus shabu-shabu; on birthdays they'll "douse you with champagne", so for a "fun party atmosphere", it's just the ticket.

Maria's Italian Kitchen *Italian* 19 | 15 | 19 | $24

Downtown | 615 Flower St. (bet. 6th St. & Wilshire Blvd.) | 213-623-4777
Brentwood | 11723 Barrington Ct. (Barrington Ave.) | 310-476-6112
West LA | 10761 W. Pico Blvd. (Malcolm Ave.) | 310-441-3663
Pasadena | Hastings Ranch Shopping Ctr. | 3537 E. Foothill Blvd. (bet. Halstead St. & Rosemead Blvd.) | 626-351-2080
Encino | 16608 Ventura Blvd. (bet. Petit & Rubio Aves.) | 818-783-2920
Northridge | 9161 Reseda Blvd. (bet. Dearborn & Nordhoff Sts.) | 818-341-5114
Sherman Oaks | 13353 Ventura Blvd. (bet. Dixie Canyon & Fulton Aves.) | 818-906-0783
Woodland Hills | El Camino Shopping Ctr. | 23331 Mulholland Dr. (Ave. San Luis) | 818-225-0586
Agoura Hills | Twin Oaks Shopping Ctr. | 29035 Thousand Oaks Blvd. (Kanan Rd.) | 818-865-8999
www.mariasitaliankitchen.com

"Red-sauce lovers unite" over "generous portions" of Italian "comfort food" at this "homey" "no-frills chain" that "feels like a mom and pop" to some with its "checked tablecloth decor"; sure, "service varies" and some find the food only "so-so", but "reasonable prices keep 'em coming back" for more.

Marino Ⓢ *Italian* 25 | 20 | 25 | $48

Hollywood | 6001 Melrose Ave. (Wilcox Ave.) | 323-466-8812 | www.marinorestaurant.net

"It feels like you're visiting friends" at this longtime family-run Italian in Hollywood that turns out "marvelous", "homestyle" Italian with "no pretense" in a "lovely" updated setting; it's not cheap, but the "comfortable", "quiet" ambiance makes it a "local treasure."

Mario's Peruvian & Seafood *Peruvian* 24 | 7 | 18 | $20

Hollywood | 5786 Melrose Ave. (Vine St.) | 323-466-4181

"It's all about the ceviche" and "addictive" pollo saltado at this Hollywood Peruvian that often hosts "lines out the door" for its inexpensive eats; even if the "decor has all the personality of a DMV", most have "no complaints"; P.S. it's also "terrific for takeout."

NEW Mari Vanna Ⓢ *Russian* - | - | - | E

West Hollywood | 8475 Melrose Pl. (bet. Alfred St. & La Cienega Blvd.) | 323-655-1977 | www.marivanna.ru

This upscale West Hollywood Russian (with siblings in St. Petersburg, London, New York and more) serves authentic flavors of the homeland

and a huge range of vodkas; the maximalist design features tchotchkes spread everywhere in the super-plush space, including throughout several indoor rooms and on the patio.

Marix Tex Mex Café *Tex-Mex* 17 | 14 | 18 | $26

West Hollywood | 1108 N. Flores St. (bet. Fountain Ave. & Santa Monica Blvd.) | 323-656-8800

Marix Tex Mex Playa *Tex-Mex*

Santa Monica | 118 Entrada Dr. (bet. Ocean Dr. & PCH) | 310-459-8596
www.marixtexmex.com

"Killer margaritas" fuel the "lively" scene at these perpetually "packed" Tex-Mex twins where solid servers deliver "plentiful" portions of "passable" Mexican fare ("but who comes here for the food?"); the Santa Monica location is a post-"beach hang" with "kids on the loose", while WeHo's happy hour hosts "hot men" and "pretty people" on the patio.

Marmalade Café *American* 17 | 15 | 18 | $26

Fairfax | Farmers Mkt. | 6333 W. Third St. (Fairfax Ave.) | 323-954-0088
Rolling Hills Estates | Avenue of the Peninsula Mall | 550 Deep Valley Dr. (Drybank Dr.) | Rolling Hills | 310-544-6700
Malibu | 3894 Cross Creek Rd. (PCH) | 310-317-4242
Santa Monica | 710 Montana Ave. (bet. Lincoln Blvd. & 7th St.) | 310-395-9196
El Segundo | Plaza El Segundo | 2014 E. Park Pl. (PCH) | 310-648-7200
Calabasas | The Commons at Calabasas Shopping Ctr. | 4783 Commons Way (bet. Civic Center Way & Commons Way) | 818-225-9092
Sherman Oaks | 14910 Ventura Blvd. (bet. Kester & Noble Aves.) | 818-905-8872
Westlake Village | Promenade at Westlake | 140 Promenade Way (Thousand Oaks Blvd.) | 805-370-1331
www.marmaladecafe.com

"A step up from a coffee shop", this SoCal chain offers a "varied menu" of American "comfort food" "with a Californian touch", including "particularly good breakfasts"; some say the food's "just ok", but with "cute" "shabby-chic" settings, a "pleasant staff" and "fair" prices, it certainly works "in a pinch."

Marouch M *Lebanese* ▽ 28 | 16 | 22 | $29

East Hollywood | 4905 Santa Monica Blvd. (Edgemont St.) | 323-662-9325 | www.marouchrestaurant.com

"Intense, creamy baba ghanoush" and "tasty" kebabs are just a few of the "authentic" affordable treats at this East Hollywood eatery considered to be "the best Lebanese" in LA; just "ignore the setting" in a nondescript mini-mall and let the "helpful staff" guide you through "the wonderful daily specials" - whatever it is "it's bound to be delicious."

Marrakesh *Moroccan* ▽ 21 | 23 | 23 | $42

Studio City | 13003 Ventura Blvd. (bet. Coldwater Canyon & Ethel Aves.) | 818-788-6354 | www.marrakeshdining.com

Think "cozy den with belly dancers" to imagine this Moroccan in Studio City serving "authentic, tasty cuisine" - and "a lot" of it - that requires "diving in" and "eating with your hands"; despite "disappearing" waiters and "outdated" digs, it's a "unique" experience, especially for a "date or group."

FOOD | DECOR | SERVICE | COST

Mar'sel *Californian* 26 | 28 | 25 | $61

Rancho Palos Verdes | Terranea Resort | 6610 Palos Verdes Dr. S. (Hawthorne Blvd.) | 310-265-2780 | www.terranea.com

Set in the "world-class" Terranea Resort, this Californian "should be on every romantic's bucket list" with its "breathtaking" ocean views from its perch atop Rancho Palos Verdes; the cuisine's as "stunning" as the setting, with "fabulous" fare made with ingredients picked straight from the chef's garden, while the service is what "you would expect at a luxury resort", and so are the prices.

Marston's *American* 21 | 16 | 18 | $22

Pasadena | 151 E. Walnut St. (bet. Marengo & Raymond Aves.) | 626-796-2459

Valencia | 24011 Newhall Ranch Rd. (McBean Pkwy.) | 661-253-9910 M

www.marstonsrestaurant.com

"Breakfasts are the bomb" at this Pasadena "institution" (and its newer Valencia spin-off) where "fresh, tasty" American fare comes served in a "quaint" "old-fashioned cottage" by a "personable" crew; just know, "it's mobbed on weekends", so "come early" or try it for lunch.

Martha's 22nd St. Grill *American* 23 | 16 | 21 | $18

Hermosa Beach | 25 22nd St. (bet. Beach Dr. & Hermosa Ave.) | 310-376-7786

"Sit on the patio and watch the world go by" at this Hermosa Beach American known for its "bountiful breakfasts" and other "solid" fare from a menu styled with a "California nod to vegetarians"; with "great service", water views ("you can hear the waves crashing") and affordable tabs, it's no surprise the "crowds line up on sunny days."

NEW **Maru** *Japanese* - | - | - | E

Santa Monica | 12400 Wilshire Blvd. (McClellan Dr.) | 310-820-7240 | www.marusantamonica.com

The sushi bar is packed at this pricey West LA Japanese, where the menu meanders from familiar creations into fusion (heirloom tomatoes in shiso pesto, crispy duck risotto); diners eat at the bar or at a handful of tables in the brightly lit, noisy room, while the chefs work away with an intense level of concentration.

Maruhide Uni Club S M *Japanese* - | - | - | M

Torrance | 2130 W. Redondo Beach Blvd. (Van Ness Ave.) | 310-323-2864 | www.maruhide.us

Heaven for sea urchin lovers, this mini-mall space - a brick-and-mortar expansion from a wholesaler of the delicacy - offers reasonably priced uni-based dishes and a few non-urchin options; there's seating in a polished wood room with unexpected chandeliers overhead, and a counter that sells pre-packed fare to go.

Masa *Pizza* 24 | 17 | 21 | $28

Echo Park | 1800 W. Sunset Blvd. (Lemoyne St.) | 213-989-1558 | www.masaofechopark.com

"If you're hankering for deep-dish" this late-night Echo Park pizzeria is considered one of "the best this side of Chicago" for "true" pies fashioned with "buttery-soft dough" and authentic toppings, plus vegan options; a "friendly" staff and a "casual, festive" setting make up for long waits and prices that can feel on the higher side for the genre; P.S. call your order ahead to skip the wait.

Mas Malo *Mexican* 18 | 20 | 17 | $34

Downtown | 515 W. Seventh St. (bet. Grand Ave. & Olive St.) | 213-985-4332 | www.masmalorestaurant.com

A "gorgeous", "energetic" setting inside a circa-1923 former jewelry store provides the backdrop for this "*muy bueno*" Downtown Mexican (sib to Silver Lake's Malo); a "tasty", "well-thought-out" menu and "extraordinary" tequila list make it a "great place to kick off your evening"; P.S. check out the "secret basement cantina."

Mastro's Steakhouse *Steak* 26 | 24 | 25 | $79

Beverly Hills | 246 N. Canon Dr. (bet. Clifton & Dayton Ways) | 310-888-8782

Thousand Oaks | 2087 E. Thousand Oaks Blvd. (bet. Conejo School Rd. & Los Feliz Dr.) | 805-418-1811

www.mastrosrestaurants.com

"Still happening", these "classic" Beverly Hills and Thousand Oaks chop shops are "always overbooked" with a "buzzing crowd" that gathers for "incredible" steaks, "memorable seafood towers" and "generous" pours that come via "attentive" servers; a "loud", "lively" piano bar and '50s supper club vibe add to an "over-the-top scene" that's matched by "over-the-top prices."

Matsuhisa *Japanese* 28 | 18 | 24 | $89

Beverly Hills | 129 N. La Cienega Blvd. (bet. Clifton Way & Wilshire Blvd.) | 310-659-9639 | www.nobumatsuhisa.com

Devotees make the "pilgrimage" to Nobu Matsuhisa's "original temple of seafood", this "still-amazing" 27-year-old Beverly Hills Japanese offering "sushi perfection" and "incredible" Peruvian-influenced fare to a "beautiful" crowd; service earns high marks while the digs are "simple and without pretense", and despite what some describe as "eyeball-popping" prices, most agree it's "worth a visit."

Matteo's 🄼 *Italian* 20 | 21 | 22 | $51

West LA | 2321 Westwood Blvd. (bet. Pico Blvd. & Tennessee Ave.) | 310-475-4521 | www.matteosla.com

This "iconic" circa-1963 Rat Pack "hangout" in West LA has an "old-school" setting but a "new-school" "pricey" menu featuring "novel takes on modern Italian cuisine" delivered by a "delightful" staff; though the decor's been freshened up, the "classic" feel remains, and you can still nab a seat in Frank Sinatra's corner booth (station eight).

Maximiliano *Italian* ▽ 22 | 18 | 20 | $32

Highland Park | 5930 York Blvd. (Figueroa St.) | 323-739-6125 | www.maximilianohp.com

Chef Andre Guerrero of The Oinkster makes Highland Park locals "happy" with his "happening" red sauce–intensive Italian serving "solid" midpriced fare like pork chops and meatballs; "well-trained" servers preside over a "trendy, yet comfortable" setting featuring an open-beam ceiling, spaghetti-themed wall art and a massive pizza oven in the open kitchen, while accessible pricing completes the package.

	FOOD	DECOR	SERVICE	COST

Maxwell's Cafe *Diner* ∇ 19 | 12 | 18 | $17

Venice | 13329 W. Washington Blvd. (Walgrove Ave.) | 310-306-7829 | www.novelcafe.com

"You can't beat it for down-home breakfasts and lunches" declare fans of this "funky", "friendly" neighborhood "staple" in Venice known for its "generous" helpings of inexpensive Americana dished out in a "cute" setting decked out with knickknacks; critics call it "nothing special", but expect "long lines" on weekends nonetheless.

M.B. Post *American* 27 | 22 | 24 | $47

Manhattan Beach | 1142 Manhattan Ave. (bet. Center Pl. & 12th St.) | 310-545-5405 | www.eatmbpost.com

"Nearly every dish is a hit" at this "not-so-hidden gem" in Manhattan Beach from chef David LeFevre (ex Water Grill) turning out "amazing", "innovative" "farm-to-table" small plates - "the bacon-cheddar biscuits are a must" - and "fun cocktails" in a "cool" setting crafted from reclaimed wood; it's not cheap and many find it "incredibly loud", "but the food makes up for it"; P.S. "brunch is fantastic" too.

M Café de Chaya *Vegetarian* 22 | 16 | 19 | $21

Melrose | 7119 Melrose Ave. (Detroit St.) | 323-525-0588
Beverly Hills | 9433 Brighton Way (bet. Beverly & Canon Drs.) | 310-858-8459
www.mcafedechaya.com

"A score for vegans and omnivores alike", these Melrose and Beverly Hills macrobiotics make "healthy food that actually tastes good" with enough "tempting" fare that "even your most food-phobic friend will be happy"; servers are helpful in making suggestions and the spare settings boast "lots of celeb sightings too", so fans only "wish it were a bit cheaper"; P.S. curbside pickup is a plus.

McCormick & Schmick's *Seafood* 18 | 19 | 19 | $44

Downtown | US Bank Tower | 633 W. Fifth St. (bet. Flower St. & Grand Ave.) | 213-629-1929
Beverly Hills | Two Rodeo | 206 N. Rodeo Dr. (Wilshire Blvd.) | 310-859-0434
El Segundo | 2101 Rosecrans Ave. (bet. Apollo & Nash Sts.) | 310-416-1123
Pasadena | 111 N. Los Robles Ave. (bet. Union & Walnut Sts.) | 626-405-0064
www.mccormickandschmicks.com

Ever "dependable", this "enjoyable", "high-end" seafood chain offers "quality" "traditional" fare in a "clubby" setting that's "great for a business lunch"; prices aren't cheap, but "happy hour is a steal" with deals on drinks and appetizers.

McKenna's on the Bay *Seafood/Steak* 21 | 24 | 21 | $43

Long Beach | 190 Marina Dr. (1st St.) | 562-342-9411 | www.mckennasonthebay.com

"Sit outside and watch the boats come and go" at this Long Beach entry overlooking Alamitos Bay purveying "good catch of the day" and other surf 'n' turf items in a "relaxing" milieu; some say the "incredible" scenery is tempered by "indifferent food at dear prices", although the "lively" bar scene and a patio that's "perfect for lunch on a sunny day" redeem it for many.

FOOD | DECOR | SERVICE | COST

Mediterraneo *Mediterranean* 23 | 19 | 22 | $32

Hermosa Beach | 73 Pier Ave. (Hermosa Ave.) | 310-318-2666 | www.themedhb.com

"Pretend you're on vacation" at this Hermosa Beach eatery on the pier, where you can sample "tasty" Med tapas that are "fun to share" and "pitchers of sangria" while "enjoying the lovely weather and the never-ending parade of beachy hipsters"; service is "friendly", prices are manageable and "if you can make happy hour, all the better!"

Mediterraneo *Mediterranean* 21 | 23 | 20 | $39

Westlake Village | 32037 Agoura Rd. (Lakeview Canyon Rd.) | 818-889-9105 | www.med-rest.com

The "charming patios" with water views may be the "highlight" at this Westlake Village Mediterranean whose upscale-modern decor creates an equally "pleasant atmosphere" indoors; most find the "varied" menu "well prepared", if "a bit pricey", although "attentive service" takes the sting off, and happy-hour specials at the bar bring some relief.

Mélisse 🅢🅜 *American/French* 28 | 26 | 27 | $121

Santa Monica | 1104 Wilshire Blvd. (11th St.) | 310-395-0881 | www.melisse.com

"Something magical happens" at Josiah Citrin's Santa Monica destination offering "exquisite" tasting menus of "fresh, market-driven" French-American cuisine (plus a "top-notch" vegetarian version) and "heavenly" wine pairings; "everything is totally polished", from the "impeccable" service (ranked No. 1 in Los Angeles) to the "elegant" setting, and while some quip that you'll need to "sell that screenplay to afford it", most agree you'll be "richly rewarded" for the expense.

Melting Pot *Fondue* 15 | 17 | 18 | $47

Torrance | 21525 Hawthorne Blvd. (Carson St.) | 310-316-7500
Pasadena | 88 W. Colorado Blvd. (bet. De Lacey & Pasadena Aves.) | 626-792-1941
Westlake Village | 3685 E. Thousand Oaks Blvd. (bet. Duesenberg Dr. & Westlake Blvd.) | 805-370-8802
www.meltingpot.com

"If melting, gooey cheese is your passion" then look no further than this fondue trio where "happy campers" enjoy "slow, leisurely meals" or the "divine combination" of "wine and melted chocolate" in "quiet", contemporary settings; "helpful" service is another plus, although a few find it "overpriced" considering you have to "cook your own food."

Mendocino Farms *Sandwiches* 24 | 16 | 21 | $16

Downtown | California Plaza | 300 S. Grand Ave. (4th St.) | 213-620-1114 🅢
Downtown | Citibank Bldg. | 444 S. Flower St. (5th St.) | 213-627-3262 🅢
NEW **Downtown** | 735. S. Figueroa Ave. (7th St.) | 213-430-9040 🅢
Fairfax | 175 S. Fairfax Ave. (3rd St.) | 323-934-4261
West Hollywood | 7100 Santa Monica Blvd. (La Brea Ave.) | 323-512-2700
Marina del Rey | 4724 Admiralty Way (PCH) | 310-822-2300
www.mendocinofarms.com

"Awesome, inventive sandwiches" stuffed with ultra-"fresh" locally sourced ingredients lure "obsessed" fans to this "eco-conscious" fast-casual chainlet famed for its "life-changing" pork-belly banh mi and "impressive vegan selections"; lunch brings "lines out the door", but the staff "keeps things moving" and "could they be any friendlier?"

	FOOD	DECOR	SERVICE	COST

Mercado *Mexican* 24 | 22 | 23 | $39

Santa Monica | 1416 Fourth St. (Santa Monica Blvd.) | 310-526-7121 | www.mercadosantamonica.com

This "upbeat, trendy" sibling of Yxta Cocina in Santa Monica offers a "high-end" Mexican menu with "creative twists"; it's all served in a "noisy" whitewashed space with high ceilings, long, distressed wood tables and a bar pouring more than 70 tequilas for its "tasty margs."

Mercato di Vetro *Italian* ∇ 22 | 22 | 21 | $53

West Hollywood | 9077 Santa Monica Blvd. (Doheny Dr.) | 310-859-8369 | www.sbe.com

This "hip" Italian from Sam Nazarian's SBE Group brings a taste of la dolce vita to West Hollywood with a moderately priced Italian menu including pizzas and vino-friendly nibbles served to a "beautiful" crowd at a counter surrounding the antipasti bar or at polished wood tables; it's a total "scene", so "go early or take earplugs" if you want to avoid the din; P.S. there's also a mercato where you can buy oils, pastas and more.

NEW **MessHall Kitchen** ◐ *American* ∇ 21 | 23 | 19 | $37

Los Feliz | 4500 Los Feliz Blvd. (Hillhurst Ave.) | 323-660-6377 | www.messhallkitchen.com

This storied Los Feliz address (it was a branch of The Brown Derby) is now home to this "fun, trendy" gastrotavern offering American fare with molecular touches and avant-garde cocktails; the modern-day mess-hall setting features long tables, a separate bar area and a domed beamed ceiling held over from when the roof was shaped like a derby hat.

Miceli's *Italian* 18 | 20 | 20 | $28

Hollywood | 1646 N. Las Palmas Ave. (Hollywood Blvd.) | 323-466-3438
Universal City | 3655 Cahuenga Blvd. W. (Regal Pl.) | 323-851-3344
www.micelisrestaurant.com

"The singing waiters are a kick" at this "corny", "old-school" Hollywood haunt and its Universal City sib slinging "saucy", inexpensive Italiana and "gooey" pizzas in "dark", moody digs that "would make Tony Soprano and his gang very comfortable"; those who are "not super-thrilled" about the menu or service say it lives off its "novelty", while defenders insist "a glass of wine will make the food more than tolerable."

Michael's on Naples Ristorante *Italian* 27 | 24 | 26 | $58

Long Beach | 5620 E. Second St. (bet. Ravenna & Tivoli Drs.) | 562-439-7080 | www.michaelsonnaples.com

Helmed by "ever-present" owner Michael Dene, this upscale Long Beach "gem" "deserves the accolades" for its "excellent", "genuine" Italian cuisine and "top-notch" wine list, served by a "charming", "professional" staff; a "sophisticated" setting with "rooftop dining" and live music also help make it an "amazing destination restaurant"; P.S. the tasting menus are "well worth the price."

Michael's Pizzeria *Pizza* 27 | 21 | 25 | $25

NEW **Long Beach** | 210 E. Third St. (bet. Long Beach Blvd. & Pine Ave.) | 562-491-2100
Long Beach | 5616 E. Second St. (Ravenna Dr.) | 562-987-4000 | www.michaelspizzeria.com

An offshoot of the venerable Michael's on Naples, this "fabulous" Long Beach pizzeria duo loads up its "heavenly", "authentic" Neapolitan pies with "fresh", homemade mozz, plus more "creative" items like clams, egg and baby artichokes; given "excellent service" and "modest prices", the "simple", "noisy" settings are easily excused.

Michael's Restaurant 🅂 *Californian* 24 | 25 | 25 | $68

Santa Monica | 1147 Third St. (bet. California Ave. & Wilshire Blvd.) | 310-451-0843 | www.michaelssantamonica.com

This longtime "icon" of Californian cuisine in Santa Monica "hasn't lost its touch", still impressing well-heeled guests with "sensational" seasonal cooking from Michael McCarty and "exquisite", "professional" service offered in an art-filled dining room or on a "transporting" patio ("one of the most beautiful on the Westside"); indeed, fans say it can be "quite expensive", but "still very good for a special evening."

Mijares Mexican Restaurant *Mexican* 18 | 15 | 19 | $22

Pasadena | 145 Palmetto Dr. (bet. Herr Alley & Pasadena Ave.) | 626-792-2763

Pasadena | 1806 E. Washington Blvd. (Allen Ave.) | 626-794-6674

www.mijaresrestaurant.com

This family-owned "Pasadena staple" has been serving "satisfying" Mexican standards and "fabulous" margaritas "for generations" in a festive indoor-outdoor milieu with "roaming mariachis"; it's a "friendly", "old-school" place, the kind "your dad expected", with a smaller offshoot in East Pasadena that's convenient for takeout.

Mike & Anne's 🄼 *American* 21 | 18 | 19 | $34

South Pasadena | 1040 Mission St. (Fairview Ave.) | 626-799-7199 | www.mikeandannes.com

Both the "beautiful" twinkle-lit patio overlooking a garden and the well-priced New American "classics with a modern touch" are a "breath of fresh air" at this South Pasadena standby that's especially "enjoyable" on "warm summer evenings"; perhaps "service can be unreliable and curt when it gets busy", but on the whole it's a "nice, neighborhood spot."

Milk *Sandwiches* 23 | 14 | 17 | $15

Mid-City | 7290 Beverly Blvd. (Poinsettia Pl.) | 323-939-6455 | www.themilkshop.com

The name says it all at this pint-sized purveyor of "melty" milky treats in Mid-City, where "fabulous shakes" and "amazing" ice creams share menu space with less-acclaimed sandwiches and other "decent" quick-bite fare at moderate cost; the setting and service aren't much to speak of, but "there are a handful of tables and some outdoor seating perfect for a sunny day."

Milky Way *Californian/Kosher* ▽ 20 | 20 | 24 | $30

Pico-Robertson | 9108 W. Pico Blvd. (bet. Doheny & Oakhurst Drs.) | 310-859-0004

"Chatty" owner Leah Adler (aka Steven Spielberg's mom) "greets you at the door" of this "lovely, little" Pico-Robertson Cal-kosher putting out dairy "comfort food" "at its finest" like blintzes, salads and pastas; a few find the eats "unremarkable", but the "welcoming" service, "homey", "comfortable" ambiance and prices deemed "very reasonable by LA standards" mean "you'll leave satisfied."

	FOOD	DECOR	SERVICE	COST

Milo & Olive *American* 24 16 19 $31

Santa Monica | 2723 Wilshire Blvd. (Harvard St.) | 310-453-6776 | www.miloandolive.com

"Wonderful" wood-fired pizzas, "finely crafted" small plates and "unbelievable baked goods" draw "lines out the door" of this "sleek" Santa Monica New American (sibling of Huckleberry and Rustic Canyon); the "crazy-small" space can get "noisy", and while some like to "socialize" at the communal tables, others find it "better for takeout."

Mi Piace ◐ *Californian/Italian* 21 19 18 $33

Pasadena | 25 E. Colorado Blvd. (bet. Fair Oaks & Raymond Aves.) | 626-795-3131 | www.mipiace.com

This "classy" Californian-Italian in Old Town Pasadena is a find for an "excellent variety" of "crave-worthy carbs" (for instance, their standout bread basket and gnocchi), plus other "tasty" fare served in a "modern" setting completed with stellar "people-watching" from the patio; true, service is "hit-or-miss" and "the tables are so close together you can partake in your neighbors conversation", but "value" prices compensate.

The Misfit ◐ *Eclectic* 22 23 20 $34

Santa Monica | 225 Santa Monica Blvd. (bet. 2nd & 4th Sts.) | 310-656-9800 | www.themisfitrestaurant.com

This "cool" Santa Monica gastropub resembling "a high-end library" is a "fun" place to graze on Eclectic small plates ("a little of this, a little of that") with "expertly mixed" cocktails to wash it all down; factor in "fair prices" and "prompt" service, and consensus is it's a "great addition to the neighborhood"; P.S. the "free chocolate chip cookies with sea salt are the perfect ending."

Mistral *French* 26 22 26 $54

Sherman Oaks | 13422 Ventura Blvd. (bet. Dixie Canyon & Greenbush Aves.) | 818-981-6650 | www.mistralrestaurant.net

"If you want to be taken care of", admirers tout this "hidden gem" in Sherman Oaks, where a "charming" staff delivers "outstanding" French bistro fare and a "pretty darn good" wine list amid "elegant" environs featuring chandeliers and a circa-1920s bar; some find it "pricey", but most deem it one of "the best" around for "special occasions."

Mo-Chica ◐ ⊠ *Peruvian* 23 16 18 $42

Downtown | 514 W. Seventh St. (bet. Grand Ave. & Olive St.) | 213-622-3744 | www.mo-chica.com

Fans want to go "mo-often" to this midpriced Downtowner on Seventh Street's Restaurant Row, where Ricardo Zarate (Picca, Paiche) creates his "modern takes on Peruvian food" with "lots of unique small plates to mix up"; the servers "know the menu inside and out", and "well-done" cocktails help fuel a "happening" vibe ("noisy" to some).

Modo Mio Cucina Rustica *Italian* 23 20 24 $38

Pacific Palisades | Pacific Palisades Commercial Vill. | 15200 W. Sunset Blvd. (La Cruz Dr.) | 310-459-0979 | www.modomiocucinarustica.com

A "solid" bet in Pacific Palisades, this "inviting" trattoria dishes out "moderately priced", "hearty" Italian in "warm" white-tablecloth environs; with "wonderful", "professional service" and a "relaxing" vibe, it's no wonder some call it the "perfect neighborhood restaurant."

	FOOD	DECOR	SERVICE	COST

Mohawk Bend ◐ *Eclectic* 21 24 19 $27

Echo Park | 2141 W. Sunset Blvd. (bet. Alvarado & Mohawk Sts.) | 213-483-2337 | www.mohawk.la

"Vegans and carnivores coexist" at this "hip" Echo Park gastropub spotlighting "inventive", well-priced Eclectic plates, plus an "unparalleled" beer selection (the "knowledgeable staff" knows its brews too); it's situated in a "magnificent" "beautifully converted" movie theater with worn brick walls and a spacious patio with an immense fireplace making for a "charming" milieu for "hanging out", day or night.

Momed *Mediterranean* 20 14 18 $25

Beverly Hills | 233 S. Beverly Dr. (bet. Charleville Blvd. & Gregory Way) | 310-270-4444 | www.atmomed.com

The name of this Bev Hills marketplace and deli is short for 'modern Mediterranean', and diners dig the "updated", "fresh", "healthy" takes on the standards like dips, meze and wraps served up "fast"; given such "great value", the all-white environs are frequently "crowded" - luckily it's also "good for takeout."

Monsieur Marcel *French* 20 16 18 $31

Fairfax | Farmers Mkt. | 6333 W. Third St. (Fairfax Ave.) | 323-939-7792

NEW **Beverly Hills** | 447 N. Canon Dr. (Santa Monica Blvd.) | 310 274 7300

Santa Monica | Third St. Promenade | 1260 Third St. Promenade (bet. Arizona Ave. & Wilshire Blvd.) | 310-587-1166

www.mrmarcel.com

"A taste of the Left Bank" can be found at these "pleasant" "cozy bistros" where locals linger over "simple" French fare and "nicely priced wines"; added perks are "prompt service" and "great people-watching" at all branches.

Monsoon Cafe ◐ *Asian* 20 23 21 $30

Santa Monica | Third St. Promenade | 1212 Third St. Promenade (bet. Arizona Ave. & Wilshire Blvd.) | 310-576-9996 | www.globaldiningca.com

"See and be seen" at this "date"-worthy Pan-Asian on The Promenade in Santa Monica with a massive space decked out like a "colonial mansion" with semi-private booths and serving a "broad", "dependable" array of eats and "exotic" cocktails; service is "hit-or-miss", but pricing's affordable and it boasts one of "the sexiest happy hours in town."

Moonshadows ◐ *American* 20 24 20 $45

Malibu | 20356 PCH (bet. Big Rock Dr. & Las Flores Canyon Rd.) | 310-456-3010 | www.moonshadowsmalibu.com

"Bring a ring - the answer will be yes" insist admirers of this ultra-"romantic" Malibu New American perched over the Pacific and offering "stunning views"; given such an "amazing" setting, many find the "pricey" food to be "an afterthought", but sipping "strong drinks" on the tiki-themed patio is always "a delight."

Morels French Steakhouse & Bistro *French/Steak* 20 22 21 $53

Fairfax | The Grove | 189 The Grove Dr. (bet. Beverly Blvd. & 3rd St.) | 323-965-9595 | www.mcchgroup.com

Bringing moules marinière and filet mignon to the masses is this pricey French steakhouse and bistro in The Grove offering "good"

FOOD	DECOR	SERVICE	COST

eats, an upscale setting and some mighty-fine "people-watching" from the outdoor patio on ground level and balcony up above; some call the food and service "hit-and-miss", although a chef change may remedy that.

More Than Waffles *American* 22 | 14 | 21 | $16

Encino | 17200 Ventura Blvd. (bet. Louise & Oak Park Aves.) | 818-789-5937 | www.morethanwaffles.com

"Light, crisp" Belgian waffles are "served a gazillion ways" at this "bang-for-the-buck" breakfast entry in Encino also offering "terrific" omelets and other American daytime fare that fans happily "scarf down"; it's "jammed on weekends", but staffers "try hard to please", and there's often even free coffee while you wait.

Mori Sushi ⊠ *Japanese* 27 | 17 | 24 | $86

West LA | 11500 W. Pico Blvd. (Gateway Blvd.) | 310-479-3939

The omakase is "incredible" at this "high-quality, traditional" West LA Japanese that wows with "delicate, delectable sushi" crafted with specially grown rice and served by an "efficient, courteous" crew on handcrafted ceramics; a few find prices "out of line" with the "understated", "casual" surroundings, but the majority insists "it's an experience that you won't soon forget."

NEW **The Morrison** ◐ *Pub Food/Scottish* - | - | - | I

Atwater Village | 3179 Los Feliz Blvd. (Glenfeliz Blvd.) | 323-667-1839 | www.themorrisonla.com

This cozy, reasonably priced Atwater Village public house isn't just another gastropub - it's a Scottish gastropub, which means an affordable menu of Northland specialties that include deep-fried Scotch eggs meat pies, all chased down with many beers, and many, many scotches; it's all served in a low-lit atmospheric setting with family crests on the walls.

Morton's The Steakhouse *Steak* 22 | 21 | 22 | $73

Downtown | Seventh and Fig | 735 S. Figueroa St. (bet. 7th & 8th Sts.) | 213-553-4566

Beverly Hills | 435 S. La Cienega Blvd. (Colgate Ave.) | 310-246-1501

Burbank | The Pinnacle | 3400 W. Olive Ave. (Lima St.) | 818-238-0424

Woodland Hills | Warner Ctr. | 6250 Canoga Ave. (bet. Erwin St. & Victory Blvd.) | 818-703-7272

www.mortons.com

This iconic, "spendy" chophouse chain caters to a "special-occasion" crowd with "high-quality" steaks, "delightful martinis" and "personal" service in "dark", "clubby" digs with a "dressed-up" vibe; while some lament "it's not quite the same" since a 2012 ownership change, others recommend it for an "elegant evening."

Mo's *American* 18 | 14 | 19 | $22

Burbank | 4301 Riverside Dr. (Rose St.) | 818-845-3009 | www.eatatmos.com

Burbank's answer to "*Cheers*" is this "friendly" American with its "inexpensive" array of "comforting" fare that's "dependable", even if it "won't set the world on fire"; the setting's "plain", and "dark", but it's a nexus for "media moguls' power breakfasts" nonetheless.

FOOD | DECOR | SERVICE | COST

Mosto Enoteca *Italian* ▽ 24 | 16 | 22 | $49

Venice | Marina Connection | 517 Washington Blvd. (Via Marina) | 310-821-3035 | www.mostoenoteca.com

A "real sleeper" "hidden" in a Venice strip mall, this "fine" dinner-only Italian is a find for "genuine" "handmade pastas like grandma would make" to go with an impressive wine list; it can be "expensive", but pays off with "polished" service and a "romantic" vibe.

Mozza to Go *Pizza* 26 | 16 | 20 | $34

West Hollywood | 6610 Melrose Ave. (Highland Ave.) | 323-297-1130 | www.mozza2go.com

Pizzeria Mozza's "fabulous" take-out sibling in West Hollywood offers the same "innovative" pizza "favorites" as the namesake along with its famous "wow"-worthy butterscotch pudding; it's a "great way to treat yourself" to the "amazing flavors" on a relative budget, and "you don't have to wait" or snag a reservation, but if you get it to go, good luck "making it home without sampling during the drive."

Mr. Chow *Chinese* 23 | 21 | 22 | $73

Beverly Hills | 344 N. Camden Dr. (bet. Brighton & Dayton Ways) | 310-278-9911 ◐

NEW **Malibu** | Malibu Country Mart | 3835 Cross Creek Rd. (Civic Center Way) | 310-456-7600

www.mrchow.com

It's "celebrity-spotting central" at this "hip", "legendary" Beverly Hills Chinese, a "high-energy" haunt ("an elegant zoo") where both stars and "normal folks" tuck into "refined" fare served in a "chic" black-and-white setting graced with original Warhols; fans call it a "must-go at least once" just to "see what the hullabaloo is all about", although many find both the "super-high" prices and the "snooty" service a little "over the top"; P.S. the Malibu branch is newer and set in a trendy shopping mall.

M Street Kitchen *American* 21 | 18 | 19 | $26

Santa Monica | 2000 N. Main St. (Bicknell Ave.) | 310-396-9145 | www.mstreetkitchen.com

This "vibrant" neighborhood American in Santa Monica dishes up a "fine, but not memorable" "comfort-food" menu morning, noon and night; "affordable" tabs, a "laid-back" staff and a pet-friendly patio keep it "buzzing" with a "great vibe."

NEW **Muddy Leek** Ⓢ Ⓜ *American/French* - | - | - | M

Culver City | 8631 Washington Blvd. (Sherbourne Dr.) | 310-838-2281 | www.muddyleek.com

This moderately priced, market-driven French-New American from the husband-and-wife Bon Melange catering team adds to the Culver City culinary explosion with a menu heavy on charcuterie and braised meats and an extensive wine list, all served in an airy, wood-paneled quasi-industrial space.

Mulberry Street Pizzeria *Pizza* 23 | 12 | 18 | $16

Beverly Hills | 240 S. Beverly Dr. (bet. Charleville Blvd. & Gregory Way) | 310-247-8100

Beverly Hills | 347 N. Canon Dr. (bet. Brighton & Dayton Ways) | 310-247-8998

(continued)

(continued)

Mulberry Street Pizzeria

Encino | 17040 Ventura Blvd. (Oak Park Ave.) | 818-906-8881
Sherman Oaks | 15136 Ventura Blvd. (bet. Columbus & Noble Aves.) | 818-784-8880
NEW **Thousand Oaks** | 1655 E. Thousand Oaks Blvd. (Erbes Rd.) | 805-379-3191
www.mulberrypizzeria.com

For "real-deal" New York pizza, it's hard to beat this "no-frills" Italian chain offering "monstrously huge" slices and pies with "crispy crusts and chewy, stretchy cheese" served in "nothing-fancy" digs with "copies of the *NY Post* laying around"; with "appropriate attitude" from the counter staff, it "feels like you're back in the city" - "fold your slice in half and *mangia.*"

Musashi *Japanese* 23 | 19 | 22 | $28

Northridge | 9046 Tampa Ave. (Nordhoff St.) | 818-701-7041 | www.musashirestaurant.com

This Northridge Japanese is "well rounded" to say the least, offering "fresh" sushi, tempura-laden platters and "fun" communal teppanyaki tables with meats cooked up "Benihana"-style right before your eyes; the casual, "comfortable" setting can be "quiet" or "boisterous" depending on the crowd, but "friendly" service and "reasonable prices" are constants.

Musha *Japanese* 23 | 14 | 19 | $35

Santa Monica | 424 Wilshire Blvd. (bet. 4th Ct. & 5th St.) | 310-576-6330 ◐
Torrance | 1725 W. Carson St. (Western Ave.) | 310-787-7344

"Innovative and different", this "small-plates Japanese" duo is "fun for groups" with an "adventurous" array of well-priced dishes ("you can't go without trying the risotto served in a Parmesan wheel the size of a table drum"); expect "cheerful service" and a "noisy", "vibrant" atmosphere that "feels like you're in Tokyo."

Musso & Frank Grill ⊠ M *American* 22 | 22 | 22 | $45

Hollywood | 6667 Hollywood Blvd. (bet. Cherokee & Las Palmas Aves.) | 323-467-7788 | www.mussoandfrankgrill.com

"Old Hollywood is alive and well" at this "charming" former literary haunt - Hollywood's oldest restaurant - where "miraculous martinis" and "simple", "well-executed" American standards are still "served by waiters in red jackets"; dark booths, wood-paneled walls and murals of English hunting scenes add to "the feeling that the ghosts of Raymond Chandler and Charlie Chaplin are not very far" away.

Nanbankan *Japanese* 27 | 16 | 23 | $36

West LA | 11330 Santa Monica Blvd. (Corinth Ave.) | 310-478-1591

A "fantastic find" for "skewer cooking over a real charcoal grill", this "tiny" West LA Japanese offers "little robata bites so tasty and reasonable, you can graze through many dishes and come away with change in your pocket"; the "welcoming" chefs "foster a party atmosphere" (it's also a "total date-night spot"), so "sit at the counter and make some new friends."

FOOD | DECOR | SERVICE | COST

Napa Valley Grille *Californian* 19 | 22 | 20 | $42

Westwood | 1100 Glendon Ave. (Lindbrook Dr.) | 310-824-3322 | www.napavalleygrille.com

It's like a road trip to "wine country" at this "sophisticated", "yuppie" Westwood mainstay offering "an aging but appealing" Cal menu incorporating "fresh, local produce" and "great wines (no surprise)"; the mood is conducive to "quiet conversation" and service is "attentive" too, although some find it "a tad overpriced" for food that's "dependable, but nothing too exciting."

Natalee Thai *Thai* 20 | 16 | 18 | $23

Beverly Hills | 998 S. Robertson Blvd. (Olympic Blvd.) | 310-855-9380

Palms | 10101 Venice Blvd. (Clarington Ave.) | 310-202-7003

www.nataleethai.com

This "sleek" Thai twosome in Beverly Hills and Palms provides "spicy", "well-prepared" dishes along with cocktails in "fun", "noisy" environs deemed "upscale" for the genre, although at fairly "reasonable" prices; it's often "bustling" and servers move the "crowds" quickly, however, some customers complain about the "hurried" pace

Nate 'n Al *Deli* 21 | 12 | 18 | $26

Beverly Hills | 414 N. Beverly Dr. (bet. Brighton Way & Santa Monica Blvd.) | 310-274-0101

LAX | LA Int'l Airport, Terminal 2 | 209 World Way (Sepulveda Blvd.) | 310-646-4680 ◐

www.natenal.com

"Showbiz" "old-timers hold court" at this "busy, buzzy" Beverly Hills "institution" (with a satellite in LAX), a source for "deli the way it should be", including "primo breakfasts", delivered by "surly" servers; "occasional celebrity sightings add to the fun", and while a few feel it's "showing its age", others point out you don't stick around since 1945 "unless you deliver the goods."

Native Foods Café *Vegan* 22 | 15 | 20 | $16

Culver City | 9343 Culver Blvd. (Canfield Ave.) | 310-559-3601

Santa Monica | 2901 Ocean Park Blvd. (bet. 29th & 30th Sts.) | 310-450-3666

Westwood | Westwood Vill. | 1114 Gayley Ave. (Wilshire Blvd.) | 310-209-1055

www.nativefoods.com

"Heaven for vegans" and anyone "looking for healthy, tasty" dining, this popular Californian-Eclectic chain "satisfies" its many fans with "big" portions of dishes that "mimic the flavors of meat"; the casual settings may not impress, but "cheery" service and affordable prices compensate.

Nawab of India *Indian* 22 | 16 | 20 | $31

Santa Monica | 1621 Wilshire Blvd. (bet. 16th & 17th Sts.) | 310-829-1106 | www.nawabindia.com

A "favorite curry house" of many, this Santa Monica Indian "standby" lures locals with "fresh", "fabulous" masalas and vindaloos that vary in heat "from mild to wow"; some find it a little "expensive" for the genre, but service is "amiable", the space is relatively "elegant" and the "bargain" weekday lunch buffet is "hard to beat."

FOOD | DECOR | SERVICE | COST

Neptune's Net 🅂🄼 *Seafood* 19 | 11 | 13 | $22

Malibu | 42505 PCH (Yerba Buena Rd.) | 310-457-3095 | www.neptunesnet.com

"Jammed on weekends", this "funky" Malibu fish shack on PCH is beloved for its "fresh" seafood matched with "beers galore" and "views of the surf"; it can be "tough to get a seat" at one of the picnic tables, though it remains a "favorite" for everyone "from bikers to ranchers to lawyers."

Newport Seafood *Chinese/Seafood* 26 | 17 | 18 | $34

Rowland Heights | 18441 Colima Rd. (bet. Batson & Jellick Aves.) | 626-839-1239

San Gabriel | 518 W. Las Tunas Dr. (Santa Anita St.) | 626-289-5998

www.newportseafood.com

"The house special lobster is the dish to get" at this midpriced Chinese duo moored in San Gabriel and Rowland Heights incorporating Vietnamese, Cambodian and Thai influences into its "excellent" menu; "massive crowds" "are the only downside", but "service is prompt" once you're seated and the settings are "tasteful" too; P.S. "bring a large group so you can try as many dishes as possible."

Newsroom Café *Vegetarian* 17 | 14 | 16 | $23

West Hollywood | 120 N. Robertson Blvd. (bet. Alden Dr. & Beverly Blvd.) | 310-652-4444 | www.thenewsroomcafe.com

For "healthy, inventive" vegetarian and organic fare, many venture out to this "lively" West Hollywood cafe set in a "cute", casual setting; stellar "people-watching" and "value" prices are perks.

Next Door by Josie 🄼 *American* 24 | 20 | 21 | $35

Santa Monica | 2420 Pico Blvd. (25th St.) | 310-581-4201 | www.nextdoorbyjosie.com

"Craft cocktails and delicious bites, both large and small", await at this "wonderful" "pocketbook-friendly" "side-car" to the upscale Josie's in Santa Monica; expect "innovative" American fare in a more "casual" gastropub with a "welcoming" vibe - just know it's often "noisy"; P.S. "the duck banh mi is mind-blowing."

Nick & Stef's Steakhouse *Steak* 23 | 21 | 23 | $62

Downtown | Wells Fargo Ctr. | 330 S. Hope St. (bet. 3rd & 4th Sts.) | 213-680-0330 | www.patinagroup.com

"They know their steak" at this "luxurious" Downtown chophouse from the Patina Group known for its "top-notch" beef dry-aged in an "impressive glass-ensconced meat locker" and a "prompt" staff accustomed to "client lunches" and curtain calls (there's a free shuttle to the Music Center); many are "enamored" with the "elegant" vibe, less so the "à la carte" pricing.

Nickel Diner 🄼 *Diner* 21 | 16 | 19 | $20

Downtown | 524 S. Main St. (bet. 5th & 6th Sts.) | 213-623-8301 | www.nickeldiner.com

The "decadent" desserts - like housemade bacon-maple donuts - inspire "OMGs" at this "affordable" Downtown diner offering "clever twists" on American "comfort food" in a "tiny" vintage-inspired setting on the edge of Skid Row; the "staff's a little quirky", but that's part of the charm.

	FOOD	DECOR	SERVICE	COST

Nic's ◐ ☒ *American* | 22 | 21 | 22 | $46

Beverly Hills | 453 N. Canon Dr. (bet. Brighton Way & Santa Monica Blvd.) | 310-550-5707 | www.nicsbeverlyhills.com

"An unending list of vodkas" keeps the mood "fun" - especially for those who don "faux fur to brave the VodBox" (a walk-in exhibition freezer) - at this Beverly Hills boîte offering a "solid" New American menu; with "warm" hospitality and a "classy" vibe, many find it "expensive", but well "worth the price", and there's also a "superior" happy hour with deals on martinis, wines and small plates.

Night + Market Ⓜ *Thai* ▽ 25 | 14 | 19 | $37

West Hollywood | 9041 W. Sunset Blvd. (bet. Doheny & Wetherly Drs.) | 310-275-9724 | www.nightmarketla.com

This well-priced offshoot of Talésai in West Hollywood spotlights chef Kris Yenbamroong's "interesting" takes on Thai street food with meaty eats like fried pig's tails and housemade Isaan sausages, with the spice turned way up; bottles of beer and ice cream sandwiches with sticky rice for dessert cool things down.

NEW Nikita *Italian/Mediterranean* - | - | - | E

Malibu | 22716 PCH (Sweetwater Canyon Dr.) | 310-456-3274 | www.nikitarestaurants.com

This Malibu entry from Larry Ellison (the CEO of Oracle) is all about the view, with floor-to-ceiling windows overlooking the Pacific in an otherwise understated room of painted brick and polished wood; the kitchen turns out pricey Med-Italian dishes for the fast-lane crowd from the adjacent Malibu Colony and other 'bu enclaves.

9021Pho *Vietnamese* 21 | 17 | 19 | $21

Beverly Hills | 490 N. Beverly Dr. (Santa Monica Blvd.) | 310-275-5277

NEW Glendale | Glendale Galleria | 1164 Glendale Galleria Way (B'way) | 818-551-9021

NEW Sherman Oaks | Westfield Fashion Square Mall | 14006 Riverside Dr. (Woodman Ave.) | 818-728-9021

Westlake Village | 30990 Russell Ranch Rd. (Lindero Canyon Rd.) | 818-597-1902

www.9021pho.com

To "satisfy pho cravings" try this "quick"-bite mini-chain offering "comforting" soups and other Vietnamese eats at "cheap" rates; some say it's "not very authentic", but it's a "solid bet "if you can't drive to the San Gabriel Valley."

Nine Thirty *American* ▽ 16 | 21 | 19 | $49

Westwood | W Los Angeles Westwood | 930 Hilgard Ave. (bet. Le Conte & Weyburn Aves.) | 310-443-8211 | www.ninethirtyw.com

The sleek, Asian-inspired dining room is "beautiful" and there's "picturesque outdoor dining" by the pool at this modern American in the W Hotel Westwood; unfortunately, some find the "upscale" fare "not fabulous", although "gooeylicious" desserts can compensate.

N/Naka ☒ Ⓜ *Japanese* 27 | 22 | 27 | $148

Palms | 3455 S. Overland Ave. (Palms Blvd.) | 310-836-6252 | www.n-naka.com

This omakase-only, ultrapricey Japanese on an industrial strip of Overland Avenue presents "perfectly crafted", "fascinating" feasts

FOOD | DECOR | SERVICE | COST

deemed "a delightful extravagance"; at the helm is Niki Nakayama - one of LA's few female Japanese chef - who uses "fabulous" ingredients, including veggies from the restaurant's garden, and oversees attentive service in the modern setting, making it an absolute "must for foodies."

Nobu Los Angeles *Japanese* 26 | 24 | 23 | $84

West Hollywood | 903 N. La Cienega Blvd. (bet. Santa Monica Blvd. & Sherwood Dr.) | 310-657-5711 | www.noburestaurants.com

"After all these years" "it's hard to top" the "exceptional" Peruvian-accented delicacies and "top-grade", "melt-in-your-mouth" sushi and sashimi from Nobu Matsuhisa at this West Hollywood Japanese where the "cutting-edge" David Rockwell-designed dining rooms are "swarming with elegant people", celebs and "wanna-be-seens"; service is "professional", but just know you're "paying a premium for the name."

Nobu Malibu *Japanese* 27 | 24 | 24 | $84

Malibu | 22706 PCH (Sweetwater Canyon Dr.) | 310-317-9140 | www.noburestaurants.com

"Simply outstanding" sums up Nobu Matsuhisa's Malibu Japanese featuring "amazing" sushi and "innovative" Peruvian-influenced plates served by a "fantastic" staff in a "lovely" oceanside setting; factor in a patio filled with "gorgeous patrons" including a smattering of celebs and fans say "if your wallet can handle it", it "never disappoints."

Noe *American* 22 | 23 | 23 | $57

Downtown | Omni Los Angeles Hotel | 251 S. Olive St. (bet. 2nd & 4th Sts.) | 213-356-4100 | www.noerestaurant.com

"Surprisingly good for a hotel restaurant" is the finding on this "pleasant pre-theater" stop in the Omni Downtown, where pricey New American fare is "creatively prepared" with Japanese flourishes in a "quiet, contemporary setting" adorned with "tasteful art"; it earns extra "points for being an overachiever" with a "lovely staff" and an "excellent late-night bar."

Nong La Cafe M *Vietnamese* - | - | - | I

West LA | 2055 Sawtelle Blvd. (Mississippi Ave.) | 310-268-1881 | www.nonglacafe.com

Adding to the Asian mix on Sawtelle Boulevard, this Vietnamese entry offers a menu built around Saigon favorites like hot steaming bowls of pho and chunky banh mi sandwiches; it's all served in a casually stylish space with reclaimed wood tables and chairs.

Nonna *Italian* ▽ 23 | 20 | 23 | $52

West Hollywood | 9255 W. Sunset Blvd. (bet. Doheny & Sierra Drs.) | 310-270-4455 | www.nonnaofitaly.com

"A restaurant for grown-ups", this "warm", "beautiful" West Hollywood trattoria puts out "excellent" "classical" Italian cuisine, including "crispy-crust" pizzas, with a menu "varied enough to inspire repeat dining"; it's not inexpensive, but service is "welcoming", there's pleasant sidewalk seating and it's often "easy to get a table" too.

Nook Bistro *American* 24 | 18 | 23 | $35

West LA | Plaza West | 11628 Santa Monica Blvd. (bet. Barry & Federal Aves.) | 310-207-5160 | www.nookbistro.com

"Hidden away in a strip mall", this West LA "gem" is "well worth the search" thanks to "wholesome", "delicious" American cooking that puts "interesting" eclectic "twists on old classics"; a "well-curated wine selection" and "attentive servers" make for a near-"perfect neighborhood spot", with a "minimal", "noisy" space as the only setback.

Noshi Sushi *Japanese* 23 | 13 | 19 | $29

Koreatown | 4430 Beverly Blvd. (bet. Harvard & Hobart Aves.) | 323-469-3458 | www.noshisushila.com

In a "highly unlikely Koreatown location" dwells this "popular" Japanese "delivering better-than-expected" sushi and sashimi for a "reasonable price"; there are "no fancy rolls", just "large portions" of "basic", "quality fish" that come out "fast" and furious in no-frills digs - for sushi-philes, "it's one of the best values in town."

NEW Nozawa Bar *Japanese* - | - | - | VE

Beverly Hills | 212 N. Canon Dr. (bet. Clifton & Dayton Ways) | 310-276-6900 | www.sugarfishsushi.com

Hidden in the back of Sugarfish Beverly Hills, this 10-seat private room brings back the 'trust me' policies of the now-closed Sushi Nozawa, with a daily 20-course omakase priced at around $150 for dinner; the fare is served in a spare, understated room reminiscent of the high-end eateries in office buildings in Tokyo.

Nyala Ethiopian *Ethiopian* 23 | 17 | 20 | $23

Mid-Wilshire | 1076 S. Fairfax Ave. (bet. Olympic Blvd. & Whitworth Dr.) | 323-936-5918 | www.nyala-la.com

"Terrific Ethiopian food" awaits at this "festive" art-filled find, in Mid-Wilshire's Little Ethiopia, known for its stews, which patrons scoop up using "excellent" injera bread; "gracious" service and "reasonable prices" also help explain why it's one of "the best in town", and "a great place for the uninitiated" to get an introduction to the cuisine.

Obikà *Italian* 21 | 17 | 19 | $32

Beverly Boulevard | Beverly Ctr. | 8500 Beverly Blvd. (San Vicente Blvd.) | 310-652-2088

Century City | Westfield Century City Shopping Ctr. | 10250 Santa Monica Blvd. (Ave. of the Stars) | 310-556-2452

www.obika.it

"You can't go wrong with a menu based on cheese" say formaggio fans who frequent this Italian duo for its "tender, fresh" mozzarella and meats "flown in from Italy", along with "simple" pizza, panini and pasta; with "courteous" service and mod decor, it's an "interesting concept" for a mall even if some call it a tad "expensive" for a "shopping break."

Ocean & Vine *Californian* ▽ 23 | 24 | 21 | $52

Santa Monica | Loews Santa Monica Beach Hotel | 1700 Ocean Ave. (Pacific Terr.) | 310-576-3180 | www.santamonicaloewshotel.com

"What a view!" exclaim fans of this oceanside restaurant in the Loews Santa Monica Beach Hotel, where the "elegant" setting also boasts a "beautiful" patio with fire pits; mix in "personal" service and "nuanced" Cal cuisine, and fans find it's "worth" the relatively high cost.

Ocean Seafood Restaurant *Chinese/Seafood* 21 | 14 | 17 | $25

Chinatown | 750 N. Hill St. (bet. Alpine & Ord Sts.) | 213-687-3088 | www.oceansf.com

"Quality" dim sum is the "favorite" attraction at this Chinatown Chinese, where "roving carts" navigate the "huge dining room" dispensing "endless choices" including "fresh" seafood specials; the atmosphere borders on "nonexistent", but it's a "popular" spot to "go in a group."

Ocean Star *Chinese* 21 | 14 | 17 | $24

Monterey Park | 145 N. Atlantic Blvd. (bet. Emerson & Garvey Aves.) | 626-308-2128 | www.oceanstarrestaurant.com

"Much cheaper than flying to Hong Kong", this "cavernous" second-floor Chinese woos Monterey Park dim sum devotees with an "impressive" "variety" of cart-borne morsels; the banquet-hall space is "always busy", so beware of "waits on the weekends."

Ocean Tava *Indian* ∇ 25 | 21 | 22 | $23

Redondo Beach | 1212 S. PCH (Ave. E) | 310-540-2240 | www.oceantava.com

Redondo Beach locals are all aglow about the "incredible" flavors at this "fantastic, neighborhood" Indian, where the "reasonably priced" dishes can be tailored "to the degree of spiciness that you want"; servers who "take care of their guests", patio seating with ocean views plus a bargain lunch buffet more than make up for the strip-mall location.

NEW Ocho 8 Taqueria & Tequila House *Mexican* - | - | - | M

Torrance | Del Amo Fashion Ctr. | 21424 Hawthorne Blvd. (Del Amo Circle) | 310-802-7960 | www.ochotaqueria.com

Adding to the burgeoning culinary scene at the sprawling Del Amo Fashion Center in Torrance's South Bay, this midpriced Mexican offers 63 tequilas to wash down a range of tacos, ceviches and entrees; the lively space is often more party than restaurant, with bright colors and loads of tables lending a never-ending fiesta effect.

Off Vine *Californian* 22 | 22 | 23 | $38

Hollywood | 6263 Leland Way (bet. El Centro Ave. & Vine St.) | 323-962-1900 | www.offvine.com

You might almost "forget you're in the heart of Hollywood" as you sit on the "charming" front porch of this "adorable" Craftsman cottage dispensing "homey" Cal-American cuisine with "gourmet" touches; "efficient, friendly servers" and "surprisingly reasonable prices" (including an "affordable" wine list) make it "perfect for pre- or post-ArcLight" dates; it's also "marvelous for brunch."

The Oinkster *BBQ* 21 | 12 | 15 | $15

Eagle Rock | 2005 Colorado Blvd. (Shearin Ave.) | 323-255-6465 | www.theoinkster.com

"Pastrami that can't be beat" and pulled pork fill the "gut-bustin' sandwiches" offered along with "mouthwatering" burgers, "perfectly crispy" fries and craft brews at Andre Guerrero's "cheap" Eagle Rock outlet for Americana; an oldfangled fast-fooder with a "nice patio", it's "always busy" with "hipsters" who deem the eating "worth the long lines."

Old Tony's ◐ *Italian/Seafood* 20 | 19 | 20 | $34

Redondo Beach | 210 Fishermans Wharf (International Boardwalk) | 310-374-1442 | www.oldtonys.com

"Old-school Redondo Beach" lives on at this "friendly" Italian seafooder that's been reeling 'em in since 1952 with "famous mai tais" and "generous" plates offered against a backdrop of "beautiful" ocean views; with weekend music, late hours and "reasonable" tabs, "you gotta love it."

	FOOD	DECOR	SERVICE	COST

Olio Pizzeria & Cafe *Italian* 23 | 13 | 18 | $21

Third Street | 8075 W. Third St. (Crescent Heights Blvd.) | 323-930-9490 | www.pizzeriaolio.com

Chef-owner Bradford Kent "seemingly slaves over each individual pie" at this rustic "little" Italian on Third Street where the "incredible pizzas" coming out of the wood-burning oven are made with "only the freshest in-season ingredients"; service can be "spotty", and with only a few seats inside and out, many "opt for takeout."

Oliva *Italian* 20 | 17 | 19 | $33

Sherman Oaks | 4449 Van Nuys Blvd. (bet. Hortense & Moorpark Sts.) | 818-789-4490 | www.olivarestaurant.com

They "treat you like *famiglia*" at this Sherman Oaks local "full of happy people" tucking into "solid" pastas, risotto and Northern Italian specialties ("a well-stocked bar" helps the mood too); it boasts a muraled dining room and "value" pricing that keeps it "packed every night."

Olive & Thyme Café Market ☒ *Eclectic* 22 | 21 | 18 | $22

Burbank | 4013 Riverside Dr. (Pass Ave.) | 818-557-1560 | www.oliveandthyme.com

"A rare stylish treat" in "chain-happy Burbank", this "cute", "high-end" cafe and market brings "delightful" Eclectic fare like sandwiches, salads, "amazing cheeses" and other "temptations" - plus Intelligentsia coffee - to a "media" crowd; the whitewashed setting stocked with gourmet goodies can feel "cramped", but many get it to go.

Oliverio *Italian* ∇ 25 | 24 | 24 | $45

Beverly Hills | Avalon Hotel | 9400 W. Olympic Blvd. (Beverly Dr.) | 310-277-5221 | www.avalonbeverlyhills.com

"Poolside dining" is de rigueur at this "retro-cool" Italian in the Avalon Hotel, where the design by Kelly Wearstler evokes "Miami minus the humidity"; it serves an "excellent" menu and "amazing drinks" that taste extra "fabulous" if you're lucky enough to dine in one of the cabanas.

Ombra Ristorante ☒ *Italian* 21 | 15 | 21 | $45

Studio City | 3737 Cahuenga Blvd. (bet. Lankershim Blvd. & Regal Pl.) | 818-985-7337 | www.ombrala.com

This Venetian Italian in Studio City turns out "delicious, distinctive" specialties - including standout pastas - at moderate prices in "lively", "casual" digs; a handful finds the fare "overrated", but service is "charming" and the low corkage fee "is a plus", so on the whole, it's "satisfying."

101 Coffee Shop ◐ *Diner* 22 | 20 | 21 | $19

Hollywood | 6145 Franklin Ave. (Vista Del Mar Ave.) | 323-467-1175 | www.the101coffeeshop.com

"Diner kitsch in its highest form" serves as a "hipster", "celebrity" and "tourist" magnet at this "late-night" Hollywood hang that dishes up plentiful portions of "spot-on" American coffee-shop eats, plus some "mean" java and "amazing" milkshakes at "fair prices"; an "enthusiastic" staff keeps it "vibrant", so it's "always hopping" whether curing "hangovers" in the morning or "getting them started" in the first place.

	FOOD	DECOR	SERVICE	COST

101 Noodle Express *Chinese*

23	16	19	$16

Culver City | Westfield Culver City | 6000 Sepulveda Blvd. (Slauson Ave.) | 310-397-2060
Arcadia | 1025 S. Baldwin Ave. (bet. Arcadia & Fairview Aves.) | 626-446-8855 ◐≠
Alhambra | 1408 E. Valley Blvd. (bet. New Ave. & Vega St.) | 626-300-8654 ◐≠
www.101noodleexpress.com

Fans "love" these late-night "mall surprises" in Arcadia, Alhambra and Culver City featuring "top-notch" dumplings and a "must-try" beef roll (like a "Chinese burrito"), "full of meaty goodness"; prices are "cheap", but with "no-frills service and digs they're "best for a quick bite."

One Pico *Mediterranean*

23	25	24	$58

Santa Monica | Shutters on the Beach | 1 Pico Blvd. (Ocean Ave.) | 310-587-1717 | www.shuttersonthebeach.com

"Stunning views over the ocean" qualify this Santa Monica hotel dining room as "one of the top places for taking visitors", and the Med menu is quite "tasty" too; with a "classy, but not stuffy", setting perfect for "lingering" and "attentive" service, most don't mind a little "overspending"; P.S. it's also "excellent" for Sunday brunch.

On Rodeo *Californian/French*

-	-	-	M

Beverly Hills | Luxe Rodeo Dr. Hotel | 360 N. Rodeo Dr. (bet. Santa Monica & Wilshire Blvds.) | 310-273-0300 | www.luxerodeo.com

Set in the Luxe Rodeo Drive Hotel, this stylish, midpriced bistro with a mixology-focused bar attracts gaggles of ladies who lunch post-shopping on Cal-French cuisine; the room is understated but elegant, with soft lighting, muffled sounds and lots of heads turning to see what famous face just walked through the door.

Open Sesame *Lebanese*

24	19	20	$24

Long Beach | 5201 E. Second St. (Nieto Ave.) | 562-621-1698
Long Beach | 5215 E. Second St. (bet. Corona & Nieto Aves.) | 562-621-1698
Manhattan Beach | 2640 N. Sepulveda Blvd. (bet. Marine Ave. & 27th St.) | 310-545-1600
www.opensesamegrill.com

"Always crowded", but "ohhhh the food" rave Med mavens who devour "perfectly prepared kebabs", "wonderful" signature fried potatoes and other "fairly priced" "garlic-infused" Lebanese eats at this bargain trio with a "cute name"; the "funky" setups with murals and throw pillows are a "welcome change" for fast-casual, as is "helpful, courteous" service.

Original Pantry Cafe ◐≠ *Diner*

18	11	18	$20

Downtown | 877 S. Figueroa St. (9th St.) | 213-972-9279 | www.pantrycafe.com

"Feel like you're in a Raymond Chandler story" at this circa-1924 Downtown "greasy spoon" owned by former mayor Richard Riordan, a 24/7 chance to savor "large portions" of "good ol' diner food", a "cheap cup of coffee and all the characters" in attendance, servers included; as the "de rigueur" lines suggest, it's "the real thing"; P.S. cash only.

	FOOD	DECOR	SERVICE	COST

The Original Tops *American* ▽ 22 | 9 | 16 | $12

Pasadena | 3838 E. Colorado Blvd. (Merlon Ave.) | 626-449-4412 | www.theoriginaltops.com

A Pasadena mainstay since 1952, this affordable spot slings "great, greasy-spoon" Americana in "hearty" helpings; the vibrant, fast-casual setup is a true throwback with "polite" service and a drive-thru window.

Ortega 120 *Mexican* 22 | 19 | 18 | $28

Redondo Beach | 1814 S. PCH (bet. Palos Verdes Blvd. & Prospect Ave.) | 310-792-4120 | www.ortega120.com

"Elegant, authentic Mexican" cuisine keeps customers coming to this "modern" Redondo Beach cantina famed for its "creative" "twists" on tradition like duck confit chilaquiles; the art-filled digs are "loud and busy", the service "spotty" and the bill might set you back, but most agree the "incredible" margaritas will ease the pain.

NEW Osek Korean M *Korean* - | - | - | M

Pasadena | 67 N. Raymond Ave. (bet. Holly & Union Sts.) | 626-644-1299 | www.osekpasadena.com

At this upscale Korean BBQ on Old Town Pasadena's culinarily diverse Raymond Avenue the cooking is done in the kitchen rather than at the table; everything is served with the requisite army of small dishes, and lots of beers and soju.

Osteria Drago *Italian* ▽ 22 | 17 | 21 | $66

West Hollywood | 8741 W. Sunset Blvd. (Holloway Dr.) | 310-657-1182 | www.osteriadrago.com

The ubiquitous Drago brothers hit the Sunset Strip with this pricey modern Italian, whose flashy menu matches the celeb-heavy crowd clustered inside; the "lovely" sun-washed space boasts floor-to-ceiling windows, wainscoting on the ceiling and Milanese pottery in nooks on the wall, while an "expert" staff caps things off.

Osteria La Buca M *Italian* 22 | 19 | 20 | $42

Hollywood | 5210 Melrose Ave. (Wilton Pl.) | 323-462-1900 | www.osterialabuca.com

Devotees "dream about the carbonara" and other "comfort food" "made with love" at this "charming" Hollywood Italian that's "affordable" too; despite some ownership changes over the years, it's frequently "crowded" with a "nice, neighborhood" feel and fittingly affable service.

Osteria Latini *Italian* 25 | 20 | 23 | $47

Brentwood | 11712 San Vicente Blvd. (bet. Barrington & Gorham Aves.) | 310-826-9222 | www.osterialatini.com

Despite "heavy competition" in Brentwood, admirers insist this "gem" is still "the Italian that Italians go to" for "amazing", "authentic" fare and "charming" hospitality from "attentive" owner Paolo Pasio; if you mind "tight" quarters and "eavesdropping" on your neighbors, "better to go during the week" when it's less crowded.

Osteria Mamma *Italian* 24 | 17 | 22 | $38

Hollywood | 5732 Melrose Ave. (Lucerne Blvd.) | 323-284-7060 | www.osteriamamma.com

"Mamma Loredana puts a lot of love" into her "fantastic, homemade" fare at this "true" Italian trattoria in Hollywood where the gnocchi, pastas and other "heavenly" treats are some of "the best this side of Napoli"; perhaps the modest decor "leaves a bit to be desired", but "everyone's treated like family" and moderate prices seal the deal.

Osteria Mozza *Italian* 27 23 23 $67

Hollywood | 6602 Melrose Ave. (Highland Ave.) | 323-297-0100 | www.osteriamozza.com

"Melt-in-your-mouth" pastas and a "to-die-for" mozzarella bar "speak volumes" about the "extraordinary" eating at this "high-end" Hollywood Italian from powerhouse pair Nancy Silverton and Mario Batali; "knowledgeable" servers tend to a "celebrity clientele" that packs the "elegant" space, and one bite of burrata ("wow!") will render the "deafening" noise and "huge prices" "worth it."

Outpost ◐ *American* - - - I

Hollywood | 1624 N. Cahuenga Blvd. (Hollywood Blvd.) | 323-464-7678 | www.outposthollywood.com

This Western-themed gastropub offers a menu of $10-and-under options like pulled pork sandwiches and oversized burgers, served by girls-next-door in Daisy Dukes; the atmosphere is pure Hollywood kitsch, with longhorn skulls, saddles and TV screens on the walls, and there's a massive wooden bar issuing giant cocktails served in glass boots.

Pace *Italian* 23 24 23 $49

Laurel Canyon | 2100 Laurel Canyon Blvd. (Kirkwood Dr.) | 323-654-8583 | www.peaceinthecanyon.com

"Tucked up in the hills" of Laurel Canyon, this "super-cute" Italian pulls a "beautiful crowd" for "excellent" Italian pizzas and pastas with an organic bent served in a "romantic", twinkle-lit setting with "atmosphere to spare"; though some grumble it's a little "pricey", service is "attentive" and it's a "great date spot if you want to get cozy."

Pacific Dining Car ◐ *Steak* 24 22 24 $60

Downtown | 1310 W. Sixth St. (Witmer St.) | 213-483-6000
Santa Monica | 2700 Wilshire Blvd. (Princeton St.) | 310-453-4000
www.pacificdiningcar.com

A well-known 24/7 "standby" for "a power breakfast" or a "properly done" "steak at 2 AM", this "old-fashioned" chophouse duo in Downtown and Santa Monica "will never go out of style" thanks to their "excellent" food, "clubby" dining-car decor, "generous" cocktails and "professional" service; just be aware that "you're going to pay for it."

Paco's Tacos *Mexican* 21 15 19 $21

Mar Vista | 4141 S. Centinela Ave. (bet. Louise Ave. & Washington Blvd.) | 310-391-9616
Westchester | 6212 W. Manchester Ave. (bet. Sepulveda Blvd. & Truxton Ave.) | 310-645-8692
www.pacoscantina.com

"Heavenly, buttery tortillas made by a cute *abuela*" add a "special" touch to the otherwise "solid" eats at this affordable Mexican duo in Mar Vista and Westchester also appreciated for its "pretty-darn-good margaritas"; it follows through with "efficient" service and an atmosphere that "feels like Cinco de Mayo" - just know "there's always a wait."

	FOOD	DECOR	SERVICE	COST

Padri ◐ *Italian* | 22 | 23 | 21 | $40

Agoura Hills | 29002 Agoura Rd. (Cornell Rd.) | 818-865-3700 | www.padrirestaurant.net

"Charming" Tuscan farmhouse decor creates a "romantic" mood at this midpriced Italian in Agoura Hills where an "attentive" staff proffers "authentic", "homestyle" fare (osso buco is a standout) in the "cozy" interior or out on the patio; although it's "quiet" early on, the adjoining martini bar hosts live music and "the Friday night scene is great spectator sport."

NEW Paiche ◐ *Japanese/Peruvian* | - | - | - | M

Marina del Rey | 13488 Maxella Ave. (Del Rey Ave.) | 310-893-6100 | www.paichela.com

Nouvelle Peruvian icon Ricardo Zarate (Mo-Chica, Picca) continues his streak with this Peruvian izakaya in the Marina, serving small dishes that blend the flavors of Peru and Japan plus a pisco-, rum- and tequila-heavy cocktail list; the stylish space is designed to reflect the nearby Pacific, with oceanic themes on every surface.

Palermo *Italian* | 22 | 20 | 24 | $23

Los Feliz | 1858 N. Vermont Ave. (bet. Franklin & Russell Aves.) | 323-663-1178 | www.palermorestaurant.net

"Go right for the pizza, baby" and the "incredible garlic bread" at this "unfussy", "old-world" Los Feliz Italian boasting "hearty" red-sauce feasts and "one of the friendliest owners in the SoCal area"; "it's as much about the atmosphere as it is the food", and the "cheap prices" don't hurt either.

The Palm *Steak* | 23 | 20 | 22 | $70

Downtown | 1100 S. Flower St. (11th St.) | 213-763-4600
West Hollywood | 9001 Santa Monica Blvd. (bet. Doheny Dr. & San Vicente Blvd.) | 310-550-8811
www.thepalm.com

"A classic", this "convivial", "old-fashioned" chophouse chain - aka "home of the giant lobsters" - impresses guests with "excellent" surf 'n' turf and "perfect martinis" served in a setting chock-full of "character"; service is "top-notch" too, so even if "it can get pricey fast", you "always leave feeling like a million bucks."

Palmeri *Italian* | 25 | 22 | 24 | $51

Brentwood | 11650 San Vicente Blvd. (bet. Barrington & Darlington Aves.) | 310-442-8446 | www.palmeriristorante.com

A "foodie haven" on "Brentwood's Italian row", this "excellent, neighborhood" ristorante is beloved for "talented" chef Ottavio Palmeri's "original", "fabulous" Sicilian-influenced recipes like "wonderful" salt-crusted branzino; "warm, welcoming" service "makes the cost worth it", so the only drawback is that it's "a bit noisy on a crowded Saturday night."

Palmilla Cocina y Tequila *Mexican* | ▽ 18 | 22 | 18 | $35

Hermosa Beach | 39 Pier Ave. (Beach Dr.) | 310-374-4440 | www.palmillarestaurant.com

This "upscale" Hermosa Beach Mexican offers "unique" regional specialties like carnitas Michoacán, camarones Veracruz and Baja-style fish in a bar-intensive space that claims one of the largest tequila collections in town; the eccentric setting features lamps that cast a mysterious glow, walls of pebbled glass and exotic swirly plasterwork on the walls.

Palms Thai ◐ *Thai* 21 | 14 | 19 | $19

East Hollywood | 5900 Hollywood Blvd. (Bronson Ave.) | 323-462-5073 | www.palmsthai.com

Karaoke and Thai food come together at this "late-night" East Hollywood mainstay for "delectable" "authentic" eats with some "wild" offerings like deer with peppercorns; service is "fast, but not terribly attentive" and the "simple" setup lends it "a get-in-and-get-out feel" - that said, the "prices can't be beat."

Palomino *American* 20 | 20 | 20 | $37

Westwood | 10877 Wilshire Blvd. (Glendon Ave.) | 310-208-1960 | www.palomino.com

The "happening" bar scene and "all-day happy hours" are the main draws at this Westwood New American whose more "relaxed, elegant" dining room is also a "go-to for business lunches" and pre-theater dinners thanks to servers who "understand tight schedules"; some say you're "paying more for mood than the food", although the Med-influenced menu is "very good" too.

Panda Inn *Chinese* 22 | 19 | 21 | $26

Pasadena | 3488 E. Foothill Blvd. (bet. Halstead St. & Rosemead Blvd.) | 626-793-7300

Glendale | 111 E. Wilson Ave. (bet. Brand Blvd. & Maryland Ave.) | 818-502-1234

Universal City | Universal Studios | 1000 Universal City Plaza (Hollywood Frwy.) | 818-487-6889

www.pandainn.com

"It may be Americanized Chinese, but it still hits the mark" swear habitués of these upscale progenitors of Panda Express presenting "well-prepared" Mandarin cuisine like honey-walnut shrimp and other "recipes lost in time from the 1970s"; if the red-and-orange-hued setting is "comfortable but not memorable", at least service is "polite" and "prices won't break the bank" either.

Panini Cafe *Italian/Mediterranean* 21 | 16 | 20 | $21

Downtown | 600 W. Ninth St. (bet. Flower & Hope Sts.) | 213-489-4200

NEW **West Hollywood** | 8054 W. Third St. (Crescent Heights Blvd.) | 323-951-1900

Beverly Hills | 9601 Santa Monica Blvd. (Camden Dr.) | 310-247-8300

Westwood | 10861 Lindbrook Dr. (bet. Glendon & Tverton Aves.) | 310-443-2100

Woodland Hills | 21600 Victory Blvd. (Owensmouth Ave.) | 818-992-3330

www.mypaninicafe.com

"Value"-seekers rely on this "casual" all-day Italian-Med chain for "fresh", "filling" and "plentiful" kebab platters, salads, wraps and "tasty" panini; the settings are nothing fancy, but service is usually "friendly" and it's "great for takeout" too.

Panzanella *Italian* 25 | 22 | 24 | $52

Sherman Oaks | 14928 Ventura Blvd. (bet. Sepulveda & Van Nuys Blvds.) | 818-784-4400 | www.giacominodrago.com

"It's one of the Drago brothers' restaurants, so you can't go wrong" assert admirers of this "high-end" Sherman Oaks Italian built around a "wonderful" selection of "traditional" Sicilian dishes and wines; "excellent service" and a setting suited to "special occasions" (including an "intimate wine cellar") make it easy to take the "expensive" tabs.

Papa Cristo's 🅼 *Greek* 22 | 12 | 18 | $20

Mid-City | 2771 W. Pico Blvd. (Normandie Ave.) | 323-737-2970 | www.papacristos.com

"The mother lode of Greek authenticity", this "quirky" Mid-City Hellenic market and eatery has been going strong for 65 years with "generous" servings of "simple" fare served off disposable plates and lots of "delicacies" available to go; it "looks like a hole-in-the-wall, but has a lot of charm and character" (Papa himself "can often be seen roaming the tables"), while already "affordable" pricing is enhanced by live bouzouki Thursdays-Sundays.

Paradise Cove *American/Seafood* 18 | 21 | 19 | $33

Malibu | 28128 PCH (Paradise Cove Rd.) | 310-457-2503 | www.paradisecovemalibu.com

"Even Matthew McConaughey-spotters need to eat" joke patrons of this surfside Malibu seafooder by Gladstone's founder Bob Morris set on a "fantastic" stretch of beachfront real estate; expect "enormous portions" of "elevated bar food" and fruity drinks, and even if some call the service "inconsistent" and the fare "mediocre and overpriced", "where else can you dig your toes in the sand and eat?"

The Parish ◐ *British* ▽ 22 | 21 | 18 | $44

Downtown | 840 S. Spring St. (Main St.) | 213-225-2400 | www.theparishla.com

Casey Lane (Tasting Kitchen) is behind this "happening" British-accented gastropub on Downtown's Gallery Row serving "impressive" midpriced fare and house-cured meats, plus a food-friendly beer and cocktail menu; the airy space features exposed ductwork, polished wood and ornate wallpaper.

The Parish Wine Bar ◐ *American* - | - | - | M

Downtown | 840 S. Spring St. (bet. Main & 9th Sts.) | 213-225-2400 | www.theparishla.com

What was a small cafe for overflow from the main dining room at The Parish has been turned into a stylish wine bar with an extensive selection of little known vintages, along with small dishes to match (at prices that can add up); the candlelit space is intimate, romantic and conveniently located near the Staples Center and Nokia Arena.

The Park *American* ▽ 25 | 15 | 22 | $29

Echo Park | 1400 W. Sunset Blvd. (Douglas St.) | 213-482-9209 | www.thepark1400sunset.com

A "neighborhood" mainstay with "lots of personality", this Echo Park eatery is a "go-to" for "inventive" Americana - plus $5 burgers on Wednesdays - in a simple bistro setting; add in "reasonable" prices and "inviting" hospitality, and insiders insist "once you find it, you'll be back."

Parkers' Lighthouse *Seafood* 22 | 24 | 22 | $39

Long Beach | 435 Shoreline Village Dr. (Shoreline Dr.) | 562-432-6500 | www.parkerslighthouse.com

"You won't find a better view" in Long Beach say fans of this seafooder overlooking the Queen Mary and the harbor, where "excellent" surf 'n' turf is set down by "professional" servers; a few find it "too expensive for what you get", but "the location can't be beat", especially at happy hour.

Park's Barbeque ◐ *Korean* 25 | 14 | 19 | $38

Koreatown | 955 S. Vermont Ave. (bet. Olympic Blvd. & San Marino St.) | 213-380-1717 | www.parksbbq.com

Devotees "dream about the galbi" at this perpetually "packed" K-town grill known for its "premium" BBQ meats (including Wagyu) and "amazing array of banchan" offered in a "slick", "not-too-smoky" setting; yes, it's "one of the more expensive" in the genre, but consensus is it's also "one of the best."

NEW The Park's Finest *BBQ* - | - | - | I

Echo Park | 1267 W. Temple St. (Edgeware Rd.) | 213-481-2800 | www.theparksfinest.com

Filipino-inspired BBQ and craft beers make up most of the menu at this funky Echo Park stop set in bright-red digs; cheap prices and communal tables create an easygoing vibe.

Parkway Grill *Californian* 26 | 25 | 25 | $53

Pasadena | 510 S. Arroyo Pkwy. (bet. California & Del Mar Blvds.) | 626-795-1001 | www.theparkwaygrill.com

Still a "favorite" "after all these years", this "Pasadena mainstay" from the Smith Brothers is admired for its "consistently" "wonderful" Cal cuisine and "gracious hospitality"; its "timeless bistro" look - think fireplaces, paintings and exposed brick - is "suitable for a special occasion" or "an adult evening out", so few protest if tabs run "a bit pricey."

Pastina ☒ *Italian* 23 | 18 | 23 | $39

West LA | 2260 Westwood Blvd. (bet. Olympic & Tennessee Blvds.) | 310-441-4655 | www.pastina.net

Exuding "family-run warmth", this "old-school" "frequent favorite" in West LA offers "excellent" Southern Italian fare - including a nightly prix fixe - at prices that "won't break you"; add in a "quiet", "pleasant" atmosphere and it's "like you're eating in your own dining room", but with "attentive" service and white tablecloths.

Patina Ⓜ *American/Californian* 26 | 26 | 27 | $90

Downtown | Walt Disney Concert Hall | 141 S. Grand Ave. (2nd St.) | 213-972-3331 | www.patinarestaurant.com

"Superb attention to detail" yields "refined dining" that's "near perfection" at this Patina Group headliner from Joachim Splichal tucked into the Walt Disney Concert Hall, where "brilliant" New American-Californian cuisine meets "gracious" service in a "quiet, elegant setting"; the "steep" price tag is equally "exceptional", but for a "sophisticated" "pre-performance" "treat" it's "among LA's finest."

Patrick's Roadhouse *Diner* ▽ 17 | 17 | 17 | $24

Santa Monica | 106 Entrada Dr. (PCH) | 310-459-4544 | www.patricksroadhouse.info

"Pretty good" breakfasts top the menu of "ok" diner food at this "atmospheric" 1970s-era American "right off the beach" in Santa Monica that's known for its "quirky" setup with antiques "hanging from the ceiling" and peek-a-boo ocean view; "don't expect lightning-fast service" or much more than "average" eats - for most "the best thing about it" is the "funky" ambiance.

	FOOD	DECOR	SERVICE	COST

Paul Martin's American Bistro *American* 22 | 22 | 22 | $41

El Segundo | 2361 Rosecrans Ave. (bet. Aviation Blvd. & Douglas St.) | 310-643-9300 | www.paulmartinsamericanbistro.com

"Local" and "organic" are the watchwords at this "pleasant" "eco"-American chain link from Paul Fleming (P.F. Chang's, Fleming's) turning out "fresh" takes on the classics like fish tacos and burgers abetted by California-centric wines, "cozy" Napa-inspired decor and a "welcoming, informative" staff; prices can be a sticking point, but then "sustainability ain't cheap."

Pearl Dragon *Asian* ▽ 20 | 18 | 19 | $36

Pacific Palisades | 15229 W. Sunset Blvd. (bet. Monument St. & Swarthmore Ave.) | 310-459-9790 | www.thepearldragon.com

"Quite the happening bar and grill" in the Palisades, this midpriced Pan-Asian "locals' place" entices with "well-executed" sushi and burgers and "sensational cocktails" in a candlelit setting; since it features "one of the few full bars in the area", it's often busy, so some say "distracted" service and "loud" acoustics come with the territory.

Pecorino *Italian* 24 | 22 | 23 | $52

Brentwood | 11604 San Vicente Blvd. (bet. Darlington & Mayfield Aves.) | 310-571-3800 | www.pecorinorestaurant.com

Flying somewhat "under the radar", this "high-end" eatery wins "neighborhood" hearts with "authentic Italian" fare, a "warm, receptive" staff and a cozy space with exposed brick and a beamed ceiling; its "tiny" dimensions can mean "little privacy" and lots of "noise", but *amici* insist it's "one of the finest" on Brentwood's Italian Row.

The Penthouse *American* 20 | 26 | 20 | $55

Santa Monica | Huntley Santa Monica Beach Hotel | 1111 Second St. (bet. California Ave. & Wilshire Blvd.) | 310-394-5454 | www.thehuntleyhotel.com

"Stunning" ocean views and "eye-poppingly gorgeous" decor - including an outdoor space with luxe white cabanas - attract a "good-looking" crowd to this "expensive" New American perched atop the Huntley Santa Monica Beach Hotel; given the "lively scene", the "artfully presented" cuisine is almost an afterthought; P.S. "brunch away your hangover" on weekends.

NEW The Penthouse at Mastro's ◐ *American* - | - | - | E

Beverly Hills | Mastro's Steakhouse | 246 N. Canon Dr., 3rd fl. (Dayton Way) | 310-888-8782 | www.mastrosrestaurants.com

Situated on the third floor of Mastro's Steakhouse in Beverly Hills, this stylish indoor-outdoor hang includes a casual dining room and spacious outdoor patio with a view of the lights of Cañon Drive and Wilshire Boulevard; expect a menu of smaller American dishes than those served at the steakhouse, plus a selection of sushi and plenty of mixology.

Peppone *Italian* 21 | 19 | 23 | $61

Brentwood | 11628 Barrington Ct. (Barrington Ave.) | 310-476-7379 | www.peppone.com

"Old-school" all the way, this "been-there-forever" Brentwood Italian "hasn't changed" in years, with "authentic", "consistently good" food like osso buco and calf's liver delivered by a "professional" staff that

FOOD | DECOR | SERVICE | COST

coddles the "regulars"; some call it "too expensive and too clubby", although it remains a "favorite of many."

Perch ◐ ☒ *French* 17 | 26 | 18 | $44

Downtown | 448 S. Hill St. (5th St.) | 213-802-1770 | www.perchla.com
"The view's unbeatable" at this "happening" "rooftop aerie" perched "high over Pershing Square", where a "hip after-work crowd" creates a "vibrant" scene stoked by live music and "happy-hour specials"; party-poopers say the French food's "only ok" and service is "spotty", but it's always a "dramatic" site to "grab a quality drink."

Pete's Cafe & Bar ◐ *American* 20 | 19 | 20 | $31

Downtown | 400 S. Main St. (4th St.) | 213-617-1000 | www.petescafe.com
There's a "cool Downtown vibe" at this atmospheric American in LA's historic bank district that "satisfies" with "classic" bites like burgers, "addictive" blue-cheese fries and other "solid" midpriced fare ("keep it simple and you can't go wrong"); it's "popular" thanks to a "comfortable, easy" ambiance that's "not too intimidating or precious", and "even when they're crowded, service isn't rushed"; added perks are a pooch-friendly patio and late-night hours.

Petros *Greek* 24 | 21 | 21 | $47

Manhattan Beach | Metlox Plaza | 451 Manhattan Beach Blvd. (bet. Morningside & Valley Drs.) | 310-545-4100 | www.petrosrestaurant.com
This "fashionable", "upscale" Hellenic in Manhattan Beach "never fails to please" with its "refined", "lighter-style California-Greek" cuisine that's "a cut above" plus "refreshing cocktails" proffered by an "upbeat" staff; it's set in a "cool" Santorini-inspired space, although some loyalists only wish it "weren't so loud."

Petrossian Paris *French* 25 | 21 | 24 | $62

West Hollywood | 321 N. Robertson Blvd. (Rosewood Ave.) | 310-271-0576 | www.petrossian.com
"Fantastic caviar" and flutes of champagne "make the time slip away" at this "wonderfully decadent" West Hollywood boutique offering delicacies to go along with an "enjoyable", abbreviated French menu; the setting's "*très* chic" and servers "try hard to please" - just remember "it's easy to run up the price quickly."

NEW Petty Cash Taqueria *Mexican* - | - | - | M

Beverly Boulevard | 7360 Beverly Blvd. (bet. Fuller & Martel Aves.) | 323-933-5300 | www.pettycashtaqueria.com
Mega-restaurateur Bill Chait has teamed up with chef Walter Manzke and fabled taco king Guillermo 'Oso' Campos at this hot-from-day-one Beverly Boulevard taqueria featuring unusual takes on street food, plus tequila and mezcal cocktails; it's built to look like a down-home eatery from south of the border, with picnic tables, a bar and cool graphic decor touches.

P.F. Chang's China Bistro *Chinese* 17 | 18 | 18 | $31

Beverly Hills | Beverly Ctr. | 121 N. La Cienega Blvd. (bet. Beverly Blvd. & 3rd St.) | 310-854-6467
Santa Monica | 326 Wilshire Blvd. (4th St.) | 310-395-1912
El Segundo | 2041 Rosecrans Ave. (Nash St.) | 310-607-9062
Long Beach | 340 S. Pine Ave. (Shoreline Dr.) | 562-308-1025

(continued)

P.F. Chang's China Bistro

Torrance | Del Amo Fashion Ctr. | 3525 W. Carson St. (bet. Hawthorne Blvd. & Madrona Ave.) | 310-793-0590
Pasadena | Paseo Colorado | 260 E. Colorado Blvd. (bet. Los Robles & Marengo Aves.) | 626-356-9760
Burbank | Burbank Town Ctr. | 201 E. Magnolia Blvd. (bet. 1st & 3rd Sts.) | 818-391-1070
Sherman Oaks | Sherman Oaks Galleria | 15301 Ventura Blvd. (Sepulveda Blvd.) | 818-784-1694
Woodland Hills | Westfield Promenade | 21821 Oxnard St. (bet. Owensmouth Ave. & Topanga Canyon Blvd.) | 818-340-0491
Thousand Oaks | 2250 E. Thousand Oaks Blvd. (Conejo School Rd.) | 805-277-5915
www.pfchangs.com
Additional locations throughout the Los Angeles area

Families swarm to this midpriced Chinese chain that plates "inventive" (some say "Americanized") eats, like its signature lettuce wraps plus gluten-free and vegetarian selections, in an "airy" setting "right out of the movies"; though cantankerous types feel they're "shouting at their dinner partners" and quibble with "commercial" fare and just-"ok" service, it's always "crowded" nonetheless.

Philippe the Original ⊭ *Sandwiches* 23 | 14 | 18 | $14

Chinatown | 1001 N. Alameda St. (Ord St.) | 213-628-3781 | www.philippes.com

Billed as "the originator of the French dip", this 1908-vintage Chinatown "landmark" still turns out "must-try" sandwiches hailed as "national treasures" (hint: "ask for it double dipped"); it's an "unorganized" "mess hall" with "communal tables, sawdust on the floor" and "long lines", but the staffers "work fast" and the "low prices" "take you back in time."

Phillips Bar-B-Que *BBQ* 24 | 6 | 16 | $19

Leimert Park | 4307 Leimert Blvd. (43rd St.) | 323-292-7613 [S]
Mid-City | 2619 Crenshaw Blvd. (Adams Blvd.) | 323-731-4772 [M]
Inglewood | 1517 Centinela Ave. (bet. Beach Ave. & Cedar St.) | 310-412-7135 [S]

"The meat just falls off the rib" at this BBQ mini-chain plying "addictive" 'cue along with "all the trimmings"; the "no-frills" settings are basically for takeout only (with some outdoor seating at the Mid-City locale), but service is "warm" and prices are a solid "value"; P.S. don't miss the signature spicy sauce.

Pho Café ◐⊭ *Vietnamese* ▽ 24 | 14 | 20 | $16

Silver Lake | 2841 W. Sunset Blvd. (Silver Lake Blvd.) | 213-413-0888

"Silver Lake twentysomethings" hunker down over "plentiful" bowls of "hot, steaming" pho at this "hipster" Vietnamese tucked in a "nondescript strip mall"; there's "no sign", but it's "always packed" because it works for a "quick, cheap and delicious" meal; P.S. cash only.

NEW Phorage *Vietnamese* - | - | - | I

Palms | 3300 Overland Ave. (Rose Ave.) | 310-876-0910 | www.phoragela.com

This wallet-friendly modern Vietnamese in Palms is the creation of Perry Cheung, a vet of San Francisco's lauded Slanted Door; the minuscule mini-mall space hosts some of the edgier Asian cooking in town.

	FOOD	DECOR	SERVICE	COST

Pho 79 *Vietnamese* 23 | 12 | 15 | $14

Alhambra | 29 S. Garfield Ave. (bet. Bay State & Main Sts.) | 626-289-0239
The "holy grail of pho" awaits at this Alhambra Vietnamese purveying "satisfying" noodle soups with "rich, flavorful" broth and other "fresh, appealing" South Asian specialties; service is "abrupt" and the setting's "not pretty", but the food's "cheap", so it's "always busy", especially on weekends.

Pho Show ◐ *Vietnamese* ▽ 19 | 13 | 17 | $13

Culver City | 4349 Sepulveda Blvd. (bet. Barman Ave. & Culver Blvd.) | 310-398-5200
NEW **Redondo Beach** | 1617 S. PCH (Ave. I) | 310-792-7800
www.phoshow.net
"Get your pho on" at this "casual" Vietnamese duo in Culver City and Redondo Beach that "satisfies cravings" with "delicious noodles" and other "basic" Pan-Asian eats; "don't expect glamour or first-class service", but the "comfortable" atmosphere makes it a "welcome" stop; P.S. "drinkers rejoice" - they're open till 2 AM most nights.

Pho So 1 *Vietnamese* 25 | 10 | 18 | $12

Gardena | 1749 W. Redondo Beach Blvd. (Western Ave.) | 310-329-7365
Reseda | 7231 Reseda Blvd. (bet. Sherman Way & Wyandotte St.) | 818-996-6515
Van Nuys | 6450 Sepulveda Blvd. (Victory Blvd.) | 818-989-6377
Simi Valley | 2837 Cochran St. (Sycamore Dr.) | 805-306-1868
www.phoso1.com
This no-frills Vietnamese mini-chain "is one of the best" for "wonderful" pho "rich in spices and beefy goodness" served up "quick"; the strip-mall settings aren't fancy, but "generous" portions at "excellent" prices keep locals coming back.

Picanha Churrascaria *Brazilian* 21 | 17 | 21 | $36

Burbank | 269 E. Palm Ave. (3rd St.) | 818-972-2100 | www.picanharestaurant.com
You "have to like meat" to appreciate this Burbank Brazilian where an "awesome variety" of "fantastically filling" rotisserie items are carved tableside by roving waiters who "don't stop serving until you put your stop sign up"; gaucho-themed decor and caipirinhas complete the package, and while some find it too "expensive", others maintain it's "worth it."

Picca ⊠ *Japanese/Peruvian* 25 | 21 | 21 | $54

Century City | 9575 W. Pico Blvd. (Edris Dr.) | 310-277-0133 | www.piccaperu.com
"See and be seen" while sampling "delightful", "adventuresome" Japanese-Peruvian small plates and "awesome" "pisco-based cocktails" via an "attentive" staff at this "energetic" Century City "foodie heaven" from Ricardo Zarate (Mo-Chica); predictably, the "ambitious menu" comes "at a price" and the space gets "super-noisy", though "quieter evenings" can be had upstairs.

Piccolo *Italian* 27 | 23 | 25 | $71

Venice | 5 Dudley Ave. (Speedway) | 310-314-3222 | www.piccolovenice.com
"Journey to Italy" via this "romantic" "jewel" just off Venice beach, where "sublime" Venetian cuisine, "amazing" wines and "smart" ser-

vice make for a "thoroughly delightful" time; yes, it's "pricey", but admirers insist it's also "one of LA's best."

Piccolo Paradiso *Italian* 24 | 19 | 24 | $51

Beverly Hills | 150 S. Beverly Dr. (bet. Charleville & Wilshire Blvds.) | 310-271-0030 | www.giacominodrago.com

"The locals fill the tables night after night" at this neighborhood Italian from Giacomino Drago serving "wonderful" fare in an "unassuming" storefront in Beverly Hills; so maybe it's not cheap, and it can "get noisy on weekends", but "warm" service makes it "always a pleasure."

NEW Pichet S M ⊭ *French* - | - | - | M

Venice | 2805 Abbot Kinney Blvd. (Garfield Ave.) | 424-259-1222

What began as a temporary pop-up in a Venice bakery (B1 Breadshop) has grown into a permanent weekend engagement, serving a small selection of midpriced French classics that change weekly for dinner on Friday and Saturday nights; part of the fun is dining at a handful of tables in a casual, candlelit room dominated by the smell of bread and pastries.

Pico Kosher Deli *Deli* 22 | 10 | 17 | $20

Century City | 8826 W. Pico Blvd. (Robertson Blvd.) | 310-273-9381 | www.pkdla.com

"Delicious" pastrami and corned beef are the specialties at this "old-style" Jewish deli on Pico's Kosher Corridor; perhaps the way-"casual" digs and "gruff" service "leave a lot to be desired", so those in the know opt to "take it home to enjoy."

Pie 'N Burger ⊭ *Diner* 20 | 10 | 19 | $17

Pasadena | 913 E. California Blvd. (bet. Catalina & Lake Aves.) | 626-795-1123 | www.pienburger.com

"What the name says is what you get" at this Pasadena "classic" that's been putting out "juicy" griddled burgers, "heavenly" pies and "superior" shakes and malts since 1963; the decor "hasn't been updated since Jimmy Carter was in office" and service "runs the gamut from accommodating to hostile", but true fans cheer that "it still delivers."

Pig 'n Whistle ◐ *Continental* 18 | 20 | 18 | $24

Hollywood | 6714 Hollywood Blvd. (McCadden Pl.) | 323-463-0000 | www.pignwhistlehollywood.com

There's "lots of character" at this "historic" "old-style Hollywood" pub dating back to 1927 that's "aimed at the tourist crowd"; yet while the "cool, classic" setting has "so much potential", detractors decry the "overpriced", "so-so" Continental fare and "weak drinks", saying "it's sad such an icon isn't better."

The Pikey ◐ *Pub Food* ▽ 18 | 22 | 18 | $37

Hollywood | 7617 W. Sunset Blvd. (Stanley Ave.) | 323-850-5400 | www.thepikeyla.com

Hearty gastropub fare plus inventive cocktails crafted from an extensive list of spirits (absinthe, anyone?) make this "trendy", well-priced Hollywood spot a happy-hour crowd-pleaser; tiled floors, dark wooden booths and "sharp" servers in suspenders add to the authentic English feel.

	FOOD	DECOR	SERVICE	COST

Pink's Famous Hot Dogs ◐⊄ *Hot Dogs* 21 10 17 $12

La Brea | 709 N. La Brea Ave. (bet. Melrose & Waring Aves.) | 323-931-4223 | www.pinkshollywood.com

An "LA treasure", this "iconic" La Brea hot dog shack is well known for its "over-the-top" chili-topped dogs, celebrity sightings and "massive" lines "wrapped around the corner", even at 2 AM; sure, some call it "overrated", but it's practically "mandatory to make at least one trip"; P.S. "have Rolaids ready."

Pink Taco *Mexican* 17 19 17 $26

West Hollywood | 8225 Sunset Blvd. (bet. Marmont Ln. & Roxbury Rd.) | 323-380-7474 ◐

Century City | Westfield Century City Shopping Ctr. | 10250 Santa Monica Blvd. (Century Park) | 310-789-1000

www.pinktaco.com

"Delightfully tacky", these "trendy", "truly LA" stops in Century City and West Hollywood are where an "eye-candy" crowd downs "strong" margaritas in a setting that's "too loud and too dark" for many; as for the food, perhaps "it's not Mexican, but it's edible", and service can be "unenthusiastic", but the "rowdy" happy hour keeps the crowds coming back.

Pitfire Artisan Pizza *Pizza* 22 17 18 $20

Downtown | 108 W. Second St. (Main St.) | 213-808-1200

West Hollywood | 801 N. Fairfax Ave. (Waring Ave.) | 323-544-6240

Culver City | 12924 W. Washington Blvd. (bet. Beethoven St. & Lyceum Ave.) | 424-835-4088

West LA | 2018 Westwood Blvd. (La Grange Ave.) | 310-481-9860

North Hollywood | 5211 Lankershim Blvd. (Magnolia Blvd.) | 818-980-2949

www.pitfirepizza.com

It's "kid central" at this "popular" chainlet specializing in "paper-thin" "crusty-edged" pizzas with "interesting toppings", "delicious" salads and other "market-fresh", "Californiaized" Italian fare brought by an "enthusiastic" staff; an "excellent tap selection" keeps the atmosphere "lively" till late, and there's also a bargain no-corkage policy; P.S. the outdoor fire pit at the North Hollywood locale is a "nice touch."

Pizzeria Mozza ◐ *Pizza* 27 19 22 $40

Hollywood | 641 N. Highland Ave. (bet. Highland & Melrose Aves.) | 323-297-0101 | www.pizzeriamozza.com

"The pizza rocks" at this still-"happening" Hollywood Italian where Mario Batali and Nancy Silverton "do it up right" with "eye-opening" antipasti, "fantastic", thin-crust pies, "delish" wines and a "dreamy butterscotch budino" dessert; you may need to "squeeze" in and overlook "rushed" service, a "noisy" room and "expensive" prices, but for most it's all "worth the hype."

Pizzicotto *Italian* 23 18 22 $35

Brentwood | 11758 San Vicente Blvd. (bet. Gorham & Montana Aves.) | 310-442-7188 | www.pizzicottorestaurant.com

Brentwood locals fill up this "rustic Italian" "neighborhood favorite" offering "simple", "authentic" pastas, pizzas and salads in a "homey" "Tuscan" setting; moderate pricing and "friendly" service make for "crowded" conditions, but "upstairs is more relaxing."

	FOOD	DECOR	SERVICE	COST

Plan Check ◐ *American* — 21 | 16 | 17 | $27

West LA | 1800 Sawtelle Blvd. (Nebraska Ave.) | 310-288-6500 | www.plancheckbar.com

Situated at the north end of West LA's Little Osaka strip, this "hip" New American offers many craft beers, mixology exotica and a casual, well-priced menu with the likes of fried chicken and a Wagyu beef burger complete with their signature ketchup leather; the room features an open truss ceiling and an open kitchen, and there's an outdoor patio in front.

Plate 38 *Eclectic* — 22 | 15 | 18 | $28

Pasadena | 2361 E. Colorado Blvd. (Sierra Madre Blvd.) | 626-793-7100 | www.plate38.com

Surveyors say they're "pleasantly surprised" by the "sophisticated" Eclectic gastropub fare like truffle burgers and fried Cornish game hen coming out of this otherwise "unassuming" Pasadena cafe set in modern-industrial digs with full table service at night; some find the food and hospitality only "so-so", but "great value" compensates.

Polo Lounge ◐ *Californian/Continental* — 22 | 26 | 24 | $62

Beverly Hills | Beverly Hills Hotel & Bungalows | 9641 W. Sunset Blvd. (bet. Crescent Dr. & Hartford Way) | 310-887-2777 | www.beverlyhillshotel.com

"Quintessential Beverly Hills", this art deco "landmark" provides "perfect" celeb-watching in a "classy", "old-style" setting that "makes you want to dress up and be pampered"; the Cal-Continental cuisine is "predictable, but well prepared" and "served with the highest level of professionalism", so even though it's "expensive, expensive, expensive", "who can resist?"; P.S. "the patio is a delight for lunch."

Poquito Más *Mexican* — 21 | 11 | 17 | $13

West Hollywood | 8555 W. Sunset Blvd. (Londonderry Pl.) | 310-652-7008
Santa Monica | 2025 Wilshire Blvd. (bet. 20th & 21st Sts.) | 310-828-1700
West LA | 2215 Westwood Blvd. (Olympic Blvd.) | 310-474-1998
Burbank | 2635 W. Olive Ave. (Naomi St.) | 818-563-2252
Chatsworth | Pacific Theatre Ctr. | 9229 Winnetka Ave. (Prairie St.) | 818-775-1555
NEW **Encino** | 16545 Ventura Blvd. (Hayvenhurst Ave.) | 818-789-9400
North Hollywood | 10651 Magnolia Blvd. (Cartwright Ave.) | 818-994-8226
Sherman Oaks | 13924 Ventura Blvd. (Colbath Ave.) | 818-981-7500
Studio City | Universal City Shopping Vill. | 3701 Cahuenga Blvd. (Regal Pl.) | 818-760-8226 ◐
Woodland Hills | 21049 Ventura Blvd. (Alhama Dr.) | 818-887-2007
www.poquitomas.com

"Freshness rules" at this "relatively healthy" Mex – one of the "best of the gringo-burrito chains" – that also pleases with its "awesome" salsa bar and complimentary tortilla soup on rainy days; the "fast-food" settings are often crammed with "noisy kids", but it makes up for it with "quick" service and "terrific value."

Porta Via *Californian* — 22 | 19 | 22 | $40

Beverly Hills | 424 N. Canon Dr. (bet. Brighton Way & Santa Monica Blvd.) | 310-274-6534 | www.portaviabh.com

A "home away from home" for Beverly Hills locals, this all-day Californian offers "dependable" fare based on organic ingredients, "warm" hospitality and an "understated, elegant" ambiance; the ample patio is a perk, and it remains an "inexpensive alternative to some of the pricier fare" nearby; P.S. picky eaters and dieters rejoice "they accommodate any and all requests."

Portillo's Hot Dogs *Hot Dogs* ∇ 25 | 25 | 24 | $12

Moreno Valley | 12840 Day St. (Gateway Dr.) | 951-653-1000 | www.portillos.com

"Authentic Chicago-style" dogs and "juicy" Italian beef sandwiches bring back "happy memories" for displaced Windy City folks at this chain link in Moreno Valley done up in a "cute", "retro" style evoking the gangster era; the line can get "long", but service is generally "efficient", and the "affordable" pricing makes it family-friendly too.

Porto's Bakery *Bakery/Cuban* 25 | 17 | 20 | $15

Downey | 8233 Firestone Blvd. (bet. Downey & Paramount Aves.) | 562-862-8888

Burbank | 3614 W. Magnolia Blvd. (Hollywood Way) | 818-846-9100

Glendale | 315 N. Brand Blvd. (bet. California Ave. & Lexington Dr.) | 818-956-5996

www.portosbakery.com

"Decadent" cakes, "heavenly" sandwiches and "addictive" cheese rolls make this "legendary" Cuban bakery trio "the closest thing to paradise" for "bargain"-hunting crowds; they're usually "insanely busy", but the "lines move fast" and "the treats waiting at the end make you forget about the wait"; P.S. "you can't leave without at least one potato ball."

Post & Beam *American* ∇ 22 | 20 | 21 | $42

Mid-City | Baldwin Hills Crenshaw Plaza | 3767 Santa Rosalia Dr. (Stocker St.) | 323-299-5599 | www.postandbeamla.com

Dreadlocked chef Govind Armstrong is behind this midpriced American in chain restaurant-heavy Baldwin Hills Crenshaw Plaza featuring "soul food with a modern twist" with an "awesome signature short-rib sandwich" plus pizzas; expect a "cool vibe", a patio for "evening summer hangouts" and a full bar with a small-plates menu that's perfect after work.

Prado *Caribbean* 23 | 18 | 24 | $32

Hancock Park | 244 N. Larchmont Blvd. (Beverly Blvd.) | 323-467-3871 | www.pradola.com

"There's something for everyone" at this "charming" little "mainstay" in Hancock Park offering "tasty, well-prepared" Caribbean-inspired cuisine like crab cakes, corn chowder and combo plates for over 20 years; service is "more than accommodating" and prices are "reasonable", and an appealingly "quiet", "laid-back" dining room seals the deal.

Primitivo Wine Bistro *Mediterranean* 22 | 19 | 21 | $42

Venice | 1025 Abbot Kinney Blvd. (bet. B'way & Westminster Ave.) | 310-396-5353 | www.primitivowinebistro.com

"Taste away" at this "fun" little tapas stop with a "cool Venice vibe" known for its varied Med small plates ("bacon-wrapped dates, anyone?"), "fantastic wine selection" and happy-hour specials; the "dark" digs can be "great for romance", but tables are "so close it's like [you're] eating dinner with the couple at the next table"; P.S. the patio provides extra elbow room.

Prosecco *Italian* 25 | 22 | 23 | $40

Toluca Lake | 10144 Riverside Dr. (bet. Forman & Talofa Aves.) | 818-505-0930 | www.proseccotrattoria.com

"Don't change a thing" plead fans of this Toluca Lake "gem" where "exceptional" Northern Italian fare comes at "moderate" prices; the "cozy" space is often "crowded", but "accommodating" waiters "who fawn over you" compensate, and many find it so "pleasant" "you hate to leave."

Providence *American/Seafood* 28 | 26 | 27 | $124

Hollywood | 5955 Melrose Ave. (Cole Ave.) | 323-460-4170 | www.providencela.com

"Seafood is the star" at this "sophisticated", "upscale" New American in Hollywood helmed by "brilliant" chef Michael Cimarusti who turns out "delectable", "wildly creative" prix fixe feasts in a "minimalist setting" that's an "oasis of tranquility"; add in "warm", "intelligent" service that "treats you like royalty" and "you won't want to leave after your meal"; P.S. "save room for the cheese cart."

P'tit Soleil *Québécois* - | - | - | I

Westwood | 1386 Westwood Blvd. (Wilkins Ave.) | 310-441-5384 | www.soleilwestwood.com

This French-Canadian lounge in Westwood specializes in no less than 10 versions of poutine, the gut-busting Québécois french fry/cheese/gravy favorite; the minimalist space - adjacent to the more formal Soleil - has bare-brick walls, a long zinc bar, and maple leaf and fleur de lis paintings on the walls.

Public Kitchen & Bar *Eclectic* ▽ 20 | 21 | 20 | $48

Hollywood | Roosevelt Hotel | 7000 Hollywood Blvd. (Orange Dr.) | 323-769-8888 | www.thompsonhotels.com

There's a real "vintage feel" at this "hip" midpriced Eclectic - "a welcome oasis" in the middle of "historic, landmark hotel" the Hollywood Roosevelt; expect "tasty" items from chef Tim Goodell like steaks, oysters and interesting bar fare that go well with classic coktails and a "see-and-be-seen" vibe.

NEW Public School 805 ◐ *American* - | - | - | M

Thousand Oaks | 120 N. Promenade Way (Thousand Oaks Blvd.) | 805-379-3909 | www.publicschool805.com

Restaurateur Bob Spivak's midpriced concept offering classic American dishes in a schoolroom setting finds an outpost in the suburbs of the Conejo Valley at this shopping-mall destination; it features fare very much unlike what you'd find in a cafeteria with Irish stout short ribs, a kale Caesar salad and artisanal beers.

NEW Public School 310 ◐ *American* ▽ 18 | 20 | 20 | $32

Culver City | 9411 Culver Blvd. (Main St.) | 310-558-0414 | www.publicschool310.com

"Your school cafeteria was never as hip" as this "hot" bar/restaurant in Downtown Culver City attracting a twentysomething crowd with "creative" American gastropub eats, "clever" decor details (like menus designed like notebooks) and a "hopping" bar scene with an ample patio; with moderate prices, it's a "swell addition" to the area.

	FOOD	DECOR	SERVICE	COST

R+D Kitchen *American* — 22 | 20 | 21 | $34

Santa Monica | 1323 Montana Ave. (bet. Euclid & 14th Sts.) | 310-395-3314 | www.hillstone.com

This "rock-solid" Santa Monica American from the Hillstone restaurant group is "always hopping" with a "good-looking" crowd there for "thick, juicy" burgers, "great salads", "refreshing" cocktails and a "lively" bar scene; a few find the no-reservations policy and subsequent "waits" "maddening", but "professional" service, "excellent value" and a "cool" setting with an open-air feel make up for it.

Racion M *Spanish* — - | - | - | M

Pasadena | 119 W. Green St. (De Lacey Ave.) | 626-396-3090 | www.racionrestaurant.com

This "exciting" entry in a narrow storefront in Pasadena is earning kudos for its well-priced Spanish tapas menu rounded out with authentic Basque specialties; the space is minimal and the vibe informal with a bar that can be used as a stopover for a quick bite and a glass of Txakolina.

Raffi's Place *Mideastern* — 26 | 17 | 19 | $28

Glendale | 211 E. Broadway (Maryland Ave.) | 818-240-7411 | www.raffisplace.com

"The king" of kebabs, this "popular" Glendale Middle Eastern offers "huge" helpings of "perfectly grilled" meats, fish and poultry and "authentic" stews; the landscaped patio offers "great atmosphere", while solid service plus "reasonable" prices ensure it's always "crowded."

Ramen Hayatemaru *Japanese* — - | - | - | I

NEW **West LA** | 11678 W. Olympic Blvd. (Barrington Ave.) | 310-444-7555

Torrance | 1644 W. Carson St. (bet. Harvard Blvd. & Western Ave.) | 310-212-0055

www.hayatemaruusa.com

This South Bay ramen specialist and its West LA offshoot specialize in several kinds of ramen and homemade gyoza; the strip-mall settings aren't much, but the price is right.

Ramen Jinya *Japanese* — 23 | 14 | 17 | $18

Studio City | Studio City Place | 11239 Ventura Blvd. (Arch Dr.) | 818-980-3977 | www.jinya-ramenbar.com

"Acolytes line up" outside this ramen chain link for "rich" "umami-bomb" broth full of "fatty porky goodness", "superb noodles" and Japanese accompaniments ("don't miss the gyoza"); the settings aren't much, but a "friendly" staff and low prices compensate, and most find they "hit the spot" anytime.

Ramenya *Japanese* — 20 | 9 | 18 | $14

West LA | 11555 W. Olympic Blvd. (bet. Colby & Federal Aves.) | 310-575-9337 | www.ramenya-usa.com

"Popular for lunch", this West LA Japanese offers a "wide selection" of "very good" ramen served in bowls so big "you can dunk your head in"; the white-walled setting with fluorescent lighting isn't exactly romantic, but with such "low prices", "you really can't go wrong"; P.S. cash only.

Ramen Yamadaya *Japanese* — 23 | 13 | 17 | $16

Culver City | 11172 Washington Blvd. (Commonwealth Ave.) | 310-815-8776

(continued)

Ramen Yamadaya

Westwood | 1248 Westwood Blvd. (Ashton Ave.) | 310-474-1600
Torrance | 3118 W. 182nd St. (Crenshaw Blvd.) | 310-380-5555 ⊄
Sherman Oaks | 15030 Ventura Blvd. (Noble Ave.) | 818-501-1115
www.ramen-yamadaya.com

"Pure heaven" proclaim ramen junkies who line up for the "unbelievable" "rich" porky broth and "perfect" noodles at this Japanese chain; just ignore the "utilitarian" digs and "erratic" service and focus on the "reasonable" prices; P.S. show a student ID and get extra noodles for free.

Raphael *American* 23 24 19 $56

Studio City | 11616 Ventura Blvd. (Colfax Ave.) | 818-505-3337 | www.raphaelonventura.com

The "Valley's dining cognoscenti" cram in to this Studio City American preparing "exciting", "well-conceived" small plates that pair with "amazing" wines; it features a "gorgeous" (some say "gaudy") interior with a "quiet" vibe making it "well worth a visit", even if a few call it "expensive for the neighborhood."

RA Sushi ◐ *Japanese* ∇ 21 19 20 $24

Torrance | Del Amo Fashion Ctr. | 3525 W. Carson St. (bet. Hawthorne Blvd. & Madrona Ave.) | 310-370-6700 | www.rasushi.com

"Great happy-hour" specials on maki rolls and appetizers are the main draw at this Torrance link in a Japanese chain from Benihana set in "hip" digs deemed "nicer than one would expect in a mall"; however, even with "amazing prices", many find the fare "run-of-the-mill."

The Raymond Ⓜ *Californian* 25 25 25 $51

Pasadena | 1250 S. Fair Oaks Ave. (Columbia St.) | 626-441-3136 | www.theraymond.com

There's "charm all over" this Californian in Pasadena, from the "romantic" Craftsman setting with a patio to the vintage bar; "thoughtfully prepared" steaks and seafood are complemented by "delightful" service making it right for a "special occasion" if you can abide the "high" prices.

Ray's & Stark Bar *Mediterranean* 23 22 20 $49

Mid-Wilshire | LACMA | 5905 Wilshire Blvd. (Fairfax Ave.) | 323-857-6180 | www.patinagroup.com

"A perfect complement" to LACMA, this somewhat "pricey" museum-restaurant "destination" is a find for "ambitious" Med dishes that are "artworks in and of themselves" set down in a "magnificent", "light-filled" setting by a "charming" staff; there's also a "beautiful outdoor lounge" named after the late movie producer Ray Stark that's "great for people-watching" with a "light bite and crazy cocktail."

Real Food Daily *Vegan* 21 16 19 $25

West Hollywood | 414 N. La Cienega Blvd. (Oakwood Ave.) | 310-289-9910
Santa Monica | 514-516 Santa Monica Blvd. (bet. 5th & 6th Sts.) | 310-451-7544
Pasadena | 899 E. Del Mar Blvd. (bet. Lake Ave. & Shoppers Ln.) | 626-844-8900
www.realfood.com

You'll "feel healthier just walking in" to this "vegan paradise", a moderately priced chainlet in Pasadena, Santa Monica and West Hollywood serving a "diverse" lineup of "surprisingly tasty" meat-free eats to a "beautiful" crowd sprinkled with celebrities; the atmosphere's "a tad New-Age-y" for some, and the staff can swing from "super-friendly" to "indifferent", but it's inevitably "packed."

Reddi Chick BBQ ⊄ *BBQ* ▽ 21 | 7 | 16 | $14

Santa Monica | Brentwood Country Mart | 225 26th St. (bet. Brentwood Terr. & San Vicente Blvd.) | 310-393-5238

Westsiders "love sitting around the fire pit and munching on delish chicken" at this "beloved" BBQ "landmark" in the old-fashioned Brentwood Country Mart featuring "finger-licking good" rotisserie birds, "tenders that are actually tender" and "mouthwatering fries"; prices are a bargain, and the setting with umbrella-topped communal tables is "great for young kids and star sightings."

Red Medicine ◐ *Vietnamese* 22 | 17 | 19 | $56

Beverly Hills | 8400 Wilshire Blvd. (Gale Dr.) | 323-651-5500 | www.redmedicinela.com

"Awaken your senses" at this "exciting" Vietnamese fusion in Beverly Hills where chef Jordan Kahn presents "wild, esoteric" dishes that "look like they came straight out of a food magazine"; all comes served against a "simple" backdrop with "amazing" cocktails, although a few take issue with "spotty" service, "noisy" acoustics and a bill that can "add up fast."

Red O *Mexican* 24 | 26 | 22 | $58

Melrose | 8155 Melrose Ave. (Kilkea Dr.) | 323-655-5009 | www.redorestaurant.com

"Haute Mexican" from celebrity chef Rick Bayless draws crowds to this "sexy" Melrose eatery matching "creative" eats to "potent" margaritas made from an "outstanding" tequila selection; it's a lot of "fun", although a few don't get "the hype" or the "high prices."

Reel Inn *Seafood* 22 | 15 | 15 | $25

Malibu | 18661 PCH (Topanga Canyon Blvd.) | 310-456-8221 | www.reelinnmalibu.com

"One of the few classic fish shacks left", this "funky" "favorite" in Malibu proffers "delicious" "fresh seafood" in way-"informal" digs with surf decor and picnic tables out back; the counter service can be hit-or-miss, but many still find it "perfect after a day at the beach."

Restaurant at The Standard ◐ *Eclectic* 18 | 21 | 18 | $45

Downtown | The Standard Downtown LA | 550 S. Flower St. (6th St.) | 213-892-8080

West Hollywood | The Standard West Hollywood | 8300 W. Sunset Blvd. (Sweetzer Ave.) | 323-650-9090

www.standardhotel.com

"Hip food for hip folks" sums up these "cool" 24/7 hotel mainstays at The Standard Downtown and in West Hollywood, where the Eclectic menu of dressed-up comfort fare takes a backseat to the "fun" scene; prices are moderate and service is "pleasant" enough, but no surprise, they get "loud" during peak hours.

Restaurant 2117 Ⓜ *Asian/European* 23 | 15 | 20 | $36

West LA | 2117 Sawtelle Blvd. (bet. Mississippi Ave. & Olympic Blvd.) | 310-477-1617 | www.restaurant2117.com

"Masterful" chef Hideyo Mitsuno fuses European and Asian traditions with "sophisticated", sometimes "spectacular" results according to

FOOD | DECOR | SERVICE | COST

acolytes of this "little-known" West LA "find" that stands out among neighboring "strip-mall noodle shops"; it "won't win any prizes for ambiance" and service can be "inconsistent", but it provides real "value for your dollar" (see the prix fixe) while "surpassing" many of its peers.

NEW Rice Thai Tapas *Thai* | - | - | - | I

Pasadena | 181 E. Glenarm St. (Marengo Ave.) | 626-799-1105 | www.ricethaitapas.com

Located in a mini-mall just off the Pasadena Freeway, this inexpensive Thai serves up both traditional and modern small plates; patrons enter the wood-lined room through a curtain, making a visit here seem a bit like a journey into a hidden culinary world.

Rick's Tavern On Main *American/Pub Food* | ∇ 21 | 18 | 23 | $21

Santa Monica | 2907 Main St. (Ashland Ave.) | 310-392-2772 | www.rtavern.com

This venerable Santa Monica pub is under new ownership, which also means a new look and a new "healthy" menu that includes edamame, crispy Brussels sprouts and veggie sliders; it's all served in a space that's been freshened up with paint and lots more big screens, though the long wooden bar remains.

NEW RivaBella Ristorante *Italian* | ∇ 20 | 27 | 22 | $68

West Hollywood | Sunset Medical Tower | 9201 Sunset Blvd. (Doheny Ave.) | 310-278-2060 | www.innovativedining.com

A "scene", this Sunset Strip Italian affords "abundant star-watching" in a "stunning" space with fireplaces and a "gorgeous" patio; it spotlights a pricey Northern-style menu by Gino Angelini (Angelini Osteria), although some "wish the food would live up to the promise of the room."

Rivera *Pan-Latin* | 26 | 24 | 23 | $62

Downtown | Met Lofts | 1050 S. Flower St. (11th St.) | 213-749-1460 | www.riverarestaurant.com

"A knockout every time", this Downtown Pan-Latin from "genius" chef John Sedlar presents "playful", "high-concept, beautifully executed" dishes that "look like art and taste like heaven" alongside "brilliant" cocktails in a "chic" dining room; service "always pleases" too, and although some complain it "needs to tone down the noise", ultimately it's a "favorite" that's "worth the high prices."

Robin's Woodfire BBQ *BBQ* | 22 | 19 | 18 | $21

Pasadena | 395 N. Rosemead Blvd. (bet. Foothill Blvd. & Sierra Madre Villa Ave.) | 626-351-8885 | www.robinsbbq.com

You can "smell the smoke a block away" at this "down-home" Pasadena BBQer dishing out "heaping" helpings of "fabulous" meats doused in "gooey, sticky" sauce sided with "tangy coleslaw" that's studded with blue cheese; service is "friendly and fast", and weekly specials (kids under 12 eat free after 4 PM some nights) plus a "fun" roadhouse setting make it fit for families.

Rock & Brews *Pub Food* | ∇ 18 | 17 | 19 | $31

El Segundo | 143 Main St. (Grand Ave.) | 310-615-9890

NEW Redondo Beach | 6300 PCH (Vista Del Mar) | 310-378-4970

www.rockandbrews.com

An "awesome place to get a beer on a sunny afternoon", this chain-in-the-making boasts 40-plus tap brews and "great music and rock 'n' roll

FOOD | DECOR | SERVICE | COST

decor"; the American grub "isn't exactly the primary focus", but "tasty" enough to "go perfectly" with the suds.

Röckenwagner Bakery Cafe *Bakery* ∇ 21 | 14 | 18 | $19

Santa Monica | 311 Arizona Ave. (3rd St. Promenade) | 310-394-4267 | www.rockenwagner.com

The "fantastic" pretzel bread gets top billing at Hans Röckenwagner's bakery/cafe on the Third Street Promenade also putting out "cute, little sandwiches", salads, pastries and other well-priced daytime Cal cuisine; expect "helpful" (if "not that friendly") service and a no-nonsense contemporary setting that caters to the grab-and-go crowd.

Rock'n Fish *Seafood* 20 | 18 | 19 | $35

Downtown | LA Live | 800 W. Olympic Blvd. (bet. Figueroa & Georgia Sts.) | 213-748-4020 | www.rocknfishlalive.com

Manhattan Beach | 120 Manhattan Beach Blvd. (Ocean Dr.) | 310-379-9900 | www.rocknfishmb.com

"The navy grog is a must" (warning: "lightweights beware") at these "hip, happening" seafooders known for a "nice variety" of "awesome" "fresh fish" and oak-grilled steaks at a "good value"; regulars report it's "tough to get a seat and kind of noisy", but most are "never disappointed" nonetheless.

RockSugar Pan Asian Kitchen *Asian* 21 | 26 | 22 | $36

Century City | Westfield Century City Center Shopping Ctr. | 10250 Santa Monica Blvd. (bet. Ave. of the Stars & Century Park) | 310-552-9988 | www.rocksugarpanasiankitchen.com

Prepare for "sensory overload" at this Cheesecake Factory offshoot in the Westfield Century City Shopping Center where the "over-the-top", "Asian Disneyland" decor is "a spectacle to behold"; the Pan-Asian fare is "surprisingly good" too, not to mention "perfect for sharing", and it comes "well served" with "fabulous drinks", so even if some say it's "a little on the expensive side", it's still "well worth checking out."

NEW ROC Star *Chinese* - | - | - | I

West LA | 2049 Sawtelle Blvd. (Mississippi Ave.) | 310-235-2089

Adding to the ethnic mix in West LA's Little Osaka is this inexpensive Chinese dumpling and noodle shop; its narrow storefront includes a handful of polished wood tables.

NEW ROFL Cafe *Eclectic* - | - | - | I

Melrose | 7661 Melrose Ave. (Stanley Ave.) | 323-951-1536 | www.roflcafe.com

'ROFL' stands for 'Republic of Laughter' at this cheery Melrose cafe from chef Govind Armstrong, who serves an Eclectic, affordable menu of pizzas and sandwiches plus beer and wine; the walls in the clean-lined space are painted with inspiring words like 'Joy', 'Love' and 'Laughter.'

Roll 'n Rye Deli *Deli* 16 | 12 | 18 | $21

Culver City | Studio Village Shopping Ctr. | 10990 W. Jefferson Blvd. (Sepulveda Blvd.) | 310-390-3497 | www.rollnrye.com

Culver City locals craving "Jewish comfort food" head to this "friendly" "New York-style" deli for "prescription-strength matzo ball soup", "decent" sandwiches and such served in a space that's like "stepping back four or five decades"; critics complain it's "past its prime", plus "at these prices you shouldn't have to ask for more pickles."

FOOD | DECOR | SERVICE | COST

Rosa Mexicano *Mexican* 20 | 21 | 21 | $41

Downtown | LA Live | 800 W. Olympic Blvd. (Figueroa St.) | 213-746-0001
West Hollywood | 8570 W. Sunset Blvd. (Alta Loma Rd.) | 310-657-4991
www.rosamexicano.com

"*Dios mio*", the tableside guacamole is "to die for" and the margaritas are "strong" at these upscale Mexican chain imports from NYC set in "eye-catching" digs in Downtown's LA Live and on the Sunset Strip; consensus is the other fare on the "extensive, creative" menu is "reliable" enough, and while prices are "not so *bueno*" for everyone, "happy hour is justifiably popular and a bargain."

Roscoe's House of Chicken 'n Waffles *Soul Food* 23 | 13 | 19 | $19

Hollywood | 1514 N. Gower St. (bet. Harold Way & Sunset Blvds.) | 323-466-7453 ◐
Mid-City | 106 W. Manchester Ave. (Main St.) | 323-752-6211
Mid-City | 5006 W. Pico Blvd. (Mansfield Ave.) | 323-934-4405 ◐
Long Beach | 730 E. Broadway (bet. Alamitos & Lime Aves.) | 562-437-8355
Pasadena | 830 N. Lake Ave. (bet. Boylston & Mountain Sts.) | 626-791-4890
www.roscoeschickenandwaffles.com

"The perfect blend of salty and sweet" awaits in the "sublime" signature dish at this "legendary" soul-food chain that "sets the standard" matching "succulent" fried chicken with "light, fluffy" waffles for a pairing that "goes together better than peanut butter and jelly"; the "old-school" digs are "not much to look at" and service can be "so-so", but even so, it "doesn't disappoint"; P.S. "prepare for a wait, especially after church on Sundays."

Rose Cafe *Californian* 21 | 19 | 19 | $23

Venice | 220 Rose Ave. (Hampton Dr.) | 310-399-0711 | www.rosecafe.com

Brunch-seekers "just love" the "inviting" patio at this otherwise "unassuming", moderately priced daytime spot that's "just a short walk away from hectic Venice Beach"; it serves a "healthy", "varied" Cal menu via sit-down service as well as "a nice selection of pick-and-choose" deli items available to go.

Rosti Tuscan Kitchen *Italian* 17 | 14 | 18 | $26

Santa Monica | 931 Montana Ave. (10th St.) | 310-393-3236
NEW **Calabasas** | Parkway Calabasas Shopping Ctr. | 23663 Calabasas Rd. (Park Granada) | 818-591-2211
Encino | 16350 Ventura Blvd. (bet. Noeline & Libbit Aves.) | 818-995-7179
www.rostituscankitchen.com

The "*perfecto*" brick-pressed chicken is the standout at this "inexpensive" chainlet specializing in "Americanized" takes on "rustic Italian food" like thin-crust pizzas, grilled salmon and panini; the vibe is "family-friendly", but some find the service and ambiance only "so-so", making it a "go-to for takeout."

NEW **The Royce Wood-Fired Steakhouse** M *Steak* 24 | 27 | 26 | $69

Pasadena | Langham Huntington | 1401 S. Oak Knoll Ave. (Huntington Circle) | 626-585-6410 | www.roycela.com

After several years of modernist cuisine (under Michael Voltaggio and then David Feau) this elegant Pasadena hotel restaurant now spotlights "excellent" steaks and chops, served in a "chic" setting with tall windows overlooking the sprawling gardens of The Langham; note: there's live jazz in the lounge next door, for those who want to make an evening of it.

Roy's *Hawaiian* 23 | 22 | 22 | $48

Downtown | 800 S. Figueroa St. (8th St.) | 213-488-4994
Pasadena | 641 E. Colorado Blvd. (El Molino Ave.) | 626-356-4066
Woodland Hills | 6363 Topanga Canyon Blvd. (Victory Blvd.) | 818-888-4801
www.roysrestaurant.com

Come for the "imaginative" Hawaiian fusion cuisine, stay for the "aloha spirit" advise aficionados of chef Roy Yamaguchi's "wonderful" "fresh" seafood, "excellent" chocolate lava cake and more, served by a "knowledgeable" staff in a "festive" island atmosphere; some find it "overpriced", but many deem it a "special-night option that can't miss"; P.S. the three-course prix fixe dinner is a "real bargain."

R23 ⊠ *Japanese* 25 | 21 | 22 | $54

Downtown | 923 E. Second St. (bet. Garey & Vignes Sts.) | 213-687-7178 | www.r23.com

"If you can find it", this "arty" Japanese in a "funky" Downtown warehouse showcases "fantastic" sushi and "seasonal creations" served on handcrafted ceramics in an "edgy" room complete with Frank Gehry chairs and a skyline view; you might have to "pay an arm and a leg", but service is solid and most find the "quality" is worth it.

Rush Street *American* 17 | 17 | 16 | $28

Culver City | 9546 Washington Blvd. (Irving Pl.) | 310-837-9546 | www.rushstreetculvercity.com

"Always hopping", this Culver City lounge is a "good meetup spot" thanks to its "all-American" "comfort-food" menu, "nicely curated" cocktail list and "jumping" bar scene; it's all "too loud and too young" for some, although the patio is slightly more sedate.

Rustic Canyon *Californian/Mediterranean* 25 | 19 | 22 | $48

Santa Monica | 1119 Wilshire Blvd. (11th St.) | 310-393-7050 | www.rusticcanyonwinebar.com

"It's like eating from the farm without the work" at this Santa Monica Cal-Med matching "phenomenal" farm-to-table small plates with "interesting wines" in a "stylish, yet casual" setting; servers are "knowledgeable" too, but "it's a little pricey" and along with the "well-heeled" crowds come "noisy" acoustics; P.S. the "fantastic" off-menu burger is a standout.

Rustico *Italian* 26 | 20 | 26 | $45

Westlake Village | 1125 Lindero Canyon Rd. (Lakeview Canyon Rd.) | 818-889-0191 | www.rustico-restaurant.com

A "go-to" in Westlake Village, this "lovely neighborhood Italian" is a find for "delicious" dishes cooked up in a wood-burning oven and set down by a "personable", "professional" staff that offers "great recommendations"; yes, it's set in a strip mall, but it's "priced better" than many and most find it a "delight" nonetheless.

Ruth's Chris Steak House *Steak* 25 | 22 | 23 | $65

Beverly Hills | 224 S. Beverly Dr. (bet. Charleville Blvd. & Gregory Way) | 310-859-8744

(continued)

Ruth's Chris Steak House

Pasadena | 369 E. Colorado Blvd. (Euclid Ave.) | 626-583-8122
Woodland Hills | Westfield Promenade | 6100 Topanga Canyon Blvd. (bet. Erwin & Oxnard Sts.) | 818-227-9505
www.ruthschris.com

For buttery "melt-in-your-mouth" steaks "served sizzling", carnivores say it's "hard to beat" this "reliable" steakhouse chain where "ample" sides, "strong" drinks and "dedicated" service also help place it "at the top of the pack"; consistent crowds ensure that "noise levels are high" in the upscale environs, and while it's "not cheap", most have themselves a "wonderfully indulgent time."

Saam at The Bazaar by José Andrés S M *Eclectic* 27 | 26 | 26 | $132

Beverly Hills | SLS at Beverly Hills | 465 S. La Cienega Blvd. (Clifton Way) | 310-246-5545 | www.thebazaar.com

Chef José Andrés will "delight all your senses" with his "exquisite" Eclectic tasting menu - "22-plus courses of molecular gastronomy at its best" - served in an "oasis of calm" inside the Bazaar in Beverly Hills; while it's "pricey", most agree it's an "incredible experience" "worth every penny"; P.S. for a "once-in-a-lifetime" event, big spenders advise "get the wine pairing and stay the night at the SLS Hotel."

Saddle Peak Lodge M *American* 26 | 27 | 26 | $69

Calabasas | 419 Cold Canyon Rd. (Piuma Rd.) | 818-222-3888 | www.saddlepeaklodge.com

An "astonishing hideaway" in the "remote" Calabasas mountains, this "romantic" New American "treasure" is "well worth the trip" for "wonderful" wild game, served in a "beautiful", "woodsy" lodge decorated with hunting trophies or on the "charming" outdoor patio; "excellent" service also makes it "perfect" for a special occasion - "just be sure to bring someone else to pay the bill."

Safire *American* 25 | 24 | 24 | $38

Camarillo | 4850 Santa Rosa Rd. (bet. Ventura Frwy. & Verdugo Way) | 805-389-1227 | www.safirebistro.com

"Excellent all around" proclaim regulars of this Camarillo bistro that "delivers the goods" with "top-drawer" New American cuisine and "excellent" service; it's "a little pricey" for the neighborhood, but it's "nicer" than most too, with a handsome, "upscale" dining room and outdoor cabanas around a fire pit; P.S. there's also live music on weekends.

Saladang *Thai* 23 | 18 | 19 | $26

Pasadena | 363 S. Fair Oaks Ave. (Waverly Dr.) | 626-793-8123

Saladang Song *Thai*

Pasadena | 383 S. Fair Oaks Ave. (bet. Bellevue & Waverly Drs.) | 626-793-5200

"Busy for a reason", these Pasadena Thais are praised for their "delicious", if "Americanized", fare presented by a "gracious" staff "at very reasonable prices"; Saladang is set in a "modern concrete setting", while the younger Saladang Song is equally "austere", but boasts a "serene" patio that's "great on a warm evening" as well as a menu that's somewhat "more adventurous" than its elder's.

	FOOD	DECOR	SERVICE	COST

NEW Salt Air *Seafood* | - | - | - | M |

Venice | 1616 Abbot Kinney Blvd. (Rialto Ave.) | 310-396-9333 | www.saltairvenice.com

This stylish seafooder on Abbot Kinney in Venice offers a midpriced menu of edgy West Coast fish fare (think fish-skin chips), along with more straightforward dishes; the bright, clean-lined space has a relaxed beach-house vibe.

Salt Creek Grille *Steak* | 19 | 20 | 19 | $35 |

El Segundo | Plaza El Segundo | 2015 E. Park Pl. (Rosecrans Ave.) | 310-335-9288

Valencia | Valencia Town Ctr. | 24415 Town Center Dr. (McBean Pkwy.) | 661-222-9999

www.saltcreekgrille.com

These "comfortable" chophouse chain links in El Segundo and Valencia are fallbacks for "casual" dining with "decent" steaks served in "lively" environs with live music on weekends; critics call the food "uninspired" and "overpriced", but happy hour by the fire pits is a lot of "fun."

Salt's Cure *American* | 22 | 16 | 20 | $38 |

West Hollywood | 7494 Santa Monica Blvd. (Vista St.) | 323-850-7258 | www.saltscure.com

"Adventurous eaters" sing the praises of this "popular" American in West Hollywood where the "inventive", "wonderfully crafted" fare is entirely California-sourced, including meat that's butchered and cured in-house ("Berkshire pork chop . . . OMG"); "fab food presentations" and an open kitchen add to the "fun" for the "cool" clientele.

Sammy's Woodfired Pizza *Pizza* | 19 | 15 | 19 | $23 |

El Segundo | Plaza El Segundo | 780 S. Sepulveda Blvd. (bet. Hughes Way & Park Pl.) | 310-335-9999

NEW Studio City | 12050 Ventura Blvd. (Laurel Canyon Blvd.) | 818-762-3330

www.sammyspizza.com

There's "something for everyone" at this casual San Diego-based 'healthy' pizza-and-more chain known for "interesting" concoctions like the popular Brie and truffle oil pie; ample "portions make sharing easy", which keeps the cost down and makes for a "great family night out"; P.S. save room for the "marvelous" hot-fudge sundae.

Sam's by the Beach M *Californian/Mediterranean* | 25 | 21 | 26 | $55 |

Santa Monica | 108 W. Channel Rd. (PCH) | 310-230-9100 | www.samsbythebeach.com

A "real treat" "hidden" just off PCH in Santa Monica, this Cal-Med offers "hands-on perfection" in the form of "wonderful" service from owner Sam Elias and his staff plus "outstanding", "fresh-from-the-market" fare; the "intimate" bistro setting is "quiet" and "peaceful" enough for a "romantic" meal, and while some find the prices "a bit high", most appreciate the "homey excellence" "without any attitude."

Sam Woo *Chinese* | 18 | 8 | 11 | $18 |

Chinatown | 803 N. Broadway (bet. Alpine & College Sts.) | 213-687-7238

Cerritos | 19008 Pioneer Blvd. (South St.) | 562-865-7278

FOOD | DECOR | SERVICE | COST

(continued)

Sam Woo

Van Nuys | Signature Plaza | 6450 Sepulveda Blvd. (bet. Haynes St. & Victory Blvd.) | 818-988-6813 ⊭
Alhambra | 514 W. Valley Blvd. (bet. 5th & 6th Sts.) | 626-281-0038 ◐⊭
San Gabriel | San Gabriel Sq. | 140 W. Valley Blvd. (bet. Abbot & Del Mar Aves.) | 626-572-8418 ◐⊭
San Gabriel | 425 S. California St. (Agostino Rd.) | 626-287-6528 ⊭
San Gabriel | 937 E. Las Tunas Dr. (Earle St.) | 626-286-3118 ◐⊭
Roast duck "done right" and other "honest", "Cantonese-style comfort food" comes at "unbeatable" prices at this "no-frills" Chinese BBQ chainlet; "the decor isn't much" and service is of the "eat and leave" variety, but takeout is "easy" and it often hits the spot late at night.

Sanamluang Cafe ◐⊭ *Thai* — 24 | 9 | 17 | $16

East Hollywood | 5176 Hollywood Blvd. (Kingsley Dr.) | 323-660-8006
North Hollywood | 12980 Sherman Way (bet. Coldwater Canyon & Ethel Aves.) | 818-764-1180
When "it's 2 AM and you need that Thai fix", these separately owned spots in East and North Hollywood are "open after the clubs close" offering "filling", "flavorful" grub; perhaps service is "meh" and decor "needs help" but the "cops, hipsters and locals" that cram in don't seem to care.

Santa Monica Seafood Café *Seafood* — 25 | 15 | 19 | $33

Santa Monica | 1000 Wilshire Blvd. (10th St.) | 310-393-5244 | www.santamonicaseafood.com
"The seafood's so fresh it's like a slap in the face" at this Santa Monica market-cum-cafe selling an "impeccable" selection of fish retail while also serving "top-flight" "straightforward" fare, including a "great cioppino" and "fantastic crab"; it's certainly "not a glamorous place", but service is "friendly", and if it's usually "loud and crowded", it's because "you can't get better for the price."

Santouka Ramen ⊭ *Japanese* — 25 | 8 | 12 | $13

Mar Vista | Mitsuwa Mktpl. | 3760 S. Centinela Ave. (Venice Blvd.) | 310-391-1101

Santouka Ramen Torrance ⊭ *Japanese*

Torrance | 21515 S. Western Ave. (214th St.) | 310-212-1101
www.santouka.co.jp
"Noodle addicts" "worship" this Japan-born chain of ramen shops for its "heavenly" broth and "meltingly tender" pork; the "no-nonsense" supermarket settings are "not the most atmospheric", but you can't beat it for a "cheap, fast and tasty" bite; P.S. cash only.

Scarpetta *Italian* — 24 | 24 | 23 | $66

Beverly Hills | Montage Beverly Hills | 225 N. Canon Dr. (bet. Dayton Way & Wilshire Blvd.) | 310-860-7970 | www.scottconant.com
The "humble" $24 spaghetti dish "is all it's cracked up to be" at this "expensive" Beverly Hills Italian from NYC, where Scott Conant's "fabulous" food is served in a "beautiful", "modern" setting with a patio affording primo people-watching; service is "pleasant" too, although a "let-down" contingent calls it "disappointing after all the hype."

FOOD | DECOR | SERVICE | COST

Sea Empress *Chinese* 21 | 14 | 17 | $25

Gardena | Pacific Sq. | 1636 W. Redondo Beach Blvd. (bet. La Salle & Normandie Aves.) | 310-538-6868

Fans say "it's hard not to stop every cart" at this Gardena dim-sum mainstay rolling out "solid" Chinese nibbles and "fantastic seafood"; the space is "huge", but the prices are so "reasonable" that "it's worth putting up with the noise and the crowds" on weekends.

Sea Harbour *Chinese/Seafood* 25 | 16 | 17 | $29

Rosemead | 3939 Rosemead Blvd. (Valley Blvd.) | 626-288-3939

"Arrive early" because "there's always a line" at this relatively "high-end" Rosemead Chinese banquet hall, a "venerable" source for "sublime" dim sum served without the carts and Cantonese seafood; service can be "borderline rude, but with dumplings like these, who cares?"

NEW Seasons 52 *American* - | - | - | M

Century City | Westfield Century City Shopping Ctr. | 10250 Santa Monica Blvd. (Century Park) | 310-277-5252

Santa Monica | 1501 Ocean Ave. (B'way) | 310-451-1152

www.seasons52.com

From the Darden-owned family of chains (which includes Red Lobster and Olive Garden) comes these entries in Century City and Santa Monica built around seasonally available fare and healthful preparations, with all plates coming in at under 475 calories; both inhabit smartly designed spaces with much gleaming wood and glass, and an open kitchen.

Seoul House of Tofu *Korean* - | - | - | M

West LA | 2101 Sawtelle Blvd. (Mississippi Ave.) | 310-444-9988 | www.seoultofuhouse.com

This oversized Sawtelle Boulevard Korean may be the fanciest option on the Asian-lined West LA street, offering a moderately priced menu of 10-plus varieties of bubbling soon tofu stew along with Korean classics like bulgogi, galbi and bibimbop; the spacious, glass-accented dining room offers views of locals bustling around the surrounding mini-mall.

Settebello Pizzeria Napoletana *Pizza* ∇ 23 | 14 | 18 | $24

NEW **Marina del Rey** | Marina Marketpl. | 13455 Maxella Ave. (Del Rey Ave.) | 310-306-8204

Pasadena | 625 E. Colorado Blvd. (bet. El Molino & Madison Aves.) | 626-765-9550

www.settebello.net

This affordable pizzeria chainlet in Pasadena and Marina del Rey boasts "authentic Neapolitan pizza" "done simply and well" the old-fashioned way - first by hand, and then in a wood-burning oven; a "welcoming" vibe and "ample seating" make it "a perfect place to relax" and enjoy a casual bite.

71 Palm Ⓢ *American/French* 24 | 22 | 22 | $44

Ventura | 71 N. Palm St. (bet. Main & Poli Sts.) | 805-653-7222 | www.71palm.com

"Magnificent" French-American fare by chef-owner Didier Poirier keeps "longtime customers" coming back to this "quaint" Craftsman cottage in Downtown Ventura that's "peaceful" and "intimate" with seating by the fireplace and "friendly" service; though "a tad expensive", it's well suited to "date nights" and "special occasions."

Shabu Shabu House Ⓜ *Japanese* 22 | 9 | 15 | $22

Little Tokyo | Japanese Village Plaza | 127 Japanese Village Plaza Mall (bet. 1st & 2nd Sts.) | 213-680-3890

Cook-it-yourself types tout the "masterful version" of the eponymous dish at this budget Little Tokyo Japanese where the "delicious" meats, sauces and condiments can be had for "bargain-basement prices"; decor isn't a strong suit, and it's always "busy", so prepare to "wait."

The Shack *Burgers* 18 | 12 | 16 | $17

Playa del Rey | 185 Culver Blvd. (Vista del Mar) | 310-823-6222 | www.theshackpdr.com

"Big, juicy" burgers - like the signature Shackburger topped with a Louisiana hot link - and lots of "cold beer" are the draws at this "laid-back" beach "dive" in Playa del Rey; there's "no frills and no fancy sides", just a "nice staff, sandy locals" and lots of TVs for Philadelphia sports fans on weekends.

Shaherzad *Persian* 22 | 15 | 19 | $28

Westwood | 1422 Westwood Blvd. (bet. Ohio & Wilkins Aves.) | 310-470-9131 | www.shaherzadrestaurant.com

Go for "anything lamb" at this Westwood Persian known for its "wonderful kebabs" and other "authentic" eats accompanied by "warm, fresh bread coming from the oven"; service can be "aloof" and "don't expect a luxury atmosphere", but low prices for "huge portions" mean for most it "never fails."

Shamshiri Grill *Persian* 23 | 17 | 20 | $25

Westwood | 1712 Westwood Blvd. (Santa Monica Blvd.) | 310-474-1410 | www.shamshiri.com

"One of the highlights of Little Tehran" in Westwood, this "welcoming" Persian "shines" with "fresh, hot bread", stews and kebabs dished out in "enormous" portions ("few leave without a Styrofoam container in their hand"); service veers from "welcoming" to attitudinal, but the "bargain" prices get no complaints.

Shin-Sen-Gumi Yakitori *Japanese* 23 | 15 | 21 | $28

Gardena | 18517 S. Western Ave. (185th St.) | 310-715-1588

Shin-Sen-Gumi Yakitori Shabu-Shabu *Japanese*

Monterey Park | 111 N. Atlantic Blvd. (Garvey Ave.) | 626-943-7956 www.shinsengumiusa.com

"A gastronomic ride from start to finish", these Gardena and Monterey Park grills serve some of "the best yakitori" around and other "A+", "authentic" Japanese items; prices are "low", while the tavern-style settings and "warm, loud" welcome from the staff transport you to "Tokyo without the jet lag."

Shiro Ⓜ *French/Japanese* 27 | 20 | 27 | $54

South Pasadena | 1505 Mission St. (bet. Fair Oaks & Mound Aves.) | 626-799-4774 | www.restaurantshiro.com

The "catfish is epic" at this "intimate" French-Japanese in South Pasadena where the "expertly prepared" deep-fried whole fish is so "*umami*-yummy" that "it's hard to order anything else"; "amazing" service is another plus, and while the setting strikes some as "stark" and

FOOD	DECOR	SERVICE	COST

others find the tabs "a bit high", fans insist it's "worth the drive"; P.S. open Wednesdays-Sundays.

NEW ShopHouse *Asian* — | — | — | I

Hollywood | 6333 W. Sunset Blvd. (Morningside Ct.) | 323-462-2856
Santa Monica | 1401 Third St. Promenade (Santa Monica Blvd.)
www.shophousekitchen.com

This Pan-Asian sibling of the Mexican Chipotle chain in Hollywood and Santa Monica allows you to build your own bowls, choosing from noodles or rice, various proteins, sundry vegetables, sauces and toppings, at inexpensive rates; you can eat in the industrial fast-food setting or take out - and there's also an attached market selling ingredients for home cooking.

Short Order *Burgers* 18 | 15 | 16 | $24

Fairfax | Farmers Mkt. | 6333 W. Third St. (Fairfax Ave.) | 323-761-7970 | www.shortorderla.com

Nancy Silverton and the late Amy Pressman are behind this burger joint in the Fairfax Farmers Market, where the offerings include "messy" burgers made with grass-fed beef, "shameful and delicious" milkshakes and "interesting sides" served in an airy space with a few tables inside and additional seating on heated patios; though the mood's "fun", "disappointed" diners say the food "falls short" and it's "expensive for what you get."

Simmzy's *American* 23 | 18 | 21 | $24

Long Beach | 5271 E. Second St. (Laverne Ave.) | 562-439-5590
Manhattan Beach | 229 Manhattan Beach Blvd. (bet. Highland & Manhattan Aves.) | 310-546-1201
www.simmzys.com

"Grab a beer and a burger" at these "loud, crowded" entries in Long Beach and Manhattan Beach matching accessible American fare with a "rotating selection" of craft brews in a "terrific location" just blocks from the water; prices are low, so "get there early" or be prepared for a "long wait."

NEW Sirena *Italian* ▽ 18 | 23 | 20 | $57

Mid-City | 8265 Beverly Blvd. (Sweetzer Ave.) | 323-852-7000 | www.sirenarestaurant.com

The "fabulous" patio is "attractive for year-round dining" at this Mid-City Italian where the decor evokes an "exotic waterworld" befitting the name (Italian for 'mermaid'); service is "lovely" and the menu offers an "amazing mix of flavors", and while a few feel the kitchen "needs to try harder at these prices", others deem this "gorgeous" spot a "wonderful addition to the neighborhood."

Sir Winston's *Californian/Continental* 24 | 27 | 25 | $61

Long Beach | Queen Mary | 1126 Queens Hwy. (Harbor Plaza) | 562-499-1657 | www.queenmary.com

This "top-flight" Cal-Continental anchored on the original Queen Mary ocean liner in Long Beach is "like a trip back in time", having charmed guests with its "perfect" coastal views and "elegant", romantic room for decades; the "excellent" cuisine and "second-to-none" service make it a "special" place where you "take someone you want to impress" - just "bring a fat wallet."

	FOOD	DECOR	SERVICE	COST

Sisley Italian Kitchen *Italian* 19 | 18 | 21 | $30

Sherman Oaks | 15300 Ventura Blvd. (Sepulveda Blvd.) | 818-905-8444
Valencia | Valencia Town Ctr. | 24201 Valencia Blvd. (McBean Pkwy.) | 661-287-4444
www.sisleykitchen.com

A "locals' place", this Sherman Oaks and Valencia pair purvey "large portions" of "old-school" Italian at "a fair price" in "family-friendly" environs with "prompt" service; consensus is it's "tasty" but "nothing spectacular", though it certainly works "in a pinch."

The Six *American* 19 | 15 | 18 | $30

Rancho Park | 10668 W. Pico Blvd. (bet. Manning & Overland Aves.) | 310-837-6662
Studio City | 12650 Ventura Blvd. (Fairway Ave.) | 818-761-2319
www.thesixrestaurant.com

These "pleasant", "neighborhood gastropubs" in Rancho Park and Studio City are designed around a "cute concept" with six apps and six entrees, as well as pizza and burgers served in an "attractive" rustic setting; "loud" acoustics can be a turnoff, but most folks "like the prices."

NEW Skewers by Morimoto *Japanese* - | - | - | I

LAX | LA Int'l Aiport, Terminal 5 | 500 World Way (PCH) | 310-337-1011

After years of delays, Iron Chef Masaharu Morimoto has opened a fast-casual Japanese street food outpost in LAX, serving grilled yakitori and kushiyaki on, naturally, skewers; prices are affordable - but you need a plane ticket for a Delta flight to get into the terminal and dine in the modern-minimalist space.

Sky Room *American* 23 | 27 | 24 | $62

Long Beach | Breakers Bldg. | 40 S. Locust Ave. (Ocean Blvd.) | 562-983-2703 | www.theskyroom.com

"Spectacular" 360-degree views of Long Beach, a "hipster" rooftop bar, and live entertainment and dancing on weekends - "how could you lose?" posit fans of this "iconic" New American atop the historic Breakers building; the 1920s setting has a "very cool" vibe, while the staff makes you feel "pampered", and though a few feel the fare "doesn't match the ambiance", others find it "delicious", albeit "expensive."

Slaw Dogs *Hot Dogs* 22 | 12 | 20 | $13

Pasadena | 720 N. Lake Ave. (bet. Boylston St. & Orange Grove Blvd.) | 626-808-9777
Woodland Hills | 19801 Ventura Blvd. (bet. Corbin & Oakdale Aves.) | 818-887-8882
Duarte | 1355 Huntington Dr. (bet. Buena Vista St. & Cotter Ave.) | 626-358-8898
www.theslawdogs.com

"The king of dogs" according to fans, this "awesome" concept elevates the humble frank to "a whole new level" with its "extensive menu" of "cleverly crafted" offerings with "untraditional" toppings like kimchi and truffle oil; service is "quick" and the picnic-seating setting's "unpretentious", although some quibble with the somewhat "steep" prices.

	FOOD	DECOR	SERVICE	COST

Smitty's Grill *American* 22 | 21 | 22 | $41

Pasadena | 110 S. Lake Ave. (bet. Cordova & Green Sts.) | 626-792-9999 | www.smittysgrill.com

"Right out of *Mad Men*", this "dark, classy" Pasadena American from the Smith brothers (Arroyo Chop House, Parkway Grill) serves "solid" "comfort-food classics" like steaks and chicken pot pie in a "lively", "noisy" setting with a "beautiful bar"; service is "welcoming" too, so even if the bills are "a little costly", most "return again and again."

Smoke City Market *BBQ* ∇ 22 | 13 | 15 | $21

Van Nuys | 5242 Van Nuys Blvd. (bet. Magnolia Blvd. & Weddington St.) | 818-855-1280 | www.smokecitymarket.com

"True Texas-style" 'cue is the specialty of this Van Nuys young 'un that's roping in customers with "heavily smoked", "tender" brisket, "notable sides" and Shiner Bock on tap; even if some call it "a little on the pricey side" for such a "casual" setting, consensus is it's "a real treat and a great addition for LA BBQ lovers."

Smoke House *Steak* 21 | 18 | 21 | $40

Burbank | 4420 W. Lakeside Dr. (Olive Ave.) | 818-845-3731 | www.smokehouse1946.com

"An institution for the studio set", this "legendary" Burbank steakhouse "hasn't changed a bit" since 1946 and "continues to shine" with "strong" martinis and "addictive", "mysteriously Day-Glo orange garlic bread" tendered alongside "decent" cuts; it's "sorta pricey", but most find it worth it thanks to the "entertaining" servers and overall "old-school charm."

Soleil Westwood *Canadian/French* 21 | 18 | 22 | $32

Westwood | 1386 Westwood Blvd. (Wilkins Ave.) | 310-441-5384 | www.soleilwestwood.com

"Affable host Luc Alarie greets guests with a smile" at his "quaint" Westwood bistro with a "dependable" French-Canadian menu featuring poutine in a dozen variations served in a "quiet" space that "feels like home"; a "low corkage fee", all-you-can-eat mussels on Wednesdays and "great" wine-tasting dinners all make it a highly "affordable" option.

Soleto Trattoria & Pizza Bar *Italian* ∇ 21 | 22 | 21 | $33

Downtown | 801 S. Figueroa St. (8th St.) | 213-622-3255 | www.soletorestaurant.com

Conveniently situated a short walk from Staples and Nokia, this "solid", moderately priced Southern Italian is a pasta and pizza concept from the team behind Sushi Roku and Boa; the "trendy, but comfortable" space has an exhibition-style pizza kitchen, bare-brick walls and a garden patio surrounded by the skyscrapers of Downtown LA; it's also open late enough to catch a bite after seeing the Lakers or the Clippers just down the street.

Sol y Luna *Mexican* 22 | 19 | 19 | $26

Tarzana | 19601 Ventura Blvd. (Melvin Ave.) | 818-343-8488 | www.solylunausa.com

"No need to make a run for the border" thanks to this "solid", sit-down Tarzana Mexican famed for its tableside guac, "excellent margaritas" and carne asada that could "make a vegetarian switch teams"; the folk art-adorned digs are "festive", but the "jet-engine roar of the crowds" can "make it impossible to talk, let alone think."

Son of a Gun *Seafood* 26 | 17 | 22 | $48

Third Street | 8370 W. Third St. (bet. Kings Rd. & Orlando Ave.) | 323-782-9033 | www.sonofagunrestaurant.com

A "deliciously fishy" concept from the chef dudes behind Animal, this "buzzy" Third Street seafooder draws "salivating" fans with its "mouth-watering" midpriced menu, featuring "stunning standouts" like a "dyn-o-mite" fried-chicken sandwich and "not-to-be-missed" shrimp toast served in a "packed" setting with a "Hemingwayesque, *Old Man and the Sea* thing going on"; "reservations are a pain", but you can expect a staff that's "at your beck and call" and an overall "good-time vibe."

Soot Bull Jeep *Korean* 24 | 9 | 16 | $33

Koreatown | 3136 W. Eighth St. (Catalina St.) | 213-387-3865

"Be ready to get smoked" at this "popular" DIY Koreatown "dive" where "delish" "flavorful meats" are cooked up over charcoal grills, which "makes all the difference" to aficionados; just ignore the "old-cafeteria" decor, "wear disposable clothes" and focus on the "real-deal", inexpensive eats.

Sor Tino *Italian* 21 | 19 | 22 | $41

Brentwood | 908 S. Barrington Ave. (bet. Darlington Ave. & San Vicente Blvd.) | 310-442-8466 | www.sortinorestaurant.com

A "reliable neighborhood trattoria", this "cozy" Brentwood spot from Agostino Sciandri (Ago) delivers "authentic", "rustic" fare via a "gracious" crew; a "lovely" all-seasons patio and "reasonable prices" seal the deal.

Sotto Ⓜ *Pizza* 22 | 18 | 20 | $45

Century City | 9575 W. Pico Blvd. (bet. Edris & Smithwood Drs.) | 310-277-0210 | www.sottorestaurant.com

A "culinary wonder" in Century City, this "dark", "trendy" "basement boîte" offers "gorgeously charred pizzas" and "really different, fantastic" Italian fare crafted from local, sustainable ingredients and complemented by "inspired" cocktails; some say it has "a few kinks to work out" with food and service and it's "a bit expensive", but on the whole, most are "thankful to have it in the neighborhood"; P.S. "definitely try the meatballs."

South Beverly Grill *American* 21 | 21 | 22 | $40

Beverly Hills | 122 S. Beverly Dr. (bet. Charleville & Wilshire Blvds.) | 310-550-0242 | www.hillstone.com

This "upmarket Houston's" from the group behind that chain (as well as Bandera and R+D Kitchen) hosts a well-heeled Beverly Hills crowd for "expertly prepared" American comfort food at "relatively reasonable" prices; it boasts "attentive" service and a "swanky, comfortable" setting, while the adjacent Honor Bar has drinks and "great hamburgers."

Spago *Californian* 27 | 25 | 26 | $80

Beverly Hills | 176 N. Canon Dr. (Wilshire Blvd.) | 310-385-0880 | www.wolfgangpuck.com

"Beautifully redone", Wolfgang Puck's Beverly Hills "classic" still attracts a "who's who" crowd thanks to its "consistently excellent", "creative"

Californian cuisine, "intense wine list", "on-point" service and "wonderful new environs" designed by Barbara Lazaroff; a few grouse about "smaller plates" and "higher prices", but to most it remains the "standard by which all other top-notch restaurants are judged."

Spark Woodfire Grill *American* 20 | 17 | 20 | $35

Studio City | 11801 Ventura Blvd. (bet. Carpenter & Colfax Aves.) | 818-623-8883 | www.sparkwoodfiregrill.com

For an "easy", "reliable" meal, try this "sophisticated, casual" American in Studio City where "hearty" grill fare is dished out in "cozy", "comfortable" environs; though it's "a tad loud", "decent" prices and "accommodating" service make it a worthy "neighborhood standby."

Spice Table ☒ *Asian* 23 | 19 | 21 | $37

Little Tokyo | 114 S. Central Ave. (1st St.) | 213-620-1840 | www.thespicetable.com

This "excellent find" "brings a little heat" to Little Tokyo with "flavor-packed" Southeast Asian small plates focusing on the flavors of Singapore and Vietnam, courtesy of chef-owner Bryant Ng; the "price/portion" ratio is an issue for some, but a "warm atmosphere" with exposed brick and candlelight keeps the mood "enjoyable"; P.S. the construction of a new underground light rail station may force it to move, so call ahead.

Spitz *Turkish* 22 | 16 | 17 | $15

Eagle Rock | 2506 Colorado Blvd. (bet. College View Ave. & Sierra Villa Dr.) | 323-257-5600

Spitz Little Tokyo *Turkish*

Little Tokyo | 371 E. Second St. (Central Ave.) | 213-613-0101

Spitz Los Feliz *Turkish*

NEW **Los Feliz** | 1725 Hillhurst Ave. (Kingswell Ave.) | 323-522-3309

www.eatatspitz.com

This casual Turkish trio in Little Tokyo, Eagle Rock and Los Feliz is a "great value" for "yummy sandwiches" with "Mediterranean flair", starring "large, tasty" doner kebabs along with "excellent" fries; a full bar at the Little Tokyo locale stirs up creative cocktails.

Square One Dining *American* 22 | 15 | 16 | $21

East Hollywood | 4854 Fountain Ave. (Catalina St.) | 323-661-1109 | www.squareonedining.com

For "brunching at its best", it's "totally worth visiting" this "cute" daytime spot in East Hollywood for reasonably priced, "well-crafted" American fare featuring mostly local and organic ingredients, plus "terrific coffee drinks" from Intelligentsia beans; a "sunny" patio caps thing off.

The Stand *Hot Dogs* 18 | 14 | 17 | $13

Century City | 2000 Ave. of the Stars (Constellation Blvd.) | 310-785-0400 ☒

Encino | 17000 Ventura Blvd. (Balboa Blvd.) | 818-788-2700

Woodland Hills | Warner Ctr. | 5780 Canoga Ave. (Burbank Blvd.) | 818-710-0400

www.thestandlink.com

"Custom" hot dogs "dressed the way you like", "big burgers" and other Americana bring out the crowds at this counter-service chainlet where free pickles "make the waits less painful"; while the inside dining areas are rather "pedestrian", it's "always a picnic" outside at wooden tables with benches, making it "great for a group with kids."

Stanley's *Californian* 20 | 16 | 19 | $26

Sherman Oaks | 13817 Ventura Blvd. (bet. Mammoth & Matilija Aves.) | 818-986-4623 | www.stanleys83.com

You "can't go wrong with the Chinese chicken salad" at this "steady-eddie" Sherman Oaks "institution" offering a "well-rounded", "fair-priced" array of "basic", "healthy" Cal cuisine; though some say "it's not what it was" in the 1980s, it boasts a "cute patio" and a "lively bar area", and regulars report there's "almost never a wait" for a table.

Stefan's at L.A. Farm *Eclectic* 22 | 21 | 20 | $50

Santa Monica | 3000 Olympic Blvd. (bet. Centinela Ave. & Stewart St.) | 310-449-4000 | www.stefansatlafarm.com

"He may rub you the wrong way, but he knows how to cook" assert fans of *Top Chef* alum Stefan Richter's "tasty", "creative" Eclectic small plates and mains (from sliders to goulash) at his somewhat pricey Santa Monica restaurant; the "modern" setting with a "beautiful" covered patio and usually "attentive" service is especially "enjoyable" for lunch.

Stella Barra Pizzeria ◐ *Pizza* 25 | 20 | 20 | $27

NEW **Hollywood** | 6372 W. Sunset Blvd. (Ivar Ave.) | 323-301-4001

Santa Monica | 2000 N. Main St. (Bicknell Ave.) | 310-396-9250

www.stellabarra.com

"A step above most", these "artisan" pizzerias in Hollywood and Santa Monica turn out such "fantastic", "thin-crust" pies, you'll almost "forget how long it took to get a table"; "cool digs" and a "huge bar" pouring "well-priced wines" and cocktails complete the "fun" ("if loud and chaotic") experience; P.S. "don't miss the burrata" appetizer.

NEW **Sticky Rice** *Thai* - | - | - | I

Downtown | Grand Central Mkt. | 317 Broadway St. (4th Ave.) | 626-872-0353

This Thai fast-fooder - one of the upgraded offerings at the venerable Grand Central Market - is like a stand in a Singapore hawker's market, with only a precious few menu items; it specializes in Hainanese chicken rice and BBQ chicken, with occasional curry dishes and salads rounding out the mix.

Stinking Rose *Italian* 21 | 21 | 22 | $37

Beverly Hills | 55 N. La Cienega Blvd. (Wilshire Blvd.) | 310-652-7673 | www.thestinkingrose.com

"There's garlic, garlic and more garlic" - even in the ice cream - at this "fun" midpriced Beverly Hills Italian providing a "fragrant night out" with "tasty" eats delivered by a "helpful" staff in a "quirky" "boudoir-like atmosphere with exotic rich reds and booths in curtains"; critics call it an "interesting concept" with "mediocre" results, though many find it worth it for the "novelty" - just "bring mints."

STK ◐ *Steak* 24 | 24 | 22 | $72

West Hollywood | 755 N. La Cienega Blvd. (Waring Ave.) | 310-659-3535 | www.stkhouse.com

"Fantastic steaks", "amazing" truffle fries and "celeb sightings" go together at this "loud", "sexy" West Hollywood chophouse for "beautiful people" with modern looks and an "amazing" DJ spinning most nights; service is usually "polished" too, so in spite of the "high prices", most call it a "whole lot of fun."

Stonefire Grill *BBQ* 21 | 16 | 18 | $19

Pasadena | 473 N. Rosemead Blvd. (bet. Foothill Blvd. & Halstead St.) | 626-921-1255
Chatsworth | Pacific Theater Ctr. | 9229 Winnetka Ave. (Prairie St.) | 818-534-3364
West Hills | Fallbrook Ctr. | 6405 Fallbrook Ave. (Victory Blvd.) | 818-887-4145
Thousand Oaks | Paseo Mktpl. | 3635 E. Thousand Oaks Blvd. (Marmon Ave.) | 805-413-0300
Valencia | Cinema Park Plaza | 23300 Cinema Dr. (bet. Bouquet Canyon Rd. & Hollywood Ct.) | 661-799-8282
www.stonefiregrill.com

"Go hungry" to this "reliable" "family-favorite" BBQ chain known for its "generous" helpings of "tender tri-tip", chicken and ribs served with "amazing" breadsticks and "bottomless" beverages; the "busy", "casual" settings are counter service only, but "you can feed a family of four for cheap" and it also makes "excellent takeout when no one wants to cook."

NEW The Stonehaus *Italian* - | - | - | M

Westlake Village | Westlake Village Inn | 31943 Agoura Rd. (Lakeview Canyon Rd.) | 818-889-0230 | www.the-stonehaus.com

This Tuscan-style villa on the grounds of the elegant Westlake Village Inn serves midpriced wood-oven pizzas, cheese and charcuterie from its neighboring restaurant, Mediterraneo, by day, before converting into a wine bar and tasting room at night; the lush grounds feature their own vineyards and waterfall, making it a popular destination for weddings and special events.

Strand House M *American* 20 | 26 | 20 | $50

Manhattan Beach | 117 Manhattan Beach Blvd. (Ocean Dr.) | 310-545-7470 | www.thestrandhousemb.com

A "fabulous view of the ocean" and a "hip" bar scene come together at this "sophisticated" Manhattan Beach New American featuring "innovative" farm-driven fare from a menu by Neal Fraser (Grace, BLD) plus "excellent cocktails"; it's not cheap, but some say the sunsets alone "make it well worth the price."

Street *Eclectic* 25 | 19 | 23 | $42

Hollywood | 742 N. Highland Ave. (Melrose Ave.) | 323-203-0500 | www.eatatstreet.com

"Tongue-tingling" small plates of "fabulous" "street food from around the world" makes this midpriced Hollywood eatery from Susan Feniger (Border Grill) a "downright exciting" eating "adventure"; it boasts a "cool space" with a patio and Susan herself often "stops by every table", making it a "fun place to take out-of-towners"; P.S. "the Kaya toast is the must-have", and the cocktails are "great" too.

Sugarfish by Sushi Nozawa *Japanese* 26 | 20 | 22 | $42

Downtown | 600 W. Seventh St. (Grand Ave.) | 213-627-3000
NEW Beverly Hills | 212 N. Canon Dr. (bet. Clifton & Dayton Ways) | 310-276-6900
Studio City | 11288 Ventura Blvd. (Vineland Ave.) | 818-762-2322

(continued)

Sugarfish by Sushi Nozawa

Brentwood | 11640 W. San Vicente Blvd. (bet. Darlington & Mayfield Aves.) | 310-820-4477

Marina del Rey | The Waterside | 4722¼ Admiralty Way (Mindanao Way) | 310-306-6300

Santa Monica | 1345 Second St. (Santa Monica Blvd.) | 310-393-3338

NEW **Calabasas** | The Commons at Calabasas Shopping Ctr. | 4799 Commons Way (bet. Civic Center Way & Commons Way) | 818-223-9966

www.sugarfishsushi.com

Voted LA's Most Popular restaurant, chef Kazunori Nozawa's "fantastic" Japanese minichain pleases "sushi snobs" who "line up" to enjoy its "traditional", "melt-in-your-mouth" fish on "amazing" warm rice, offered à la carte or in set menus ("order one of the 'trust me' options and you can't go wrong"); an "inviting" "modern" ambiance and "fast, efficient" service help offset the "no-reservations" policy, and most find prices "affordable" given the quality.

Sunnin *Lebanese* 23 | 13 | 18 | $23

Westwood | 1776 Westwood Blvd. (Santa Monica Blvd.) | 310-475-3358 | www.sunnin.com

"First-rate" kebabs and other "traditional", "homestyle" dishes with "exquisite spicing" plus "lots of vegetarian options" make this inexpensive Lebanese in Westwood "worth regular visits"; the crew of servers is "friendly" and "ultraquick", and though the large, informal space is essentially devoid of ambiance, it's a "go-to" spot for many.

Sunny Spot ◐ *Caribbean/Eclectic* 21 | 20 | 20 | $35

Venice | 822 Washington Blvd. (Abbot Kinney Blvd.) | 310-448-8884 | www.sunnyspotvenice.com

"Westside hipsters" sip rum cocktails and tuck into Eclectic-Caribbean dishes at this "cool" Venice entry from "genius" chef Roy Choi (of Kogi BBQ truck fame); the "vibrant" setting with a patio means "just being there makes you feel happy", and the affordable prices don't hurt either.

Superba Snack Bar *American/Italian* ▽ 21 | 18 | 18 | $44

Venice | 533 Rose Ave. (Dimmick Ave.) | 310-399-6400 | www.superbasnackbar.com

"Farm-to-table" small plates and "homemade pastas" with "intensely flavorful sauces" draw a "hip, lively crowd" to this "trendy" yet "easygoing" Italian-New American parked on Venice's "emerging Restaurant Row"; a "modern" "bistro setting" with "communal" tables and a "cool front patio" boosts the "social" vibe.

Sushi Gen ☒ *Japanese* 26 | 17 | 21 | $47

Little Tokyo | 422 E. Second St. (bet. Alameda St. & Central Ave.) | 213-617-0552

"Simplicity" rules at this Little Tokyo Japanese "stalwart" where "superb", "super-fresh" slabs of fish are fashioned into "fine pieces of art" and the prices are very "fair" for the quality; both service and decor are understated, but "be prepared to wait unless you come at off hours"; P.S. lunch offers "unbelievable deals."

	FOOD	DECOR	SERVICE	COST

Sushi Masu Ⓜ *Japanese* 27 | 15 | 25 | $48

West LA | 1911 Westwood Blvd. (bet. La Grange & Missouri Aves.) | 310-446-4368

"Lots of loyal regulars" count on this West LA Japanese, a "quiet, neighborhood" "gem" for "fresh, delish", "expertly prepared" sushi at an "ideal cost/quality ratio"; though the simple space is "not fancy", chef Hiroshi Masuko is an "engaging host" who "makes you feel at home"; P.S. "sit at the bar" if you can.

Sushi Roku *Japanese* 22 | 22 | 21 | $51

Third Street | 8445 W. Third St. (bet. Croft Ave. & La Cienega Blvd.) | 323-655-6767

Pasadena | One Colorado | 33 Miller Alley (Union St.) | 626-683-3000

www.sushiroku.com

"See and be seen" at this "rollicking" Japanese set on Third Street and in Pasadena, where a "cool" staff proffers "innovative", "expensive" sushi and "fun" drinks in a "chic" setting; waits can be a "hassle" and critics claim it's "better suited to tourists than serious aficionados", but it's still a "favorite" for many.

Sushi Sasabune Ⓢ *Japanese* 26 | 16 | 22 | $70

NEW **Beverly Hills** | 9162 W. Olympic Blvd. (Doheny Rd.) | 310-859-3878

West LA | 11917 Wilshire Blvd. (Armacost Ave.) | 310-478-3596

Sasabune Express *Japanese*

Pacific Palisades | 970 Monument St. (bet. Bashford St. & Sunset Blvd.) | 310-454-6710

www.trustmesushi.com

"Impeccably fresh", "exquisite" fish is served in "traditional" preparations (aka no California rolls) at these "expensive" Beverly Hills and West LA Japanese spots and their takeout-focused Pacific Palisades offshoot; perhaps service could use "more flexibility" and the settings aren't much to speak of, but it still comes "highly recommended."

Sushi Sushi Ⓢ Ⓜ *Japanese* ▽ 27 | 19 | 24 | $66

Beverly Hills | 326½ S. Beverly Dr. (bet. Gregory Way & Olympic Blvd.) | 310-277-1165 | www.sushisushibh.com

Loyalists insist this "small, refined" Beverly Hills Japanese is "a winner" for its "creative", "top-quality" sushi, with a "first-class omakase" from chef Hiroshige Yamada; the only downside is that the creations are "a bit on the pricey side" in contrast with the rather nondescript setting.

Sushi Zo Ⓢ *Japanese* 28 | 14 | 20 | $117

West LA | 9824 National Blvd. (Castle Heights Ave.) | 310-842-3977

The "incredible parade" of "exceptional" sushi makes a visit to this omakase-only West LA Japanese feel "like a trip to Tokyo", complete with almost "over-attentive" service; aficionados "who don't care too much about ambiance" are rewarded with "bits of bliss" that "make it hard to know when to stop" – no wonder it's "zo expensive."

Susina Bakery & Cafe *Bakery* 23 | 20 | 19 | $18

Beverly Boulevard | 7122 Beverly Blvd. (La Brea Ave.) | 323-934-7900 | www.susinabakery.com

"A vision of decadence" with rows upon rows of "gorgeous" cakes and tarts, this Beverly Boulevard bakery/cafe also purveys "fantastic coffee" along with "good" sandwiches, salads, omelets and such; service is "professional", the setting's "quaint" and "at night, it becomes a bit of a de facto office for the local scenesters."

Sweet Lady Jane *Bakery* 23 | 16 | 17 | $19

Melrose | 8360 Melrose Ave. (bet. Kings Rd. & Orlando Ave.) | 323-653-7145
Santa Monica | 1631 Montana Ave. (bet. 16th & 17th Sts.) | 310-254-9499
www.sweetladyjane.com

For "gorgeous", "decadent" pastries, birthday cakes and pies that "taste as good as they look", patrons pop into this "expensive, but worth it" Melrose and Santa Monica bakery/cafe duo that also serves "fab" sandwiches and salads washed down with "strong, delicious java"; although some grumble about "ornery" service and limited seating, most are "grateful to have this top-notch [spot], so no real complaints."

Swingers ◐ *Diner* 19 | 17 | 18 | $16

Beverly Boulevard | Beverly Laurel Motor Hotel | 8020 Beverly Blvd. (Laurel Ave.) | 323-653-5858
Santa Monica | 802 Broadway St. (Lincoln Blvd.) | 310-393-9793
www.swingersdiner.com

Boasting "the perfect LA vibe", these "hip", "rock 'n' roll" coffee shops on Beverly Boulevard and in Santa Monica sling all the "old standards" plus other inexpensive items "leaning toward the healthier side" and "lots of vegetarian options" too; sure, the service often comes "without a smile" and some say it's "all style and no substance", but for the "late-night munchies", it's hard to beat.

The Sycamore Kitchen *American* 24 | 18 | 18 | $23

Mid-City | 143 S. La Brea Ave. (bet. 1st & 2nd Sts.) | 323-939-0151 | www.thesycamorekitchen.com

"Buttery baked goods" and "sublime" sandwiches on housemade bread make for "happy" customers at this moderately priced Mid-City American cafe from Karen and Quinn Hatfield (Hatfield's) with daily specials worth "exploring"; order at the counter and grab one of the few wooden tables inside or relax on the large patio.

NEW Taberna Arros y Vi *Spanish* - | - | - | M

Santa Monica | 1403 Second St. (Santa Monica Blvd.) | 310-393-3663 | www.tabernala.com

Restaurateur Michael Cardenas (Aburiya Toranoko, BOA, Lazy Ox, Sushi Roku) has opened this moderately priced Barcelona-style taverna featuring paella and tapas with seasonal sangrias; just a short walk from the Pacific in Santa Monica, the space has a long bar and tables and lots of music wafting through the air.

NEW Tacos Punta Cabras ⊠ *Mexican* - | - | - | I

Santa Monica | 2311 Santa Monica Blvd. (Cloverfield Blvd.) | 310-917-2244

This down-home taqueria convenient to Santa Monica City College has a blackboard menu of authentic Mexican street food, served at rock bottom prices; the largely nondescript space and counter service make it ideal for scholars who want to grab and go.

Tagine Ⓜ *Moroccan* 25 | 21 | 24 | $59

Beverly Hills | 132 N. Robertson Blvd. (Wilshire Blvd.) | 310-360-7535 | www.taginebeverlyhills.com

At this "dark", "cozy" Beverly Hills Moroccan co-owned by chef Ben Benameur and actor Ryan Gosling, the "delicious" dishes include "au-

FOOD | DECOR | SERVICE | COST

thentic tagines and couscous" offered à la carte or in a multicourse tasting menu that's "a treat"; although it's not inexpensive, "attentive" service and an "intimate, romantic atmosphere" with plush banquettes make it well-tailored to "dates."

Taiko Ⓜ *Japanese* 22 | 17 | 21 | $35

Brentwood | Madison Brentwood | 11677 San Vicente Blvd. (bet. Barrington & Darlington Aves.) | 310-207-7782

An "unusually extensive" Japanese menu featuring "amazing" udon and soba "hits the spot every time" at this "economical" eatery in Brentwood that's "popular" with the college crowd and "kid-friendly" too; the decor is sparse, but pleasant, and service is generally "pretty good", so most are "never disappointed."

Taix *French* 20 | 19 | 24 | $34

Echo Park | 1911 W. Sunset Blvd. (Glendale Blvd.) | 213-484-1265 | www.taixfrench.com

"However you pronounce it, it's been in Echo Park forever", and the "charming" staff enhances the "old-world" atmosphere at this "excellent-value" French from 1927 featuring reliable bistro "staples" accompanied by tureens of soup; though some pan the "dated" decor, others find the "few wrinkles" it has acquired "add character" and make this family-owned "institution" "better than expected."

Takami Sushi & Robata *Japanese* 22 | 25 | 21 | $46

Downtown | 811 Wilshire Blvd. (bet. Figueroa & Flower Sts.) | 213-236-9600 | www.takamisushi.com

Perched on the 21st floor of a Downtown skyscraper, this "fancy" Japanese "has it all": "incredible" 360-degree views of the city and "amazing" sushi and lychee martinis served by a "friendly" staff in a contemporary setting; despite somewhat high prices many find it a "wonderful place to treat yourself."

Takao *Japanese* 26 | 16 | 24 | $66

Brentwood | 11656 San Vicente Blvd. (bet. Barrington & Darlington Aves.) | 310-207-8636 | www.takaobrentwood.com

This "quietly elegant" Japanese in Brentwood delivers "fabulous, high-quality" fare via an "exceptional" omakase, "wonderful sushi" and other "unique" dishes; perhaps the "understated" setting won't win any awards, but the staff is "charming and helpful", and "if you're willing to spend, you can have a first-rate experience."

Take a Bao *Asian* 19 | 13 | 17 | $18

Century City | Century City Center Shopping Ctr. | 10250 Santa Monica Blvd. (bet. Ave. of the Stars & Century Park) | 310-551-1100

Studio City | 11838 Ventura Blvd. (Carpenter Ave.) | 818-691-7223 www.takeabao.com

For a "quick", "low-priced" bite, customers turn to this duo in Century City and Studio City offering Pan-Asian noodles, salads and "unique takes" on the bao that are "not really authentic", but "tasty" nonetheless, plus a full lineup of cocktails, craft beer and wine at the more-upscale Ventura Boulevard locale; the staff is "courteous", although some find the concept "disappointing", insisting "the name is cuter than the rest."

FOOD	DECOR	SERVICE	COST

Talésai *Thai* 22 | 17 | 21 | $34

West Hollywood | 9043 W. Sunset Blvd. (Doheny Dr.) | 310-275-9724 | www.talesai.com M

Studio City | 11744 Ventura Blvd. (bet. Blue Canyon Dr. & Carpenter Ave.) | 818-753-1001 | www.talesairestaurant.com

Café Talésai *Thai*

Beverly Hills | 9198 W. Olympic Blvd. (Palm Dr.) | 310-271-9345 | www.cafetalesai.com

"More people should know" about these "hidden" Thai "treasures" and their "wide variety" of "sophisticated" takes on the standards "artfully prepared" and served in "upscale, hip" surroundings by a "helpful" staff; they're a "reliable" "take-out staple" too; P.S. Night + Market is an offshoot specializing in street fare.

Tam O'Shanter ◐ *Scottish* 22 | 24 | 23 | $41

Atwater Village | 2980 Los Feliz Blvd. (Boyce Ave.) | 323-664-0228 | www.lawrysonline.com

If you "come in a tartan kilt you'll feel at home" at this 90-plus year-old Scottish scion of the Lawry's chain in Atwater Village, housed in a "quaint" pub where "friendly" plaid-clad waiters proffer "classic" prime rib and the like; it's "not cheap eats", but the "quality has remained high" so "you always come out satisfied."

Tanino *Italian* 22 | 23 | 22 | $48

Westwood | 1043 Westwood Blvd. (bet. Kinross & Weyburn Aves.) | 310-208-0444 | www.tanino.com

Set in a "romantic" Florentine-style building (circa 1929) with antique chandeliers and high ceilings, this Westwood Italian from Tanino Drago is a "reliable" pre-theater pick for "well-prepared" cuisine served by a staff that "always seems happy to see you"; though some regulars grouse about "pricey" bills, its "convenient" proximity to the UCLA campus and the Geffen Playhouse keeps it "extremely busy."

Tanzore *Indian* 21 | 24 | 21 | $41

Beverly Hills | 50 N. La Cienega Blvd. (bet. Clifton Way & Wilshire Blvd.) | 310-652-3838 | www.tanzore.com

For "upscale Indian" in a "lovely", "color-saturated" setting, try this Beverly Hills respite, an "excellent" option for "standard curries" as well as other "flavorful", "specialty" items; a usually "attentive" staff helps make up for some complaints about "pricey" bills for "small portions."

NEW Tapenade *Californian/Mediterranean* - | - | - | M

West LA | Olympic Collection | 11301 W. Olympic Blvd. (bet. Corinth Ave. & Sawtelle Blvd.) | 310-312-6233 | www.tapenade.la

Situated in a mall at the southern edge of West LA's Little Osaka, this moderately priced Cal-Med is an unexpected destination for burrata and gnocchi on a street dominated by small Asian eateries; the dining room is done up in black and tan hues with long communal tables and an elegant bar offering a global assortment of wines.

Tar & Roses *American* 24 | 19 | 22 | $53

Santa Monica | 602 Santa Monica Blvd. (6th St.) | 310-587-0700 | www.tarandroses.com

"A culinary treat" "from start to finish", this "addictive" Santa Monica "up-and-comer" from chef-owner Andrew Kirschner (Joe's, Wilshire)

turns out "memorable" New American plates both small and large via a wood-burning oven; tables can be "hard to come by" since the "elevated gastropub" setting is "always busy" (and "noisy"), so "book well in advance."

NEW Tartine O Chocolat *Bakery/French* — | — | — | M

Beverly Hills | 8556 W. Third St. (Holt Ave.) | 310-275-4235 | www.tartineochocolat-hub.com

This quiet and elegant mini-mall French cafe - where the chef proudly displays a photo of himself with his idol, Joël Robuchon - offers cases filled with pastries, chocolates and various sweet things, along with midpriced breakfast, lunch and dinner options for light meals; there are tables for eating in, plus sidewalk seating.

Tasting Kitchen ◐ *Mediterranean* 25 | 21 | 21 | $57

Venice | 1633 Abbot Kinney Blvd. (Venice Blvd.) | 310-392-6644 | www.thetastingkitchen.com

"Everything is amazing, even down to the bread and butter" at this "cool", upscale Venice Med that's "packed elbow to elbow with beautiful people" tucking into "wonderful, creative" dishes elevated by "great wines" and some of "the best mixed cocktails west of the 405"; you'll need to deal with "so-so" service, "loud" acoustics and "difficult-to-get reservations", but even so, it's worth "every bit of trouble"; P.S. "for those on a budget, the front room is lovely for brunch on weekends."

Tatsu Ramen ◐ *Japanese* — | — | — | I

West LA | 2123 Sawtelle Blvd. (bet. Mississippi Ave. & Olympic Blvd.) | 310-684-2889 | www.tatsuramen.com

Little Osaka may have to be renamed Ramen Row, as yet another noodle shop has opened, this one featuring a brightly lit modernist space with a long counter and an iPad ordering system; there are several choices of ramen - with meat and without - and you can add extras and toppings, plus there's beer and sake.

Tavern *Californian/Mediterranean* 24 | 25 | 22 | $53

Brentwood | 11648 San Vicente Blvd. (bet. Barrington & Darlington Aves.) | 310-806-6464 | www.tavernla.com

This "neighborhood favorite" from Suzanne Goin and Caroline Styne attracts "foodies and A-listers" with "scrumptious" Cal-Med fare and "suave cocktails" served in a "bright, beautiful" space that defines "elegance in Brentwood"; while it's "fairly expensive", it pays off with "graceful" service, and budget-conscious types can try a "luscious" burger at the bar, the "lovely brunch" or the "casual" Larder cafe, offering "light meals" and gourmet goodies at cheaper prices.

Taverna Tony *Greek* 22 | 21 | 22 | $42

Malibu | Malibu Country Mart | 23410 Civic Center Way (Cross Creek Rd.) | 310-317-9667 | www.tavernatony.com

"Malibu locals hang out" at this "hospitable" Greek moving "huge portions" of "flavorful" eats like moussaka and spanakopita in a "celebratory" setting with belly dancers and live music that "can get quite noisy"; it's not cheap and some find the food and service "hit-or-miss", but it "can't be beat on a warm summer evening" if you "sit outside" with a glass of wine.

	FOOD	DECOR	SERVICE	COST

Taylor's Steak House *Steak* 23 | 20 | 22 | $43

Koreatown | 3361 W. Eighth St. (Ardmore Ave.) | 213-382-8449
La Cañada Flintridge | 901 Foothill Blvd. (Beulah Dr.) | 818-790-7668
www.taylorssteakhouse.com

"Steaks and drinks are done right" at this "thoroughly charming, old-school" steakhouse duo in Koreatown and La Cañada Flintridge set in "clubby", vintage digs like something "out of Mike Hammer detective novels"; with a "pleasant" staff, "quiet" atmosphere and "reasonable" tabs, it's "always a treat."

Tender Greens *American* 23 | 17 | 18 | $18

NEW **Downtown** | PacMutual Bldg. | 523 W. Sixth St. (bet. Grand Ave. & Olive St.) | no phone
Hollywood | 6290 W. Sunset Blvd. (Vine St.) | 323-382-0380
West Hollywood | 8759 Santa Monica Blvd. (Hancock Ave.) | 310-358-1919
Culver City | 9523 Culver Boulevard (bet. Cardiff & Watseka Aves.) | 310-842-8300
NEW **Marina del Rey** | Marina Mktpl. | 13455 Maxella Ave. (Del Rey Ave.) | 310-827-3777
Santa Monica | 201 Arizona Ave. (2nd St.) | 310-587-2777
NEW **Westwood** | 1109 Glendon Ave. (Kinross Ave.) | no phone
Pasadena | 621 E. Colorado Blvd. (bet. El Molino & Madison Aves.) | 626-405-1511
www.tendergreens.com

"It's easy eating green" thanks to this "virtuous, semi-fast food" chainlet - a "smart concept" - turning out "mix-and-match" salads, sandwiches and platters crafted from "exceptionally fresh" "high-quality" organic ingredients; "long lines are the norm, but they move fast", while the spare settings are augmented by "pleasant outdoor seating" at all locales.

Terroni *Italian* 22 | 20 | 19 | $35

Beverly Boulevard | 7605 Beverly Blvd. (Curson Ave.) | 323-954-0300 | www.terroni.ca
NEW **Downtown** | 802 S. Spring St. (8th St.) | 323-954-0300 | www.terroni.com

"Fabulous pasta done right" brings in a "young industry crowd" to these "scene-y" Southern Italians Downtown and on Beverly Boulevard - outposts of a Toronto mini-chain - also purveying "first-rate" pizzas; despite some gripes about service, "pricey" tabs and an "ear-splitting noise level", on the whole, fans insist "they nail it."

Teru Sushi *Japanese* 21 | 18 | 20 | $36

Studio City | 11940 Ventura Blvd. (bet. Carpenter Ave. & Laurel Canyon Blvd.) | 818-763-6201 | www.terusushi.com

"Still reliable" is the word on this midpriced Japanese stalwart in Studio City, "one of the originals on sushi row" turning out "fresh" fish and "playfully named special rolls" for a neighborhood crowd; some surveyors say it's "not as good as some of its competition" nearby, but the chefs are "friendly" and the "attractive" landscaped patio is a plus.

Thai Dishes *Thai* 20 | 15 | 18 | $22

Malibu | 22333 PCH (bet. Carbon Canyon Rd. & Sweetwater Canyon Dr.) | 310-456-6592 | www.thaidishesmaliburestaurant.com

(continued)

(continued)

Thai Dishes

Santa Monica | 123 Broadway (2nd St.) | 310-394-6189 | www.thaidishessantamonica.com
Santa Monica | 1910 Wilshire Blvd. (19th St.) | 310-828-5634 | www.thaidisheswilshire.com
Inglewood | 11934 Aviation Blvd. (119th Pl.) | 310-643-6199
LAX | 6234 W. Manchester Ave. (bet. Sepulveda Blvd. & Truxton Ave.) | 310-342-0046 | www.thaidishesmanchester.com
Manhattan Beach | 1015 N. Sepulveda Blvd. (bet. 10th & 11th Sts.) | 310-546-4147 | www.thaidishesmb.com
Valencia | Valencia Mart Shopping Ctr. | 23328 Valencia Blvd. (bet. Bouquet Canyon Rd. & Cinema Dr.) | 661-253-3663 | www.thaidishesscv.com

This "venerable" Thai chain is a "reliable" pick for "unimaginative, but well-prepared" curries and noodles priced for "those on a budget"; the service is "fair", but the atmosphere, while "family-friendly", has little to speak of in the ambiance department, so many "get it for takeout."

Think Café *American/Eclectic* ∇ 23 | 19 | 23 | $21

San Pedro | 302 W. Fifth St. (Centre St.) | 310-519-3662 | www.thinkcafe5thst.com

"Casual" dining in Downtown San Pedro comes via this "homey" all-day spot with an American-Eclectic menu featuring breakfast fare, sandwiches, salads and heartier items at dinner; solid service, decent prices and music on the weekends keep it "crowded."

3 Square Cafe + Bakery *Sandwiches* 23 | 18 | 20 | $23

Venice | 1121 Abbot Kinney Blvd. (bet. San Juan & Westminster Aves.) | 310-399-6504 | www.rockenwagner.com

"Hans still rocks" attest acolytes of chef Röckenwagner and his "cool" cafe/bakery in Venice serving "Germanesque" breakfasts, "tantalizing" pretzel burgers, "mini-sandwiches" and "neat" pastries in a "sleek" space where patrons can "watch the Abbot Kinney world go by"; some say it's a "long" wait for "nothing extraordinary", but most surveyors dig it for "something LA and different" that's "not too pricey."

Tierra Sur at Herzog Wine Cellars *Kosher/Mediterranean* ∇ 28 | 23 | 27 | $51

Oxnard | Herzog Wine Cellars | 3201 Camino Del Sol (Del Norte St.) | 805-983-1560 | www.tierrasuratherzog.com

At this "unique", "upscale" kosher restaurant in Oxnard's Herzog winery, the kitchen puts out "fabulous" dairy-free Med cuisine matched with "excellent wines" (tours and tastings are also available); service is "excellent", and the "lovely ambiance" is "great for a date", especially if you sit on the terrace; P.S. hours are limited, so call ahead.

Tinga *Mexican* 22 | 17 | 18 | $19

La Brea | 142 S. La Brea Ave. (1st St.) | 323-954-9566
NEW **Santa Monica** | 522 Wilshire Blvd. (5th Ct.) | 310-451-9341
www.tingabuena.com

"Gourmet tacos" and other "tasty", "interesting" Mex eats - like cochinita pibil "with a kick" and a dirty horchata with a double-shot of espresso - garner "rave reviews" at these "gems" on La Brea and in Santa Monica; cheery, "casual" environs and midlevel pricing make them a "solid" bet all around.

	FOOD	DECOR	SERVICE	COST

Tin Roof Bistro *American* 23 | 20 | 21 | $34

Manhattan Beach | Manhattan Vill. | 3500 N. Sepulveda Blvd. (33rd St.) | 310-939-0900 | www.tinroofbistro.com

A South Bay "favorite", this upscale Manhattan Beach cousin of Simmzy's features a "dynamite" New American menu with spicy tuna spring rolls and "fabulous burgers" - all "totally affordable" - plus "impressive" wines and cocktails and a "reasonable corkage policy"; inside is "convivial" with a "noisy", "crowded bar scene", while the "charming patio" presents a more "relaxed atmosphere" with a bocce court.

Tito's Tacos ⊄ *Mexican* 21 | 7 | 16 | $10

Culver City | 11222 Washington Pl. (Tuller Ave.) | 310-391-5780 | www.titostacos.com

"The long lines don't lie" at this inexpensive circa-1959 Culver City Mexican, a "local treasure" beloved for its "unbelievably fresh and delicious" "crispy-style" tacos and "heavenly" burritos; "you don't go for the ambiance" and "seating can be challenging", so "be patient, or get takeout."

Tlapazola Grill *Mexican* 23 | 14 | 23 | $31

Venice | 636 N. Venice Blvd. (Abbot Kinney Blvd.) | 310-822-7561 | www.tlapazolagrill.com

West LA | 11676 Gateway Blvd. (bet. Barrington Ave. & Pearl Pl.) | 310-477-1577 | www.tlapazola.com M

It's "not your garden-variety Mexican" at this separately owned pair in Venice and West LA lauded for "superb Oaxacan cooking" like "transporting" moles and other "wonderful" dishes with "interesting twists" plus "unbeatable margaritas" that "pack a wallop"; the setting's "casual and relaxed", the staff "couldn't be nicer" and prices aren't bad either.

Toast *American* 18 | 16 | 16 | $23

Third Street | 8221 W. Third St. (Harper Ave.) | 323-655-5018 | www.toastbakerycafe.net

"Quite a scene", this breakfast and brunch mainstay on Third Street hosts the "*US* magazine crowd" for "original spins on breakfast burritos, Benedicts, big salads" and other "fresh" American fare at a "fair price"; "expect a wait" - especially for a coveted sidewalk table - and don't be surprised if the staffers seem "more concerned with their hair and next audition than refilling your cup."

Tofu Ya *Korean* 20 | 10 | 16 | $16

West LA | 2021 Sawtelle Blvd. (bet. La Grange & Mississippi Aves.) | 310-473-2627

This West LA Korean is a "cheap, cheerful" stop for "fill-your-belly" "comfort-food" standards like "spicy, bubbling hot tofu soup", bulgogi and bibimbop at "economical" prices; there's "zero ambiance", but it's frequently "packed" with "workers during lunch and hipsters in the evening" and takeout is popular too.

Toi on Sunset ◐ *Thai* ▽ 19 | 20 | 18 | $22

West Hollywood | 7505½ Sunset Blvd. (bet. Gardner St. & Sierra Bonita Ave.) | 323-874-8062 | www.toirockinthaifood.com

Set amid a cluster of guitar shops in West Hollywood, this "cool", little spot offers an "awesome", "extensive" Thai menu in a "fun" space that's a veritable "shrine" to rock 'n' roll; "inexpensive" prices and late hours (till 4 AM) make it a "go-to" for many.

Tomato Pie *Pizza* 22 | 12 | 18 | $15

Melrose | 7751 Melrose Ave. (Genesee Ave.) | 323-653-9993
Silver Lake | 2457 Hyperion Ave. (Tracy St.) | 323-661-6474
www.tomatopiepizzajoint.com

Those who crave a "slice of New York in LA" say you "can't go wrong" with the "authentic", "thin-crust" pizzas at these limited-seating, no-frills Melrose and Silver Lake parlors; delivery is a plus, and it won't cost you a lot of dough, either.

Tommy's ◐⊄ *Burgers/Hot Dogs* 24 | 9 | 19 | $10

Downtown | 2575 W. Beverly Blvd. (bet. Coronado St. & Rampart Blvd.) | 213-389-9060 | www.originaltommys.com

"They don't make 'em like this anymore" declare devotees of this 1940s Downtown "shack", an "LA classic" famed for its "sloppy", "delightfully disgusting" chili-burgers and hot dogs served 24/7 and especially cherished "after a night of drinking"; there are "long lines" and little seating, but for most that's "part of the charm."

Torafuku Japanese Restaurant *Japanese* ▽ 21 | 16 | 19 | $36

West LA | 10914 W. Pico Blvd. (Westwood Blvd.) | 310-470-0014 | www.torafuku-usa.com

At this West LA outpost of a Tokyo-based chain, the menu offers "unique" Japanese specialties like *kamado* (iron-pot) rice - which arrives "fragrant" and "piping hot" - as well as grilled items and sushi in a sleek, minimalist setting; it's not inexpensive, but service is professional and lunch and happy-hour drink specials provide some relief.

Tortilla Republic *Mexican* ▽ 20 | 21 | 20 | $45

West Hollywood | 616 N. Robertson Blvd. (Melrose Ave.) | 310-657-9888 | www.tortillarepublic.com

The original location of this chic West Hollywood Mexican grill is in Hawaii, but the modern, midpriced menu translates just fine on the mainland: duck-confit tacos and such join an impressive selection of bespoke margaritas; the dramatic space is outfitted with lanterns and glittering mirrors, with a fine view of the crowds on Robertson Boulevard.

Toscana *Italian* 25 | 19 | 22 | $56

Brentwood | 11633 San Vicente Blvd. (Darlington Ave.) | 310-820-2448 | www.toscanabrentwood.com

"A real showbiz hangout", this "star-studded" Brentwood trattoria "maintains its standards" year after year with "delicious", "rustic" Tuscan cuisine and "lovely" service that "couldn't be more friendly despite the 1% crowd"; it's too "loud", "crowded" and "expensive" for some, but for "special occasions", many find it an "absolute delight"; P.S. Bar Toscana next door has nibbles and drinks.

Toscanova *Italian* 19 | 19 | 19 | $40

Century City | Westfield Century City Shopping Ctr. | 10250 Santa Monica Blvd. (Ave. of the Stars) | 310-551-0499
Calabasas | 4799 Commons Way (Calabasas Rd.) | 818-225-0499
www.toscanova.com

A "dependable" "respite" in the Westfield Century City Shopping Center, this Italian from Agostino Sciandri (Ago) provides "consistent" fare in a contempo setting with a "lovely" patio; perhaps it's "not terribly authentic" and some find it "pricey", but the staff's "accommodating" making for a "comfortable" stop; P.S. the Calabasas branch is newer.

Totoraku *Japanese* - | - | - | E

West LA | 10610 W. Pico Blvd. (bet. Manning & Parnel Aves.) | 310-838-9881

The sign in front says 'Teriyaki House Pico', a decoy title to dissuade lookie-loos from meandering into this eccentric meat-obsessed kaiseki restaurant in West LA, where the all-beef options are partly served raw, and partly served yakiniku-style, grilled over live coals; the cost runs around $140 a pop - and there's a good chance you'll run into regulars like Nobu Matsuhisa and José Andrés.

Tower Bar ◐ *American* ▽ 25 | 27 | 26 | $55

West Hollywood | Sunset Tower Hotel | 8358 W. Sunset Blvd. (bet. La Cienega Blvd. & Sweetzer Ave.) | 323-848-6677 | www.sunsettowerhotel.com

"Movers and shakers" fill up this "sophisticated" lounge - a "big celebrity hangout" - in West Hollywood's Sunset Tower Hotel; "excellent" American fare and an "impeccable" staff steered by maitre d' Dimitri Dimitrov help justify the bills.

NEW Tower 8 *Californian* - | - | - | E

Santa Monica | Oceana Beach Club Hotel | 849 Ocean Ave. (Idaho Ave.) | 310-393-0486 | www.hoteloceanasantamonica.com

At Santa Monica's stylish Oceana Beach Club Hotel, chef Josiah Citrin (Mélisse) turns out pricey, locally sourced Californian cuisine matched with inventive cocktails; the contemporary, ocean-view space is a breezy escape from the hustle and bustle of the nearby Third Street Promenade.

Trader Vic's *Polynesian* 18 | 21 | 19 | $45

Downtown | LA Live | 800 W. Olympic Blvd. (Figueroa St.) | 213-785-3330 | www.tradervicsla.com

Beverly Hills | Beverly Hilton | 9876 Wilshire Blvd. (bet. Merv Griffin Way & Santa Monica Blvd.) | 310-285-1300 | www.tradervics.com ◐

"More tikis!" clamor fans of this "transformed" Beverly Hills poolside lounge and Downtown location in LA Live, where the "kitschy" islands-themed setting, "tasty" Polynesian eats and "rummy drinks" - including "killer mai tais" - plus "excellent" service leave "nostalgic" fans feeling "like celebrities"; lei-abouts point to "overpriced", "mediocre" munchies, noting it's "not what it was", but because it's a "classic", "you have to go here at least once."

Tra di Noi Ristorante *Italian* 23 | 20 | 22 | $46

Malibu | Malibu Country Mart | 3835 Cross Creek Rd. (bet. Civic Center Way & PCH) | 310-456-0169 | www.tradinoimalibu.com

"The stars come out to eat" at this "warm, welcoming" "slice of Italy in Malibu" offering "enjoyable" pastas, risottos and entrees at prices deemed moderate for the area; although it's set in a shopping center, the dining room is modern and "comfortable" and it's "particularly pleasant to eat outdoors in good weather."

Trastevere *Italian* 18 | 19 | 18 | $35

Hollywood | Hollywood & Highland Ctr. | 6801 Hollywood Blvd. (bet. Highland Ave. & Orange Dr.) | 323-962-3261

(continued)

(continued)

Trastevere

Santa Monica | Third St. Promenade | 1360 Third St. Promenade (Santa Monica Blvd.) | 310-319-1985
www.trastevereristorante.com

"It's wonderful to sit outside on a warm summer night" at these "energetic", "touristy" Italians whose prime locales in the heart of Hollywood and Santa Monica provide ideal "people-watching"; opinions on the food - pastas, wood-fired pizzas, fish and meat - range from "good" to "underwhelming", but at least service is solid and the prices are "fair."

Traxx ⊠ *American* 21 | 21 | 21 | $42

Downtown | Union Station | 800 N. Alameda St. (Cesar E. Chavez Ave.) | 213-625-1999 | www.traxxrestaurant.com

A "well-kept secret", this "unique" destination in Downtown's "beautiful" art deco Union Station provides "satisfying" New American fare in a "memorable" setting with a "fabulous garden in summer"; the staff is "professional and takes care of you without hovering", so even though some call it "a bit pricey", it's a "fun alternative" in the area.

Tres by José Andrés *Eclectic* 23 | 21 | 20 | $55

Beverly Hills | SLS at Beverly Hills | 465 S. La Cienega Blvd. (Clifton Way) | 310-246-5551

Situated off the lobby of the *très soigne* SLS at Beverly Hills, this breakfast, lunch, afternoon tea, dinner and brunch sibling of The Bazaar shares the same elegant-quirky Philippe Starck decor, but is more "relaxing" with a "fun" menu that runs the gamut from granola to molecular mac 'n' cheese; prices suit the upmarket setting, while exceptional service flatters an environment ripe with movers and shakers.

The Tripel *Eclectic* ▽ 25 | 19 | 21 | $29

Playa del Rey | 333 Culver Blvd. (Pershing Dr.) | 310-821-0333 | www.thetripel.com

The burger is a "glorious creation" at this "teeny-tiny" Eclectic gastropub near the beach in Playa del Rey that "lives up to the hype" with "amazing", "unique" eats from husband-and-wife chefs Brooke Williamson and Nick Roberts (Hudson House), plus "a beer to go with everything"; prices are "affordable" too, but you'll need "good luck getting a seat."

NEW Trois Mec ⊠ *Eclectic/French* - | - | - | E

Hollywood | 718 N. Highland Ave. (Melrose Ave.) | www.troismec.com

A trio of celebrity chefs - Ludo Lefebvre, Jon Shook and Vinny Dotolo - oversees this hot ticket in a tiny 26-seat space in a mini-mall behind a gas station at the corner of Melrose and Highland; expect pricey French-Eclectic creations cooked by Lefebvre in the open kitchen - that is, if you can score a much-coveted reservation.

NEW True Burger *Burgers* - | - | - | I

Mid-City | 850 S. La Brea Ave. (bet. 8th & 9th Sts.) | 323-549-9488 | www.true-burger.net

This family-friendly burger outlet in Mid-City touts its burgers made from grass-fed, hormone-free beef, which are served along with free-range chicken, fries, salads and desserts in a space that's casual inside and out; the costs are low too.

True Food Kitchen *Health Food* 23 | 20 | 20 | $28

Santa Monica | 395 Santa Monica Pl. (bet. B'way & Colorado Ave.) | 310-593-8300 | www.truefoodkitchen.com

"See and be seen" at this "healthy hot spot" in Santa Monica from wellness guru Dr. Andrew Weil providing "guilt-free eating" with "fabulous, flavorful" organic New American items, fresh-squeezed juices and even cocktails all deemed "a bit pricey", but worth it for the "variety"; service is "friendly, but sporadic", but a "bright, modern" setting with pleasant patio seating compensates.

Truxton's American Bistro *American* 20 | 16 | 21 | $24

NEW **Santa Monica** | 1329 Santa Monica Blvd. (14th St.) | 310-393-8789

Westchester | 8611 Truxton Ave. (Manchester Ave.) | 310-417-8789

www.truxtonsamericanbistro.com

"A local favorite since it opened", this "family-friendly" American duo in Westchester near LAX and in Santa Monica offers a "something-for-everyone" menu of "creative" comfort food in a modern, warehouselike space; the noise level can be "a little much", but with low prices, most call it a "great place to grab a bite when you don't feel like cooking."

Tsujita LA ◐ *Japanese* 26 | 17 | 19 | $25

West LA | 2057 Sawtelle Blvd. (Mississippi Ave.) | 310-231-7373

Tsujita LA Annex ◐ *Japanese*

West LA | 2050 Sawtelle Blvd. (Mississippi Ave.) | 310-231-7373

www.tsujita-la.com

Offering "Japan in a bowl with every sip", these "spectacular" noodle shops in West LA (branches of a Tokyo original) bring "ramen to a whole other level" with "amazing" specialty *tsukemen* served with a dipping sauce; perhaps the dinner offerings of sashimi and small plates don't "quite match up" to the soups, but with sleek compact settings and moderate prices, most find them "well worth" the trip; P.S. ramen served at lunch only at 2057 Sawtelle, and waits are the norm.

Tuk Tuk Thai *Thai* 22 | 17 | 20 | $24

Pico-Robertson | 8875 W. Pico Blvd. (bet. Clark & Swall Drs.) | 310-860-1872 | www.tuktukthaila.com

A "cute" "little oasis" for Thai-food lovers in Pico-Robertson, this "neighborhood place" whips up "wonderfully fresh" recipes with "a few surprises" along with fruity cocktails; an "attentive" staff and affordable prices - plus lunch and happy-hour specials - keep it tried-and-true.

Tuscany Il Ristorante *Italian* 26 | 23 | 26 | $50

Westlake Village | Westlake Plaza | 968 S. Westlake Blvd. (bet. Agoura & Townsgate Rds.) | 805-495-2768 | www.tuscany-restaurant.com

"It's the details that delight" at this "excellent" "classic" Italian in Westlake Village kicking meals off with a "wonderful basket of fine bread"; its white-tablecloth setting and "fabulous" service make for a tab that's a "bit pricey", so some save it for "special occasions or to impress out-of-town guests."

Tutti Mangia Italian Grill *Italian* ▽ 22 | 23 | 22 | $43

Claremont | 102 Harvard Ave. (1st St.) | 909-625-4669 | www.tuttimangia.com

A "gem" in Claremont, this upmarket Italian earns high marks across the board for its "fantastic", "classic" fare - including a standout roast chicken - "romantic" ambiance and "lovely" staff; although critics call it "too expensive", the majority maintains it "never disappoints."

25 Degrees ◐ *Burgers* 23 | 20 | 20 | $26

Hollywood | Roosevelt Hotel | 7000 Hollywood Blvd. (Orange Dr.) | 323-785-7244 | www.25degreesrestaurant.com

"Decadent" burgers "kick buns" at this "hip" 24/7 hamburger joint in Hollywood's Roosevelt Hotel that's also sought out for "wonderful" sweet-potato fries and Guinness milkshakes; with bordello-style red-flocked wallpaper, the "groovy" setting completes your "rock 'n' roll midnight snack", so most are willing to put up with "infernal waits", "high noise levels" and "add-ons" that up the price.

22nd Street Landing Seafood Grill M *Seafood* 22 | 20 | 20 | $31

San Pedro | 141 W. 22nd St. (bet. Miner St. & Via Cabrilla-Marina) | 310-548-4400 | www.22ndstlandingrestaurant.com

"Fantastic marina views" are accompanied by "excellent", "straightforward" seafood at this open harbor setting in San Pedro that's a prime "place to celebrate"; the "festive atmosphere", "competent" service and "comfortable" prices are all pluses, and if it's a little "old-school" in feel, that's part of the "charm."

26 Beach *Californian* 23 | 20 | 22 | $29

Venice | 3100 Washington Blvd. (Yale Ave.) | 310-823-7526 | www.26beach.com

"Locals" are "hooked" on this Venice Californian flipping "out-of-this-world" burgers on house-baked buns, "flavorful, filling" salads and "insane" French-toast combos for brunch in a "quirky", "dollhouse"-like space flowing out to a "delightful" patio; given the "fair prices" for "gigantic" plates, most find it an "old faithful that never disappoints."

Twin Palms M *American* - | - | - | M

Pasadena | 101 W. Green St. (bet. De Lacey & Pasadena Aves.) | 626-577-4555 | www.twinpalmsrl.com

After being closed for several years, this iconic Old Pasadena space is back open with a fresh paint job and a sizable shaded patio with twin palms as the centerpiece; it turns out a menu of reasonably priced New American fare with a few edgy dishes like sweetbread corn dogs.

NEW Twist Eatery *Californian/Eclectic* - | - | - | I

La Brea | 344 S. La Brea Ave. (bet. 3rd & 4th Sts.) | 323-938-9478 | www.twisteateryla.com

This Cal-Eclectic restaurant and bakery on La Brea serves affordable and health-minded breakfasts, lunches and early dinners, including pastries, sandwiches, salads and grain bowls (such as salmon with lentils and quinoa); the casual-chic space features industrial fixtures and marble countertops.

	FOOD	DECOR	SERVICE	COST

Twohey's *American* 17 | 15 | 20 | $16

Alhambra | 1224 N. Atlantic Blvd. (Huntington Dr.) | 626-284-7387 | www.twoheys.com

"A classic", this "popular" circa-1943 diner in Alhambra is considered a "cut above" with its "big menu" of "hearty" Americana where the "burgers and hot-fudge sundaes reign supreme"; a few find it's "not what it used to be", but the "fun" retro setting and low prices make it a "pleasantly reliable" place to take the kids.

Typhoon *Asian* 20 | 21 | 20 | $37

Santa Monica | Santa Monica Airport | 3221 Donald Douglas Loop S. (Airport Ave.) | 310-390-6565 | www.typhoon.biz

"Eat the weirdest thing you can if only for the bragging rights" at this midpriced Pan-Asian at the Santa Monica Airport featuring an "adventurous" bill of fare that includes "exotic" specialties like crickets and scorpions as well as more conventional items like fried catfish; it's especially "fantastic at sunset" ("it's also nice to watch the planes take off"), and the weekly live jazz alone makes it "worth it."

Umami Burger *Burgers* 23 | 16 | 18 | $21

NEW **Fairfax** | The Grove | 189 The Grove Dr. (bet. Beverly Blvd. & 3rd St.) | 323-954-8626

Hollywood | 1520 N. Cahuenga Blvd. (bet. Selma Ave. & Sunset Blvd.) | 323-469-3100

Hollywood | 4655 Hollywood Blvd. (bet. Rodney Dr. & Vermont Ave.) | 323-669-3922

Mid-Wilshire | 850 S. La Brea Ave. (bet. 8th & 9th Sts.) | 323-931-3000

Santa Monica | Fred Segal | 500 Broadway (5th St.) | 310-451-1300

Hermosa Beach | 1040 Hermosa Ave. (bet. Pier Ave. & 10th St.) | 310-214-8626

NEW **Pasadena** | 49 E. Colorado Blvd. (bet. Fair Oaks & Raymond Aves.) | 626-799-8626

North Hollywood | 12159 Ventura Blvd. (bet. Laurel Canyon Blvd. & Laurelgrove Ave.) | 818-286-9004 ◐

www.umamiburger.com

The "unforgettable" burgers "live up to the hype" at this "must-try", "hipster" chain where the "addictive" truffle fries and other "interesting sides" ensure that "even non-meat eaters leave happy"; there are "friendly" staffers and "modern", "pleasant" surroundings too, and though some may fault "tiny" portions, judging by the crowds, "whatever they're doing, it works."

Umamicatessen *Eclectic* 22 | 19 | 17 | $27

Downtown | 852 S. Broadway (bet. 8th & 9th Sts.) | 213-413-8626 | www.umami.com

This "trendy" food hall spin-off of famed Umami Burger is set in a massive Downtown LA space offering a pleasantly "schizophrenic" array of Eclectic eats, from the signature "juicy" Umami burger to kosher-style deli eats and gourmet donuts - plus beer, cocktails and Handsome coffee - all ordered at the table off of one menu; the high-ceilinged room has a "fun, loud vibe", though it works equally well for a "quick bite"; P.S. look for chef pop-up nights too.

FOOD | DECOR | SERVICE | COST

Uncle Bill's Pancake House *Diner* 22 | 14 | 19 | $16

Manhattan Beach | 1305 Highland Ave. (13th St.) | 310-545-5177 | www.unclebills.net

The "perfect lazy brunch spot", this "cute, homey" Manhattan Beach nook is an area "institution" thanks to its "delish", "old-fashioned" omelets and pancakes offered at a "great value"; though the line can be "longer than Disneyland's" on weekends, it "moves pretty well", and besides, most agree the eats and ocean views from the patio are "worth the wait."

Uncle Darrow's *Cajun/Creole* 21 | 13 | 20 | $19

Marina del Rey | 2560 S. Lincoln Blvd. (Harrison Ave.) | 310-306-4862 | www.uncledarrows.com

"When you want a little Cajun to spice up your day", try this "little corner of Louisiana" in Marina del Rey where the catfish and po' boys are "guaranteed to pique your taste buds"; although many opt for takeout, the vibe is "pleasant" in the casual space and prices "won't break the bank."

Upstairs 2 S M *Mediterranean* 24 | 20 | 24 | $47

West LA | Wine House | 2311 Cotner Ave. (bet. Olympic & Pico Blvds.) | 310-231-0316 | www.upstairs2.com

Though it's "off the radar", fans tout this "cozy" tapas stop above a West LA wine shop offering "tasty" Med-influenced small plates "that ain't so small" alongside "fabulous wines" in "intelligent" pairings; with "unpretentious" service and "reasonable prices", "what more could you want?"

Urasawa S M *Japanese* 28 | 24 | 27 | $514

Beverly Hills | 218 N. Rodeo Dr. (Wilshire Blvd.) | 310-247-8939

Truly "memorable", this intimate Beverly Hills Japanese showcases an "amazing" omakase-only parade of small plates and sushi crafted by "perfectionist" chef Hiro Urasawa; "nothing is spared" when it comes to service either, so if you can "afford the luxury", it's "an experience worth having at least once in your lifetime."

Urth Caffé *American* 22 | 18 | 18 | $20

Downtown | 451 S. Hewitt St. (5th St.) | 213-797-4534

West Hollywood | 8565 Melrose Ave. (bet. Westbourne & Westmount Drs.) | 310-659-0628

Beverly Hills | 267 S. Beverly Dr. (bet. Charleville Blvd. & Gregory Way) | 310-205-9311

Santa Monica | 2327 Main St. (Hollister Ave.) | 310-314-7040

NEW **Pasadena** | 594 E. Colorado Blvd. (bet. Madison & Molino Aves.) | no phone

www.urthcaffe.com

"Such a scene", this "quintessential LA" cafe chain attracts a "gorgeous" crowd with "amazing Spanish lattes", "healthy juices", "gargantuan salads" and other "fresh" American fare, plus "decadent" desserts; the patio makes it a "go-to on a sunny day", even if the perpetual crowds "make you wonder, 'shouldn't these people be at work or something?'"

Ushuaia Argentinean Steakhouse *Argentinean/Steak* ▽ 23 | 20 | 21 | $52

Santa Monica | 2628 Wilshire Blvd. (Princeton St.) | 310-315-5457 | www.ushuaiasteakhouse.com

Named after Argentina's southernmost city, this Santa Monica steakhouse serves a moderately priced menu of traditional grilled meats with spicy sauces and South American wines; the vibe is steakhouse-cozy, with cork ceilings and handsome wood furnishings befitting the upper-end prices.

U-Zen *Japanese* 24 | 15 | 23 | $40

West LA | 11951 Santa Monica Blvd. (Brockton Ave.) | 310-477-1390 | www.u-zenrestaurant.com

"Been here forever and still terrific", this West LA Japanese is a source for "ample cuts" of "fresh" fish (the "toro is tops") at "reasonable prices"; chef-owner Masa Mizokami and his "accommodating" crew create a "welcoming" atmosphere, and just about all agree it's "one of the best in town."

Valentino ☒ *Italian* 26 | 24 | 26 | $74

Santa Monica | 3115 Pico Blvd. (bet. 31st & 32nd Sts.) | 310-829-4313 | www.valentinorestaurants.com

"Still excellent", this "classic" Santa Monica Italian from chef-owner Piero Selvaggio presents "refined" contemporary cuisine and "captivating" wines in an "elegant", "quiet" setting; yes, it's "pricey", but service is "impeccable" and even after 40 years the overall package is "hard to beat"; P.S. the small-plates menu at the Vin Bar is a "more affordable" option.

Valentino's *Pizza* ▽ 22 | 10 | 18 | $15

El Segundo | 150 S. Sepulveda Blvd. (El Segundo Blvd.) | 310-426-9494
Manhattan Beach | 975 N. Aviation Blvd. (10th St.) | 310-318-5959
www.valentinospizza.net

"Large slices" of "New York-style pizza" with "abundant cheese and great sauce" are the thing at these "cheap" mostly "take-out joints", where the "incredible" sausage rolls also get a shout-out; don't expect much in the way of decor, but "easy" takeaway and delivery is a plus.

Vegan Glory *Vegan* 21 | 13 | 20 | $18

Beverly Boulevard | 8393 Beverly Blvd. (Orlando Ave.) | 323-653-4900 | www.veganglory.com

"Who knew vegan food could taste this good?" ask fans of the "fresh", "flavorful options" at this "affordable" Thai-Asian eatery on Beverly Boulevard known for its "excellent fake meats"; service is "quick", but some find the fluorescent-lit strip-mall location best suited for takeout.

Veggie Grill *Vegan* 22 | 17 | 20 | $16

Fairfax | Farmers Mkt. | 110 S. Fairfax Ave. (Farmers Market Pl.) | 323-933-3997
NEW **Hollywood** | Arclight Complex | 6374 Sunset Blvd. (Ivar Ave.) | 323-962-3354
West Hollywood | 8000 W. Sunset Blvd. (Laurel Ave.) | 323-822-7575
Santa Monica | 2025 Wilshire Blvd. (bet. 20th & 21st Sts.) | 310-829-1155
NEW **Westwood** | 10916 Lindbrook Dr. (Westwood Blvd.) | 310-209-6070
El Segundo | 720 S. Allied Way (Hughes Way) | 310-535-0025
Long Beach | Long Beach Mktpl. | 6451 E. PCH (2nd St.) | 562-430-4986
Torrance | 2533 PCH (bet. Crenshaw Blvd. & Pennsylvania Ave.) | 310-325-6689
NEW **Encino** | 16542 Ventura Blvd. (Rubio Ave.) | 818-788-2621
www.veggiegrill.com

"Surprisingly tasty", "guilt-free" vegan eats - including "delicious" faux-chicken sandwiches, "craveable kale" and sweet potato fries -

	FOOD	DECOR	SERVICE	COST

make this fast-casual chain a "go-to" for "skinny yoga types"; the service is "fast and friendly" and the look is "simple, clean and modern", making it a "great place to meet for cheap."

Versailles *Cuban* | 22 | 12 | 19 | $21

Mid-City | 1415 S. La Cienega Blvd. (bet. Alcott St. & Pico Blvd.) | 310-289-0392
Palms | 10319 Venice Blvd. (bet. Motor & Vinton Aves.) | 310-558-3168
Manhattan Beach | 1000 N. Sepulveda Blvd. (bet. 10th & 11th Sts.) | 310-937-6829
Encino | 17410 Ventura Blvd. (bet. Louise & White Oak Aves.) | 818-906-0756
www.versaillescuban.com

"The garlic chicken is heaven" at this "high-energy" Cuban chain beloved by many for its "soul-satisfying" fare that "tastes like abuela's in the kitchen"; service is "welcoming" despite the "barren", "cafeteria-style" setting, and prices are a downright "bargain", so it "hits the spot" every time; P.S. "bring Tic Tacs!"

Vertical Wine Bistro ◐ M *Eclectic/Mediterranean* | 21 | 23 | 21 | $42

Pasadena | 70 N. Raymond Ave. (Union St.) | 626-795-3999 | www.verticalwinebistro.com

There's "always a vibrant crowd" at this "'in' place" for oenophiles in Pasadena owned by movie producer Gale Anne Hurd, where "tasty", "approachable" Eclectic-Med small plates are matched with "amazing wines" and a "good selection of flights" in a "stylish, modern" setting; though some caution that the tabs can "add up", happy hour offers one of the "best deals in town."

Via Alloro *Italian* | 22 | 20 | 21 | $47

Beverly Hills | 301 N. Canon Dr. (Dayton Way) | 310-275-2900 | www.viaalloro.com

An upmarket "Italian sports bar", this Beverly Hills standby from the Drago brothers "gets it right" for fans with "great food" from a "wonderful" staff in a "relaxing" atmosphere; those who want to avoid the TVs inside can opt for some stellar "people-watching on the patio."

Via Veneto *Italian* | 26 | 22 | 24 | $65

Santa Monica | 3009 Main St. (bet. Marine St. & Pier Ave.) | 310-399-1843 | www.viaveneto.us

"Every bite's a dream" at this Santa Monica Italian laying out an "amazing", "authentic" array of pastas and roasts in a setting that's "noisy, happy and full of life"; service is "attentive" too, so while it's "pricey", most find the overall atmosphere "so charming" that it's "worth it."

Vibrato Grill Jazz M *American/Steak* | 22 | 25 | 23 | $61

Bel-Air | 2930 N. Beverly Glen Circle (Beverly Glen Blvd.) | 310-474-9400 | www.vibratogrilljazz.com

This "old-fashioned supper club" in Bel-Air co-owned by trumpet great Herb Alpert is an "elegant place" with "real-life chanteuses and jazz singers" performing while you tuck into "better-than-expected" American steakhouse fare in a "lovely" setting with a "thriving bar scene"; it's "expensive", but "interesting for a change of pace."

Village Pizzeria *Pizza* | 25 | 13 | 19 | $16

Hancock Park | 131 N. Larchmont Blvd. (bet. Beverly Blvd. & 1st St.) | 323-465-5566

(continued)

Village Pizzeria

Hollywood | 6363 Yucca St. (bet. Cahuenga Blvd. & Ivar St.) | 323-790-0763 www.villagepizzeria.net

Totally "legit" "New York-style" pizza pleases the masses at this inexpensive quick-bite pair in Hollywood and Hancock Park whose "crust has just the right balance of crispy and chewy"; sure, some could "do without the attitude" from the counter staff, but the Big Apple decor "is a hoot", and most are content to just "indulge in a slice" - "fold it in half, shove it in your mouth and be happy."

Villetta *Italian* 20 | 23 | 20 | $66

Santa Monica | 246 26th St. (bet. Georgina Ave. & San Vicente Blvd.) | 310-394-8455 | www.villetta.us

"For lunch the garden can't be beat" at this "vibrant" Santa Monica Italian set in a historic building, purveying a varied lineup of pizzas, pastas, fish and chops; however, despite the "cozy" setting, many find the food and service "inconsistent", especially given the "steep" pricing.

Vincenti ☒ *Italian* 26 | 24 | 24 | $70

Brentwood | 11930 San Vicente Blvd. (bet. Bundy Dr. & Montana Ave.) | 310-207-0127 | www.vincentiristorante.com

"A star among the many Italian options in Brentwood", this "top-notch" entry matches its "superb" cuisine "prepared with minimal fuss" with "excellent" wines in an "inviting", "elegant" atmosphere; yes, it's "expensive", but there's "wonderful hospitality", making it the "perfect spot for a special quiet dinner."

Vito *Italian* 23 | 21 | 24 | $43

Santa Monica | 2807 Ocean Park Blvd. (28th St.) | 310-450-4999 | www.vitorestaurant.com

"About as old-school Italian as you can get", this "romantic" Santa Monica hideaway is a "step back in time" where "wonderful" red-sauce fare is proffered by tuxedoed waiters who "make a mean table-side Caesar salad" and "even the diners look like a casting call for a 1950s movie"; though it's "a bit pricey", most find it "delightful" and are "thankful a place like this still exists."

Vito's *Pizza* 26 | 12 | 21 | $19

West Hollywood | 846 N. La Cienega Blvd. (Willoughby Ave.) | 310-652-6859 | www.vitopizza.com

"A favorite for New York transplants", this West Hollywood pizzeria puts out "authentic" 'za that's "a slice of heaven", along with sandwiches and pastas; although the setting's modest and it's "not a bargain", "Vito and the whole crew are amazing" and fans "leave well fed and entertained"; P.S. "save room for the knockout cannoli."

Vivoli Café & Trattoria Ⓜ *Italian* 21 | 15 | 20 | $34

West Hollywood | 7994 Sunset Blvd. (Laurel Ave.) | 323-656-5050 | www.vivolicafe.com

Surveyors throw a "thumbs-up" for this "cozy, little" "neighborhood favorite" in West Hollywood, where "authentically Italian" homemade pastas and such come at "reasonable" prices; add in a "warm reception", and "the biggest challenge is to save room for dessert."

FOOD | DECOR | SERVICE | COST

Wabi-Sabi *Japanese* 22 | 18 | 19 | $41

Venice | 1635 Abbot Kinney Blvd. (Venice Blvd.) | 310-314-2229 | www.wabisabisushi.com

"A longtime fixture on Abbot Kinney", this "trusty" Venice Japanese pulls in a "young" crowd with "fresh" "Cal-style" slabs and rolls plus "innovative" small plates washed down with "good" martinis at happy hour; with a "fun", "local vibe" and "sincere" service, it's a "reliable" bet in spite of the somewhat "expensive" tabs.

The Waffle *American* 20 | 16 | 18 | $20

Hollywood | 6255 W. Sunset Blvd. (Ivar Ave.) | 323-465-6901 | www.thewafflehollywood.com

"Decadent" sweet and savory waffles lead the lineup at this "busy breakfast joint" in Hollywood that also "hits the spot" late at night; some say service "needs to get it together" and "execution is lacking" for the prices, but the retro space with a dog-friendly patio is often "jumping" nonetheless.

Wahib's Middle East *Mideastern* ▽ 20 | 14 | 20 | $20

Alhambra | 910 E. Main St. (Granada Ave.) | 626-576-1048 | www.wahibmiddleeast.com

It's "worth a drive for pigging out" at the "great-value" lunch and dinner buffets at this Alhambra Middle Eastern, an area "institution" where it's easy to "over-indulge"; while the setting and service may be unremarkable, outdoor seating is a plus, and you can light up a hookah on the patio in the evening.

Walter's *Eclectic* 20 | 17 | 20 | $26

Claremont | 310 Yale Ave. (Bonita Ave.) | 909-624-4914 | www.waltersrestaurant.biz

"Everyone can find something they like" at this "neighborhood favorite" "for budget-conscious diners in Claremont" boasting a "wildly varied" Eclectic menu peppered with "unusual" Afghan specialties at dinner; the mood's "friendly and comfortable" with patio seating that's especially "pleasant" and a "delightful" Sunday brunch buffet.

Warszawa M *Polish* 22 | 19 | 22 | $36

Santa Monica | 1414 Lincoln Blvd. (Santa Monica Blvd.) | 310-393-8831 | www.warszawarestaurant.com

"It's old world" all the way at this "*gemütlich*" Santa Monica standby where "hearty", "authentic Polish" "delicacies" are "reasonably priced" and washed down with glasses of vodka; it's set in a "charming old house" with a "fun" outdoor lounge, all boosted by "warm" hospitality; P.S. "get the duck – it's fab."

Water Grill *Seafood* 26 | 24 | 25 | $64

Downtown | 544 S. Grand Ave. (bet. 5th & 6th Sts.) | 213-891-0900

NEW **Santa Monica** | 1401 Ocean Ave. (Santa Monica Blvd.) | 310-394-5669

www.watergrill.com

"Seafood so fresh it seems as if they just fished it out of the ocean" is the hook at these upscale-casual Downtown and Santa Monica eateries also featuring "just about every kind of oyster you can imagine"; no, the Downtown branch is "not as elegant as it used to be", but service is still "lovely" and it's not as expensive, either.

	FOOD	DECOR	SERVICE	COST

Waterloo & City ◐ *British* 23 | 19 | 21 | $43

Culver City | 12517 W. Washington Blvd. (Mildred Ave.) | 310-391-4222 | www.waterlooandcity.com

"LA meets London gastropub" at this "hip" Culver City "favorite" from "innovative chef" Brendan Collins spotlighting a "sophisticated" Modern British menu "heavy on meat" with "lots of surprises", elevated by "awesome" beers and a "nicely curated" cocktail list; prices are "reasonable", the servers are "savvy" and the space has a pleasantly "ramshackle feel", although it's frequently "jam-packed."

Watermark on Main Ⓜ *American* ▽ 22 | 26 | 23 | $44

Ventura | 598 E. Main St. (Chesnut St.) | 805-643-6800 | www.watermarkonmain.com

A "beautifully restored" bank building with mahogany woodwork and dramatic chandeliers is the setting for this "upscale" Ventura American providing "excellent" food and service; it's not inexpensive, but works for a "special evening", thanks in part to its noteworthy bar pouring "imaginative" cocktails and "wonderful" live music on weekends.

Westside Tavern *Californian* 22 | 21 | 21 | $36

West LA | Westside Pavilion | 10850 W. Pico Blvd. (Westwood Blvd.) | 310-470-1539 | www.westsidetavernla.com

Groupies "go as much as possible" to this "attractive" Westside Pavilion "favorite" for "rock-solid, high-end pub food" featuring "modern", "seasonal" Californian items, from "amazing" flatbreads to "fantastic cocktails"; service is "pleasant" and prices relatively "affordable" too, so don't be surprised by the frequently "long waits"; P.S. it's especially "dependable before or after a movie."

Whale & Ale *Pub Food* ▽ 19 | 18 | 19 | $29

San Pedro | 327 W. Seventh St. (bet. Centre & Mesa Sts.) | 310-832-0363 | www.whaleandale.com

"If you want real fish 'n' chips", this "proper" San Pedro tavern is a "solid" bet with "authentic English pub grub" and "some great ales" on tap in a "charming" environment; moderate pricing and frequent live music make it a "fun place to hang out."

NEW Willie Jane ◐Ⓜ *Southern* - | - | - | M

Venice | 1031 Abbot Kinney Blvd. (bet. B'way & Westminster Ave.) | 310-392-2425 | www.williejane.com

After their success at Post & Beam, chef Govind Armstrong and restaurateur Brad Johnson have teamed up again at this eatery on Abbot Kinney with modern takes on traditional Southern cooking and cocktails; the upscale shedlike setting has lots of greenery, wicker furniture and a sense of ease not found in most hot Venice destinations.

Wilshire ⊠ *American* 22 | 24 | 22 | $55

Santa Monica | 2454 Wilshire Blvd. (bet. Chelsea Ave. & 25th St.) | 310-586-1707 | www.wilshirerestaurant.com

"The scene is good, but the food's much better" at this "modern, trendy" Santa Monican featuring "delicious" seasonal New American with "creative" touches elevated by "fantastic" cocktails; it's "expensive", but pays off with "engaging" service and an "elegant" atmosphere with a "lovely" patio (one of the "best in LA"), plus a "high-energy" bar that gets hopping late at night.

	FOOD	DECOR	SERVICE	COST

Wirtshaus ◐ *German* 19 | 17 | 19 | $24

La Brea | 345 N. La Brea Ave. (Oakwood Ave.) | 323-931-9291 | www.wirtshausla.com

Expect a "good variety of German deliciousness" at this "friendly" La Brea "beer house" with a sheltered outdoor patio, a Ping-Pong table and a polished bar with a score of suds to choose from; foodwise, there are "epic platters" of wursts, "dreamy potatoes" and such, and with modest tabs, fans can think of no better place "to spend a Saturday afternoon."

Wokcano Restaurant ◐ *Asian* 19 | 20 | 19 | $29

Downtown | 800 W. Seventh St. (Flower St.) | 213-623-2288
West Hollywood | 8408 W. Third St. (bet. La Cienega Blvd. & Orlando Ave.) | 323-951-1122
Santa Monica | 1413 Fifth St. (bet. B'way & Santa Monica Blvd.) | 310-458-3080
Long Beach | 199 The Promenade N. (B'way) | 562-951-9652
Pasadena | 33 S. Fair Oaks Ave. (bet. Colorado Blvd. & Green St.) | 626-578-1818
Burbank | 150 S. San Fernando Blvd. (Angeleno Ave.) | 818-524-2288
Santa Clarita | Valencia Mall Shopping Ctr. | 24201 Valencia Blvd. (McBean Pkwy.) | 661-288-1913
www.wokcanorestaurant.com

There are "lots of choices" on the Asian-fusion menu at this "surprisingly cool" chain that's a "reliable option for upscale Chinese, sushi" and Thai at "non-upscale prices"; late hours, a full bar and DJs are perks at some locations, but some find the "Vegas" feel and "loud" rock soundtrack less than appealing; P.S. "the happy-hour specials are your friend."

Wolfgang Puck at Hotel Bel-Air *Californian/Mediterranean* 24 | 25 | 25 | $87

Bel-Air | Hotel Bel-Air | 701 Stone Canyon Rd. (Chalon Rd.) | 310-909-1644 | www.hotelbelair.com

An "idyllic" setting is the backdrop for this ultrapricey "jewel" in the Hotel Bel-Air showcasing Wolfgang Puck's "delicious", "beautifully presented" Cal-Med cuisine; service is "outstanding" and "unrushed" too, making it a "favorite place to celebrate an event, even if you have to make one up"; P.S. breakfast is popular with industry types.

Wolfgang Puck Express *Californian* 21 | 17 | 19 | $33

Santa Monica | 1315 Third St. Promenade (Arizona Ave.) | 310-576-4770

Wolfgang Puck LA Bistro *Californian*

Universal City | Universal CityWalk | 1000 Universal Studios Blvd. (Coral Dr.) | 818-985-9653
www.wolfgangpuck.com

These "convenient" "fast-food" outlets from Wolfgang Puck offer a "something-for-everyone" array of "light" Cal sandwiches and salads to shoppers, moviegoers and travelers at "decent prices"; even if many call the food "nothing special" and say they're "certainly not destinations on their own accord", it works if you're "on the go."

Wolfgang's Steakhouse *Steak* 24 | 23 | 23 | $73

Beverly Hills | 445 N. Canon Dr. (Santa Monica Blvd.) | 310-385-0640 | www.wolfgangssteakhouse.net

One of the "best steaks this side of the Williamsburg Bridge" turns up at this "Manhattan"-style chophouse in Beverly Hills from Peter Luger alum Wolfgang Zwiener, pulling a "sophisticated crowd" for "amazing porterhouses" and other "excellent", "expensive" eats; a "manly", "upscale" ambiance and servers who "greet regulars and newbies alike with warm familiarity" complete the "old-school" package.

Wolfslair Biergarten ◐ *German* ▽ 22 | 18 | 22 | $23

Hollywood | 1521 N. Vine St. (Sunset Blvd.) | 323-467-9653 | www.wolfslairla.com

Top Chef contestant Jamie Lauren reappears at this Hollywood beer and sausage shop, where the brews are Teutonic, and so is the sausage-heavy menu; it's the latest in an increasingly large number of bierhauses where the tables are shared, the beer is cold and the toppings for the wursts tend to be exotic.

Wood & Vine ◐ *American* 20 | 21 | 20 | $40

Hollywood | Taft Bldg. | 6280 Hollywood Blvd. (bet. Argyle Ave. & Vine St.) | 323-334-3360 | www.woodandvine.com

This restaurant in the historic Taft Building in Hollywood offers "amazing" classic cocktails and "tasty little plates" of American comfort fare - from chicken 'n' waffles to pork rillette - at "reasonable prices"; the "cool" "old-industrial" interior with tin ceilings and a "beautiful bar" opens onto a "rustic patio", while its location near the theaters makes it a convenient pick "before or after shows."

Wood Ranch BBQ & Grill *BBQ* 20 | 17 | 19 | $28

Fairfax | The Grove | 189 The Grove Dr. (bet. Beverly Blvd. & 3rd St.) | 323-937-6800

Cerritos | Cerritos Towne Ctr. | 12801 Towne Center Dr. (bet. Bloomfield Ave. & 183rd St.) | 562-865-0202

Arcadia | Westfield Santa Anita Mall | 400 S. Baldwin Ave. (Huntington Dr.) | 626-447-4745

Northridge | Northridge Fashion Ctr. | 9301 Tampa Ave. (bet. Nordhoff & Plummer Sts.) | 818-886-6464

Agoura Hills | Whizins Ctr. | 5050 Cornell Rd. (Roadside Dr.) | 818-597-8900

Camarillo | 1101 E. Daily Dr. (Lantana St.) | 805-482-1202

Moorpark | 540 New Los Angeles Ave. (Spring Rd.) | 805-523-7253

Ventura | Pacific View Mall | 3449 E. Main St. (Mills Rd.) | 805-620-4500

Newhall | Valencia Mktpl. | 25580 The Old Rd. (bet. McBean Pkwy. & Pico Canyon Rd.) | 661-222-9494

www.woodranch.com

"Always a crowd-pleaser", this "wildly popular" 'cue chain inspires "pig-outs" with "tender tri-tips" and other "meaty, flavorful" fare at "fair prices"; there's "prompt" table service and a "comfy", "family-friendly" setting, but "lines can be overwhelming", so many rely on the curbside takeout.

Woody's Bar-B-Que *BBQ* 24 | 10 | 18 | $22

Mid-City | 3446 W. Slauson Ave. (Crenshaw Blvd.) | 323-294-9443

Inglewood | 475 S. Market St. (bet. Hillcrest Blvd. & La Brea Ave.) | 310-672-4200 Ⓢ

www.woodysbarbquela.com

"Right up there" with the best BBQ in town, this "no-frills" duo doles out "delicious", "finger-licking" ribs "worth traveling to" Mid-City or Inglewood for; it's primarily takeout, but you'll "get in and get out" "fast", and "you can't beat the price."

	FOOD	DECOR	SERVICE	COST

WP24 *Chinese* 25 | 27 | 25 | $91

Downtown | Ritz-Carlton | 900 W. Olympic Blvd. (Figueroa St.) | 213-743-8824 | www.wolfgangpuck.com

The towering views from the 24th floor of Downtown's Ritz-Carlton are "straight out of a *Batman* movie" at this "breathtaking" restaurant spotlighting Wolfgang Puck's "incredible", "creative" Chinese tasting menus; service is "superb" too, just "increase the limit on your credit card in advance"; P.S. the lounge offers more-affordable small plates, sushi and cocktails.

W's China Bistro *Chinese* 21 | 18 | 21 | $28

Redondo Beach | 1410 S. PCH (bet. F & G Aves.) | 310-792-1600 | www.wschinabistro.com

It's "not your usual Chinese" at this Redondo eatery presenting "elevated" eats "with a California attitude" in a "casual, but well-designed" setting; service can be variable, but tabs are "reasonable", and on the whole you really "can't go wrong here"; P.S. happy hour has "great deals."

Wurstküche ◐ *European* 23 | 18 | 17 | $19

Downtown | 800 E. Third St. (Traction Ave.) | 213-687-4444
Venice | 625 Lincoln Blvd. (bet. Sunset Ct. & Vernon Ave.) | 213-687-4444
www.wurstkucherestaurant.com

"Exactly what a modern bierhall should be", this Downtown-Venice duo dispenses "exotic tubular meat concoctions" (rattlesnake, rabbit and even vegan) and "crispy fries" with "dipping sauces galore", washed down with "fab", "unusual" Belgian and German brews in a "trendy", "loud" industrial setting with communal tables and DJs spinning; sure, the "cafeteria-style" service and "hipper-than-thou" vibe's not for everyone, but it's "fun" "with a group", and especially "packed" late at night.

Xi'an *Chinese* 21 | 19 | 20 | $37

Beverly Hills | 362 N. Canon Dr. (bet. Brighton & Dayton Ways) | 310-275-3345 | www.xian90210.com

The "default Sunday night Chinese" for many Beverly Hills denizens, this longtime venue is a find for "fresh", "creative" takes on the classics with a "healthy", "Americanized" bent; with "moderate prices", "gracious" service and contemporary digs, most don't mind the "noisy" acoustics.

Xiomara *Californian/Cuban* 21 | 24 | 23 | $46

Hollywood | 6101 Melrose Ave. (Seward St.) | 323-461-0601 | www.xiomararestaurant.com

Xiomara Ardolina turns out an "eclectic" array of "well-executed" Californian cuisine with Cuban touches at this "easygoing" spot in Hollywood; a "friendly staff", "jazzy" soundtrack and "cozy" Havana-style setup create a "romantic" mood, and almost all agree it has one of "the best mojitos in town"; P.S. it's also a lunch mainstay near Paramount Studios.

Yabu *Japanese* 23 | 15 | 20 | $35

West Hollywood | 521 N. La Cienega Blvd. (bet. Melrose & Rosewood Aves.) | 310-854-0400
West LA | 11820 W. Pico Blvd. (Granville Ave.) | 310-473-9757
www.yaburestaurant.com

"People rave about the soba", homemade tofu and other "Japanese delicacies" at this "real-deal" pair in West Hollywood and West LA also purveying "solid" sushi; the settings are "casual", but "gracious" servers offer "spot-on" recommendations, and prices are relatively modest given the "high-end" grub.

Yamashiro *Asian* 21 | 27 | 23 | $46

Hollywood | 1999 N. Sycamore Ave. (Franklin Ave.) | 323-466-5125 | www.yamashirohollywood.com

"Enjoy the scenery from high in the Hollywood Hills" at this veteran Cal-Asian boasting a "tranquil" pagoda setting with "lush gardens" that "takes you back to Japan of the 1940s"; service "excels", and if many find the "lovely location" "upstages" the "pricey" sushi, at least "you can't beat it for drinks."

Yang Chow *Chinese* 22 | 13 | 19 | $26

Chinatown | 819 N. Broadway (bet. Alpine & College Sts.) | 213-625-0811
Pasadena | 3777 E. Colorado Blvd. (Quigley Ave.) | 626-432-6868
Canoga Park | 6443 Topanga Canyon Blvd. (Victory Blvd.) | 818-347-2610
www.yangchow.com

"The slippery shrimp dish is a must-have" at this "nostalgic, old-school" Chinese trio cherished for its "comforting", "Americanized" eats like "you grew up with" in "plentiful" portions; just overlook the "noisy" somewhat "run-down" settings and "efficient, but rushed" service and focus on the way-"reasonable" prices.

Yen Sushi & Sake Bar *Japanese* 22 | 20 | 19 | $32

Little Tokyo | California Market Ctr. | 110 E. Ninth St. (bet. Los Angeles & Main Sts.) | 213-627-9709 ⊠
Pico-Robertson | 9618 W. Pico Blvd. (bet. Beverwil & Edris Drs.) | 310-278-0691
Brentwood | Granville Plaza | 11819 Wilshire Blvd. (bet. Granville & Westgate Aves.) | 310-996-1313
Long Beach | 4905 E. Second St. (bet. Argonne & St. Joseph Aves.) | 562-434-5757
Studio City | 12930 Ventura Blvd. (bet. Coldwater Canyon & Van Noord Aves.) | 818-907-6400
www.yenrestaurants.com

"Load up on sushi without breaking the bank" at this Japanese chain where the "big", "innovative" rolls are priced to move during the all-day happy hours; service is solid and the atmosphere's vaguely "hip", although many get it "to go."

Ye Olde King's Head *Pub Food* 17 | 17 | 18 | $27

Santa Monica | 116 Santa Monica Blvd. (bet. Ocean Ave. & 2nd St.) | 310-451-1402 | www.yeoldekingshead.com

"Brits and lovers of all things British" tuck into "filling" fare like fish 'n' chips at this "real-deal" Santa Monica pub (aka "Oxford on the Pacific") also featuring a "tremendous beer and ale selection", all "cheerfully served"; sure, some "can think of better places to eat", but with moderate prices, a "quaint, cozy" setting and football on the telly, it's a "sentimental favorite" for many.

Yuca's *Mexican* 25 | 9 | 21 | $11

Los Feliz | 2056 Hillhurst Ave. (bet. Ambrose Ave. & Price St.) | 323-662-1214 ⊠ ≠

(continued)

FOOD	DECOR	SERVICE	COST

(continued)

Yuca's

Los Feliz | 4666 Hollywood Blvd. (bet. Rodney Dr. & Vermont Ave.) | 323-661-0523

www.yucasla.com

"Tiny but amazing", this taco-shack duo in Los Feliz is famed for its "melt-in-your-mouth" cochinita pibil and "outrageous" carnitas as well as some of "the best cheapo burritos in town"; it's primarily take-out at both locales, but fans still call it "a must-visit" for anyone seeking a "real LA" experience.

Yxta Cocina Mexicana *Mexican* 24 | 21 | 19 | $28

Downtown | 601 S. Central Ave. (6th St.) | 213-596-5579 | www.yxta.net

A "hidden oasis in a rough part of town", this "modern" Mexican Downtown "utilizes the freshest of ingredients" in its "terrific", "original" south-of-the-border fare; moderate pricing, "professional" service and an "energetic" vibe make it "well worth the trip to find it"; P.S. there's also a "fabulous happy hour" daily.

Zane's *Italian/Steak* ∇ 21 | 18 | 21 | $41

Hermosa Beach | 1150 Hermosa Ave. (Pier Ave.) | 310-374-7488 | www.zanesrestaurant.com

"Sophisticated yet economical", this "unpretentious" Hermosa Beach spot is a "solid" bet for "well-prepared" steakhouse and Italian fare - plus burgers - backed by a "comprehensive wine list" and "smart cocktails"; service is "attentive" while the "lively", "adult" setting provides "interesting people-watching" through plate-glass windows, and being within "walking distance to the beach for an after-dinner stroll" is a plus.

Zankou Chicken *Mediterranean* 21 | 7 | 13 | $14

East Hollywood | 5065 W. Sunset Blvd. (Normandie Ave.) | 323-665-7845 ◐

West LA | 1716 S. Sepulveda Blvd. (Santa Monica Blvd.) | 310-444-0550

Pasadena | 1296 E. Colorado Blvd. (bet. Chester & Holliston Aves.) | 626-405-1502

Burbank | 1001 N. San Fernando Blvd. (Walnut Ave.) | 818-238-0414

Glendale | 1415 E. Colorado Blvd. (Verdugo Rd.) | 818-244-1937

Glendale | 901 W. Glenoaks Blvd. (Highland Ave.) | 818-244-0492

North Hollywood | 10760 Riverside Dr. (Lankershim Blvd.) | 818-655-0469

Tarzana | 19598 Ventura Blvd. (bet. Corbin & Shirley Aves.) | 818-345-1200

Van Nuys | 5658 Sepulveda Blvd. (bet. Burbank Blvd. & Hatteras St.) | 818-781-0615

Montebello | Downtown Plaza | 125 N. Montebello Blvd. (Whittier Blvd.) | 323-722-7200

www.zankouchicken.com

Devotees "dream about" the "juicy, flavorful" rotisserie chicken at this "popular" Mediterranean fast-food chain cherished for its "glorious", "kick-ass" "garlic sauce of the gods" that will make you want to "buy a tub, take it home and put it on everything you eat for the next week"; "morose" service plus "over-bright fluorescent lighting" add up to "zero atmosphere, but who cares when the food rocks?"

	FOOD	DECOR	SERVICE	COST

Zazou *Mediterranean* 25 | 21 | 22 | $41

Redondo Beach | 1810 S. Catalina Ave. (Vista Del Mar) | 310-540-4884 | www.zazourestaurant.com

"Pretty restaurant, pretty food and pretty clientele" sums up this lively Redondo Beacher that "fills a niche" in the area with an "excellent" Med menu and "terrific" wines; it can get "crowded" and "noisy", however, "timely, considerate service" smoothes things over, as do the moderate bills.

Zeke's Smokehouse *BBQ* 19 | 14 | 18 | $22

Montrose | 2209 Honolulu Ave. (bet. Montrose Ave. & Thompson Ct.) | 818-957-7045 | www.zekessmokehouse.com

"Well-executed BBQ standards" are dressed up with "some of the zingiest sauces you can find" at this "solid" Montrose entry set in a contemporary Southern-themed space with a sidewalk patio; service is "happy and quick", although a few find prices "too high" for the genre; P.S. weekend breakfast is an option too.

Zelo Pizzeria *Pizza* ▽ 21 | 14 | 18 | $17

Arcadia | 328 E. Foothill Blvd. (bet. 5th & Northview Aves.) | 626-358-8298 | www.zelopizzeria.com

"Amazing, unusual pizzas" with "abundant toppings" (corn is a favorite) are the thing at this "funky neighborhood gathering place" in Arcadia that's also "easy for takeout"; it isn't fancy, but with "friendly" service and low prices for slices and pies, it's an area "favorite."

Zengo *Asian/Nuevo Latino* 21 | 22 | 21 | $40

Santa Monica | Dining Deck, Santa Monica Pl. | 395 Santa Monica Pl. (bet. B'way & Colorado Ave.) | 310-899-1000 | www.richardsandoval.com

Nibblers "love the menu" at Richard Sandoval's moderately expensive Asian-Nuevo Latino in Santa Monica Place, where there are "lots of choices" of "fun", "unique" small plates and "powerful" cocktails; the "hip" setting includes a "beautiful patio", and there's both an "epic" Sunday brunch and a "good happy hour."

Zephyr Vegetarian *Vegetarian* ▽ 25 | 17 | 20 | $14

Long Beach | 340 E. Fourth St. (Roble Way) | 562-435-7113

This Long Beach oasis for vegans produces casual fare like portobello burgers and tempeh Reubens that might fool even the staunchest carnivores; the earthy-meets-rustic vibe is just as inviting as the affable service and favorable prices.

Zin Bistro Americana *American* 20 | 21 | 21 | $41

Westlake Village | 32131 Lindero Canyon Rd. (Summershore Ln.) | 818-865-0095 | www.zinwestlake.com

Lauded for its "stunning" lakefront views, this Westlake Village bistro offers "very good" New Americana in a "relaxing, romantic" atmosphere; "if you're watching your pennies, try it for lunch", when the "lovely location" and "charming" staff are still intact.

INDEXES

LOCATION MAPS

Special Features

Listings cover the best in each category and include names, locations and Food ratings. Multi-location restaurants' features may vary by branch.

BREAKFAST

(See also Hotel Dining)

Alcove | **Los Feliz** 21
Art's | **Studio City** 21
Auntie Em's | **Eagle Rock** 22
Barney Greengrass | **Beverly Hills** 22
BLD | **Beverly Blvd** 21
CaCao | **Eagle Rock** 24
Café Laurent | **Culver City** 20
Cecconi's | **W Hollywood** 22
Clementine | **Century City** 25
Cora's | **Santa Monica** 23
Doughboys | **Third St** 23
Du-par's | **Fairfax** 17
Farm/Bev. Hills | **Beverly Hills** 18
Farmshop | **Santa Monica** 25
Fred 62 | **Los Feliz** 18
Griddle Cafe | **Hollywood** 25
Huckleberry | **Santa Monica** 23
Hugo's | **multi.** 21
Jinky's | **multi.** 20
John O'Groats | **Rancho Pk** 20
Julienne | **San Marino** 25
La Dijonaise | **Culver City** 19
NEW Larder/Burton | **Beverly Hills** -
Larder/Maple | **Beverly Hills** 20
Lemon Moon | **West LA** 20
Maison Giraud | **Pacific Palisades** 24
Marmalade | **multi.** 17
Marston's | **Pasadena** 21
Martha's 22nd St. | **Hermosa Bch** 23
Maxwell's | **Venice** 19
Milo & Olive | **Santa Monica** 24
Nickel Diner | **Downtown** 21
Olio/Cafe | **Third St** 23
101 Coffee | **Hollywood** 22
Pacific Dining Car | **multi.** 24
Patrick's | **Santa Monica** 17
Square One | **E Hollywood** 22
Susina | **Beverly Blvd** 23
Sweet Lady | **Melrose** 23
Sycamore Kit. | **Mid-City** 24
Tavern | **Brentwood** 24
3 Square | **Venice** 23
Uncle Bill's | **Manhattan Bch** 22

BRUNCH

Abigaile | **Hermosa Bch** 19
Ammo | **Hollywood** 22
Axe | **Venice** 23
Belvedere | **Beverly Hills** 26
Blu Jam Café | **Melrose** 25
Bottega Louie | **Downtown** 23
Bouchon | **Beverly Hills** 25
Cafe Verde | **Pasadena** 23
Canelé | **Atwater Vill** 23
Churchill | **W Hollywood** 15
Cliff's Edge | **Silver Lake** 21
Comme Ça | **W Hollywood** 23
Cooks County | **Beverly Blvd** 23
Dusty's | **Silver Lake** 22
Eveleigh | **W Hollywood** 20
Farmshop | **Santa Monica** 25
Fat Dog | **multi.** 20
Fig | **Santa Monica** 22
Firefly Bistro | **S Pasadena** 19
Gjelina | **Venice** 26
Grub | **Hollywood** 24
Home | **multi.** 20
House Café | **Beverly Blvd** 20
Hugo's | **multi.** 21
Jer-ne | **Marina del Rey** 18
Joe's | **Venice** 26
Larry's | **Venice** 23
Little Dom's/Deli | **Los Feliz** 22
NEW Littlefork | **Hollywood** 24
Luna Park | **La Brea** 19
M.B. Post | **Manhattan Bch** 27
McCormick/Schmick | **El Segundo** 18
NEW MessHall Kitchen | **Los Feliz** 21
Napa Valley | **Westwood** 19
Nickel Diner | **Downtown** 21
Nine Thirty | **Westwood** 16
Ocean Seafood | **Chinatown** 21
One Pico | **Santa Monica** 23
Polo | **Beverly Hills** 22
Porta Via | **Beverly Hills** 22
Raymond | **Pasadena** 25
Saddle Peak | **Calabasas** 26
Salt's Cure | **W Hollywood** 22
Square One | **E Hollywood** 22
Superba | **Venice** 21
Tasting Kitchen | **Venice** 25
Tavern | **Brentwood** 24
3 Square | **Venice** 23
26 Beach | **Venice** 23
Twin Palms | **Pasadena** -
Twohey's | **Alhambra** 17
Waffle | **Hollywood** 20

BUFFET

(Check availability)

All India | **West LA** 21
Bombay Palace | **Beverly Hills** 24
Burger Continental | **Pasadena** 18
Chakra | **Beverly Hills** 23
Frida | **Glendale** 19
India's Tandoori | **multi.** 23
Inn/Seventh Ray | **Topanga** 20
Maison Akira | **Pasadena** 26
Mijares | **Pasadena** 18
Nawab | **Santa Monica** 22
Ocean Tava | **Redondo Bch** 25
Panda Inn | **Pasadena** 22
Picanha | **Burbank** 21
Salt Creek | **Valencia** 19
Smoke Hse. | **Burbank** 21
Tanzore | **Beverly Hills** 21
Twin Palms | **Pasadena** -
Wahib's | **Alhambra** 20
Walter's | **Claremont** 20

BUSINESS DINING

Arroyo | **Pasadena** 25
Barney Greengrass | **Beverly Hills** 22
Belvedere | **Beverly Hills** 26
Bistro 45 | **Pasadena** 25
Blvd | **Beverly Hills** 22
Bouchon | **Beverly Hills** 25
Catch | **Santa Monica** 22
Caulfield's | **Beverly Hills** 23
Celestino | **Pasadena** 25
Chaya | **Downtown** 23
Checkers | **Downtown** 22
Cheval Bistro | **Pasadena** 23
NEW chi SPACCA | **Hollywood** -
Cicada | **Downtown** 25
Coast | **Santa Monica** 22
Coco Laurent | **Downtown** -
Craft | **Century City** 25
Culina | **Beverly Hills** 23
Cut | **Beverly Hills** 27
Dan Tana's | **W Hollywood** 23
Drago Centro | **Downtown** 26
Fig & Olive | **W Hollywood** 22
FigOly | **Downtown** -
555 East | **Long Bch** 25
Fleming's | **multi.** 23
Gordon Ramsay | **W Hollywood** 23
Grill on Alley | **Beverly Hills** 25
Grill on Hollywood | **Hollywood** 24
Hatfield's | **Melrose** 27
Il Grano | **West LA** 25
Il Moro | **West LA** 21
Jar | **Beverly Blvd.** 24
Josie | **Santa Monica** 26
Kincaid's | **Redondo Bch** 22
La Botte | **Santa Monica** 22
L.A. Market | **Downtown** 19
Lucques | **W Hollywood** 27
Madeo | **W Hollywood** 26
Mar'sel | **Rancho Palos Verdes** 26
Mélisse | **Santa Monica** 28
Michael's Rest. | **Santa Monica** 24
Mistral | **Sherman Oaks** 26
Morton's | **multi.** 22
Nick & Stef's | **Downtown** 23
Nic's | **Beverly Hills** 22
Nobu | **W Hollywood** 26
Ocean & Vine | **Santa Monica** 23
Ombra | **Studio City** 21
One Pico | **Santa Monica** 23
Patina | **Downtown** 26
Paul Martin's | **El Segundo** 22
Peppone | **Brentwood** 21
Petros | **Manhattan Bch** 24
Polo | **Beverly Hills** 22
Providence | **Hollywood** 28
Public Kitchen | **Hollywood** 20
NEW RivaBella Ristorante | **W Hollywood** 20
Rivera | **Downtown** 26
Roy's | **Downtown** 23
Rustic Canyon | **Santa Monica** 25
Ruth's Chris | **multi.** 25
Safire | **Camarillo** 25
Scarpetta | **Beverly Hills** 24
Spago | **Beverly Hills** 27
Stefan's/L.A. Farm | **Santa Monica** 22
STK | **W Hollywood** 24
Taylor's | **multi.** 23
NEW Tower 8 | **Santa Monica** -
Valentino | **Santa Monica** 26
Water Grill | **Downtown** 26
Westside Tav. | **West LA** 22
Wilshire | **Santa Monica** 22
Wolfgang Puck/Hotel Bel-Air | **Bel-Air** 24
Wolfgang's | **Beverly Hills** 24
WP24 | **Downtown** 25

CELEBRITY CHEFS

José Andrés

Bazaar/José Andrés | **Beverly Hills** 27
Saam/The Bazaar | **Beverly Hills** 27
Tres/José Andrés | **Beverly Hills** 23

SPECIAL FEATURES

Gino Angelini
- Angelini | **Beverly Blvd** 28
- **NEW** RivaBella Ristorante | **W Hollywood** 20

Govind Armstrong
- Post & Beam | **Mid-City** 22
- **NEW** ROFL Cafe | **Melrose** -
- **NEW** Willie Jane | **Venice** -

Mario Batali
- **NEW** chi SPACCA | **Hollywood** -
- Osteria Mozza | **Hollywood** 27
- Pizzeria Mozza | **Hollywood** 27

Rick Bayless
- Red O | **Melrose** 24

Josef Centeno
- Bäco Mercat | **Downtown** 25
- **NEW** Bar Amá | **Downtown** 23

Jeff Cerciello
- Farmshop | **Santa Monica** 25

Roy Choi
- A-Frame | **Culver City** 23
- **NEW** Chego! | **Chinatown** 23
- Kogi | **Location Varies** 26
- Sunny Spot | **Venice** 21

Michael Cimarusti
- **NEW** Connie/Ted's | **W Hollywood** -
- Providence | **Hollywood** 28

Josiah Citrin
- Lemon Moon | **West LA** 20
- Mélisse | **Santa Monica** 28
- **NEW** Tower 8 | **Santa Monica** -

Tom Colicchio
- Craft | **Century City** 25

Brendan Collins
- Larry's | **Venice** 23
- Waterloo & City | **Culver City** 23

Scott Conant
- Scarpetta | **Beverly Hills** 24

Vinny Dotolo, Jon Shook
- Animal | **Fairfax** 27
- Son of a Gun | **Third St** 26
- **NEW** Trois Mec | **Hollywood** -

Celestino Drago
- Drago Centro | **Downtown** 26

Todd English
- Beso | **Hollywood** 18

Susan Feniger
- Border Grill | **multi.** 22
- Street | **Hollywood** 25

Ben Ford
- Ford's | **Culver City** 20

Neal Fraser
- BLD | **Beverly Blvd** 21
- Cole's | **Downtown** 17
- Strand House | **Manhattan Bch** 20

Alain Giraud
- Maison Giraud | **Pacific Palisades** 24

Suzanne Goin
- A.O.C. | **Beverly Blvd** 25
- **NEW** Larder/Burton | **Beverly Hills** -
- Larder/Maple | **Beverly Hills** 20
- Lucques | **W Hollywood** 27
- Tavern | **Brentwood** 24

Andre Guerrero
- Little Bear | **Downtown** 22
- Maximiliano | **Highland Pk** 22
- Oinkster | **Eagle Rock** 21

Ilan Hall
- Gorbals | **Downtown** 20

Thomas Keller
- Bar Bouchon | **Beverly Hills** 23
- Bouchon | **Beverly Hills** 25
- Bouchon Bakery | **Beverly Hills** 25

Casey Lane
- Parish | **Downtown** 22
- Parish Wine Bar | **Downtown** -

Ludo Lefebvre
- LudoTruck | **Location Varies** 24
- **NEW** Trois Mec | **Hollywood** -

David LeFevre
- **NEW** Fishing/Dynamite | **Manhattan Bch** -
- M.B. Post | **Manhattan Bch** 27

David Lentz
- Hungry Cat | **multi.** 23

Bruce Marder
- **NEW** Cafe Brentwood | **Brentwood** -
- Capo | **Santa Monica** 26
- Cora's | **Santa Monica** 23
- House Café | **Beverly Blvd** 20

Nobu Matsuhisa
- Matsuhisa | **Beverly Hills** 28
- Nobu | **W Hollywood** 26
- Nobu | **Malibu** 27

Joe Miller
- Bar Pintxo | **Santa Monica** 21
- Joe's | **Venice** 26

Masaharu Morimoto
- **NEW** Skewers/Morimoto | **LAX** -

David Myers

Comme Ça | **W Hollywood** 23

NEW Hinoki/The Bird | **Century City** 23

Wolfgang Puck

Chinois | **Santa Monica** 26

Cut | **Beverly Hills** 27

Spago | **Beverly Hills** 27

Wolfgang Puck/Hotel Bel-Air | **Bel-Air** 24

Wolfgang Puck Express/Bistro | **multi.** 21

WP24 | **Downtown** 25

Gordon Ramsay

Fat Cow | **Fairfax** 18

Gordon Ramsay | **W Hollywood** 23

Akasha Richmond

Akasha | **Culver City** 22

Stefan Richter

Stefan's/L.A. Farm | **Santa Monica** 22

Hans Röckenwagner

Röckenwagner | **Santa Monica** 21

3 Square | **Venice** 23

Richard Sandoval

La Sandia | **Santa Monica** 21

Zengo | **Santa Monica** 21

John Sedlar

Rivera | **Downtown** 26

Michael Shafer

Buffalo Fire Dept. | **Torrance** 22

Jimmy Shaw

Lotería! | **multi.** 22

Nancy Silverton

NEW chi SPACCA | **Hollywood** -

Osteria Mozza | **Hollywood** 27

Pizzeria Mozza | **Hollywood** 27

Short Order | **Fairfax** 18

Kerry Simon

L.A. Market | **Downtown** 19

Joachim Splichal

Patina | **Downtown** 26

Ari Taymor

NEW Alma | **Downtown** 26

Suzanne Tracht

Jar | **Beverly Blvd.** 24

Michael Voltaggio

Ink | **W Hollywood** 26

Ink Sack | **W Hollywood** -

Roy Yamaguchi

Roy's | **multi.** 23

Sang Yoon

Father's Office | **multi.** 23

Lukshon | **Culver City** 24

Ricardo Zarate

Mo-Chica | **Downtown** 23

NEW Paiche | **Marina del Rey** -

Picca | **Century City** 25

CHILD-FRIENDLY

(Alternatives to the usual fast-food places)

Abbot's Pizza | **Venice** 23

Trattoria Amici | **multi.** 21

Apple Pan | **West LA** 23

Babalu | **Santa Monica** 18

Barney's | **Santa Monica** 21

BLD | **Beverly Blvd** 21

Bluewater | **Redondo Bch** 21

Bouchon | **Beverly Hills** 25

Bravo | **Santa Monica** 20

Brent's Deli | **multi.** 26

Burger Continental | **Pasadena** 18

Caffé Delfini | **Santa Monica** 24

Caffe Pinguini | **Playa del Rey** 21

Carnival | **Sherman Oaks** 25

Casa Bianca | **Eagle Rock** 23

Cha Cha Chicken | **Santa Monica** 22

Cheesecake | **multi.** 18

Counter | **Santa Monica** 19

Din Tai Fung | **Arcadia** 26

Dish | **La Cañada Flintridge** 20

Duke's | **Malibu** 17

800 Degrees | **Westwood** 23

El Coyote | **Beverly Blvd** 16

Fabiolus Cucina | **Hollywood** 21

Farfalla/Vinoteca | **Los Feliz** 22

Fat Cow | **Fairfax** 18

Feast/East | **West LA** 22

Five Guys | **multi.** 16

Fritto Misto | **multi.** 22

Fromin's | **Santa Monica** 16

Gaucho | **Brentwood** 21

Gladstones | **Pacific Palisades** 17

Hop Li | **multi.** 20

Il Forno Caldo | **Beverly Hills** 21

Jack's/Montana | **Santa Monica** 20

Jinky's | **multi.** 20

Jody Maroni's | **multi.** 20

Johnnie's Pastrami | **Culver City** 21

John O'Groats | **Rancho Pk** 20

Kay 'n Dave's | **multi.** 18

La Grande Orange | **Pasadena** 20

Langer's | **Downtown** 26

Le Petit Greek | **Hancock Pk** 22

Les Sisters | **Chatsworth** 23

NEW Little Beast | **Eagle Rock** -

Lotería! | **multi.** 22

Louise's | **Pasadena** 19

SPECIAL FEATURES

Lucille's | **multi.** 22
Mama D's | **Manhattan Bch** 23
Maria's Italian | **multi.** 19
Marston's | **Pasadena** 21
Martha's 22nd St. | **Hermosa Bch** 23
Maxwell's | **Venice** 19
Miceli's | **Hollywood** 18
Milo & Olive | **Santa Monica** 24
Mi Piace | **Pasadena** 21
Mo's | **Burbank** 18
Mulberry St. Pizzeria | **multi.** 23
Oinkster | **Eagle Rock** 21
Paco's Tacos | **Westchester** 21
Palms Thai | **E Hollywood** 21
Panda Inn | **multi.** 22
P.F. Chang's | **multi.** 17
Philippe/Original | **Chinatown** 23
Pie 'N Burger | **Pasadena** 20
Pitfire | **multi.** 22
Pizzeria Mozza | **Hollywood** 27
Pizzicotto | **Brentwood** 23
Poquito Más | **multi.** 21
Robin's BBQ | **Pasadena** 22
Sammy's Pizza | **El Segundo** 19
Stanley's | **Sherman Oaks** 20
Thai Dishes | **multi.** 20
22nd St. Landing | **San Pedro** 22
Umami Burger | **multi.** 23
Versailles | **multi.** 22
Wabi-Sabi | **Venice** 22
Wood Ranch | **multi.** 20
Zankou | **multi.** 21

COCKTAIL SPECIALISTS

AKA Bistro | **Pasadena** 23
Akasha | **Culver City** 22
A.O.C. | **Beverly Blvd** 25
Bäco Mercat | **Downtown** 25
NEW Bank/Venice | **Venice** -
NEW Bar Amá | **Downtown** 23
Bar Bouchon | **Beverly Hills** 23
Bar Toscana | **Brentwood** 23
Bazaar/José Andrés | **Beverly Hills** 27
Bel Air B&G | **Bel-Air** 21
NEW Bestia | **Downtown** 25
Black Market | **Studio City** 23
Bouchon | **Beverly Hills** 25
Brentwood | **Brentwood** 23
NEW Bucato | **Culver City** -
Cafe Del Rey | **Marina del Rey** 23
NEW Cast | **Santa Monica** -
Caulfield's | **Beverly Hills** 23
Cecconi's | **W Hollywood** 22
NEW Chez Soi | **Manhattan Bch** -
Church/State | **Downtown** 24
Churchill | **W Hollywood** 15
NEW Circa | **Manhattan Bch** -
Cliff's Edge | **Silver Lake** 21
Cole's | **Downtown** 17
Comme Ça | **W Hollywood** 23
Craft | **Century City** 25
Craig's | **W Hollywood** 22
NEW Crossroads Vegan | **W Hollywood** -
Cut | **Beverly Hills** 27
Dan Tana's | **W Hollywood** 23
Drago Centro | **Downtown** 26
El Cholo | **multi.** 19
NEW Esterel | **W Hollywood** -
Eveleigh | **W Hollywood** 20
Federal Bar | **multi.** 19
Fig | **Santa Monica** 22
NEW Fishing/Dynamite | **Manhattan Bch** -
Freddy Smalls | **West LA** 23
Gjelina | **Venice** 26
Hatfield's | **Melrose** 27
Hillstone/Houston's | **multi.** 22
NEW Hinoki/The Bird | **Century City** 23
Hungry Cat | **multi.** 23
Ink | **W Hollywood** 26
Joe's | **Venice** 26
Katsuya | **multi.** 24
La Sandia | **Santa Monica** 21
Laurel Hardware | **W Hollywood** 19
Lukshon | **Culver City** 24
Mastro's | **multi.** 26
M.B. Post | **Manhattan Bch** 27
Mercado | **Santa Monica** 24
Mercato di Vetro | **W Hollywood** 22
NEW MessHall Kitchen | **Los Feliz** 21
Misfit | **Santa Monica** 22
NEW Nikita | **Malibu** -
Nine Thirty | **Westwood** 16
NEW Ocho 8 Taqueria | **Torrance** -
Ortega 120 | **Redondo Bch** 22
NEW Paiche | **Marina del Rey** -
Palm | **multi.** 23
Parish Wine Bar | **Downtown** -
Parkway Grill | **Pasadena** 26
Paul Martin's | **El Segundo** 22
Penthouse | **Santa Monica** 20
NEW Penthouse/Mastro's | **Beverly Hills** -
NEW Petty Cash | **Beverly Blvd** -
Picca | **Century City** 25
Pikey | **Hollywood** 18
Plan Check | **West LA** 21

Ray's/Stark Bar | **Mid-Wilshire** 23
Red Medicine | **Beverly Hills** 22
Red O | **Melrose** 24
Rivera | **Downtown** 26
NEW Royce Wood-Fired | **Pasadena** 24
Rustic Canyon | **Santa Monica** 25
Sky Room | **Long Bch** 23
South Beverly Grill | **Beverly Hills** 21
Sunny Spot | **Venice** 21
NEW Taberna Arros | **Santa Monica** –
Tar & Roses | **Santa Monica** 24
Trader Vic's | **multi.** 18
Water Grill | **Santa Monica** 26
Waterloo & City | **Culver City** 23
Westside Tav. | **West LA** 22

DANCING

Buffalo Club | **Santa Monica** 19
Cafe Fiore | **Ventura** 22
El Pollo Inka | **Gardena** 21
Monsoon | **Santa Monica** 20
Padri | **Agoura Hills** 22
Rush St. | **Culver City** 17
Smoke Hse. | **Burbank** 21
Twin Palms | **Pasadena** –
Wahib's | **Alhambra** 20
Watermark on Main | **Ventura** 22
Whale & Ale | **San Pedro** 19

DESSERT SPECIALISTS

Akasha | **Culver City** 22
Alcove | **Los Feliz** 21
Auntie Em's | **Eagle Rock** 22
Babalu | **Santa Monica** 18
Bottega Louie | **Downtown** 23
Bouchon | **Beverly Hills** 25
Bouchon Bakery | **Beverly Hills** 25
Cafe Montana | **Santa Monica** 20
Cheesecake | **multi.** 18
Clementine | **Century City** 25
Doughboys | **Third St** 23
Farm/Bev. Hills | **multi.** 18
Forage | **Silver Lake** 25
Huckleberry | **Santa Monica** 23
Jack's/Montana | **Santa Monica** 20
Joan's/Third | **Third St** 24
Josie | **Santa Monica** 26
La Crêperie | **Long Bch** 23
L.A. Market | **Downtown** 19
LAMILL | **Silver Lake** 22
Le Pain Quotidien | **multi.** 18
Melting Pot | **multi.** 15
Milo & Olive | **Santa Monica** 24
Mi Piace | **Pasadena** 21
Nickel Diner | **Downtown** 21
Porto's | **multi.** 25
Providence | **Hollywood** 28
Spago | **Beverly Hills** 27
Susina | **Beverly Blvd** 23
Sweet Lady | **Melrose** 23
Urth | **multi.** 22

DINING AT THE BAR

A.O.C. | **Beverly Blvd** 25
AKA Bistro | **Pasadena** 23
NEW Bar Amá | **Downtown** 23
NEW Barnyard | **Venice** –
NEW Bestia | **Downtown** 25
Bouchon | **Beverly Hills** 25
Brentwood | **Brentwood** 23
Chaya | **W Hollywood** 23
NEW Chez Soi | **Manhattan Bch** –
Church/State | **Downtown** 24
NEW Circa | **Manhattan Bch** –
NEW Crossroads Vegan | **W Hollywood** –
Drago Centro | **Downtown** 26
Father's Office | **multi.** 23
Firefly | **Studio City** 20
NEW Fishing/Dynamite | **Manhattan Bch** –
Gjelina | **Venice** 26
Hillstone/Houston's | **multi.** 22
NEW Hinoki/The Bird | **Century City** 23
Hungry Cat | **multi.** 23
Jar | **Beverly Blvd.** 24
Joe's | **Venice** 26
Lazy Ox | **Little Tokyo** 24
Lucques | **W Hollywood** 27
Lukshon | **Culver City** 24
M.B. Post | **Manhattan Bch** 27
NEW MessHall Kitchen | **Los Feliz** 21
NEW Ocho 8 Taqueria | **Torrance** –
Osteria Mozza | **Hollywood** 27
NEW Paiche | **Marina del Rey** –
Parkway Grill | **Pasadena** 26
Pizzeria Mozza | **Hollywood** 27
Rivera | **Downtown** 26
Roy's | **Downtown** 23
NEW Taberna Arros | **Santa Monica** –
Water Grill | **multi.** 26
Waterloo & City | **Culver City** 23
Westside Tav. | **West LA** 22

ENTERTAINMENT

(Call for types and times of performances)

Alegria | **Long Bch** 23
Antonio's | **Melrose** 20
Arroyo | **Pasadena** 25
Bandera | **West LA** 23
Buffalo Club | **Santa Monica** 19
Carlitos Gardel | **Melrose** 24
Carousel | **Glendale** 25
Catch | **Santa Monica** 22
El Pollo Inka | **multi.** 21
Galletto | **Westlake Vill** 24
Great Greek | **Sherman Oaks** 22
Hal's | **Venice** 20
Lucille's | **Long Bch** 22
Mastro's | **Beverly Hills** 26
Moonshadows | **Malibu** 20
One Pico | **Santa Monica** 23
Padri | **Agoura Hills** 22
Papa Cristo's | **Mid-City** 22
Parkers' Lighthouse | **Long Bch** 22
Parkway Grill | **Pasadena** 26
Polo | **Beverly Hills** 22
Sky Room | **Long Bch** 23
Twin Palms | **Pasadena** -
Vibrato Grill Jazz | **Bel-Air** 22

FIREPLACES

Abigaile | **Hermosa Bch** 19
Admiral Risty | **Rancho Palos Verdes** 22
Amalfi | **La Brea** 20
Arroyo | **Pasadena** 25
Bar | Kitchen | **Downtown** 24
Bel Air B&G | **Bel-Air** 21
Berlin Currywurst | **Hollywood** 21
Bistro Gdn. | **Studio City** 21
Bluewater | **Redondo Bch** 21
Buggy Whip | **Westchester** 19
Ca' del Sole | **N Hollywood** 22
Cafe Del Rey | **Marina del Rey** 23
Cafe Fiore | **Ventura** 22
Cafe Firenze | **Moorpark** 22
Cafe La Boheme | **W Hollywood** 20
Capo | **Santa Monica** 26
Culina | **Beverly Hills** 23
Dal Rae | **Pico Rivera** 25
Dan Tana's | **W Hollywood** 23
Derby | **Arcadia** 23
Dish | **La Cañada Flintridge** 20
Dominick's | **W Hollywood** 20
El Cholo | **multi.** 19
El Coyote | **Beverly Blvd** 16
Eveleigh | **W Hollywood** 20
Gonpachi | **Torrance** 19
Guido's | **West LA** 21
Hamburger Hamlet | **Pasadena** 18
Haven Gastropub | **Pasadena** 19
Hillstone/Houston's | **multi.** 22
Home | **multi.** 20
Il Cielo | **Beverly Hills** 23
Il Fornaio | **multi.** 20
Inn/Seventh Ray | **Topanga** 20
Ivy | **W Hollywood** 22
James' | **Venice** 20
Jer-ne | **Marina del Rey** 18
Josie | **Santa Monica** 26
Koi | **W Hollywood** 24
Larchmont Bungalow | **Hancock Pk** 19
Lawry's Prime | **Beverly Hills** 26
Literati | **West LA** 18
Little Door | **Third St** 23
Lucques | **W Hollywood** 27
Maison Akira | **Pasadena** 26
Marrakesh | **Studio City** 21
Mar'sel | **Rancho Palos Verdes** 26
Mastro's | **Thousand Oaks** 26
McCormick/Schmick | **Pasadena** 18
Mediterraneo | **Westlake Vill** 21
Mélisse | **Santa Monica** 28
Mercato di Vetro | **W Hollywood** 22
Michael's Rest. | **Santa Monica** 24
Napa Valley | **Westwood** 19
Ocean & Vine | **Santa Monica** 23
Off Vine | **Hollywood** 22
Old Tony's | **Redondo Bch** 20
One Pico | **Santa Monica** 23
Osteria La Buca | **Hollywood** 22
Outpost | **Hollywood** -
Paradise Cove | **Malibu** 18
Parkway Grill | **Pasadena** 26
Penthouse | **Santa Monica** 20
Perch | **Downtown** 17
Pitfire | **West LA** 22
R+D Kitchen | **Santa Monica** 22
Raymond | **Pasadena** 25
Reel Inn | **Malibu** 22
NEW RivaBella Ristorante | **W Hollywood** 20
Saddle Peak | **Calabasas** 26
Safire | **Camarillo** 25
Salt Creek | **El Segundo** 19
71 Palm | **Ventura** 24
Smoke Hse. | **Burbank** 21
Stinking Rose | **Beverly Hills** 21
Taix | **Echo Pk** 20
Tanino | **Westwood** 22
Tower Bar | **W Hollywood** 25

Vertical Wine | **Pasadena** 21
Walter's | **Claremont** 20
Waterloo & City | **Culver City** 23
Watermark on Main | **Ventura** 22
Whale & Ale | **San Pedro** 19
Wolfgang Puck/Hotel Bel-Air | **Bel-Air** 24
Ye Olde King's | **Santa Monica** 17
Zengo | **Santa Monica** 21
Zin | **Westlake Vill** 20

FOOD TRUCKS

Baby's/Burgers | **Location Varies** 24
Frysmith | **Location Varies** 23
Grilled Cheese Truck | **Location Varies** 24
Kogi | **Location Varies** 26
Let's Be Frank | **Culver City** 17
LudoTruck | **Location Varies** 24
Pie 'N Burger | **Pasadena** 20

GLUTEN-FREE OPTIONS

(Call to discuss specific needs)

Akasha | **Culver City** 22
Ammo | **multi.** 22
Auntie Em's | **Eagle Rock** 22
A Votre Sante | **Brentwood** 21
Axe | **Venice** 23
NEW Barnyard | **Venice** -
Blue Plate Oysterette | **Santa Monica** 22
Blu Jam Café | **multi.** 25
Caffe Luxxe | **multi.** 21
Catch | **Santa Monica** 22
Chaya | **W Hollywood** 23
Cooks County | **Beverly Blvd** 23
Coral Tree | **multi.** 19
NEW Crossroads Vegan | **W Hollywood** -
Cube Cafe | **La Brea** 24
Doughboys | **Third St** 23
Euro Pane | **Pasadena** 25
Farmshop | **Santa Monica** 25
Flore | **Silver Lake** 20
Gjelina Take Away | **Venice** 27
NEW Goldie's | **Third St** -
Good Girl | **Highland Pk** 22
Greenleaf Gourmet | **multi.** 21
Homeboy/girl | **multi.** 22
Huckleberry | **Santa Monica** 23
Hugo's | **multi.** 21
Industriel | **Downtown** 20
Joan's/Third | **Third St** 24
LAMILL | **Silver Lake** 22
Larchmont Bungalow | **Hancock Pk** 19
NEW Larder/Burton | **Beverly Hills** -
Larder/Maple | **Beverly Hills** 20
Lemonade | **multi.** 21
Lemon Moon | **West LA** 20
M.A.K.E. | **Santa Monica** 15
M Café | **multi.** 22
More Than Waffles | **Encino** 22
NEW Muddy Leek | **Culver City** -
Native Foods | **multi.** 22
Olive/Thyme | **Burbank** 22
Osteria La Buca | **Hollywood** 22
Porta Via | **Beverly Hills** 22
Ray's/Stark Bar | **Mid-Wilshire** 23
NEW ROFL Cafe | **Melrose** -
Sammy's Pizza | **El Segundo** 19
NEW Seasons 52 | **multi.** -
Stefan's/L.A. Farm | **Santa Monica** 22
Tavern | **Brentwood** 24
Tender Greens | **multi.** 23
3 Square | **Venice** 23
True Food | **Santa Monica** 23
Vegan Glory | **Beverly Blvd** 21
Veggie Grill | **multi.** 22

GREEN/LOCAL/ORGANIC

Akasha | **Culver City** 22
Ammo | **Hollywood** 22
Animal | **Fairfax** 27
A Votre Sante | **Brentwood** 21
Axe | **Venice** 23
Bashan | **Montrose** 27
Bloom | **Mid-City** 23
Blue Hen | **Eagle Rock** 21
Café Gratitude | **multi.** 23
Cooks County | **Beverly Blvd** 23
NEW Crossroads Vegan | **W Hollywood** -
Cube Cafe | **La Brea** 24
Elf Café | **Echo Pk** 25
Farmshop | **Santa Monica** 25
Farm Stand | **El Segundo** 22
Fig | **Santa Monica** 22
Forage | **Silver Lake** 25
Gjelina | **Venice** 26
Gjelina Take Away | **Venice** 27
Golden State | **Fairfax** 25
Greenleaf Gourmet | **multi.** 21
Hatfield's | **Melrose** 27
Huckleberry | **Santa Monica** 23
Hungry Cat | **Hollywood** 23
Inn/Seventh Ray | **Topanga** 20
Jar | **Beverly Blvd.** 24
Joe's | **Venice** 26

Larchmont Bungalow | **Hancock Pk** 19
Lazy Ox | **Little Tokyo** 24
Le Pain Quotidien | **multi.** 18
Literati | **West LA** 18
Lucques | **W Hollywood** 27
M Café | **multi.** 22
Mélisse | **Santa Monica** 28
Michael's Rest. | **Santa Monica** 24
Milo & Olive | **Santa Monica** 24
M Street | **Santa Monica** 21
Native Foods | **Westwood** 22
Providence | **Hollywood** 28
Real Food | **multi.** 21
Rustic Canyon | **Santa Monica** 25
Salt's Cure | **W Hollywood** 22
Simmzy's | **Manhattan Bch** 23
Son of a Gun | **Third St** 26
Square One | **E Hollywood** 22
Tavern | **Brentwood** 24
Tender Greens | **multi.** 23
True Food | **Santa Monica** 23
Urth | **multi.** 22
Vegan Glory | **Beverly Blvd** 21
Waterloo & City | **Culver City** 23

HISTORIC PLACES

(Year opened; * building)

1900 | Raymond* | **Pasadena** 25
1900 | Saddle Peak* | **Calabasas** 26
1902 | L'Opera* | **Long Bch** 23
1906 | Pete's* | **Downtown** 20
1907 | Watermark on Main* | **Ventura** 22
1908 | Cole's* | **Downtown** 17
1908 | Off Vine* | **Hollywood** 22
1908 | Philippe/Original | **Chinatown** 23
1910 | 71 Palm* | **Ventura** 24
1910 | Via Veneto* | **Santa Monica** 26
1910 | Warszawa* | **Santa Monica** 22
1911 | Pitfire* | **Downtown** 22
1912 | Engine Co. 28* | **Downtown** 20
1912 | Polo* | **Beverly Hills** 22
1914 | Yamashiro* | **Hollywood** 21
1916 | Alcove* | **Los Feliz** 21
1919 | Musso & Frank* | **Hollywood** 22
1920 | Farm/Bev. Hills* | **Beverly Hills** 18
1920 | Haven Gastropub* | **Pasadena** 19
1920 | La Paella* | **Beverly Hills** 22
1920 | Mijares | **Pasadena** 18
1920 | Salt's Cure* | **W Hollywood** 22
1921 | Pacific Dining Car | **Downtown** 24
1922 | Derby* | **Arcadia** 23
1922 | Tam O'Shanter | **Atwater Vill** 22
1923 | Farfalla/Vinoteca* | **Los Feliz** 22
1923 | El Cholo | **Mid-City** 19
1923 | Mas Malo* | **Downtown** 18
1923 | Wood & Vine* | **Hollywood** 20
1924 | Grub* | **Hollywood** 24
1924 | Original Pantry | **Downtown** 18
1925 | Bay Cities | **Santa Monica** 26
1925 | Church/State* | **Downtown** 24
1925 | Palm* | **Downtown** 23
1926 | Greenblatt's | **Hollywood** 19
1926 | Sky Room* | **Long Bch** 23
1927 | Far Niente* | **Glendale** 24
1927 | Pig 'n Whistle* | **Hollywood** 18
1927 | Public Kitchen* | **Hollywood** 20
1927 | Taix | **Echo Pk** 20
1929 | Tanino* | **Westwood** 22
1929 | Tower Bar* | **W Hollywood** 25
1930 | Brighton Coffee | **Beverly Hills** 19
1931 | Lucques* | **W Hollywood** 27
1933 | Michael's Rest.* | **Santa Monica** 24
1934 | Galley* | **Santa Monica** 19
1934 | Luggage Room* | **Pasadena** 23
1936 | Sir Winston's* | **Long Bch** 24
1938 | Du-par's | **multi.** 17
1938 | Lawry's Prime | **Beverly Hills** 26
1939 | Bistro 45* | **Pasadena** 25
1939 | Formosa | **W Hollywood** 14
1939 | Luna Park* | **La Brea** 19
1939 | Pink's Hot Dogs | **La Brea** 21
1939 | Traxx* | **Downtown** 21
1940 | Il Cielo* | **Beverly Hills** 23
1940 | Tommy's* | **Downtown** 24
1942 | Beckers Bakery | **Manhattan Bch** 21
1943 | Twohey's | **Alhambra** 17
1945 | Nate 'n Al | **Beverly Hills** 21
1946 | Billingsley's | **West LA** 17
1946 | Gus's | **S Pasadena** 19
1946 | Paradise Cove* | **Malibu** 18
1946 | Smoke Hse. | **Burbank** 21
1946 | Uncle Bill's | **Manhattan Bch** 22
1947 | Apple Pan | **West LA** 23
1947 | Langer's | **Downtown** 26
1948 | Canter's | **Fairfax** 20
1948 | Dominick's | **W Hollywood** 20

1948 | Factor's | **Pico-Robertson** 19
1948 | Geoffrey's Malibu | **Malibu** 22
1948 | Papa Cristo's | **Mid-City** 22
1948 | Reddi Chick | **Santa Monica** 21
1949 | Miceli's | **Hollywood** 18
1950 | Rock & Brews* | **El Segundo** 18
1951 | El Coyote | **Beverly Blvd** 16
1952 | Buggy Whip | **Westchester** 19
1952 | Johnnie's Pastrami | **Culver City** 21
1952 | Old Tony's | **Redondo Bch** 20
1952 | Original Tops | **Pasadena** 22
1953 | Father's Office | **Santa Monica** 23
1954 | Angelini* | **Beverly Blvd** 28
1955 | Casa Bianca | **Eagle Rock** 23
1955 | El Tepeyac | **Boyle Hts** 26
1955 | Trader Vic's | **Beverly Hills** 18
1956 | Antonio's | **Melrose** 20
1956 | Casa Vega | **Sherman Oaks** 19
1956 | La Scala | **Beverly Hills** 21
1957 | Art's | **Studio City** 21
1957 | Walter's | **Claremont** 20
1958 | Dal Rae | **Pico Rivera** 25
1959 | Chez Jay | **Santa Monica** 20
1959 | Dinah's | **Westchester** 18
1959 | Tito's Tacos | **Culver City** 21
1960 | Porto's | **Glendale** 25
1960 | Tuscany* | **Westlake Vill** 26
1960 | Waterloo & City* | **Culver City** 23

HOTEL DINING

Alexandria Hotel
Gorbals | **Downtown** 20
Alhambra Renaissance Ctr.
NEW Grill 'Em All | **Alhambra** 19
Avalon Hotel
Oliverio | **Beverly Hills** 25
Hotel Bel-Air
Wolfgang Puck/Hotel Bel-Air | **Bel-Air** 24
Beverly Hills Hotel & Bungalows
Polo | **Beverly Hills** 22
Beverly Hilton
Trader Vic's | **Beverly Hills** 18
Beverly Laurel Motor Hotel
Swingers | **Beverly Blvd** 19
Beverly Terrace Hotel
Trattoria Amici | **Beverly Hills** 21
Beverly Wilshire
Blvd | **Beverly Hills** 22
Cut | **Beverly Hills** 27
Burbank Marriott
Daily Grill | **Burbank** 19
Hotel Casa del Mar
Catch | **Santa Monica** 22
Fairmont Miramar Hotel
Fig | **Santa Monica** 22
Four Seasons Beverly Hills
Culina | **Beverly Hills** 23
Hilton Checkers
Checkers | **Downtown** 22
Huntley Santa Monica Beach
Penthouse | **Santa Monica** 20
JW Marriott at LA Live
L.A. Market | **Downtown** 19
Langham Huntington
NEW Royce Wood-Fired | **Pasadena** 24
L'Ermitage Beverly Hills
Livello | **Beverly Hills** 23
Loews Santa Monica Beach
Ocean & Vine | **Santa Monica** 23
London West Hollywood
Gordon Ramsay | **W Hollywood** 23
Luxe City Center Hotel
FigOly | **Downtown** -
Luxe Rodeo Dr. Hotel
On Rodeo | **Beverly Hills** -
Hotel Maya
Fuego/Maya | **Long Bch** 22
Miyako Hybrid Hotel
Gonpachi | **Torrance** 19
Oceana Beach Club Hotel
NEW Tower 8 | **Santa Monica** -
O Hotel
Bar | Kitchen | **Downtown** 24
Omni Los Angeles Hotel
Noe | **Downtown** 22
Orlando Hotel
Churchill | **W Hollywood** 15
Palihotel
NEW Hart/Hunter | **W Hollywood** 23
Peninsula Beverly Hills
Belvedere | **Beverly Hills** 26
Redbury Hotel
Cleo | **Hollywood** 26
Ritz-Carlton
WP24 | **Downtown** 25
Ritz-Carlton, Marina del Rey
Jer-ne | **Marina del Rey** 18
Roosevelt Hotel
Public Kitchen | **Hollywood** 20
25 Degrees | **Hollywood** 23

Shore Hotel
NEW Blue Plate Taco | **Santa Monica** 16
Shutters on the Beach
Coast | **Santa Monica** 22
One Pico | **Santa Monica** 23
SLS at Beverly Hills
Bazaar/José Andrés | **Beverly Hills** 27
Saam/The Bazaar | **Beverly Hills** 27
Tres/José Andrés | **Beverly Hills** 23
Sofitel LA
NEW Esterel | **W Hollywood** -
Terranea Resort
Bashi | **Rancho Palos Verdes** -
Mar'sel | **Rancho Palos Verdes** 26
The Standard
Restaurant/Standard | **W Hollywood** 18
The Standard Downtown LA
Restaurant/Standard | **Downtown** 18
Thompson Beverly Hills
Caulfield's | **Beverly Hills** 23
Viceroy Santa Monica
NEW Cast | **Santa Monica** -
Westlake Village Inn
NEW Stonehaus | **Westlake Vill** -
W Hollywood Hotel
Delphine | **Hollywood** 21
W Los Angeles Westwood
Nine Thirty | **Westwood** 16

LATE DINING

(Weekday closing hour)
Alcove | 12 AM | **Los Feliz** 21
Apple Pan | 12 AM | **West LA** 23
NEW Bank/Venice | varies | **Venice** -
Bar Hayama | 11:15 PM | **West LA** 24
BCD Tofu | varies | **Koreatown** 22
Beer Belly | 1 AM | **Koreatown** 23
Berlin Currywurst | varies | **Hollywood** 21
BierBeisl | varies | **Beverly Hills** 22
Black Market | 2 AM | **Studio City** 23
Blvd | varies | **Beverly Hills** 22
Boneyard | 2 AM | **Sherman Oaks** 22
Bossa Nova | varies | **multi.** 22
BottleRock | varies | **Downtown** 18
Bow & Truss | 2 AM | **N Hollywood** 18
Bowery | 2 AM | **Hollywood** 22
Bravo | 1:30 AM | **Santa Monica** 20
Brentwood | 12 AM | **Brentwood** 23
Brewco | 1 AM | **Manhattan Bch** 19
NEW Bucato | 12 AM | **Culver City** -
Buffalo Club | 2 AM | **Santa Monica** 19
Café Habana | varies | **Malibu** 20
Caffe Roma | varies | **Beverly Hills** 22
Canter's | 24 hrs. | **Fairfax** 20
NEW Carson House | 2:30 AM | **Beverly Hills** -
Casa Bianca | varies | **Eagle Rock** 23
Casa Vega | 1 AM | **Sherman Oaks** 19
Chez Jay | varies | **Santa Monica** 20
Churchill | varies | **W Hollywood** 15
NEW Circa | varies | **Manhattan Bch** -
Cole's | varies | **Downtown** 17
Congregation Ale | 1 AM | **multi.** 18
Corner Door | varies | **Culver City** -
Daikokuya | 12 AM | **multi.** 24
Daily Grill | 12:30 AM | **Burbank** 19
Dan Tana's | 1 AM | **W Hollywood** 23
Dominick's | 12:45 AM | **W Hollywood** 20
Du-par's | 24 hrs. | **multi.** 17
Duplex/Third | 1 AM | **W Hollywood** -
Eat.Drink.Americano | varies | **Downtown** -
800 Degrees | 2 AM | **Westwood** 23
Fab Hot Dogs | varies | **Westwood** 22
Farfalla/Vinoteca | 12 AM | **Glendale** 22
Fat Dog | 1 AM | **multi.** 20
Father's Office | varies | **multi.** 23
NEW Fatty's Public | 12 AM | **W Hollywood** -
Federal Bar | 1 AM | **N Hollywood** 19
Firefly | 12 AM | **Studio City** 20
Fishbar | varies | **Manhattan Bch** 22
Formosa | varies | **W Hollywood** 14
Freddy Smalls | varies | **West LA** 23
Fred 62 | 24 hrs. | **Los Feliz** 18
Gaby's | varies | **multi.** 20
Galletto | 12:30 AM | **Westlake Vill** 24
Gjelina | varies | **Venice** 26
Gorbals | 12 AM | **Downtown** 20
Gordon Biersch | varies | **Burbank** 18
Gordon Ramsay | 12 AM | **W Hollywood** 23

NEW Gorge | 12 AM | W Hollywood –
Gottsui | 12 AM | **West LA** 21
Greenblatt's | 1:30 AM | **Hollywood** 19
Hal's | 12:30 AM | **Venice** 20
Haven Gastropub | 1 AM | **Pasadena** 19
Honda-Ya | varies | **multi.** 21
Hudson Hse. | varies | **Redondo Bch** 21
Hummus B&G | 1 AM | **Tarzana** 21
Il Tiramisù | varies | **Sherman Oaks** 22
In-N-Out | varies | **multi.** 23
Iroha | 12 AM | **Studio City** 24
Jerry's Deli | varies | **multi.** 15
Joe's Pizza | varies | **multi.** 23
Johnnie's Pastrami | varies | **Culver City** 21
Katsuya | varies | **Hollywood** 24
Killer Shrimp | 12 AM | **Marina del Rey** 21
Kitchen 24 | 24 hrs. | **multi.** 19
Lago d'Argento | 12 AM | **Silver Lake** –
Lamonica's | varies | **Westwood** 23
Larry's | varies | **Venice** 23
Laurel Hardware | 2 AM | **W Hollywood** 19
Lazy Ox | 12 AM | **Little Tokyo** 24
NEW Le Ka | varies | **Downtown** –
Le Petit Bistro | 12 AM | **W Hollywood** 24
Little Bear | 2 AM | **Downtown** 22
Little Door | varies | **Third St** 23
NEW Louie's Old School | 12 AM | **Mar Vista** –
NEW MessHall Kitchen | varies | **Los Feliz** 21
Misfit | varies | **Santa Monica** 22
Mo-Chica | 12 AM | **Downtown** 23
Mohawk Bend | varies | **Echo Pk** 21
Monsoon | 1:30 AM | **Santa Monica** 20
Moonshadows | 1:30 AM | **Malibu** 20
NEW Morrison | 1 AM | **Atwater Vill** –
Nate 'n Al | 1 AM | **LAX** 21
Nic's | varies | **Beverly Hills** 22
Old Tony's | 2 AM | **Redondo Bch** 20
101 Coffee | 3 AM | **Hollywood** 22
101 Noodle | 1 AM | **multi.** 23
Original Pantry | 24 hrs. | **Downtown** 18
Outpost | 2 AM | **Hollywood** –
Pacific Dining Car | 24 hrs. | **multi.** 24
Padri | varies | **Agoura Hills** 22
Palms Thai | 12 AM | **E Hollywood** 21
Parish | 2 AM | **Downtown** 22
Parish Wine Bar | varies | **Downtown** –
Park's BBQ | 1 AM | **Koreatown** 25
NEW Penthouse/Mastro's | 2 AM | **Beverly Hills** –
Perch | varies | **Downtown** 17
Pete's | 2 AM | **Downtown** 20
Pho Café | 12 AM | **Silver Lake** 24
Pho Show | varies | **multi.** 19
Pig 'n Whistle | 1:30 AM | **Hollywood** 18
Pikey | 2 AM | **Hollywood** 18
Pink's Hot Dogs | 2 AM | **La Brea** 21
Pink Taco | 2 AM | **W Hollywood** 17
Pizzeria Mozza | 12 AM | **Hollywood** 27
Plan Check | varies | **West LA** 21
Polo | 1:30 AM | **Beverly Hills** 22
Poquito Más | varies | **Studio City** 21
NEW Public School 805 | 12 AM | **Thousand Oaks** –
NEW Public School 310 | 1:45 AM | **Culver City** 18
RA Sushi | 1 AM | **Torrance** 21
Red Medicine | 2 AM | **Beverly Hills** 22
Restaurant/Standard | 24 hrs. | **multi.** 18
Rick's Tavern | 2 AM | **Santa Monica** 21
Rock & Brews | 12 AM | **Redondo Bch** 18
Roscoe's | varies | **multi.** 23
Sam Woo | 12 AM | **multi.** 18
Sanamluang Cafe | 3:30 AM | **multi.** 24
Stella Barra Pizza | varies | **multi.** 25
Sunny Spot | varies | **Venice** 21
Swingers | varies | **multi.** 19
Tam O'Shanter | varies | **Atwater Vill** 22
Tatsu Ramen | 2 AM | **West LA** –
Tinga | 2 AM | **Santa Monica** 22
Toi on Sunset | 4 AM | **W Hollywood** 19
Tommy's | 24 hrs. | **Downtown** 24
Trader Vic's | varies | **Beverly Hills** 18
Tsujita LA | varies | **West LA** 26
25 Degrees | 1:30 AM | **Hollywood** 23
Umami Burger | 1 AM | **N Hollywood** 23
Vertical Wine | varies | **Pasadena** 21
Waterloo & City | 12 AM | **Culver City** 23

SPECIAL FEATURES

NEW Willie Jane | 12 AM | **Venice** -
Wirtshaus | 12 AM | **La Brea** 19
Wokcano | varies | **multi.** 19
Wolfslair | 2 AM | **Hollywood** 22
Wood & Vine | varies | **Hollywood** 20
Wurstküche | varies | **multi.** 23
Zankou | 11:45 PM | **E Hollywood** 21

NEWCOMERS

Allumette | **Echo Pk** -
Alma | **Downtown** 26
Ara's Tacos | **Glendale** -
Aventine | **Hollywood** -
Bamboo Izakaya | **Santa Monica** -
Bank/Venice | **Venice** -
Bar Amá | **Downtown** 23
Barnyard | **Venice** -
Bestia | **Downtown** 25
Blaze | **multi.** -
Blue Plate Taco | **Santa Monica** 16
Bunker Hill | **Downtown** -
Cafe Brentwood | **Brentwood** -
Carson House | **Beverly Hills** -
Cast | **Santa Monica** -
Chego! | **Chinatown** 23
Chez Mimi | **Pacific Palisades** 19
Chez Soi | **Manhattan Bch** -
Chi-Lin | **W Hollywood** -
chi SPACCA | **Hollywood** -
Circa | **Manhattan Bch** -
Clusi Batusi | **West LA** -
Connie/Ted's | **W Hollywood** -
Corazon y Miel | **Bell** -
Creation Grill | **Santa Monica** -
Crossroads Vegan | **W Hollywood** -
Del Frisco's | **Santa Monica** -
The Doughroom | **Palms** -
Esterel | **W Hollywood** -
Fatty's Public | **W Hollywood** -
Figaro | **Downtown** -
Fishing/Dynamite | **Manhattan Bch** -
Flores | **West LA** -
Girasol | **Studio City** -
Goldie's | **Third St** -
Gorge | **W Hollywood** -
Grill 'Em All | **Alhambra** 19
Hart/Hunter | **W Hollywood** 23
Hinoki/The Bird | **Century City** 23
Hole in the Wall | **Santa Monica** 23
Horse Thief BBQ | **Downtown** -
Il Piccolo Ritrovo | **multi.** 26
Jackson's Food/Drink | **El Segundo** 17
Kaishin | **Malibu** -
Kal's Bistro | **Pasadena** -
Kitchen/Perfecto | **Hermosa Bch** -
Larder/Burton | **Beverly Hills** -
Le Ka | **Downtown** -
Lenny's Deli | **West LA** -
Little Beast | **Eagle Rock** -
Littlefork | **Hollywood** 24
Little Sister | **Manhattan Bch** -
Louie's Old School | **Mar Vista** -
Maccheroni Republic | **Downtown** -
Mari Vanna | **W Hollywood** -
Maru | **Santa Monica** -
MessHall Kitchen | **Los Feliz** 21
Morrison | **Atwater Vill** -
Muddy Leek | **Culver City** -
Nikita | **Malibu** -
Nozawa Bar | **Beverly Hills** -
Ocho 8 Taqueria | **Torrance** -
Osek Korean | **Pasadena** -
Paiche | **Marina del Rey** -
Park's Finest | **Echo Pk** -
Penthouse/Mastro's | **Beverly Hills** -
Petty Cash | **Beverly Blvd** -
Phorage | **Palms** -
Pichet | **Venice** -
Public School 805 | **Thousand Oaks** -
Public School 310 | **Culver City** 18
Rice Thai | **Pasadena** -
RivaBella Ristorante | **W Hollywood** 20
ROC Star | **West LA** -
ROFL Cafe | **Melrose** -
Royce Wood-Fired | **Pasadena** 24
Salt Air | **Venice** -
Seasons 52 | **multi.** -
ShopHouse | **multi.** -
Sirena | **Mid-City** 18
Skewers/Morimoto | **LAX** -
Sticky Rice | **Downtown** -
Stonehaus | **Westlake Vill** -
Taberna Arros | **Santa Monica** -
Tacos Punta Cabras | **Santa Monica** -
Tapenade | **West LA** -
Tartine O | **Beverly Hills** -
Tower 8 | **Santa Monica** -
Trois Mec | **Hollywood** -
True Burger | **Mid-City** -
Twist Eatery | **La Brea** -
Willie Jane | **Venice** -

OUTDOOR DINING

Ago | **W Hollywood** 22
Alcove | **Los Feliz** 21

- A.O.C. | **Beverly Blvd** 25
- **NEW** Aventine | **Hollywood** -
- **NEW** Bamboo Izakaya | **Santa Monica** -
- Bar Bouchon | **Beverly Hills** 23
- Barney Greengrass | **Beverly Hills** 22
- Barney's | **multi.** 21
- Bar Pintxo | **Santa Monica** 21
- Belvedere | **Beverly Hills** 26
- Buffalo Club | **Santa Monica** 19
- Ca' del Sole | **N Hollywood** 22
- Café Habana | **Malibu** 20
- Cafe Med | **W Hollywood** 20
- Cafe Pinot | **Downtown** 24
- Cecconi's | **W Hollywood** 22
- Cliff's Edge | **Silver Lake** 21
- Cora's | **Santa Monica** 23
- Culina | **Beverly Hills** 23
- **NEW** Del Frisco's | **Santa Monica** -
- Dominick's | **W Hollywood** 20
- Eveleigh | **W Hollywood** 20
- Fat Dog | **multi.** 20
- **NEW** Figaro | **Downtown** -
- Firefly Bistro | **S Pasadena** 19
- Gjelina | **Venice** 26
- Hungry Cat | **Hollywood** 23
- Inn/Seventh Ray | **Topanga** 20
- Ivy | **W Hollywood** 22
- **NEW** Jackson's Food/Drink | **El Segundo** 17
- James' | **Venice** 20
- Joe's | **Venice** 26
- Katana | **W Hollywood** 25
- Koi | **W Hollywood** 24
- La Grande Orange | **Pasadena** 20
- **NEW** Little Beast | **Eagle Rock** -
- Little Door | **Third St** 23
- Locanda/Lago | **Santa Monica** 23
- Lucques | **W Hollywood** 27
- Lukshon | **Culver City** 24
- Malibu Seafood | **Malibu** 24
- Martha's 22nd St. | **Hermosa Bch** 23
- Mediterraneo | **Hermosa Bch** 23
- Mediterraneo | **Westlake Vill** 21
- Michael's Rest. | **Santa Monica** 24
- Mike & Anne's | **S Pasadena** 21
- Mi Piace | **Pasadena** 21
- Mohawk Bend | **Echo Pk** 21
- Nobu | **Malibu** 27
- Oinkster | **Eagle Rock** 21
- **NEW** Penthouse/Mastro's | **Beverly Hills** -
- Perch | **Downtown** 17
- Polo | **Beverly Hills** 22
- **NEW** Public School 310 | **Culver City** 18
- Raymond | **Pasadena** 25
- Ray's/Stark Bar | **Mid-Wilshire** 23
- Reel Inn | **Malibu** 22
- Restaurant/Standard | **W Hollywood** 18
- **NEW** RivaBella Ristorante | **W Hollywood** 20
- Rose Cafe | **Venice** 21
- Saddle Peak | **Calabasas** 26
- Safire | **Camarillo** 25
- Scarpetta | **Beverly Hills** 24
- Shack | **Playa del Rey** 18
- **NEW** Sirena | **Mid-City** 18
- Spago | **Beverly Hills** 27
- Square One | **E Hollywood** 22
- Street | **Hollywood** 25
- Sunny Spot | **Venice** 21
- Superba | **Venice** 21
- 26 Beach | **Venice** 23
- Twin Palms | **Pasadena** -
- Uncle Bill's | **Manhattan Bch** 22
- Urth | **multi.** 22
- Wilshire | **Santa Monica** 22
- Wirtshaus | **La Brea** 19
- Zengo | **Santa Monica** 21

PARTIES/ PRIVATE ROOMS

(Restaurants charge less at off times; call for capacity)

- Antonio's | **Melrose** 20
- Belvedere | **Beverly Hills** 26
- Bistro Gdn. | **Studio City** 21
- Buffalo Club | **Santa Monica** 19
- Ca'Brea | **La Brea** 20
- Ca' del Sole | **N Hollywood** 22
- Cafe Bizou | **multi.** 22
- Cafe Del Rey | **Marina del Rey** 23
- Cafe Pinot | **Downtown** 24
- Canal Club | **Venice** 20
- Checkers | **Downtown** 22
- Cicada | **Downtown** 25
- Dal Rae | **Pico Rivera** 25
- Depot | **Torrance** 25
- Duke's | **Malibu** 17
- El Cholo | **Santa Monica** 19
- Enoteca Drago | **Beverly Hills** 22
- Fleming's | **El Segundo** 23
- Getty Ctr. | **Brentwood** 23
- Giorgio Baldi | **Santa Monica** 25
- Gladstones | **Pacific Palisades** 17
- Hal's | **Venice** 20
- Hatfield's | **Melrose** 27
- Il Cielo | **Beverly Hills** 23

SPECIAL FEATURES

Il Fornaio | **multi.** 20
Il Moro | **West LA** 21
Inn/Seventh Ray | **Topanga** 20
James' | **Venice** 20
Katana | **W Hollywood** 25
Kendall's | **Downtown** 19
King's Fish | **Long Bch** 21
Lawry's Prime | **Beverly Hills** 26
Little Door | **Third St** 23
L'Opera | **Long Bch** 23
Mastro's | **Beverly Hills** 26
Matsuhisa | **Beverly Hills** 28
McCormick/Schmick | **multi.** 18
McKenna's | **Long Bch** 21
Mélisse | **Santa Monica** 28
Michael's Rest. | **Santa Monica** 24
Monsoon | **Santa Monica** 20
Morels French Steak | **Fairfax** 20
Morton's | **multi.** 22
Napa Valley | **Westwood** 19
Nick & Stef's | **Downtown** 23
Off Vine | **Hollywood** 22
One Pico | **Santa Monica** 23
Pacific Dining Car | **multi.** 24
Palm | **multi.** 23
Parkway Grill | **Pasadena** 26
Polo | **Beverly Hills** 22
Red Medicine | **Beverly Hills** 22
RockSugar | **Century City** 21
Ruth's Chris | **Beverly Hills** 25
Saam/The Bazaar | **Beverly Hills** 27
Spago | **Beverly Hills** 27
Spice Table | **Little Tokyo** 23
Tanino | **Westwood** 22
Tavern | **Brentwood** 24
Valentino | **Santa Monica** 26
Vibrato Grill Jazz | **Bel-Air** 22

PEOPLE-WATCHING

NEW Allumette | **Echo Pk** -
NEW Alma | **Downtown** 26
Ammo | **Westwood** 22
Animal | **Fairfax** 27
A.O.C. | **Beverly Blvd** 25
Apple Pan | **West LA** 23
NEW Aventine | **Hollywood** -
Bäco Mercat | **Downtown** 25
NEW Bamboo Izakaya | **Santa Monica** -
NEW Bar Amá | **Downtown** 23
Barney Greengrass | **Beverly Hills** 22
Bashi | **Rancho Palos Verdes** -
Bay Cities | **Santa Monica** 26
Bazaar/José Andrés | **Beverly Hills** 27
NEW Bestia | **Downtown** 25
Black Hogg | **Silver Lake** 22
Black Market | **Studio City** 23
Bludso's BBQ | **Mid-City** 25
NEW Blue Plate Taco | **Santa Monica** 16
Bow & Truss | **N Hollywood** 18
Brentwood | **Brentwood** 23
NEW Cafe Brentwood | **Brentwood** -
Canter's | **Fairfax** 20
Ado/Casa Ado | **Marina del Rey** 25
Cecconi's | **W Hollywood** 22
Chaya | **W Hollywood** 23
Chaya | **Venice** 23
Chez Mélange | **Redondo Bch** 26
NEW Chi-Lin | **W Hollywood** -
NEW chi SPACCA | **Hollywood** -
Church/State | **Downtown** 24
NEW Circa | **Manhattan Bch** -
Coco Laurent | **Downtown** -
Craft | **Century City** 25
Culina | **Beverly Hills** 23
Cut | **Beverly Hills** 27
Dan Tana's | **W Hollywood** 23
NEW Fatty's Public | **W Hollywood** -
NEW Figaro | **Downtown** -
NEW Fishing/Dynamite | **Manhattan Bch** -
Freddy Smalls | **West LA** 23
Giorgio Baldi | **Santa Monica** 25
Gjelina | **Venice** 26
Griddle Cafe | **Hollywood** 25
NEW Grill 'Em All | **Alhambra** 19
Grill on Alley | **Beverly Hills** 25
Gumbo Pot | **Fairfax** 20
NEW Hart/Hunter | **W Hollywood** 23
NEW Hinoki/The Bird | **Century City** 23
Ink | **W Hollywood** 26
Ivy | **W Hollywood** 22
Ivy/Shore | **Santa Monica** 22
Joan's/Third | **Third St** 24
Katana | **W Hollywood** 25
Katsu-ya | **multi.** 27
Katsuya | **multi.** 24
Koi | **W Hollywood** 24
L&E Oyster | **Silver Lake** 25
Larry's | **Venice** 23
Laurel Hardware | **W Hollywood** 19
Lazy Ox | **Little Tokyo** 24
Le Pain Quotidien | **multi.** 18
Little Dom's/Deli | **Los Feliz** 22
Little Door | **Third St** 23
NEW Littlefork | **Hollywood** 24

Madeo | **W Hollywood** 26
Mastro's | **Beverly Hills** 26
Matsuhisa | **Beverly Hills** 28
M.B. Post | **Manhattan Bch** 27
Mercado | **Santa Monica** 24
NEW MessHall Kitchen | **Los Feliz** 21
Michael's/Naples | **Long Bch** 27
Michael's Rest. | **Santa Monica** 24
Misfit | **Santa Monica** 22
Mo-Chica | **Downtown** 23
Mr. Chow | **Beverly Hills** 23
Nate 'n Al | **Beverly Hills** 21
Neptune's Net | **Malibu** 19
NEW Nikita | **Malibu** -
Nobu | **Malibu** 27
Osteria Drago | **W Hollywood** 22
Osteria Mozza | **Hollywood** 27
NEW Paiche | **Marina del Rey** -
Palm | **W Hollywood** 23
Parish | **Downtown** 22
Penthouse | **Santa Monica** 20
NEW Penthouse/Mastro's | **Beverly Hills** -
Perch | **Downtown** 17
Pete's | **Downtown** 20
Petros | **Manhattan Bch** 24
NEW Pichet | **Venice** -
Pikey | **Hollywood** 18
Pink's Hot Dogs | **La Brea** 21
Pink Taco | **multi.** 17
Pizzeria Mozza | **Hollywood** 27
Polo | **Beverly Hills** 22
Ray's/Stark Bar | **Mid-Wilshire** 23
Red O | **Melrose** 24
Restaurant/Standard | **W Hollywood** 18
Rick's Tavern | **Santa Monica** 21
NEW RivaBella Ristorante | **W Hollywood** 20
Rivera | **Downtown** 26
RockSugar | **Century City** 21
NEW ROC Star | **West LA** -
NEW ROFL Cafe | **Melrose** -
Rustic Canyon | **Santa Monica** 25
Scarpetta | **Beverly Hills** 24
Short Order | **Fairfax** 18
Soleto Trattoria | **Downtown** 21
Son of a Gun | **Third St** 26
Spago | **Beverly Hills** 27
Spice Table | **Little Tokyo** 23
Spitz | **Los Feliz** 22
Stefan's/L.A. Farm | **Santa Monica** 22
STK | **W Hollywood** 24
NEW Stonehaus | **Westlake Vill** -
Strand House | **Manhattan Bch** 20
Sunny Spot | **Venice** 21
Superba | **Venice** 21
Sushi Roku | **multi.** 22
Tortilla Rep. | **W Hollywood** 20
Tower Bar | **W Hollywood** 25
NEW Tower 8 | **Santa Monica** -
Tripel | **Playa del Rey** 25
NEW Trois Mec | **Hollywood** -
Umamicatessen | **Downtown** 22
Uncle Bill's | **Manhattan Bch** 22
Urth | **multi.** 22
Wolfgang Puck/Hotel Bel-Air | **Bel-Air** 24
Wood & Vine | **Hollywood** 20

POWER SCENES

Ago | **W Hollywood** 22
Akasha | **Culver City** 22
Angelini | **Beverly Blvd** 28
NEW Aventine | **Hollywood** -
NEW Bamboo Izakaya | **Santa Monica** -
Bar Bouchon | **Beverly Hills** 23
Barney Greengrass | **Beverly Hills** 22
Bar Toscana | **Brentwood** 23
Belvedere | **Beverly Hills** 26
NEW Bestia | **Downtown** 25
Bouchon | **Beverly Hills** 25
Caffe Luxxe | **multi.** 21
Cecconi's | **W Hollywood** 22
Chaya | **Downtown** 23
NEW Chi-Lin | **W Hollywood** -
Cleo | **Hollywood** 26
Coco Laurent | **Downtown** -
Comme Ça | **W Hollywood** 23
Craft | **Century City** 25
Craig's | **W Hollywood** 22
Culina | **Beverly Hills** 23
Cut | **Beverly Hills** 27
Dan Tana's | **W Hollywood** 23
Drago Centro | **Downtown** 26
NEW Esterel | **W Hollywood** -
FigOly | **Downtown** -
Gordon Ramsay | **W Hollywood** 23
Grill on Alley | **Beverly Hills** 25
Grill on Hollywood | **Hollywood** 24
NEW Hinoki/The Bird | **Century City** 23
Hungry Cat | **Santa Monica** 23
Ink | **W Hollywood** 26
Ivy/Shore | **Santa Monica** 22
Katsu-ya | **multi.** 27
Katsuya | **multi.** 24
Livello | **Beverly Hills** 23

SPECIAL FEATURES

Mastro's | **Beverly Hills** 26
Matsuhisa | **Beverly Hills** 28
M.B. Post | **Manhattan Bch** 27
Michael's Rest. | **Santa Monica** 24
Morton's | **multi.** 22
Mr. Chow | **Beverly Hills** 23
Nick & Stef's | **Downtown** 23
NEW Nikita | **Malibu** -
Nobu | **W Hollywood** 26
Nobu | **Malibu** 27
Osteria Drago | **W Hollywood** 22
Osteria Mozza | **Hollywood** 27
Palm | **W Hollywood** 23
Parkway Grill | **Pasadena** 26
Patina | **Downtown** 26
NEW Penthouse/Mastro's | **Beverly Hills** -
Pizzeria Mozza | **Hollywood** 27
Polo | **Beverly Hills** 22
Providence | **Hollywood** 28
Red Medicine | **Beverly Hills** 22
Restaurant/Standard | **Downtown** 18
Restaurant 2117 | **West LA** 23
NEW RivaBella Ristorante | **W Hollywood** 20
Rivera | **Downtown** 26
Scarpetta | **Beverly Hills** 24
NEW Sirena | **Mid-City** 18
Spago | **Beverly Hills** 27
Stefan's/L.A. Farm | **Santa Monica** 22
STK | **W Hollywood** 24
Strand House | **Manhattan Bch** 20
Tavern | **Brentwood** 24
Toscana | **Brentwood** 25
NEW Tower 8 | **Santa Monica** -
Valentino | **Santa Monica** 26
Vincenti | **Brentwood** 26
Water Grill | **Downtown** 26
Wilshire | **Santa Monica** 22
Wolfgang Puck/Hotel Bel-Air | **Bel-Air** 24

QUIET CONVERSATION

Ammo | **Westwood** 22
NEW Aventine | **Hollywood** -
Bashi | **Rancho Palos Verdes** -
Belvedere | **Beverly Hills** 26
Blossom | **multi.** 21
Blvd | **Beverly Hills** 22
Bottle Inn | **Hermosa Bch** 21
Bouchon | **Beverly Hills** 25
Bouchon Bakery | **Beverly Hills** 25
Cafe Fiore | **Ventura** 22
Café 14 | **Agoura Hills** 26
Ado/Casa Ado | **Marina del Rey** 25
Checkers | **Downtown** 22
NEW Chez Mimi | **Pacific Palisades** 19
Coast | **Santa Monica** 22
Culina | **Beverly Hills** 23
Dusty's | **Silver Lake** 22
Enzo/Angela | **West LA** 21
FigOly | **Downtown** -
Float | **Pasadena** -
Fuego/Maya | **Long Bch** 22
Gordon Ramsay | **W Hollywood** 23
Hatfield's | **Melrose** 27
NEW Hinoki/The Bird | **Century City** 23
Il Grano | **West LA** 25
La Botte | **Santa Monica** 22
NEW Le Ka | **Downtown** -
Livello | **Beverly Hills** 23
Madeo | **W Hollywood** 26
Mama Terano | **Rolling Hills Estates** 22
Marino | **Hollywood** 25
Mar'sel | **Rancho Palos Verdes** 26
Mélisse | **Santa Monica** 28
Michael's Rest. | **Santa Monica** 24
Momed | **Beverly Hills** 20
NEW Muddy Leek | **Culver City** -
Ocean & Vine | **Santa Monica** 23
Oliva | **Sherman Oaks** 20
Ombra | **Studio City** 21
Polo | **Beverly Hills** 22
Providence | **Hollywood** 28
Raymond | **Pasadena** 25
Ray's/Stark Bar | **Mid-Wilshire** 23
NEW RivaBella Ristorante | **W Hollywood** 20
Saam/The Bazaar | **Beverly Hills** 27
71 Palm | **Ventura** 24
Spago | **Beverly Hills** 27
Stefan's/L.A. Farm | **Santa Monica** 22
NEW Stonehaus | **Westlake Vill** -
Tierra Sur/Herzog | **Oxnard** 28
NEW Tower 8 | **Santa Monica** -
Tres/José Andrés | **Beverly Hills** 23
Upstairs 2 | **West LA** 24
Valentino | **Santa Monica** 26
Villetta | **Santa Monica** 20
Vito | **Santa Monica** 23
Wolfgang Puck/Hotel Bel-Air | **Bel-Air** 24
Wolfgang's | **Beverly Hills** 24

RAW BARS

Blue Plate Oysterette | **Santa Monica** 22
Bluewater | **Redondo Bch** 21

Brophy Bros. | **Ventura** 21
Canal Club | **Venice** 20
Coast | **Santa Monica** 22
Comme Ça | **W Hollywood** 23
NEW Fishing/Dynamite | **Manhattan Bch** -
Gulfstream | **Century City** 22
Hungry Cat | **multi.** 23
Joe's | **Venice** 26
Kendall's | **Downtown** 19
King's Fish | **multi.** 21
L&E Oyster | **Silver Lake** 25
NEW Littlefork | **Hollywood** 24
Lobster | **Santa Monica** 23
McKenna's | **Long Bch** 21
NEW Salt Air | **Venice** -
Santa Monica Seafood | **Santa Monica** 25
Sky Room | **Long Bch** 23
Water Grill | **multi.** 26

ROMANTIC PLACES

Ammo | **Westwood** 22
NEW Aventine | **Hollywood** -
Ba Restaurant | **Highland Pk** -
Bashi | **Rancho Palos Verdes** -
Bazaar/José Andrés | **Beverly Hills** 27
Belvedere | **Beverly Hills** 26
NEW Bestia | **Downtown** 25
Bistro/Gare | **S Pasadena** 20
Bistro 45 | **Pasadena** 25
Blvd | **Beverly Hills** 22
Bouchon | **Beverly Hills** 25
Bouchon Bakery | **Beverly Hills** 25
Brandywine | **Woodland Hills** 27
Brentwood | **Brentwood** 23
Cafe Del Rey | **Marina del Rey** 23
Cafe Fiore | **Ventura** 22
Cafe La Boheme | **W Hollywood** 20
Café Laurent | **Culver City** 20
Caffe Roma | **Beverly Hills** 22
Capo | **Santa Monica** 26
Ado/Casa Ado | **Marina del Rey** 25
Catch | **Santa Monica** 22
Checkers | **Downtown** 22
NEW Chez Mimi | **Pacific Palisades** 19
Cicada | **Downtown** 25
Cleo | **Hollywood** 26
Cliff's Edge | **Silver Lake** 21
Comme Ça | **W Hollywood** 23
Craft | **Century City** 25
Culina | **Beverly Hills** 23
Dominick's | **W Hollywood** 20
Drago Centro | **Downtown** 26
Duplex/Third | **W Hollywood** -
NEW Esterel | **W Hollywood** -
Fig & Olive | **W Hollywood** 22
FigOly | **Downtown** -
Fuego/Maya | **Long Bch** 22
Geoffrey's Malibu | **Malibu** 22
Getty Ctr. | **Brentwood** 23
Gordon Ramsay | **W Hollywood** 23
Hatfield's | **Melrose** 27
NEW Hinoki/The Bird | **Century City** 23
Il Cielo | **Beverly Hills** 23
Inn/Seventh Ray | **Topanga** 20
Jer-ne | **Marina del Rey** 18
JiRaffe | **Santa Monica** 26
Josie | **Santa Monica** 26
La Botte | **Santa Monica** 22
Le Chêne | **Saugus** 24
NEW Le Ka | **Downtown** -
Little Door | **Third St** 23
Livello | **Beverly Hills** 23
Lucques | **W Hollywood** 27
Mar'sel | **Rancho Palos Verdes** 26
Mélisse | **Santa Monica** 28
Michael's/Naples | **Long Bch** 27
Michael's Rest. | **Santa Monica** 24
NEW Muddy Leek | **Culver City** -
Noe | **Downtown** 22
NEW Ocho 8 Taqueria | **Torrance** -
Ombra | **Studio City** 21
Osteria Drago | **W Hollywood** 22
Pace | **Laurel Canyon** 23
Patina | **Downtown** 26
Penthouse | **Santa Monica** 20
Perch | **Downtown** 17
Piccolo | **Venice** 27
Providence | **Hollywood** 28
Raymond | **Pasadena** 25
Ray's/Stark Bar | **Mid-Wilshire** 23
NEW RivaBella Ristorante | **W Hollywood** 20
Rivera | **Downtown** 26
Saddle Peak | **Calabasas** 26
71 Palm | **Ventura** 24
Sir Winston's | **Long Bch** 24
Sky Room | **Long Bch** 23
Soleto Trattoria | **Downtown** 21
Spago | **Beverly Hills** 27
Stefan's/L.A. Farm | **Santa Monica** 22
NEW Stonehaus | **Westlake Vill** -
Strand House | **Manhattan Bch** 20
Taix | **Echo Pk** 20
NEW Tapenade | **West LA** -

SPECIAL FEATURES

Tierra Sur/Herzog | **Oxnard** 28
NEW Tower 8 | **Santa Monica** -
Tres/José Andrés | **Beverly Hills** 23
Valentino | **Santa Monica** 26
Vertical Wine | **Pasadena** 21
Via Alloro | **Beverly Hills** 22
Villetta | **Santa Monica** 20
Vito | **Santa Monica** 23
Wolfgang Puck/Hotel Bel-Air | **Bel-Air** 24
Yamashiro | **Hollywood** 21

SINGLES SCENES

A.O.C. | **Beverly Blvd** 25
NEW Bank/Venice | **Venice** -
NEW Bar Amá | **Downtown** 23
Boa | **multi.** 24
Border Grill | **multi.** 22
Bouzy | **Redondo Bch** 22
Bowery | **Hollywood** 22
Caffe Roma | **Beverly Hills** 22
Canal Club | **Venice** 20
Cecconi's | **W Hollywood** 22
Chaya | **W Hollywood** 23
Chaya | **Venice** 23
City Tavern | **Culver City** 19
Comme Ça | **W Hollywood** 23
Corkbar | **Downtown** 21
Dominick's | **W Hollywood** 20
Father's Office | **multi.** 23
Ford's | **Culver City** 20
Freddy Smalls | **West LA** 23
Hal's | **Venice** 20
Hama | **Venice** 23
Haven Gastropub | **Pasadena** 19
Hudson Hse. | **Redondo Bch** 21
James' | **Venice** 20
Katsu-ya | **multi.** 27
Katsuya | **multi.** 24
Kitchen 24 | **Hollywood** 19
Koi | **W Hollywood** 24
Larry's | **Venice** 23
M.B. Post | **Manhattan Bch** 27
Mercado | **Santa Monica** 24
NEW MessHall Kitchen | **Los Feliz** 21
NEW Paiche | **Marina del Rey** -
Parish | **Downtown** 22
Parkway Grill | **Pasadena** 26
Penthouse | **Santa Monica** 20
Pikey | **Hollywood** 18
Pizzeria Mozza | **Hollywood** 27
Primitivo | **Venice** 22
Public Kitchen | **Hollywood** 20
Restaurant/Standard | **multi.** 18
Restaurant 2117 | **West LA** 23
Rock'n Fish | **Manhattan Bch** 20
Rush St. | **Culver City** 17
Rustic Canyon | **Santa Monica** 25
Safire | **Camarillo** 25
Soleto Trattoria | **Downtown** 21
Spitz | **Los Feliz** 22
STK | **W Hollywood** 24
Superba | **Venice** 21
Sushi Roku | **multi.** 22
25 Degrees | **Hollywood** 23
Twin Palms | **Pasadena** -
Umamicatessen | **Downtown** 22
Wood & Vine | **Hollywood** 20

SPECIAL OCCASIONS

Bashi | **Rancho Palos Verdes** -
Bazaar/José Andrés | **Beverly Hills** 27
Belvedere | **Beverly Hills** 26
Bistro 45 | **Pasadena** 25
Bouchon | **Beverly Hills** 25
Ado/Casa Ado | **Marina del Rey** 25
Cecconi's | **W Hollywood** 22
Chinois | **Santa Monica** 26
NEW chi SPACCA | **Hollywood** -
Cicada | **Downtown** 25
Coco Laurent | **Downtown** -
Comme Ça | **W Hollywood** 23
Craft | **Century City** 25
Culina | **Beverly Hills** 23
Cut | **Beverly Hills** 27
Drago Centro | **Downtown** 26
NEW Esterel | **W Hollywood** -
FigOly | **Downtown** -
Fleming's | **multi.** 23
Gordon Ramsay | **W Hollywood** 23
Hatfield's | **Melrose** 27
NEW Hinoki/The Bird | **Century City** 23
Ink | **W Hollywood** 26
Jar | **Beverly Blvd.** 24
JiRaffe | **Santa Monica** 26
Josie | **Santa Monica** 26
NEW Le Ka | **Downtown** -
Livello | **Beverly Hills** 23
Marino | **Hollywood** 25
Mar'sel | **Rancho Palos Verdes** 26
Mastro's | **Beverly Hills** 26
Matsuhisa | **Beverly Hills** 28
NEW Nikita | **Malibu** -
Nobu | **W Hollywood** 26
Noe | **Downtown** 22
NEW Nozawa Bar | **Beverly Hills** -
Ocean & Vine | **Santa Monica** 23

Osteria Mozza | **Hollywood** 27
Palm | **W Hollywood** 23
Patina | **Downtown** 26
NEW Penthouse/Mastro's | **Beverly Hills** -
Petros | **Manhattan Bch** 24
Providence | **Hollywood** 28
NEW RivaBella Ristorante | **W Hollywood** 20
Roy's | **multi.** 23
Saam/The Bazaar | **Beverly Hills** 27
Saddle Peak | **Calabasas** 26
Scarpetta | **Beverly Hills** 24
NEW Sirena | **Mid-City** 18
Sir Winston's | **Long Bch** 24
Sky Room | **Long Bch** 23
Soleto Trattoria | **Downtown** 21
Spago | **Beverly Hills** 27
Stefan's/L.A. Farm | **Santa Monica** 22
Strand House | **Manhattan Bch** 20
Taix | **Echo Pk** 20
NEW Tapenade | **West LA** -
Tar & Roses | **Santa Monica** 24
Tierra Sur/Herzog | **Oxnard** 28
NEW Tower 8 | **Santa Monica** -
Tres/José Andrés | **Beverly Hills** 23
NEW Trois Mec | **Hollywood** -
Tuscany | **Westlake Vill** 26
Ushuaia | **Santa Monica** 23
Valentino | **Santa Monica** 26
Water Grill | **Downtown** 26
Wolfgang Puck/Hotel Bel-Air | **Bel-Air** 24
Wolfgang's | **Beverly Hills** 24

STARGAZING

Axe | **Venice** 23
Bar Toscana | **Brentwood** 23
Black Market | **Studio City** 23
Boa | **multi.** 24
Brentwood | **Brentwood** 23
Café Habana | **Malibu** 20
Cecconi's | **W Hollywood** 22
Craft | **Century City** 25
Craig's | **W Hollywood** 22
Culina | **Beverly Hills** 23
Cut | **Beverly Hills** 27
Dan Tana's | **W Hollywood** 23
Eveleigh | **W Hollywood** 20
Fig & Olive | **W Hollywood** 22
Giorgio Baldi | **Santa Monica** 25
Griddle Cafe | **Hollywood** 25
Grill on Alley | **Beverly Hills** 25
Hamasaku | **West LA** 28
Ivy | **W Hollywood** 22
Ivy/Shore | **Santa Monica** 22
Katsuya | **multi.** 24
Koi | **W Hollywood** 24
Madeo | **W Hollywood** 26
Matsuhisa | **Beverly Hills** 28
M.B. Post | **Manhattan Bch** 27
Misfit | **Santa Monica** 22
Mr. Chow | **Beverly Hills** 23
NEW Nikita | **Malibu** -
Nobu | **W Hollywood** 26
Nobu | **Malibu** 27
Osteria Mozza | **Hollywood** 27
Pizzeria Mozza | **Hollywood** 27
Polo | **Beverly Hills** 22
Sotto | **Century City** 22
Spago | **Beverly Hills** 27
Sushi Roku | **multi.** 22
Tavern | **Brentwood** 24
Taverna Tony | **Malibu** 22
Tower Bar | **W Hollywood** 25
Tra di Noi | **Malibu** 23
Urasawa | **Beverly Hills** 28

TRENDY

Aburiya Toranoko | **Downtown** 22
A-Frame | **Culver City** 23
Ago | **W Hollywood** 22
Akasha | **Culver City** 22
Animal | **Fairfax** 27
Bäco Mercat | **Downtown** 25
NEW Bamboo Izakaya | **Santa Monica** -
NEW Bar Amá | **Downtown** 23
Bar Bouchon | **Beverly Hills** 23
Bar Toscana | **Brentwood** 23
Bazaar/José Andrés | **Beverly Hills** 27
NEW Bestia | **Downtown** 25
Black Hogg | **Silver Lake** 22
Bludso's BBQ | **Mid-City** 25
Bouchon | **Beverly Hills** 25
Bow & Truss | **N Hollywood** 18
Ado/Casa Ado | **Marina del Rey** 25
Cecconi's | **W Hollywood** 22
Chaya | **Venice** 23
NEW chi SPACCA | **Hollywood** -
Churchill | **W Hollywood** 15
City Tavern | **Culver City** 19
Cole's | **Downtown** 17
Corner Door | **Culver City** -
Craft | **Century City** 25
Cut | **Beverly Hills** 27
800 Degrees | **Westwood** 23
Eveleigh | **W Hollywood** 20
Fat Cow | **Fairfax** 18
Father's Office | **Culver City** 23

NEW Fishing/Dynamite | **Manhattan Bch** –
Forage | **Silver Lake** 25
Freddy Smalls | **West LA** 23
Gjelina | **Venice** 26
Gorbals | **Downtown** 20
NEW Grill 'Em All | **Alhambra** 19
Hama | **Venice** 23
NEW Hinoki/The Bird | **Century City** 23
Hungry Cat | **multi.** 23
Ink | **W Hollywood** 26
Jar | **Beverly Blvd.** 24
Jitlada | **E Hollywood** 27
Katana | **W Hollywood** 25
Katsu-ya | **multi.** 27
Katsuya | **multi.** 24
Kitchen 24 | **Hollywood** 19
Kogi | **Location Varies** 26
Koi | **W Hollywood** 24
Langer's | **Downtown** 26
Larry's | **Venice** 23
Laurel Hardware | **W Hollywood** 19
Lazy Ox | **Little Tokyo** 24
Little Door | **Third St** 23
LudoTruck | **Location Varies** 24
Lukshon | **Culver City** 24
Mastro's | **Beverly Hills** 26
M.B. Post | **Manhattan Bch** 27
Mercado | **Santa Monica** 24
NEW MessHall Kitchen | **Los Feliz** 21
Misfit | **Santa Monica** 22
Mo-Chica | **Downtown** 23
Mohawk Bend | **Echo Pk** 21
Mr. Chow | **Beverly Hills** 23
Talésai/Night | **W Hollywood** 25
N/Naka | **Palms** 27
Nobu | **W Hollywood** 26
Nobu | **Malibu** 27
Osteria Mozza | **Hollywood** 27
Parish | **Downtown** 22
Parkway Grill | **Pasadena** 26
Penthouse | **Santa Monica** 20
NEW Pichet | **Venice** –
Pizzeria Mozza | **Hollywood** 27
Plan Check | **West LA** 21
Public Kitchen | **Hollywood** 20
NEW Public School 310 | **Culver City** 18
Red O | **Melrose** 24
NEW RivaBella Ristorante | **W Hollywood** 20
Rock & Brews | **multi.** 18
Rock'n Fish | **Manhattan Bch** 20
NEW ROC Star | **West LA** –
Saam/The Bazaar | **Beverly Hills** 27
Scarpetta | **Beverly Hills** 24
Short Order | **Fairfax** 18
Soleto Trattoria | **Downtown** 21
Son of a Gun | **Third St** 26
Spago | **Beverly Hills** 27
Spice Table | **Little Tokyo** 23
Stefan's/L.A. Farm | **Santa Monica** 22
Strand House | **Manhattan Bch** 20
Street | **Hollywood** 25
Superba | **Venice** 21
Sushi Roku | **multi.** 22
Tar & Roses | **Santa Monica** 24
Tasting Kitchen | **Venice** 25
Tavern | **Brentwood** 24
Tin Roof | **Manhattan Bch** 23
NEW Tower 8 | **Santa Monica** –
Tripel | **Playa del Rey** 25
NEW Trois Mec | **Hollywood** –
Umamicatessen | **Downtown** 22
Wolfgang Puck/Hotel Bel-Air | **Bel-Air** 24
Wood & Vine | **Hollywood** 20
Wurstküche | **Downtown** 23

VIEWS

Boa | **Santa Monica** 24
Brophy Bros. | **Ventura** 21
Cheebo | **Hollywood** 21
Coast | **Santa Monica** 22
Duke's | **Malibu** 17
FigOly | **Downtown** –
Fuego/Maya | **Long Bch** 22
Geoffrey's Malibu | **Malibu** 22
Getty Ctr. | **Brentwood** 23
Hostaria/Piccolo | **Santa Monica** 24
Jinky's | **Agoura Hills** 20
Katana | **W Hollywood** 25
Kincaid's | **Redondo Bch** 22
Lobster | **Santa Monica** 23
Malibu Seafood | **Malibu** 24
Mar'sel | **Rancho Palos Verdes** 26
McKenna's | **Long Bch** 21
Moonshadows | **Malibu** 20
M Street | **Santa Monica** 21
NEW Nikita | **Malibu** –
Nobu | **Malibu** 27
Ocean Tava | **Redondo Bch** 25
Old Tony's | **Redondo Bch** 20
One Pico | **Santa Monica** 23
Raymond | **Pasadena** 25
Ray's/Stark Bar | **Mid-Wilshire** 23
Reel Inn | **Malibu** 22
NEW Royce Wood-Fired | **Pasadena** 24

Rustico | **Westlake Vill** 26
Saddle Peak | **Calabasas** 26
Salt's Cure | **W Hollywood** 22
Sam's/Beach | **Santa Monica** 25
71 Palm | **Ventura** 24
Sir Winston's | **Long Bch** 24
Sky Room | **Long Bch** 23
Strand House | **Manhattan Bch** 20
Tower Bar | **W Hollywood** 25
22nd St. Landing | **San Pedro** 22
Typhoon | **Santa Monica** 20
Water Grill | **Santa Monica** 26
Whale & Ale | **San Pedro** 19
WP24 | **Downtown** 25
Yamashiro | **Hollywood** 21
Zengo | **Santa Monica** 21
Zin | **Westlake Vill** 20

VISITORS ON EXPENSE ACCOUNT

Ago | **W Hollywood** 22
Arroyo | **Pasadena** 25
Bar Bouchon | **Beverly Hills** 23
Bashi | **Rancho Palos Verdes** –
Bazaar/José Andrés | **Beverly Hills** 27
Belvedere | **Beverly Hills** 26
Beso | **Hollywood** 18
Blvd | **Beverly Hills** 22
Boa | **multi.** 24
Bouchon | **Beverly Hills** 25
Buffalo Club | **Santa Monica** 19
Capo | **Santa Monica** 26
Catch | **Santa Monica** 22
Cecconi's | **W Hollywood** 22
Celestino | **Pasadena** 25
Chaya | **W Hollywood** 23
Chaya | **Downtown** 23
Checkers | **Downtown** 22
Chinois | **Santa Monica** 26
Cicada | **Downtown** 25
Comme Ça | **W Hollywood** 23
Craft | **Century City** 25
Crustacean | **Beverly Hills** 25
Culina | **Beverly Hills** 23
Cut | **Beverly Hills** 27
Dominick's | **W Hollywood** 20
Drago Centro | **Downtown** 26
Fig & Olive | **W Hollywood** 22
FigOly | **Downtown** –
Fleming's | **multi.** 23
Fogo de Chão | **Beverly Hills** 23
Geoffrey's Malibu | **Malibu** 22
Gordon Ramsay | **W Hollywood** 23
Grill on Hollywood | **Hollywood** 24
Hatfield's | **Melrose** 27
NEW Hinoki/The Bird | **Century City** 23
Ink | **W Hollywood** 26
Ivy | **W Hollywood** 22
Ivy/Shore | **Santa Monica** 22
Jar | **Beverly Blvd.** 24
Jer-ne | **Marina del Rey** 18
JiRaffe | **Santa Monica** 26
Joe's | **Venice** 26
Josie | **Santa Monica** 26
Livello | **Beverly Hills** 23
Lobster | **Santa Monica** 23
L'Opera | **Long Bch** 23
Lucques | **W Hollywood** 27
Mar'sel | **Rancho Palos Verdes** 26
Mastro's | **Beverly Hills** 26
Matsuhisa | **Beverly Hills** 28
Mélisse | **Santa Monica** 28
Michael's Rest. | **Santa Monica** 24
Morton's | **multi.** 22
Mr. Chow | **Beverly Hills** 23
Nick & Stef's | **Downtown** 23
Nic's | **Beverly Hills** 22
Nobu | **W Hollywood** 26
Nobu | **Malibu** 27
Ombra | **Studio City** 21
One Pico | **Santa Monica** 23
Osteria Drago | **W Hollywood** 22
Osteria Mozza | **Hollywood** 27
Pacific Dining Car | **multi.** 24
Palm | **W Hollywood** 23
Parkway Grill | **Pasadena** 26
Patina | **Downtown** 26
Petros | **Manhattan Bch** 24
Polo | **Beverly Hills** 22
Providence | **Hollywood** 28
Raymond | **Pasadena** 25
Red O | **Melrose** 24
NEW RivaBella Ristorante | **W Hollywood** 20
Rivera | **Downtown** 26
Roy's | **multi.** 23
Saam/The Bazaar | **Beverly Hills** 27
Saddle Peak | **Calabasas** 26
Scarpetta | **Beverly Hills** 24
Shiro | **S Pasadena** 27
Sky Room | **Long Bch** 23
Spago | **Beverly Hills** 27
Stefan's/L.A. Farm | **Santa Monica** 22
STK | **W Hollywood** 24
Strand House | **Manhattan Bch** 20
Sushi Roku | **multi.** 22
Tavern | **Brentwood** 24

Tierra Sur/Herzog | **Oxnard** 28
Tres/José Andrés | **Beverly Hills** 23
NEW Trois Mec | **Hollywood** -
Valentino | **Santa Monica** 26
Water Grill | **Downtown** 26
Wilshire | **Santa Monica** 22
Wolfgang Puck/Hotel Bel-Air | **Bel-Air** 24
Wolfgang's | **Beverly Hills** 24
Zengo | **Santa Monica** 21

WATERSIDE

Belmont Brewing | **Long Bch** 20
Bluewater | **Redondo Bch** 21
Boa | **Santa Monica** 24
Brophy Bros. | **Ventura** 21
Cafe Del Rey | **Marina del Rey** 23
Catch | **Santa Monica** 22
Cheesecake | **Redondo Bch** 18
Coast | **Santa Monica** 22
Duke's | **Malibu** 17
Fuego/Maya | **Long Bch** 22
Geoffrey's Malibu | **Malibu** 22
Gladstones | **multi.** 17
Ivy/Shore | **Santa Monica** 22
Jer-ne | **Marina del Rey** 18
Jody Maroni's | **Venice** 20
Killer Shrimp | **Marina del Rey** 21
Kincaid's | **Redondo Bch** 22
Lobster | **Santa Monica** 23
Mar'sel | **Rancho Palos Verdes** 26
Martha's 22nd St. | **Hermosa Bch** 23
McKenna's | **Long Bch** 21
Mediterraneo | **Westlake Vill** 21
Moonshadows | **Malibu** 20
Neptune's Net | **Malibu** 19
NEW Nikita | **Malibu** -
Nobu | **Malibu** 27
One Pico | **Santa Monica** 23
Paradise Cove | **Malibu** 18
Parkers' Lighthouse | **Long Bch** 22
Sir Winston's | **Long Bch** 24
22nd St. Landing | **San Pedro** 22
Zin | **Westlake Vill** 20

WINE BARS

Bar Bouchon | **Beverly Hills** 23
Bar Pintxo | **Santa Monica** 21
Bar Toscana | **Brentwood** 23
NEW Bestia | **Downtown** 25
Bistro/Gare | **S Pasadena** 20
NEW Blue Plate Taco | **Santa Monica** 16
Boneyard | **Sherman Oaks** 22
BottleRock | **Culver City** 18
Ca'Brea | **La Brea** 20
Cole's | **Downtown** 17
Corkbar | **Downtown** 21
Counter | **Century City** 19
Cube Cafe | **La Brea** 24
Daily Grill | **Brentwood** 19
Enoteca Drago | **Beverly Hills** 22
Firefly | **Studio City** 20
Fleming's | **multi.** 23
Gaucho | **multi.** 21
Holdren's | **Thousand Oaks** 24
Hungry Cat | **Hollywood** 23
La Paella | **Beverly Hills** 22
Larry's | **Venice** 23
La Scala | **Brentwood** 21
La Serenata | **West LA** 23
Leila's | **Oak Pk** 27
Michael's Rest. | **Santa Monica** 24
Monsieur Marcel | **Fairfax** 20
Parish Wine Bar | **Downtown** -
Petrossian | **W Hollywood** 25
Pho Show | **Culver City** 19
Porta Via | **Beverly Hills** 22
Primitivo | **Venice** 22
Rustic Canyon | **Santa Monica** 25
Spark | **Studio City** 20
NEW Tapenade | **West LA** -
25 Degrees | **Hollywood** 23
Upstairs 2 | **West LA** 24
Valentino | **Santa Monica** 26
Vertical Wine | **Pasadena** 21

WINNING WINE LISTS

Ago | **W Hollywood** 22
AKA Bistro | **Pasadena** 23
Akasha | **Culver City** 22
A.O.C. | **Beverly Blvd** 25
Arroyo | **Pasadena** 25
Bar Bouchon | **Beverly Hills** 23
Bar Toscana | **Brentwood** 23
Bazaar/José Andrés | **Beverly Hills** 27
Bistro 45 | **Pasadena** 25
Bistro Provence | **Burbank** 23
Blvd | **Beverly Hills** 22
Boa | **multi.** 24
Bouchon | **Beverly Hills** 25
Bouzy | **Redondo Bch** 22
Cafe Del Rey | **Marina del Rey** 23
Cafe Pinot | **Downtown** 24
Cecconi's | **W Hollywood** 22
Chaya | **Downtown** 23
Chez Mélange | **Redondo Bch** 26
Chinois | **Santa Monica** 26
NEW chi SPACCA | **Hollywood** -
Cleo | **Hollywood** 26
Comme Ça | **W Hollywood** 23

Corkbar | **Downtown** 21
Craft | **Century City** 25
Culina | **Beverly Hills** 23
Cut | **Beverly Hills** 27
Delphine | **Hollywood** 21
Drago Centro | **Downtown** 26
Eveleigh | **W Hollywood** 20
Fig & Olive | **W Hollywood** 22
FigOly | **Downtown** -
555 East | **Long Bch** 25
Fleming's | **multi.** 23
Foundry/Melrose | **Melrose** 23
Gorbals | **Downtown** 20
Gordon Ramsay | **W Hollywood** 23
Grill on Alley | **Beverly Hills** 25
NEW Hinoki/The Bird | **Century City** 23
Hungry Cat | **Santa Monica** 23
Il Moro | **West LA** 21
Ink | **W Hollywood** 26
Jer-ne | **Marina del Rey** 18
JiRaffe | **Santa Monica** 26
Kendall's | **Downtown** 19
King's Fish | **Calabasas** 21
La Botte | **Santa Monica** 22
Larsen's | **Encino** 24
Livello | **Beverly Hills** 23
Lucques | **W Hollywood** 27
Mar'sel | **Rancho Palos Verdes** 26
Mélisse | **Santa Monica** 28
Michael's Rest. | **Santa Monica** 24
Mosto | **Venice** 24
Napa Valley | **Westwood** 19
Nick & Stef's | **Downtown** 23
Nobu | **W Hollywood** 26
Ombra | **Studio City** 21
Osteria Drago | **W Hollywood** 22
Pacific Dining Car | **multi.** 24
Parkway Grill | **Pasadena** 26
Patina | **Downtown** 26
Paul Martin's | **El Segundo** 22
Peppone | **Brentwood** 21
Primitivo | **Venice** 22
Raymond | **Pasadena** 25
Red O | **Melrose** 24
NEW RivaBella Ristorante | **W Hollywood** 20
Rivera | **Downtown** 26
Roy's | **multi.** 23
Saam/The Bazaar | **Beverly Hills** 27
Safire | **Camarillo** 25
Scarpetta | **Beverly Hills** 24
Sky Room | **Long Bch** 23
Soleto Trattoria | **Downtown** 21
Spago | **Beverly Hills** 27
STK | **W Hollywood** 24
Strand House | **Manhattan Bch** 20
Street | **Hollywood** 25
Tar & Roses | **Santa Monica** 24
Tavern | **Brentwood** 24
Tierra Sur/Herzog | **Oxnard** 28
Tin Roof | **Manhattan Bch** 23
NEW Tower 8 | **Santa Monica** -
Tres/José Andrés | **Beverly Hills** 23
Upstairs 2 | **West LA** 24
Valentino | **Santa Monica** 26
Vertical Wine | **Pasadena** 21
Via Alloro | **Beverly Hills** 22
Water Grill | **Downtown** 26
Westside Tav. | **West LA** 22
Wilshire | **Santa Monica** 22
Wolfgang Puck/Hotel Bel-Air | **Bel-Air** 24
Wolfgang's | **Beverly Hills** 24

Cuisines

Includes names, locations and Food ratings.

Hatfield's | **Melrose** 27
Haven Gastropub | **Pasadena** 19
Hillstone/Houston's | **multi.** 22
Homeboy/girl | **Chinatown** 22
Huckleberry | **Santa Monica** 23
Hudson Hse. | **Redondo Bch** 21
Ink | **W Hollywood** 26
NEW Jackson's Food/Drink | **El Segundo** 17
James' | **Venice** 20
Jar | **Beverly Blvd.** 24
Jinky's | **multi.** 20
JiRaffe | **Santa Monica** 26
Joan's/Third | **Third St** 24
John O'Groats | **multi.** 20
Josie | **Santa Monica** 26
Julienne | **San Marino** 25
Kate Mantilini | **multi.** 20
Killer Cafe | **Marina del Rey** -
Kings Rd. | **W Hollywood** 17
Kitchen 24 | **multi.** 19
Larchmont Bungalow | **Hancock Pk** 19
NEW Larder/Burton | **Beverly Hills** -
Larder/Maple | **Beverly Hills** 20
Larry's | **Venice** 23
Laurel Hardware | **W Hollywood** 19
Lawry's Carvery | **Downtown** 22
NEW Little Beast | **Eagle Rock** -
Little Dom's/Deli | **Los Feliz** 22
NEW Louie's Old School | **Mar Vista** -
Lulu's Cafe | **W Hollywood** 23
Luna Park | **La Brea** 19
Marmalade | **multi.** 17
Marston's | **multi.** 21
Martha's 22nd St. | **Hermosa Bch** 23
Maxwell's | **Venice** 19
M.B. Post | **Manhattan Bch** 27
Mélisse | **Santa Monica** 28
NEW MessHall Kitchen | **Los Feliz** 21
Mike & Anne's | **S Pasadena** 21
Milo & Olive | **Santa Monica** 24
Moonshadows | **Malibu** 20
More Than Waffles | **Encino** 22
Mo's | **Burbank** 18
M Street | **Santa Monica** 21
NEW Muddy Leek | **Culver City** -
Musso & Frank | **Hollywood** 22
Next Door/Josie | **Santa Monica** 24
Nickel Diner | **Downtown** 21
Nic's | **Beverly Hills** 22
Nine Thirty | **Westwood** 16
Noe | **Downtown** 22
Nook | **West LA** 24
Off Vine | **Hollywood** 22
Oinkster | **Eagle Rock** 21
Original Tops | **Pasadena** 22
Outpost | **Hollywood** -
Palomino | **Westwood** 20
Paradise Cove | **Malibu** 18
Parish Wine Bar | **Downtown** -
Park | **Echo Pk** 25
Patina | **Downtown** 26
Paul Martin's | **El Segundo** 22
Penthouse | **Santa Monica** 20
NEW Penthouse/Mastro's | **Beverly Hills** -
Pete's | **Downtown** 20
Plan Check | **West LA** 21
Post & Beam | **Mid-City** 22
Providence | **Hollywood** 28
NEW Public School 805 | **Thousand Oaks** -
NEW Public School 310 | **Culver City** 18
R+D Kitchen | **Santa Monica** 22
Raphael | **Studio City** 23
Rick's Tavern | **Santa Monica** 21
NEW Royce Wood-Fired | **Pasadena** 24
Rush St. | **Culver City** 17
Saddle Peak | **Calabasas** 26
Safire | **Camarillo** 25
Salt's Cure | **W Hollywood** 22
NEW Seasons 52 | **multi.** -
71 Palm | **Ventura** 24
Shack | **Playa del Rey** 18
Short Order | **Fairfax** 18
Simmzy's | **multi.** 23
Six | **multi.** 19
Sky Room | **Long Bch** 23
Smitty's | **Pasadena** 22
South Beverly Grill | **Beverly Hills** 21
Spark | **Studio City** 20
Square One | **E Hollywood** 22
Stand | **multi.** 18
Strand House | **Manhattan Bch** 20
Superba | **Venice** 21
Swingers | **multi.** 19
Sycamore Kit. | **Mid-City** 24
Tar & Roses | **Santa Monica** 24
Tender Greens | **multi.** 23
Tin Roof | **Manhattan Bch** 23
Toast | **Third St** 18
Tower Bar | **W Hollywood** 25
Traxx | **Downtown** 21

- Truxton's | **multi.** 20
- Twin Palms | **Pasadena** -
- Twohey's | **Alhambra** 17
- Uncle Bill's | **Manhattan Bch** 22
- Urth | **multi.** 22
- Vibrato Grill Jazz | **Bel-Air** 22
- Waffle | **Hollywood** 20
- Watermark on Main | **Ventura** 22
- Wilshire | **Santa Monica** 22
- Wolfgang's | **Beverly Hills** 24
- Wood & Vine | **Hollywood** 20
- Wood Ranch | **multi.** 20
- Zin | **Westlake Vill** 20

ARGENTINEAN

- Carlitos Gardel | **Melrose** 24
- Gaucho | **multi.** 21
- Malbec | **multi.** 23
- Ushuaia | **Santa Monica** 23

ASIAN

- Bashi | **Rancho Palos Verdes** -
- Buddha's Belly | **multi.** 20
- Chaya | **W Hollywood** 23
- Chaya | **Downtown** 23
- Chaya | **Venice** 23
- Chin Chin | **multi.** 19
- Chinois | **Santa Monica** 26
- Feast/East | **West LA** 22
- Formosa | **W Hollywood** 14
- Gina Lee's | **Redondo Bch** 24
- NEW Little Sister | **Manhattan Bch** -
- Lukshon | **Culver City** 24
- Monsoon | **Santa Monica** 20
- Pearl Dragon | **Pacific Palisades** 20
- Restaurant 2117 | **West LA** 23
- RockSugar | **Century City** 21
- Roy's | **multi.** 23
- NEW ShopHouse | **multi.** -
- Take a Bao | **multi.** 19
- Typhoon | **Santa Monica** 20
- Wokcano | **multi.** 19
- Yamashiro | **Hollywood** 21
- Zengo | **Santa Monica** 21

AUSTRIAN

- BierBeisl | **Beverly Hills** 22

BAKERIES

- Auntie Em's | **Eagle Rock** 22
- Baker | **Woodland Hills** 24
- Beckers Bakery | **Manhattan Bch** 21
- Bouchon Bakery | **Beverly Hills** 25
- Breadbar | **Century City** 18
- Clementine | **Century City** 25
- Doughboys | **Third St** 23
- Du-par's | **Studio City** 17
- Euro Pane | **Pasadena** 25
- Huckleberry | **Santa Monica** 23
- Joan's/Third | **Third St** 24
- Le Pain Quotidien | **multi.** 18
- Porto's | **multi.** 25
- Röckenwagner | **Santa Monica** 21
- Susina | **Beverly Blvd** 23
- Sweet Lady | **multi.** 23
- NEW Tartine O | **Beverly Hills** -
- 3 Square | **Venice** 23
- Toast | **Third St** 18
- NEW Twist Eatery | **La Brea** -

BARBECUE

- Baby Blues | **multi.** 21
- Beachwood BBQ | **Long Bch** 23
- Bludso's BBQ | **multi.** 25
- Boneyard | **Sherman Oaks** 22
- Dr. Hogly Wogly's | **Van Nuys** 22
- Gus's | **S Pasadena** 19
- NEW Horse Thief BBQ | **Downtown** -
- Johnny Rebs' | **multi.** 23
- JR's | **Culver City** 23
- Lucille's | **multi.** 22
- Oinkster | **Eagle Rock** 21
- NEW Park's Finest | **Echo Pk** -
- Phillips BBQ | **multi.** 24
- Reddi Chick | **Santa Monica** 21
- Robin's BBQ | **Pasadena** 22
- Smoke City | **Van Nuys** 22
- Stonefire | **multi.** 21
- Wood Ranch | **multi.** 20
- Woody's BBQ | **multi.** 24
- Zeke's | **Montrose** 19

BELGIAN

- Le Pain Quotidien | **multi.** 18
- Little Bear | **Downtown** 22
- Wurstküche | **Downtown** 23

BRAZILIAN

- Bossa Nova | **multi.** 22
- Café Brasil | **multi.** 22
- Fogo de Chão | **Beverly Hills** 23
- Galletto | **Westlake Vill** 24
- Picanha | **Burbank** 21

BRITISH

- Parish | **Downtown** 22
- Waterloo & City | **Culver City** 23
- Whale & Ale | **San Pedro** 19
- Ye Olde King's | **Santa Monica** 17

BURGERS

Apple Pan | **West LA** 23
Baby's/Burgers | **Location Varies** 24
Barney's | **multi.** 21
Bowery | **Hollywood** 22
NEW Bunker Hill | **Downtown** -
Burger Lounge | **multi.** -
Comme Ça | **W Hollywood** 23
Counter | **multi.** 19
Fab Hot Dogs | **multi.** 22
Father's Office | **multi.** 23
Five Guys | **multi.** 16
Ford's | **Culver City** 20
Go Burger | **Hollywood** 20
Golden State | **Fairfax** 25
NEW Grill 'Em All | **Alhambra** 19
Hamburger Hamlet | **Sherman Oaks** 18
NEW Hole in the Wall | **Santa Monica** 23
Hot's Kitchen | **Hermosa Bch** 25
Hungry Cat | **multi.** 23
In-N-Out | **multi.** 23
King's Burgers | **Northridge** 25
Lazy Ox | **Little Tokyo** 24
Little Bear | **Downtown** 22
Mo's | **Burbank** 18
Oinkster | **Eagle Rock** 21
Pie 'N Burger | **Pasadena** 20
Rustic Canyon | **Santa Monica** 25
Shack | **Playa del Rey** 18
Short Order | **Fairfax** 18
Stand | **multi.** 18
Tommy's | **Downtown** 24
NEW True Burger | **Mid-City** -
25 Degrees | **Hollywood** 23
26 Beach | **Venice** 23
Umami Burger | **multi.** 23

CAJUN

Boiling Crab | **multi.** 24
Gumbo Pot | **Fairfax** 20
Uncle Darrow's | **Marina del Rey** 21

CALIFORNIAN

Ammo | **multi.** 22
A.O.C. | **Beverly Blvd** 25
Axe | **Venice** 23
Babalu | **Santa Monica** 18
Basix | **W Hollywood** 19
Bel Air B&G | **Bel-Air** 21
Bistro 45 | **Pasadena** 25
Bloom | **Mid-City** 23
Blvd | **Beverly Hills** 22
Cafe Del Rey | **Marina del Rey** 23
Cafe La Boheme | **W Hollywood** 20
Cafe Montana | **Santa Monica** 20
Cafe Pinot | **Downtown** 24
Cafe Verde | **Pasadena** 23
Canal Club | **Venice** 20
NEW Cast | **Santa Monica** -
Checkers | **Downtown** 22
Chef Melba's | **Hermosa Bch** 26
NEW Chez Soi | **Manhattan Bch** -
Cicada | **Downtown** 25
Cliff's Edge | **Silver Lake** 21
Coast | **Santa Monica** 22
Cooks County | **Beverly Blvd** 23
Cuvée | **W Hollywood** 21
Emle's | **Northridge** 23
Farmshop | **Santa Monica** 25
FigOly | **Downtown** -
Food + Lab | **multi.** 21
Forage | **Silver Lake** 25
Geoffrey's Malibu | **Malibu** 22
Getty Ctr. | **Brentwood** 23
Gina Lee's | **Redondo Bch** 24
NEW Goldie's | **Third St** -
Gordon Ramsay | **W Hollywood** 23
Green St. | **Pasadena** 21
Green St. Tavern | **Pasadena** 23
Hugo's | **multi.** 21
Inn/Seventh Ray | **Topanga** 20
Ivy | **W Hollywood** 22
Ivy/Shore | **Santa Monica** 22
Jack's/Montana | **Santa Monica** 20
Jer-ne | **Marina del Rey** 18
Joe's | **Venice** 26
La Grande Orange | **Pasadena** 20
L.A. Market | **Downtown** 19
LAMILL | **Silver Lake** 22
Leila's | **Oak Pk** 27
Lemonade | **multi.** 21
Lemon Moon | **West LA** 20
Literati | **West LA** 18
Louise's | **multi.** 19
Lucques | **W Hollywood** 27
Mar'sel | **Rancho Palos Verdes** 26
Michael's Rest. | **Santa Monica** 24
Milky Way | **Pico-Robertson** 20
Milo & Olive | **Santa Monica** 24
Mi Piace | **Pasadena** 21
Napa Valley | **Westwood** 19
Ocean & Vine | **Santa Monica** 23
Off Vine | **Hollywood** 22
On Rodeo | **Beverly Hills** -
Parkway Grill | **Pasadena** 26
Patina | **Downtown** 26
Polo | **Beverly Hills** 22

Porta Via | **Beverly Hills** 22
Raymond | **Pasadena** 25
Röckenwagner | **Santa Monica** 21
NEW ROFL Cafe | **Melrose** -
Rose Cafe | **Venice** 21
Rustic Canyon | **Santa Monica** 25
Sam's/Beach | **Santa Monica** 25
Sir Winston's | **Long Bch** 24
Spago | **Beverly Hills** 27
Stanley's | **Sherman Oaks** 20
NEW Tapenade | **West LA** -
Tavern | **Brentwood** 24
NEW Tower 8 | **Santa Monica** -
26 Beach | **Venice** 23
NEW Twist Eatery | **La Brea** -
Westside Tav. | **West LA** 22
Wolfgang Puck/Hotel Bel-Air | **Bel-Air** 24
Wolfgang Puck Express/Bistro | **multi.** 21
Xiomara | **Hollywood** 21

CANADIAN

Soleil | **Westwood** 21

CARIBBEAN

Bamboo Restaurant | **Culver City** 21
Cha Cha Cha | **Silver Lake** 21
Cha Cha Chicken | **Santa Monica** 22
Prado | **Hancock Pk** 23
Sunny Spot | **Venice** 21

CHINESE

(* dim sum specialist)

Bamboo Cuisine | **Sherman Oaks** 23
Bao* | **Beverly Blvd** 21
Chi Dynasty | **multi.** 20
NEW Chi-Lin | **W Hollywood** -
Chin Chin* | **multi.** 19
Din Tai Fung | **Arcadia** 26
Duck Hse. | **Monterey Pk** 22
888 Seafood | **Rosemead** 23
Elite* | **Monterey Pk** 25
Hop Li | **multi.** 20
NEW Kaishin* | **Malibu** -
Mandarette | **Beverly Blvd.** 19
Mr. Chow | **multi.** 23
Newport Seafood | **multi.** 26
Ocean Seafood | **Chinatown** 21
Ocean Star | **Monterey Pk** 21
101 Noodle | **multi.** 23
Panda Inn* | **multi.** 22
P.F. Chang's | **multi.** 17
NEW ROC Star | **West LA** -
Sam Woo | **multi.** 18
Sea Empress* | **Gardena** 21
Sea Harbour* | **Rosemead** 25
WP24* | **Downtown** 25
W's China Bistro | **Redondo Bch** 21
Xi'an | **Beverly Hills** 21
Yang Chow | **multi.** 22

COFFEEHOUSES

Black Dog Coffee | **Mid-City** 21
Caffe Luxxe | **multi.** 21
LAMILL | **Silver Lake** 22
Literati | **West LA** 18
Urth | **multi.** 22

CONTINENTAL

Bistro Gdn. | **Studio City** 21
Brandywine | **Woodland Hills** 27
Café 14 | **Agoura Hills** 26
Dal Rae | **Pico Rivera** 25
NEW Le Ka | **Downtown** -
Lulu's Cafe | **W Hollywood** 23
Pig 'n Whistle | **Hollywood** 18
Polo | **Beverly Hills** 22
Sir Winston's | **Long Bch** 24

CREOLE

Harold & Belle's | **Mid-City** 24
Uncle Darrow's | **Marina del Rey** 21

CRÊPES

Café Laurent | **Culver City** 20
La Crêperie | **Long Bch** 23

CUBAN

Café Habana | **Malibu** 20
Porto's | **multi.** 25
Versailles | **multi.** 22
Xiomara | **Hollywood** 21

DELIS

Art's | **Studio City** 21
Barney Greengrass | **Beverly Hills** 22
Bay Cities | **Santa Monica** 26
Beckers Bakery | **Manhattan Bch** 21
Brent's Deli | **multi.** 26
Canter's | **Fairfax** 20
Factor's | **Pico-Robertson** 19
Fromin's | **Santa Monica** 16
Greenblatt's | **Hollywood** 19
Jerry's Deli | **multi.** 15
Langer's | **Downtown** 26
NEW Lenny's Deli | **West LA** -
Little Dom's/Deli | **Los Feliz** 22
Nate 'n Al | **multi.** 21

Pico Kosher Deli | **Century City** 22
Roll 'n Rye | **Culver City** 16

DINER

Brighton Coffee | **Beverly Hills** 19
Cora's | **Santa Monica** 23
Dinah's | **Westchester** 18
Du-par's | **multi.** 17
Eat Well | **multi.** 20
Fred 62 | **Los Feliz** 18
Hamburger Hamlet | **multi.** 18
Homeboy/girl | **Downtown** 22
Jinky's | **multi.** 20
Johnnie's Pastrami | **Culver City** 21
Kate Mantilini | **multi.** 20
Nickel Diner | **Downtown** 21
101 Coffee | **Hollywood** 22
Original Pantry | **Downtown** 18
Patrick's | **Santa Monica** 17
Pie 'N Burger | **Pasadena** 20
Swingers | **multi.** 19
Uncle Bill's | **Manhattan Bch** 22

EASTERN EUROPEAN

Aroma | **West LA** 20

ECLECTIC

Abricott | **Pasadena** 22
A-Frame | **Culver City** 23
Beer Belly | **Koreatown** 23
Black Market | **Studio City** 23
BottleRock | **Downtown** 18
Caffe Opera | **Monrovia** 21
Canal Club | **Venice** 20
Chez Mélange | **Redondo Bch** 26
Corkbar | **Downtown** 21
Depot | **Torrance** 25
Farm Stand | **El Segundo** 22
Gorbals | **Downtown** 20
Home | **multi.** 20
Hot's Kitchen | **Hermosa Bch** 25
House Café | **Beverly Blvd** 20
Ink | **W Hollywood** 26
Lazy Ox | **Little Tokyo** 24
Literati | **West LA** 18
NEW Littlefork | **Hollywood** 24
Livello | **Beverly Hills** 23
LudoTruck | **Location Varies** 24
Misfit | **Santa Monica** 22
Mohawk Bend | **Echo Pk** 21
Olive/Thyme | **Burbank** 22
Plate 38 | **Pasadena** 22
Public Kitchen | **Hollywood** 20
Restaurant/Standard | **multi.** 18
NEW ROFL Cafe | **Melrose** -
Saam/The Bazaar | **Beverly Hills** 27
Stefan's/L.A. Farm | **Santa Monica** 22
Street | **Hollywood** 25
Sunny Spot | **Venice** 21
Think Café | **San Pedro** 23
Tres/José Andrés | **Beverly Hills** 23
Tripel | **Playa del Rey** 25
NEW Trois Mec | **Hollywood** -
NEW Twist Eatery | **La Brea** -
Umamicatessen | **Downtown** 22
Vertical Wine | **Pasadena** 21
Walter's | **Claremont** 20

ETHIOPIAN

Nyala | **Mid-Wilshire** 23

EUROPEAN

Blu Jam Café | **multi.** 25
BottleRock | **Downtown** 18
Euro Pane | **Pasadena** 25
Gorbals | **Downtown** 20
NEW Little Sister | **Manhattan Bch** -
Restaurant 2117 | **West LA** 23
Wurstküche | **Venice** 23

FILIPINO

NEW Park's Finest | **Echo Pk** -

FONDUE

Melting Pot | **multi.** 15

FRENCH

A.O.C. | **Beverly Blvd** 25
Ba Restaurant | **Highland Pk** -
Café Laurent | **Culver City** 20
Cafe Pinot | **Downtown** 24
Chaya | **W Hollywood** 23
Chaya | **Downtown** 23
Chaya | **Venice** 23
NEW Chez Mimi | **Pacific Palisades** 19
Chinois | **Santa Monica** 26
Coco Laurent | **Downtown** -
Comme Ça | **W Hollywood** 23
Dusty's | **Silver Lake** 22
NEW Esterel | **W Hollywood** -
Fig | **Santa Monica** 22
NEW Figaro | **Downtown** -
Figaro | **Los Feliz** 22
Gordon Ramsay | **W Hollywood** 23
NEW Gorge | **W Hollywood** -
Industriel | **Downtown** 20

JiRaffe | **Santa Monica** 26
Joe's | **Venice** 26
Kendall's | **Downtown** 19
La Dijonaise | **Culver City** 19
Le Chêne | **Saugus** 24
NEW Le Ka | **Downtown** –
Le Sanglier | **Tarzana** 24
Little Door | **Third St** 23
Maison Akira | **Pasadena** 26
Maison Giraud | **Pacific Palisades** 24
Mélisse | **Santa Monica** 28
Mi Piace | **Pasadena** 21
Monsieur Marcel | **multi.** 20
Morels French Steak | **Fairfax** 20
NEW Muddy Leek | **Culver City** –
On Rodeo | **Beverly Hills** –
Perch | **Downtown** 17
Petrossian | **W Hollywood** 25
NEW Pichet | **Venice** –
71 Palm | **Ventura** 24
Shiro | **S Pasadena** 27
Soleil | **Westwood** 21
Taix | **Echo Pk** 20
NEW Tartine O | **Beverly Hills** –
NEW Trois Mec | **Hollywood** –

FRENCH (BISTRO)

Bar Bouchon | **Beverly Hills** 23
Bistro/Gare | **S Pasadena** 20
Bistro Provence | **Burbank** 23
Bouchon | **Beverly Hills** 25
Café Beaujolais | **Eagle Rock** 26
Cafe Bizou | **multi.** 22
Café Pierre | **Manhattan Bch** 24
Cheval Bistro | **Pasadena** 23
Church/State | **Downtown** 24
Julienne | **San Marino** 25
La Crêperie | **Long Bch** 23
Le Petit Bistro | **W Hollywood** 24
Le Petit Cafe | **Santa Monica** 24
Le Petit Rest. | **Sherman Oaks** 23
Mistral | **Sherman Oaks** 26

GASTROPUB

AKA Bistro | Amer. | **Pasadena** 23
NEW Bank/Venice | Amer. | **Venice** –
Beer Belly | Eclectic | **Koreatown** 23
Black Market | Eclectic | **Studio City** 23
Bouzy | Amer. | **Redondo Bch** 22
Churchill | Amer. | **W Hollywood** 15
Congregation Ale | Amer. | **multi.** 18
NEW The Doughroom | Italian | **Palms** –
Eat.Drink.Americano | Amer. | **Downtown** –
Fat Cow | Amer. | **Fairfax** 18
Fat Dog | Amer. | **multi.** 20
Father's Office | Amer. | **multi.** 23
NEW Fatty's Public | Amer. | **W Hollywood** –
Federal Bar | Amer. | **multi.** 19
Ford's | Amer. | **Culver City** 20
Haven Gastropub | Amer. | **Pasadena** 19
Hudson Hse. | Amer. | **Redondo Bch** 21
Larry's | Amer. | **Venice** 23
Little Bear | Belgian | **Downtown** 22
NEW MessHall Kitchen | Amer. | **Los Feliz** 21
Misfit | Eclectic | **Santa Monica** 22
Mohawk Bend | Eclectic | **Echo Pk** 21
NEW Morrison | Scottish | **Atwater Vill** –
Next Door/Josie | Amer. | **Santa Monica** 24
Outpost | Amer. | **Hollywood** –
Parish | British | **Downtown** 22
Plate 38 | Eclectic | **Pasadena** 22
NEW Public School 310 | Amer. | **Culver City** 18
R+D Kitchen | Amer. | **Santa Monica** 22
Six | Amer. | **multi.** 19
Tar & Roses | Eclectic | **Santa Monica** 24
Tripel | Eclectic | **Playa del Rey** 25
Waterloo & City | British | **Culver City** 23

GERMAN

Berlin Currywurst | **multi.** 21
Brats Brothers | **multi.** 22
Wirtshaus | **La Brea** 19
Wolfslair | **Hollywood** 22
Wurstküche | **Downtown** 23

GREEK

Great Greek | **Sherman Oaks** 22
Le Petit Greek | **Hancock Pk** 22
Limani Taverna | **San Pedro** 18
Papa Cristo's | **Mid-City** 22
Petros | **Manhattan Bch** 24
Taverna Tony | **Malibu** 22

HAWAIIAN

Roy's | **multi.** 23

HOT DOGS

Fab Hot Dogs | **multi.** 22
Five Guys | **multi.** 16

Jody Maroni's | **multi.** 20
Let's Be Frank | **Culver City** 17
Pink's Hot Dogs | **La Brea** 21
Portillo's | **Moreno Valley** 25
Slaw Dogs | **multi.** 22
Stand | **multi.** 18
Tommy's | **Downtown** 24
Wirtshaus | **La Brea** 19

INDIAN

Addi's | **Redondo Bch** 26
Agra Cafe | **Silver Lake** 22
Akbar Cuisine | **multi.** 22
All India | **multi.** 21
Bollywood | **multi.** 24
Bombay Cafe | **West LA** 22
Bombay Palace | **Beverly Hills** 24
Chakra | **Beverly Hills** 23
Clay Oven | **Sherman Oaks** 23
India's Tandoori | **multi.** 23
Jaipur | **West LA** 22
Nawab | **Santa Monica** 22
Ocean Tava | **Redondo Bch** 25
Tanzore | **Beverly Hills** 21

ISRAELI

Itzik Hagadol | **Encino** 20

ITALIAN

(N=Northern; S=Southern)

Adagio | N | **Woodland Hills** 22
Ado/Casa Ado | **multi.** 25
Ago | N | **W Hollywood** 22
Alejo's/Eddie's italian | **Westchester** 21
Alessio/Bistro | **multi.** 21
Amalfi | **La Brea** 20
Amarone | N | **W Hollywood** 24
Trattoria Amici | **multi.** 21
Angelini | **Beverly Blvd** 28
Aroma | **Silver Lake** 24
NEW Aventine | **Hollywood** -
Barbrix | **Silver Lake** 24
Bar Toscana | **Brentwood** 23
Basix | **W Hollywood** 19
NEW Bestia | **Downtown** 25
Bottega Louie | **Downtown** 23
Bottle Inn | **Hermosa Bch** 21
Bravo | **Santa Monica** 20
Brunello | **Culver City** 22
NEW Bucato | **Culver City** -
Ca'Brea | **La Brea** 20
Ca' del Sole | N | **N Hollywood** 22
Cafe Angelino | **Mid-City** 23
Cafe Fiore | S | **Ventura** 22
Cafe Firenze | N | **Moorpark** 22
Cafe Med | **W Hollywood** 20
Café Piccolo | N | **Long Bch** 24
Cafe Verde | **Pasadena** 23
Caffé Delfini | **Santa Monica** 24
Caffe Pinguini | **Playa del Rey** 21
Caffe Roma | **Beverly Hills** 22
C & O | **Marina del Rey** 21
Capo | **Santa Monica** 26
Cecconi's | N | **W Hollywood** 22
Celestino | **Pasadena** 25
Cheebo | **Hollywood** 21
NEW chi SPACCA | **Hollywood** -
Cicada | N | **Downtown** 25
Cliff's Edge | **Silver Lake** 21
NEW Clusi Batusi | **West LA** -
Cube Cafe | **La Brea** 24
Culina | **Beverly Hills** 23
Cuvée | **Century City** 21
Dan Tana's | **W Hollywood** 23
Da Pasquale | S | **Beverly Hills** 24
Divino | **Brentwood** 24
Dominick's | **W Hollywood** 20
NEW The Doughroom | **Palms** -
Drago Centro | **Downtown** 26
Eatalian | **Gardena** 24
E. Baldi | N | **Beverly Hills** 23
Enoteca Drago | **Beverly Hills** 22
Enzo/Angela | **West LA** 21
Fabiolus Cucina | N | **Hollywood** 21
Farfalla/Vinoteca | **multi.** 22
Far Niente | N | **Glendale** 24
FigOly | **Downtown** -
Firenze | **N Hollywood** 22
Fritto Misto | **multi.** 22
Gale's Restaurant | N | **Pasadena** 22
Galletto | **Westlake Vill** 24
Giorgio Baldi | **Santa Monica** 25
Giovanni Ristorante | **Woodland Hills** 21
Grissini Ristorante | **Agoura Hills** 21
Guido's | N | **West LA** 21
Gusto | **Third St** 23
Hostaria/Piccolo | **multi.** 24
Il Buco Cucina | **W Hollywood** 21
Il Cielo | N | **Beverly Hills** 23
Il Fornaio | **multi.** 20
Il Forno | **Santa Monica** 22
Il Forno Caldo | **Beverly Hills** 21
Il Grano | **West LA** 25
Il Moro | **West LA** 21
Il Pastaio | **Beverly Hills** 26
Il Piccolino | **W Hollywood** 23

CUISINES

NEW Il Piccolo Ritrovo | **multi.** 26
Il Tiramisù | **Sherman Oaks** 22
Il Tramezzino | **multi.** 22
Ivy/Shore | **Santa Monica** 22
La Botte | **Santa Monica** 22
La Bottega | **West LA** 21
La Bruschetta | **Westwood** 23
La Dolce Vita | **Beverly Hills** 24
Lago d'Argento | **Silver Lake** -
La Parolaccia | **multi.** 24
La Pergola | **Sherman Oaks** 25
La Scala | **multi.** 21
La Vecchia | **Santa Monica** 24
Little Dom's/Deli | **Los Feliz** 22
Locanda/Lago | N | **Santa Monica** 23
Locanda Positano | **Marina del Rey** 25
Locanda Veneta | N | **Third St** 24
L'Opera | N | **Long Bch** 23
Louise's | **multi.** 19
Luggage Room | **Pasadena** 23
NEW Maccheroni Republic | **Downtown** -
Madeo | N | **W Hollywood** 26
Mama D's | **Manhattan Bch** 23
Mama Terano | **Rolling Hills Estates** 22
Maria's Italian | **multi.** 19
Marino | **Hollywood** 25
Matteo's | **West LA** 20
Maximiliano | **Highland Pk** 22
Mercato di Vetro | **W Hollywood** 22
Miceli's | **multi.** 18
Michael's/Naples | **Long Bch** 27
Mi Piace | S | **Pasadena** 21
Modo Mio | **Pacific Palisades** 23
Mosto | **Venice** 24
Mulberry St. Pizzeria | **multi.** 23
NEW Nikita | **Malibu** -
Nonna | **W Hollywood** 23
Obikà | **multi.** 21
Old Tony's | **Redondo Bch** 20
Olio/Cafe | **Third St** 23
Oliva | N | **Sherman Oaks** 20
Oliverio | **Beverly Hills** 25
Ombra | **Studio City** 21
Osteria Drago | **W Hollywood** 22
Osteria La Buca | N | **Hollywood** 22
Osteria Latini | **Brentwood** 25
Osteria Mamma | **Hollywood** 24
Osteria Mozza | **Hollywood** 27
Pace | **Laurel Canyon** 23
Padri | **Agoura Hills** 22
Palermo | **Los Feliz** 22
Palmeri | S | **Brentwood** 25
Panini Cafe | **multi.** 21
Panzanella | S | **Sherman Oaks** 25
Pastina | S | **West LA** 23
Pecorino | **Brentwood** 24
Peppone | **Brentwood** 21
Piccolo | N | **Venice** 27
Piccolo Paradiso | **Beverly Hills** 24
Pizzeria Mozza | **Hollywood** 27
Pizzicotto | **Brentwood** 23
Prosecco | N | **Toluca Lake** 25
NEW RivaBella Ristorante | **W Hollywood** 20
Rosti | N | **multi.** 17
Rustico | **Westlake Vill** 26
Scarpetta | **Beverly Hills** 24
Settebello Pizzeria | **Pasadena** 23
NEW Sirena | **Mid-City** 18
Sisley | **multi.** 19
Soleto Trattoria | **Downtown** 21
Sor Tino | **Brentwood** 21
Sotto | S | **Century City** 22
Stinking Rose | **Beverly Hills** 21
NEW Stonehaus | **Westlake Vill** -
Superba | **Venice** 21
Tanino | S | **Westwood** 22
NEW Tapenade | **West LA** -
Terroni | S | **multi.** 22
Tomato Pie | **multi.** 22
Toscana | N | **Brentwood** 25
Toscanova | N | **multi.** 19
Tra di Noi | **Malibu** 23
Trastevere | **multi.** 18
Tuscany | **Westlake Vill** 26
Tutti Mangia | **Claremont** 22
Valentino | **Santa Monica** 26
Via Alloro | **Beverly Hills** 22
Via Veneto | **Santa Monica** 26
Villetta | **Santa Monica** 20
Vincenti | **Brentwood** 26
Vito | **Santa Monica** 23
Vito's | **W Hollywood** 26
Vivoli | **W Hollywood** 21
Zane's | **Hermosa Bch** 21

JAPANESE

(* sushi specialist)

Aburiya Toranoko | **Downtown** 22
Ahi* | **Studio City** 23
Asahi | **West LA** 20
Asaka* | **multi.** 22
Asakuma* | **multi.** 22
Asanebo* | **Studio City** 29
B.A.D. Sushi* | **multi.** 22
NEW Bamboo Izakaya* | **Santa Monica** -

Bar Hayama | **West LA** 24
Boss Sushi* | **Beverly Hills** 24
Brother Sushi* | **Woodland Hills** 25
Crazy Fish | **Beverly Hills** 21
Daikokuya | **multi.** 24
Echigo* | **West LA** 26
Gin Sushi* | **Pasadena** 22
Gonpachi | **Torrance** 19
Gottsui | **West LA** 21
Gyu-Kaku | **multi.** 20
Hakata | **Gardena** 25
Hamasaku* | **West LA** 28
Hama* | **Venice** 23
Hannosuke | **Mar Vista** –
Hide* | **West LA** 24
NEW Hinoki/The Bird | **Century City** 23
Hirosuke* | **Encino** 22
Hirozen* | **Beverly Blvd.** 26
Honda-Ya* | **multi.** 21
Iroha* | **Studio City** 24
Izaka-ya/Katsu-ya | **multi.** 25
Kabuki* | **multi.** 21
Katana* | **W Hollywood** 25
Katsu-ya* | **multi.** 27
Katsuya* | **multi.** 24
Kiriko | **West LA** 26
Kiwami | **Studio City** 27
Koi* | **W Hollywood** 24
K-Zo* | **Culver City** 26
Maison Akira | **Pasadena** 26
NEW Maru | **Santa Monica** –
Maruhide | **Torrance** –
Matsuhisa* | **Beverly Hills** 28
Mori Sushi* | **West LA** 27
Musashi | **Northridge** 23
Musha | **multi.** 23
Nanbankan | **West LA** 27
N/Naka | **Palms** 27
Nobu | **W Hollywood** 26
Nobu | **Malibu** 27
Noshi Sushi | **Koreatown** 23
NEW Nozawa Bar* | **Beverly Hills** –
NEW Paiche | **Marina del Rey** –
Ramen Hayatemaru | **multi.** –
Ramen Jinya | **Studio City** 23
Ramenya | **West LA** 20
Ramen Yamadaya | **multi.** 23
RA Sushi* | **Torrance** 21
R23* | **Downtown** 25
Santouka Ramen | **multi.** 25
Shabu Shabu | **Little Tokyo** 22
Shin-Sen-Gumi Yakitori | **multi.** 23
Shiro | **S Pasadena** 27
NEW Skewers/Morimoto | **LAX** –
Sugarfish* | **multi.** 26
Sushi Gen* | **Little Tokyo** 26
Sushi Masu* | **West LA** 27
Sushi Roku* | **multi.** 22
Sushi Sasabune* | **multi.** 26
Sushi Sushi* | **Beverly Hills** 27
Sushi Zo* | **West LA** 28
Taiko* | **Brentwood** 22
Takami* | **Downtown** 22
Takao* | **Brentwood** 26
Tatsu Ramen | **West LA** –
Teru Sushi* | **Studio City** 21
Torafuku* | **West LA** 21
Totoraku | **West LA** –
Tsujita LA | **West LA** 26
Urasawa* | **Beverly Hills** 28
U-Zen* | **West LA** 24
Wabi-Sabi* | **Venice** 22
Yabu* | **multi.** 23
Yen* | **multi.** 22

KOREAN

(* barbecue specialist)

BCD Tofu | **multi.** 22
NEW Chego! | **Chinatown** 23
ChoSun Galbee* | **Koreatown** 24
Genwa | **multi.** 25
Kogi | **Location Varies** 26
Manna* | **Downtown** 17
NEW Osek Korean | **Pasadena** –
Park's BBQ* | **Koreatown** 25
Seoul House/Tofu | **West LA** –
Soot Bull Jeep* | **Koreatown** 24
Tofu Ya* | **West LA** 20

KOSHER/ KOSHER-STYLE

Fish Grill | **multi.** 22
Milky Way | **Pico-Robertson** 20
Real Food | **multi.** 21
Tierra Sur/Herzog | **Oxnard** 28

LEBANESE

Carnival | **Sherman Oaks** 25
Marouch | **E Hollywood** 28
Open Sesame | **multi.** 24
Sunnin | **Westwood** 23

MEDITERRANEAN

Barbrix | **Silver Lake** 24
Cafe Del Rey | **Marina del Rey** 23
Cafe La Boheme | **W Hollywood** 20
Café Santorini | **Pasadena** 21
Canelé | **Atwater Vill** 23
Christine | **Torrance** 27

Cleo | **Hollywood** 26
NEW Creation Grill | **Santa Monica** -
Elf Café | **Echo Pk** 25
Emle's | **Northridge** 23
Falafel Palace | **Northridge** 22
Fig & Olive | **W Hollywood** 22
Gaby's | **multi.** 20
NEW Kal's Bistro | **Pasadena** -
Lemon Moon | **West LA** 20
Le Petit Greek | **Hancock Pk** 22
Little Door | **Third St** 23
Lucques | **W Hollywood** 27
Mediterraneo | **Hermosa Bch** 23
Mediterraneo | **Westlake Vill** 21
Momed | **Beverly Hills** 20
NEW Nikita | **Malibu** -
One Pico | **Santa Monica** 23
Open Sesame | **Long Bch** 24
Palomino | **Westwood** 20
Panini Cafe | **multi.** 21
Primitivo | **Venice** 22
Ray's/Stark Bar | **Mid-Wilshire** 23
Rustic Canyon | **Santa Monica** 25
Sam's/Beach | **Santa Monica** 25
NEW Tapenade | **West LA** -
Tasting Kitchen | **Venice** 25
Tavern | **Brentwood** 24
Tierra Sur/Herzog | **Oxnard** 28
Upstairs 2 | **West LA** 24
Vertical Wine | **Pasadena** 21
Wolfgang Puck/Hotel Bel-Air | **Bel-Air** 24
Zankou | **multi.** 21
Zazou | **Redondo Bch** 25

MEXICAN

Alegria/Sunset | **Silver Lake** 24
Alfredo's | **Lomita** 26
Antonio's | **Melrose** 20
NEW Ara's Tacos | **Glendale** -
Babita | **San Gabriel** 27
NEW Blue Plate Taco | **Santa Monica** 16
Border Grill | **multi.** 22
CaCao | **Eagle Rock** 24
Café Habana | **Malibu** 20
Casa Vega | **Sherman Oaks** 19
NEW Chego! | **Chinatown** 23
Chichen Itza | **Downtown** 25
Cook's Tortas | **Monterey Pk** 23
El Cholo | **multi.** 19
El Coyote | **Beverly Blvd** 16
El Tepeyac | **Boyle Hts** 26
Frida | **multi.** 19
Fuego/Maya | **Long Bch** 22
Guelaguetza | **Koreatown** 24
Homeboy/girl | **Chinatown** 22
Kay 'n Dave's | **multi.** 18
Kogi | **Location Varies** 26
La Sandia | **Santa Monica** 21
La Serenata | **multi.** 23
Lotería! | **multi.** 22
Malo | **Silver Lake** 19
Mas Malo | **Downtown** 18
Mercado | **Santa Monica** 24
Mijares | **Pasadena** 18
NEW Ocho 8 Taqueria | **Torrance** -
Ortega 120 | **Redondo Bch** 22
Paco's Tacos | **multi.** 21
Palmilla | **Hermosa Bch** 18
NEW Petty Cash | **Beverly Blvd** -
Pink Taco | **multi.** 17
Poquito Más | **multi.** 21
Red O | **Melrose** 24
Rosa Mexicano | **multi.** 20
Sol y Luna | **Tarzana** 22
NEW Tacos Punta Cabras | **Santa Monica** -
Tinga | **multi.** 22
Tito's Tacos | **Culver City** 21
Tlapazola | **multi.** 23
Tortilla Rep. | **W Hollywood** 20
Yuca's | **Los Feliz** 25
Yxta | **Downtown** 24

MIDDLE EASTERN

Bäco Mercat | **Downtown** 25
Burger Continental | **Pasadena** 18
Carousel | **multi.** 25
Falafel King | **multi.** 18
Falafel Palace | **Northridge** 22
Hummus B&G | **Tarzana** 21
Raffi's Place | **Glendale** 26
Wahib's | **Alhambra** 20

MOROCCAN

Marrakesh | **Studio City** 21
Tagine | **Beverly Hills** 25

NOODLE SHOPS

Absolutely Pho | **multi.** 20
Asahi | **West LA** 20
Daikokuya | **multi.** 24
Golden Deli | **San Gabriel** 25
Hakata | **Gardena** 25
Nong La | **West LA** -
101 Noodle | **multi.** 23

Pho Café | **Silver Lake** 24
Pho Show | **multi.** 19
Pho So 1 | **multi.** 25
Ramen Jinya | **Studio City** 23
Ramenya | **West LA** 20
Ramen Yamadaya | **multi.** 23
Santouka Ramen | **multi.** 25
Tatsu Ramen | **West LA** -
Tsujita LA | **West LA** 26

NUEVO LATINO

Alegria | **Long Bch** 23
Zengo | **Santa Monica** 21

PACIFIC RIM

Christine | **Torrance** 27
Duke's | **Malibu** 17

PAN-LATIN

Beso | **Hollywood** 18
Cafe Verde | **Pasadena** 23
Cha Cha Chicken | **Santa Monica** 22
NEW Corazon y Miel | **Bell** -
Fuego/Maya | **Long Bch** 22
Rivera | **Downtown** 26

PERSIAN

Javan | **West LA** 22
Shaherzad | **Westwood** 22
Shamshiri Grill | **Westwood** 23

PERUVIAN

El Pollo Inka | **multi.** 21
El Rocoto | **multi.** 23
Louie's | **Hollywood** 20
Mario's Peruvian | **Hollywood** 24
Mo-Chica | **Downtown** 23
NEW Paiche | **Marina del Rey** -
Picca | **Century City** 25

PIZZA

Abbot's Pizza | **Venice** 23
NEW Blaze | **multi.** -
Bottega Louie | **Downtown** 23
Bravo | **Santa Monica** 20
Caioti Pizza | **Studio City** 21
Casa Bianca | **Eagle Rock** 23
Cheebo | **Hollywood** 21
NEW Clusi Batusi | **West LA** -
800 Degrees | **Westwood** 23
Farfalla/Vinoteca | **Los Feliz** 22
Gjelina | **Venice** 26
Joe's Pizza | **multi.** 23
Lamonica's | **Westwood** 23
Luggage Room | **Pasadena** 23
Masa | **Echo Pk** 24
Michael's Pizzeria | **Long Bch** 27
Milo & Olive | **Santa Monica** 24
Mozza to Go | **W Hollywood** 26
Mulberry St. Pizzeria | **multi.** 23
Olio/Cafe | **Third St** 23
Pace | **Laurel Canyon** 23
Pitfire | **multi.** 22
Pizzeria Mozza | **Hollywood** 27
Sammy's Pizza | **multi.** 19
Settebello Pizzeria | **Marina del Rey** 23
Soleto Trattoria | **Downtown** 21
Sotto | **Century City** 22
Stella Barra Pizza | **multi.** 25
Terroni | **Beverly Blvd** 22
Tomato Pie | **multi.** 22
Valentino's | **multi.** 22
Village Pizzeria | **multi.** 25
Vito's | **W Hollywood** 26
Zelo Pizzeria | **Arcadia** 21

POLISH

Warszawa | **Santa Monica** 22

POLYNESIAN

Trader Vic's | **multi.** 18

PUB FOOD

Gordon Biersch | **Burbank** 18
Pikey | **Hollywood** 18
Rick's Tavern | **Santa Monica** 21
Rock & Brews | **multi.** 18
Whale & Ale | **San Pedro** 19
Ye Olde King's | **Santa Monica** 17

QUÉBÉCOIS

P'tit Soleil | **Westwood** -

RUSSIAN

NEW Mari Vanna | **W Hollywood** -

SANDWICHES

(See also Delis)
Artisan | **Studio City** 24
Bäco Mercat | **Downtown** 25
Baker | **Woodland Hills** 24
BlueCow Kitchen | **Downtown** 22
Breadbar | **Century City** 18
Brent's Deli | **multi.** 26
Clementine | **Century City** 25
Cole's | **Downtown** 17
Cook's Tortas | **Monterey Pk** 23
Coral Tree | **multi.** 19
Factor's | **Pico-Robertson** 19

Food | **Rancho Pk** 22
Food + Lab | **multi.** 21
Fromin's | **Santa Monica** 16
Fundamental LA | **Westwood** 22
Grilled Cheese Truck | **Location Varies** 24
Ink Sack | **W Hollywood** -
Johnnie's Pastrami | **Culver City** 21
Label's Table | **multi.** 22
Langer's | **Downtown** 26
Lawry's Carvery | **Downtown** 22
Lemon Moon | **West LA** 20
Little Dom's/Deli | **Los Feliz** 22
Mendocino Farms | **multi.** 24
Milk | **Mid-City** 23
Nate 'n Al | **multi.** 21
Philippe/Original | **Chinatown** 23
Porta Via | **Beverly Hills** 22
Porto's | **multi.** 25
Roll 'n Rye | **Culver City** 16
3 Square | **Venice** 23

SCOTTISH

NEW Morrison | **Atwater Vill** -
Tam O'Shanter | **Atwater Vill** 22

SEAFOOD

Admiral Risty | **Rancho Palos Verdes** 22
Blue Plate Oysterette | **Santa Monica** 22
Bluewater | **multi.** 21
Boiling Crab | **multi.** 24
Brophy Bros. | **Ventura** 21
Buggy Whip | **Westchester** 19
Catch | **Santa Monica** 22
CBS Seafood | **Chinatown** 20
Coast | **Santa Monica** 22
NEW Connie/Ted's | **W Hollywood** -
Delmonico's | **Encino** 23
Duke's | **Malibu** 17
888 Seafood | **Rosemead** 23
Fishbar | **Manhattan Bch** 22
Fish Grill | **multi.** 22
NEW Fishing/Dynamite | **Manhattan Bch** -
Galley | **Santa Monica** 19
Gladstones | **multi.** 17
Gulfstream | **Century City** 22
Holdren's | **Thousand Oaks** 24
Hop Li | **multi.** 20
Hungry Cat | **multi.** 23
Killer Shrimp | **Marina del Rey** 21
Kincaid's | **Redondo Bch** 22
King's Fish | **multi.** 21
L&E Oyster | **Silver Lake** 25
NEW Littlefork | **Hollywood** 24
Lobster | **Santa Monica** 23
Lure Fish Hse. | **Camarillo** 24
Malibu Seafood | **Malibu** 24
McCormick/Schmick | **multi.** 18
McKenna's | **Long Bch** 21
Neptune's Net | **Malibu** 19
Newport Seafood | **multi.** 26
Ocean Seafood | **Chinatown** 21
Old Tony's | **Redondo Bch** 20
One Pico | **Santa Monica** 23
Paradise Cove | **Malibu** 18
Parkers' Lighthouse | **Long Bch** 22
Providence | **Hollywood** 28
Reel Inn | **Malibu** 22
Rock'n Fish | **multi.** 20
NEW Salt Air | **Venice** -
Salt Creek | **Valencia** 19
Santa Monica Seafood | **Santa Monica** 25
Sea Harbour | **Rosemead** 25
Sol y Luna | **Tarzana** 22
Son of a Gun | **Third St** 26
22nd St. Landing | **San Pedro** 22
Water Grill | **multi.** 26

SINGAPOREAN

Spice Table | **Little Tokyo** 23

SMALL PLATES

(See also Spanish tapas specialist)
NEW Alma | Amer. | **Downtown** 26
NEW Bamboo Izakaya | Japanese | **Santa Monica** -
NEW Bar Amá | Tex-Mex | **Downtown** 23
Bar Bouchon | French | **Beverly Hills** 23
Bar Hayama | Japanese | **West LA** 24
Bazaar/José Andrés | Spanish | **Beverly Hills** 27
Cleo | Med. | **Hollywood** 26
Corkbar | Eclectic | **Downtown** 21
Cube Cafe | Italian | **La Brea** 24
Fundamental LA | Sandwiches | **Westwood** 22
Gjelina | Amer. | **Venice** 26
Gorbals | Eclectic | **Downtown** 20
Izaka-ya/Katsu-ya | Japanese | **multi.** 25
K-Zo | Japanese | **Culver City** 26
Lazy Ox | Eclectic | **Little Tokyo** 24
Leila's | Cal. | **Oak Pk** 27
NEW Littlefork | Seafood | **Hollywood** 24

M.B. Post | Amer. | **Manhattan Bch** 27
Mediterraneo | Med. | **Hermosa Bch** 23
Musha | Japanese | **multi.** 23
Talésai/Night | Thai | **W Hollywood** 25
NEW Paiche | Japanese/Peruvian | **Marina del Rey** -
NEW Petty Cash | Mex. | **Beverly Blvd** -
Primitivo | Med. | **Venice** 22
Rustic Canyon | Med. | **Santa Monica** 25
Street | Eclectic | **Hollywood** 25
Upstairs 2 | Med. | **West LA** 24
Vertical Wine | Eclectic/Med. | **Pasadena** 21
Zengo | Asian/Nuevo Latino | **Santa Monica** 21

SOUL FOOD/ SOUTHERN

Johnny Rebs' | **multi.** 23
Les Sisters | **Chatsworth** 23
Roscoe's | **multi.** 23
NEW Willie Jane | **Venice** -

SOUTHWESTERN

Bandera | **West LA** 23
Coyote Cantina | **Redondo Bch** 21

SPANISH

(* tapas specialist)
Bäco Mercat | **Downtown** 25
Bar Pintxo* | **Santa Monica** 21
Bazaar/José Andrés | **Beverly Hills** 27
Bow & Truss | **N Hollywood** 18
NEW Kitchen/Perfecto | **Hermosa Bch** -
La Paella* | **Beverly Hills** 22
Racion | **Pasadena** -
NEW Taberna Arros* | **Santa Monica** -

STEAKHOUSES

Arroyo | **Pasadena** 25
Billingsley's | **West LA** 17
Boa | **multi.** 24
Buggy Whip | **Westchester** 19
Capital Grille | **Beverly Hills** 22
Carlitos Gardel | **Melrose** 24
Chez Jay | **Santa Monica** 20
Cut | **Beverly Hills** 27
NEW Del Frisco's | **Santa Monica** -
Delmonico's | **Encino** 23
Derby | **Arcadia** 23
555 East | **Long Bch** 25
Fleming's | **multi.** 23
Fogo de Chão | **Beverly Hills** 23
Galley | **Santa Monica** 19
Gaucho | **multi.** 21
Grill on Alley | **Beverly Hills** 25
Holdren's | **Thousand Oaks** 24
Jar | **Beverly Blvd.** 24
Kincaid's | **Redondo Bch** 22
Larsen's | **Encino** 24
Lawry's Prime | **Beverly Hills** 26
Malbec | **multi.** 23
Mastro's | **multi.** 26
McKenna's | **Long Bch** 21
Morels French Steak | **Fairfax** 20
Morton's | **multi.** 22
Nick & Stef's | **Downtown** 23
Pacific Dining Car | **multi.** 24
Palm | **multi.** 23
Parkers' Lighthouse | **Long Bch** 22
Rock'n Fish | **multi.** 20
Ruth's Chris | **multi.** 25
Salt Creek | **multi.** 19
Smoke Hse. | **Burbank** 21
STK | **W Hollywood** 24
Taylor's | **multi.** 23
Vibrato Grill Jazz | **Bel-Air** 22
Wolfgang's | **Beverly Hills** 24
Zane's | **Hermosa Bch** 21

TEX-MEX

NEW Bar Amá | **Downtown** 23
Marix | **multi.** 17

THAI

Ayara Thai | **Westchester** 24
Bangkok West | **Santa Monica** 23
Chadaka | **Burbank** 21
Chan Dara | **multi.** 22
Cholada | **multi.** 23
Jitlada | **E Hollywood** 27
Natalee | **multi.** 20
Talésai/Night | **W Hollywood** 25
Palms Thai | **E Hollywood** 21
NEW Rice Thai | **Pasadena** -
Saladang | **Pasadena** 23
Sanamluang Cafe | **multi.** 24
NEW Sticky Rice | **Downtown** -
Talésai | **multi.** 22
Thai Dishes | **multi.** 20
Toi on Sunset | **W Hollywood** 19
Tuk Tuk | **Pico-Robertson** 22
Vegan Glory | **Beverly Blvd** 21

TURKISH

Spitz | **multi.** 22

VEGETARIAN

(* vegan)

Café Gratitude* | **multi.** 23

NEW Crossroads Vegan* | **W Hollywood** -

Elf Café | **Echo Pk** 25

Flore* | **Silver Lake** 20

M.A.K.E.* | **Santa Monica** 15

M Café* | **multi.** 22

Native Foods* | **multi.** 22

Newsroom Café | **W Hollywood** 17

Real Food* | **multi.** 21

True Food | **Santa Monica** 23

Urth* | **multi.** 22

Vegan Glory* | **Beverly Blvd** 21

Veggie Grill* | **multi.** 22

Zephyr* | **Long Bch** 25

VIETNAMESE

Absolutely Pho | **multi.** 20

Benley | **Long Bch** 27

Blossom | **multi.** 21

Blue Hen | **Eagle Rock** 21

Crustacean | **Beverly Hills** 25

Gingergrass | **Silver Lake** 22

Golden Deli | **San Gabriel** 25

Good Girl | **Highland Pk** 22

9021Pho | **multi.** 21

Nong La | **West LA** -

Pho Café | **Silver Lake** 24

NEW Phorage | **Palms** -

Pho 79 | **Alhambra** 23

Pho Show | **multi.** 19

Pho So 1 | **multi.** 25

Red Medicine | **Beverly Hills** 22

Locations

Includes names, cuisines and Food ratings.

LA Central

ATWATER VILLAGE

Canelé | *Med.* 23
NEW Morrison | *Pub/Scottish* -
Tam O'Shanter | *Scottish* 22

BEVERLY BLVD.

(bet. La Brea & La Cienega)
Angelini | *Italian* 28
A.O.C. | *Cal./French* 25
Bao | *Chinese* 21
BLD | *Amer.* 21
Buddha's Belly | *Asian* 20
Cooks County | *Cal.* 23
El Coyote | *Mex.* 16
Fish Grill | *Seafood* 22
Hirozen | *Japanese* 26
House Café | *Eclectic* 20
Jar | *Amer.* 24
Mandarette | *Chinese* 19
Obikà | *Italian* 21
NEW Petty Cash | *Mex.* -
Susina | *Bakery* 23
Swingers | *Diner* 19
Terroni | *Italian* 22
Vegan Glory | *Vegan* 21

CHINATOWN

CBS Seafood | *Seafood* 20
NEW Chego! | *Korean/Mex.* 23
Homeboy/girl | *Amer./Mex.* 22
Hop Li | *Chinese/Seafood* 20
Ocean Seafood | *Chinese/Seafood* 21
Philippe/Original | *Sandwiches* 23
Sam Woo | *Chinese* 18
Yang Chow | *Chinese* 22

DOWNTOWN

Aburiya Toranoko | *Japanese* 22
NEW Alma | *Amer.* 26
Bäco Mercat | *Sandwiches* 25
NEW Bar Amá | *Tex-Mex* 23
Bar | Kitchen | *Amer.* 24
NEW Bestia | *Italian* 25
Blossom | *Viet.* 21
BlueCow Kitchen | *Amer.* 22
Border Grill | *Mex.* 22
Bottega Louie | *Italian* 23
BottleRock | *Euro.* 18
NEW Bunker Hill | *Amer.* -
Cafe Pinot | *Cal./French* 24
Chaya | *Asian/French* 23
Checkers | *Cal.* 22
Chichen Itza | *Mex.* 25
Church/State | *French* 24
Cicada | *Cal./Italian* 25
Coco Laurent | *French* -
Cole's | *Sandwiches* 17
Corkbar | *Eclectic* 21
Daily Grill | *Amer.* 19
Drago Centro | *Italian* 26
Eat.Drink.Americano | *Amer.* -
El Cholo | *Mex.* 19
Engine Co. 28 | *Amer.* 20
Farm/Bev. Hills | *Amer.* 18
NEW Figaro | *French* -
FigOly | *Cal./Italian* -
First & Hope | *Amer.* 17
Fleming's | *Steak* 23
Gorbals | *Eclectic* 20
Homeboy/girl | *Sandwiches* 22
NEW Horse Thief BBQ | *BBQ* -
Industriel | *French* 20
Katsuya | *Japanese* 24
Kendall's | *French* 19
L.A. Market | *Amer./Cal.* 19
Langer's | *Deli* 26
Lawry's Carvery | *Amer.* 22
NEW Le Ka | *Continental* -
Lemonade | *Cal.* 21
Little Bear | *Belgian* 22
NEW Maccheroni Republic | *Italian* -
Manna | *Korean* 17
Maria's Italian | *Italian* 19
Mas Malo | *Mex.* 18
McCormick/Schmick | *Seafood* 18
Mendocino Farms | *Sandwiches* 24
Mo-Chica | *Peruvian* 23
Morton's | *Steak* 22
Nick & Stef's | *Steak* 23
Nickel Diner | *Diner* 21
Noe | *Amer.* 22
Original Pantry | *Diner* 18
Pacific Dining Car | *Steak* 24
Palm | *Steak* 23
Panini Cafe | *Italian/Med.* 21
Parish | *British* 22
Parish Wine Bar | *Amer.* -
Patina | *Amer./Cal.* 26
Perch | *French* 17
Pete's | *Amer.* 20

Pitfire | *Pizza* 22
Restaurant/Standard | *Eclectic* 18
Rivera | *Pan-Latin* 26
Rock'n Fish | *Seafood* 20
Rosa Mexicano | *Mex.* 20
Roy's | *Hawaiian* 23
R23 | *Japanese* 25
Soleto Trattoria | *Italian* 21
NEW Sticky Rice | *Thai* -
Sugarfish | *Japanese* 26
Takami | *Japanese* 22
Tender Greens | *Amer.* 23
Terroni | *Italian* 22
Tommy's | *Burgers/Hot Dogs* 24
Trader Vic's | *Polynesian* 18
Traxx | *Amer.* 21
Umamicatessen | *Eclectic* 22
Urth | *Amer.* 22
Water Grill | *Seafood* 26
Wokcano | *Asian* 19
WP24 | *Chinese* 25
Wurstküche | *Euro.* 23
Yxta | *Mex.* 24

EAST HOLLYWOOD

Carousel | *Mideast.* 25
Jitlada | *Thai* 27
Marouch | *Lebanese* 28
Palms Thai | *Thai* 21
Sanamluang Cafe | *Thai* 24
Square One | *Amer.* 22
Zankou | *Med.* 21

ECHO PARK

NEW Allumette | *Amer.* -
Elf Café | *Med./Veg.* 25
Masa | *Pizza* 24
Mohawk Bend | *Eclectic* 21
Park | *Amer.* 25
NEW Park's Finest | *BBQ* -
Taix | *French* 20

FAIRFAX

Animal | *Amer.* 27
Canter's | *Deli* 20
Cheesecake | *Amer.* 18
Du-par's | *Diner* 17
Fat Cow | *Amer.* 18
Golden State | *Burgers* 25
Gumbo Pot | *Cajun* 20
Lotería! | *Mex.* 22
Marmalade | *Amer.* 17
Mendocino Farms | *Sandwiches* 24
Monsieur Marcel | *French* 20
Morels French Steak | *French/Steak* 20

Short Order | *Burgers* 18
Umami Burger | *Burgers* 23
Veggie Grill | *Vegan* 22
Wood Ranch | *BBQ* 20

HANCOCK PARK/ LARCHMONT VILLAGE

Café Gratitude | *Amer.* 23
Chan Dara | *Thai* 22
Genwa | *Korean* 25
Larchmont Bungalow | *Amer.* 19
Le Petit Greek | *Greek* 22
Louise's | *Cal./Italian* 19
Prado | *Carib.* 23
Village Pizzeria | *Pizza* 25

HIGHLAND PARK

Ba Restaurant | *French* -
Good Girl | *Viet.* 22
Maximiliano | *Italian* 22

HOLLYWOOD

Ammo | *Cal.* 22
NEW Aventine | *Italian* -
Berlin Currywurst | *German* 21
Beso | *Pan-Latin* 18
Bossa Nova | *Brazilian* 22
Bowery | *Amer.* 22
Chan Dara | *Thai* 22
Cheebo | *Italian* 21
NEW chi SPACCA | *Italian* -
Cleo | *Med.* 26
Delphine | *Amer.* 21
Fabiolus Cucina | *Italian* 21
Go Burger | *Burgers* 20
Greenblatt's | *Deli* 19
Griddle Cafe | *Amer.* 25
Grill on Hollywood | *Amer.* 24
Grub | *Amer.* 24
Hungry Cat | *Seafood* 23
In-N-Out | *Burgers* 23
Joe's Pizza | *Pizza* 23
Kabuki | *Japanese* 21
Katsuya | *Japanese* 24
Kitchen 24 | *Amer.* 19
NEW Littlefork | *Seafood* 24
Louie's | *Peruvian* 20
Lotería! | *Mex.* 22
Marino | *Italian* 25
Mario's Peruvian | *Peruvian* 24
Miceli's | *Italian* 18
Musso & Frank | *Amer.* 22
Off Vine | *Cal.* 22
101 Coffee | *Diner* 22
Osteria La Buca | *Italian* 22
Osteria Mamma | *Italian* 24

Osteria Mozza | *Italian* 27
Outpost | *Amer.* -
Pig 'n Whistle | *Continental* 18
Pikey | *Pub* 18
Pizzeria Mozza | *Pizza* 27
Providence | *Amer./Seafood* 28
Public Kitchen | *Eclectic* 20
Roscoe's | *Soul Food* 23
NEW ShopHouse | *Asian* -
Stella Barra Pizza | *Pizza* 25
Street | *Eclectic* 25
Tender Greens | *Amer.* 23
Trastevere | *Italian* 18
NEW Trois Mec | *Eclectic/French* -
25 Degrees | *Burgers* 23
Umami Burger | *Burgers* 23
Veggie Grill | *Vegan* 22
Village Pizzeria | *Pizza* 25
Waffle | *Amer.* 20
Wolfslair | *German* 22
Wood & Vine | *Amer.* 20
Xiomara | *Cal./Cuban* 21
Yamashiro | *Asian* 21

KOREATOWN

BCD Tofu | *Korean* 22
Beer Belly | *Eclectic* 23
Boiling Crab | *Cajun/Seafood* 24
ChoSun Galbee | *Korean* 24
Guelaguetza | *Mex.* 24
Noshi Sushi | *Japanese* 23
Park's BBQ | *Korean* 25
Soot Bull Jeep | *Korean* 24
Taylor's | *Steak* 23

LA BREA

Amalfi | *Italian* 20
Ca'Brea | *Italian* 20
Cube Cafe | *Italian* 24
Luna Park | *Amer.* 19
Pink's Hot Dogs | *Hot Dogs* 21
Tinga | *Mex.* 22
NEW Twist Eatery | *Cal./Eclectic* -
Wirtshaus | *German* 19

LAUREL CANYON

Pace | *Italian* 23

LEIMERT PARK

Phillips BBQ | *BBQ* 24

LITTLE TOKYO

Daikokuya | *Japanese* 24
Honda-Ya | *Japanese* 21
Lazy Ox | *Eclectic* 24
Shabu Shabu | *Japanese* 22
Spice Table | *Asian* 23

Spitz | *Turkish* 22
Sushi Gen | *Japanese* 26
Yen | *Japanese* 22

LOS FELIZ

Alcove | *Amer.* 21
Chi Dynasty | *Chinese* 20
Farfalla/Vinoteca | *Italian* 22
Figaro | *French* 22
Fred 62 | *Diner* 18
Home | *Eclectic* 20
Little Dom's/Deli | *Italian* 22
Louise's | *Cal./Italian* 19
NEW MessHall Kitchen | *Amer.* 21
Palermo | *Italian* 22
Spitz | *Turkish* 22
Yuca's | *Mex.* 25

MELROSE

Antonio's | *Mex.* 20
Blu Jam Café | *Amer./Euro.* 25
Carlitos Gardel | *Argent./Steak* 24
Foundry/Melrose | *Amer.* 23
Frida | *Mex.* 19
Hatfield's | *Amer.* 27
M Café | *Veg.* 22
Red O | *Mex.* 24
NEW ROFL Cafe | *Eclectic* -
Sweet Lady | *Bakery* 23
Tomato Pie | *Pizza* 22

MID-CITY

Black Dog Coffee | *Coffee* 21
Bloom | *Cal.* 23
Bludso's BBQ | *BBQ* 25
Cafe Angelino | *Italian* 23
El Cholo | *Mex.* 19
Harold & Belle's | *Creole* 24
Milk | *Sandwiches* 23
Papa Cristo's | *Greek* 22
Phillips BBQ | *BBQ* 24
Post & Beam | *Amer.* 22
Roscoe's | *Soul Food* 23
NEW Sirena | *Italian* 18
Sycamore Kit. | *Amer.* 24
NEW True Burger | *Burgers* -
Versailles | *Cuban* 22
Woody's BBQ | *BBQ* 24

MID-WILSHIRE

Counter | *Burgers* 19
Five Guys | *Burgers* 16
India's Tandoori | *Indian* 23
Nyala | *Ethiopian* 23
Ray's/Stark Bar | *Med.* 23
Umami Burger | *Burgers* 23

PICO-ROBERTSON

Factor's | *Deli* 19
Fish Grill | *Seafood* 22
Hop Li | *Chinese/Seafood* 20
Milky Way | *Cal./Kosher* 20
Tuk Tuk | *Thai* 22
Yen | *Japanese* 22

SILVER LAKE

Agra Cafe | *Indian* 22
Alegria/Sunset | *Mex.* 24
Aroma | *Italian* 24
Barbrix | *Italian/Med.* 24
Berlin Currywurst | *German* 21
Black Hogg | *Amer.* 22
Blair's | *Amer.* 24
Blossom | *Viet.* 21
Cha Cha Cha | *Carib.* 21
Cliff's Edge | *Cal./Italian* 21
Dusty's | *Amer./French* 22
Flore | *Vegan* 20
Food + Lab | *Cal.* 21
Forage | *Cal.* 25
Gingergrass | *Viet.* 22
Home | *Eclectic* 20
Lago d'Argento | *Italian* -
LAMILL | *Cal./Coffee* 22
L&E Oyster | *Seafood* 25
Malo | *Mex.* 19
Pho Café | *Viet.* 24
Tomato Pie | *Pizza* 22

THIRD STREET

(bet. La Brea & Robertson)

Doughboys | *Amer.* 23
NEW Goldie's | *Cal.* -
Gusto | *Italian* 23
Izaka-ya/Katsu-ya | *Japanese* 25
Joan's/Third | *Amer.* 24
Little Door | *French/Med.* 23
Locanda Veneta | *Italian* 24
Olio/Cafe | *Italian* 23
Son of a Gun | *Seafood* 26
Sushi Roku | *Japanese* 22
Toast | *Amer.* 18

WEST HOLLYWOOD

Absolutely Pho | *Viet.* 20
Ago | *Italian* 22
Amarone | *Italian* 24
Baby Blues | *BBQ* 21
Basix | *Cal./Italian* 19
Boa | *Steak* 24
Bossa Nova | *Brazilian* 22
Burger Lounge | *Burgers* -
Cafe La Boheme | *Cal.* 20
Cafe Med | *Italian* 20
Cecconi's | *Italian* 22
Chaya | *Asian/French* 23
NEW Chi-Lin | *Chinese* -
Chin Chin | *Asian* 19
Churchill | *Amer.* 15
Comme Ça | *French* 23
NEW Connie/Ted's | *Seafood* -
Counter | *Burgers* 19
Craig's | *Amer.* 22
NEW Crossroads Vegan | *Vegan* -
Cuvée | *Cal.* 21
Dan Tana's | *Italian* 23
Dominick's | *Italian* 20
Duplex/Third | *Amer.* -
Eat Well | *Amer.* 20
NEW Esterel | *French* -
Eveleigh | *Amer./Euro.* 20
Fat Dog | *Amer.* 20
NEW Fatty's Public | *Amer.* -
Fig & Olive | *Med.* 22
Food + Lab | *Cal.* 21
Formosa | *Asian* 14
Gaby's | *Med.* 20
Gordon Ramsay | *Cal./French* 23
NEW Gorge | *French* -
NEW Hart/Hunter | *Amer.* 23
Hugo's | *Cal.* 21
Il Buco Cucina | *Italian* 21
Il Piccolino | *Italian* 23
Ink | *Amer./Eclectic* 26
Ink Sack | *Sandwiches* -
Ivy | *Cal.* 22
Joe's Pizza | *Pizza* 23
Katana | *Japanese* 25
Kings Rd. | *Amer.* 17
Kitchen 24 | *Amer.* 19
Koi | *Japanese* 24
Laurel Hardware | *Amer.* 19
Lemonade | *Cal.* 21
Le Pain Quotidien | *Bakery* 18
Le Petit Bistro | *French* 24
Lucques | *Cal./Med.* 27
Lulu's Cafe | *Amer.* 23
Madeo | *Italian* 26
NEW Mari Vanna | *Russian* -
Marix | *Tex-Mex* 17
Mendocino Farms | *Sandwiches* 24
Mercato di Vetro | *Italian* 22
Mozza to Go | *Pizza* 26
Newsroom Café | *Veg.* 17
Talésai/Night | *Thai* 25
Nobu | *Japanese* 26
Nonna | *Italian* 23

Osteria Drago | *Italian* 22
Palm | *Steak* 23
Panini Cafe | *Italian/Med.* 21
Petrossian | *French* 25
Pink Taco | *Mex.* 17
Pitfire | *Pizza* 22
Poquito Más | *Mex.* 21
Real Food | *Vegan* 21
Restaurant/Standard | *Eclectic* 18
NEW RivaBella Ristorante | *Italian* 20
Rosa Mexicano | *Mex.* 20
Salt's Cure | *Amer.* 22
STK | *Steak* 24
Talésai | *Thai* 22
Tender Greens | *Amer.* 23
Toi on Sunset | *Thai* 19
Tortilla Rep. | *Mex.* 20
Tower Bar | *Amer.* 25
Urth | *Amer.* 22
Veggie Grill | *Vegan* 22
Vito's | *Pizza* 26
Vivoli | *Italian* 21
Wokcano | *Asian* 19
Yabu | *Japanese* 23

LA East

BOYLE HEIGHTS

El Tepeyac | *Mex.* 26
La Serenata | *Mex.* 23

HACIENDA HEIGHTS

Daikokuya | *Japanese* 24

LA South

BELL

NEW Corazon y Miel | *Pan-Latin* -

BELLFLOWER

Johnny Rebs' | *BBQ* 23

CARSON

Five Guys | *Burgers* 16

CERRITOS

BCD Tofu | *Korean* 22
El Rocoto | *Peruvian* 23
Five Guys | *Burgers* 16
Lucille's | *BBQ* 22
Sam Woo | *Chinese* 18
Wood Ranch | *BBQ* 20

COMPTON

Bludso's BBQ | *BBQ* 25

LAWNDALE

El Pollo Inka | *Peruvian* 21

LOMITA

Alfredo's | *Mex.* 26

PALOS VERDES PENINSULA/ ROLLING HILLS

Admiral Risty | *Seafood* 22
Asaka | *Japanese* 22
Bashi | *Asian* -
Mama Terano | *Italian* 22
Marmalade | *Amer.* 17
Mar'sel | *Cal.* 26

LA West

BEL-AIR

Bel Air B&G | *Cal.* 21
Vibrato Grill Jazz | *Amer./Steak* 22
Wolfgang Puck/Hotel Bel-Air | *Cal./Med.* 24

BEVERLY HILLS

Asakuma | *Japanese* 22
Bar Bouchon | *French* 23
Barney Greengrass | *Deli* 22
Bazaar/José Andrés | *Spanish* 27
Belvedere | *Amer.* 26
BierBeisl | *Austrian* 22
Blvd | *Cal.* 22
Bombay Palace | *Indian* 24
Boss Sushi | *Japanese* 24
Bouchon | *French* 25
Bouchon Bakery | *Bakery* 25
Brighton Coffee | *Diner* 19
Burger Lounge | *Burgers* -
Caffe Roma | *Italian* 22
Capital Grille | *Steak* 22
NEW Carson House | *Amer.* -
Caulfield's | *Amer.* 23
Chakra | *Indian* 23
Cheesecake | *Amer.* 18
Chin Chin | *Asian* 19
Crazy Fish | *Japanese* 21
Crustacean | *Asian/Viet.* 25
Culina | *Italian* 23
Cut | *Steak* 27
Da Pasquale | *Italian* 24
E. Baldi | *Italian* 23
Enoteca Drago | *Italian* 22
Farm/Bev. Hills | *Amer.* 18
Fleming's | *Steak* 23
Fogo de Chão | *Brazilian/Steak* 23
Frida | *Mex.* 19

Genwa | *Korean* 25
Greenleaf Gourmet | *Amer.* 21
Grill on Alley | *Amer.* 25
Gyu-Kaku | *Japanese* 20
Il Cielo | *Italian* 23
Il Fornaio | *Italian* 20
Il Forno Caldo | *Italian* 21
Il Pastaio | *Italian* 26
Il Tramezzino | *Italian* 22
Kate Mantilini | *Amer.* 20
La Dolce Vita | *Italian* 24
La Paella | *Spanish* 22
NEW Larder/Burton | *Amer.* -
Larder/Maple | *Amer.* 20
La Scala | *Italian* 21
Lawry's Prime | *Steak* 26
Le Pain Quotidien | *Bakery* 18
Livello | *Eclectic* 23
Mastro's | *Steak* 26
Matsuhisa | *Japanese* 28
M Café | *Veg.* 22
McCormick/Schmick | *Seafood* 18
Momed | *Med.* 20
Monsieur Marcel | *French* 20
Morton's | *Steak* 22
Mr. Chow | *Chinese* 23
Mulberry St. Pizzeria | *Pizza* 23
Natalee | *Thai* 20
Nate 'n Al | *Deli* 21
Nic's | *Amer.* 22
9021Pho | *Viet.* 21
NEW Nozawa Bar | *Japanese* -
Oliverio | *Italian* 25
On Rodeo | *Cal./French* -
Panini Cafe | *Italian/Med.* 21
NEW Penthouse/Mastro's | *Amer.* -
P.F. Chang's | *Chinese* 17
Piccolo Paradiso | *Italian* 24
Polo | *Cal./Continental* 22
Porta Via | *Cal.* 22
Red Medicine | *Viet.* 22
Ruth's Chris | *Steak* 25
Saam/The Bazaar | *Eclectic* 27
Scarpetta | *Italian* 24
South Beverly Grill | *Amer.* 21
Spago | *Cal.* 27
Stinking Rose | *Italian* 21
Sugarfish | *Japanese* 26
Sushi Sasabune | *Japanese* 26
Sushi Sushi | *Japanese* 27
Tagine | *Moroccan* 25
Talésai | *Thai* 22
Tanzore | *Indian* 21
NEW Tartine O | *Bakery/French* -
Trader Vic's | *Polynesian* 18
Trattoria Amici | *Italian* 21
Tres/José Andrés | *Eclectic* 23
Urasawa | *Japanese* 28
Urth | *Amer.* 22
Via Alloro | *Italian* 22
Wolfgang's | *Steak* 24
Xi'an | *Chinese* 21

BRENTWOOD

Trattoria Amici | *Italian* 21
A Votre Sante | *Health* 21
Barney's | *Burgers* 21
Bar Toscana | *Italian* 23
Brentwood | *Amer.* 23
Burger Lounge | *Burgers* -
NEW Cafe Brentwood | *Amer.* -
Caffe Luxxe | *Coffee* 21
Chin Chin | *Asian* 19
Coral Tree | *Sandwiches* 19
Daily Grill | *Amer.* 19
Divino | *Italian* 24
Fish Grill | *Seafood* 22
Gaucho | *Argent./Steak* 21
Getty Ctr. | *Cal.* 23
NEW Il Piccolo Ritrovo | *Italian* 26
India's Tandoori | *Indian* 23
Katsuya | *Japanese* 24
La Scala | *Italian* 21
Lemonade | *Cal.* 21
Le Pain Quotidien | *Bakery* 18
Maria's Italian | *Italian* 19
Osteria Latini | *Italian* 25
Palmeri | *Italian* 25
Pecorino | *Italian* 24
Peppone | *Italian* 21
Pizzicotto | *Italian* 23
Sor Tino | *Italian* 21
Sugarfish | *Japanese* 26
Taiko | *Japanese* 22
Takao | *Japanese* 26
Tavern | *Cal./Med.* 24
Toscana | *Italian* 25
Vincenti | *Italian* 26
Yen | *Japanese* 22

CENTURY CITY

Breadbar | *Bakery* 18
Clementine | *Amer.* 25
Coral Tree | *Sandwiches* 19
Counter | *Burgers* 19
Craft | *Amer.* 25
Cuvée | *Cal.* 21
Greenleaf Gourmet | *Amer.* 21
Gulfstream | *Amer./Seafood* 22

NEW Hinoki/The Bird | *Japanese* 23
Joe's Pizza | *Pizza* 23
Label's Table | *Sandwiches* 22
Obikà | *Italian* 21
Picca | *Japanese/Peruvian* 25
Pico Kosher Deli | *Deli* 22
Pink Taco | *Mex.* 17
RockSugar | *Asian* 21
NEW Seasons 52 | *Amer.* -
Sotto | *Pizza* 22
Stand | *Hot Dogs* 18
Take a Bao | *Asian* 19
Toscanova | *Italian* 19

CULVER CITY

A-Frame | *Eclectic* 23
Akasha | *Amer.* 22
Bamboo Restaurant | *Carib.* 21
BottleRock | *Euro.* 18
Brunello | *Italian* 22
NEW Bucato | *Italian* -
Café Brasil | *Brazilian* 22
Café Laurent | *French* 20
City Tavern | *Amer.* 19
Corner Door | *Amer.* -
Father's Office | *Amer.* 23
Five Guys | *Burgers* 16
Ford's | *Amer.* 20
Gaby's | *Med.* 20
In-N-Out | *Burgers* 23
Johnnie's Pastrami | *Diner* 21
JR's | *BBQ* 23
Kay 'n Dave's | *Mex.* 18
K-Zo | *Japanese* 26
La Dijonaise | *French* 19
Let's Be Frank | *Hot Dogs* 17
Lucille's | *BBQ* 22
Lukshon | *Asian* 24
NEW Muddy Leek | *Amer./French* -
Native Foods | *Vegan* 22
101 Noodle | *Chinese* 23
Pho Show | *Viet.* 19
Pitfire | *Pizza* 22
NEW Public School 310 | *Amer.* 18
Ramen Yamadaya | *Japanese* 23
Roll 'n Rye | *Deli* 16
Rush St. | *Amer.* 17
Tender Greens | *Amer.* 23
Tito's Tacos | *Mex.* 21
Waterloo & City | *British* 23

MALIBU

Café Habana | *Cuban/Mex.* 20
Cholada | *Thai* 23
Duke's | *Pac. Rim* 17
Fish Grill | *Seafood* 22
Geoffrey's Malibu | *Cal.* 22
NEW Kaishin | *Chinese* -
Malibu Seafood | *Seafood* 24
Marmalade | *Amer.* 17
Moonshadows | *Amer.* 20
Mr. Chow | *Chinese* 23
Neptune's Net | *Seafood* 19
NEW Nikita | *Italian/Med.* -
Nobu | *Japanese* 27
Paradise Cove | *Amer./Seafood* 18
Reel Inn | *Seafood* 22
Taverna Tony | *Greek* 22
Thai Dishes | *Thai* 20
Tra di Noi | *Italian* 23

MARINA DEL REY

Akbar Cuisine | *Indian* 22
Cafe Del Rey | *Cal./Med.* 23
C & O | *Italian* 21
Ado/Casa Ado | *Italian* 25
Cheesecake | *Amer.* 18
Counter | *Burgers* 19
Gaby's | *Med.* 20
Jer-ne | *Amer.* 18
Jerry's Deli | *Deli* 15
Killer Cafe | *Amer.* -
Killer Shrimp | *Seafood* 21
Locanda Positano | *Italian* 25
Mendocino Farms | *Sandwiches* 24
NEW Paiche | *Japanese/Peruvian* -
Settebello Pizzeria | *Pizza* 23
Sugarfish | *Japanese* 26
Tender Greens | *Amer.* 23
Uncle Darrow's | *Cajun/Creole* 21

MAR VISTA

Hannosuke | *Japanese* -
NEW Louie's Old School | *Amer.* -
Paco's Tacos | *Mex.* 21
Santouka Ramen | *Japanese* 25

PACIFIC PALISADES

NEW Chez Mimi | *French* 19
Gladstones | *Seafood* 17
NEW Il Piccolo Ritrovo | *Italian* 26
Kay 'n Dave's | *Mex.* 18
Maison Giraud | *French* 24
Modo Mio | *Italian* 23
Pearl Dragon | *Asian* 20
Sushi Sasabune | *Japanese* 26

PALMS

Café Brasil | *Brazilian* 22
NEW The Doughroom | *Italian* -
Gaby's | *Med.* 20

In-N-Out | *Burgers* 23
Natalee | *Thai* 20
N/Naka | *Japanese* 27
NEW Phorage | *Viet.* -
Versailles | *Cuban* 22

PLAYA DEL REY

Caffe Pinguini | *Italian* 21
Shack | *Burgers* 18
Tripel | *Eclectic* 25

RANCHO PARK

Food | *Amer.* 22
John O'Groats | *Amer.* 20
Six | *Amer.* 19

SANTA MONICA

Akbar Cuisine | *Indian* 22
Babalu | *Cal.* 18
NEW Bamboo Izakaya | *Japanese* -
Bangkok West | *Thai* 23
Barney's | *Burgers* 21
Bar Pintxo | *Spanish* 21
Bay Cities | *Deli* 26
Blue Plate | *Amer.* 20
Blue Plate Oysterette | *Seafood* 22
NEW Blue Plate Taco | *Mex.* 16
Boa | *Steak* 24
Border Grill | *Mex.* 22
Bravo | *Italian/Pizza* 20
Bru's Wiffle | *Amer.* 22
Buddha's Belly | *Asian* 20
Buffalo Club | *Amer.* 19
Burger Lounge | *Burgers* -
Cafe Bizou | *French* 22
Cafe Montana | *Cal.* 20
Caffé Delfini | *Italian* 24
Caffe Luxxe | *Coffee* 21
Capo | *Italian* 26
NEW Cast | *Cal.* -
Catch | *Seafood* 22
Cha Cha Chicken | *Carib.* 22
Chez Jay | *Steak* 20
Chinois | *Asian/French* 26
Coast | *Cal./Seafood* 22
Cora's | *Diner* 23
Counter | *Burgers* 19
NEW Creation Grill | *Med.* -
Daily Grill | *Amer.* 19
NEW Del Frisco's | *Steak* -
El Cholo | *Mex.* 19
Falafel King | *Mideast.* 18
Farmshop | *Amer.* 25
Father's Office | *Amer.* 23
Fig | *Amer./French* 22
Frida | *Mex.* 19
Fritto Misto | *Italian* 22
Fromin's | *Deli* 16
Galley | *Seafood/Steak* 19
Giorgio Baldi | *Italian* 25
Hillstone/Houston's | *Amer.* 22
NEW Hole in the Wall | *Burgers* 23
Hostaria/Piccolo | *Italian* 24
Huckleberry | *Amer.* 23
Hungry Cat | *Seafood* 23
Il Forno | *Italian* 22
Ivy/Shore | *Cal.* 22
Jack's/Montana | *Cal.* 20
Jinky's | *Diner* 20
JiRaffe | *Amer./French* 26
Joe's Pizza | *Pizza* 23
Josie | *Amer.* 26
Kay 'n Dave's | *Mex.* 18
La Botte | *Italian* 22
La Sandia | *Mex.* 21
La Vecchia | *Italian* 24
Le Pain Quotidien | *Bakery* 18
Le Petit Cafe | *French* 24
Lobster | *Seafood* 23
Locanda/Lago | *Italian* 23
Lotería! | *Mex.* 22
Louise's | *Cal./Italian* 19
M.A.K.E. | *Vegan* 15
Marix | *Tex-Mex* 17
Marmalade | *Amer.* 17
NEW Maru | *Japanese* -
Mélisse | *Amer./French* 28
Mercado | *Mex.* 24
Michael's Rest. | *Cal.* 24
Milo & Olive | *Amer.* 24
Misfit | *Eclectic* 22
Monsieur Marcel | *French* 20
Monsoon | *Asian* 20
M Street | *Amer.* 21
Musha | *Japanese* 23
Native Foods | *Vegan* 22
Nawab | *Indian* 22
Next Door/Josie | *Amer.* 24
Ocean & Vine | *Cal.* 23
One Pico | *Med.* 23
Pacific Dining Car | *Steak* 24
Patrick's | *Diner* 17
Penthouse | *Amer.* 20
P.F. Chang's | *Chinese* 17
Poquito Más | *Mex.* 21
R+D Kitchen | *Amer.* 22
Real Food | *Vegan* 21
Reddi Chick | *BBQ* 21
Rick's Tavern | *Amer./Pub* 21

Röckenwagner | *Bakery* 21
Rosti | *Italian* 17
Rustic Canyon | *Cal./Med.* 25
Sam's/Beach | *Cal./Med.* 25
Santa Monica Seafood | *Seafood* 25
NEW Seasons 52 | *Amer.* -
NEW ShopHouse | *Asian* -
Stefan's/L.A. Farm | *Eclectic* 22
Stella Barra Pizza | *Pizza* 25
Sugarfish | *Japanese* 26
Sweet Lady | *Bakery* 23
Swingers | *Diner* 19
NEW Taberna Arros | *Spanish* -
NEW Tacos Punta Cabras | *Mex.* -
Tar & Roses | *Amer.* 24
Tender Greens | *Amer.* 23
Thai Dishes | *Thai* 20
Tinga | *Mex.* 22
NEW Tower 8 | *Cal.* -
Trastevere | *Italian* 18
True Food | *Health* 23
Truxton's | *Amer.* 20
Typhoon | *Asian* 20
Umami Burger | *Burgers* 23
Urth | *Amer.* 22
Ushuaia | *Argent./Steak* 23
Valentino | *Italian* 26
Veggie Grill | *Vegan* 22
Via Veneto | *Italian* 26
Villetta | *Italian* 20
Vito | *Italian* 23
Warszawa | *Polish* 22
Water Grill | *Seafood* 26
Wilshire | *Amer.* 22
Wokcano | *Asian* 19
Wolfgang Puck Express/Bistro | *Cal.* 21
Ye Olde King's | *Pub* 17
Zengo | *Asian/Nuevo Latino* 21

TOPANGA

Inn/Seventh Ray | *Cal.* 20

VENICE

Abbot's Pizza | *Pizza* 23
Ado/Casa Ado | *Italian* 25
Asakuma | *Japanese* 22
Axe | *Cal.* 23
Baby Blues | *BBQ* 21
NEW Bank/Venice | *Amer.* -
NEW Barnyard | *Amer.* -
Café Gratitude | *Amer.* 23
Canal Club | *Cal./Eclectic* 20
Chaya | *Asian/French* 23
Gjelina | *Amer.* 26
Gjelina Take Away | *Amer.* 27
Hal's | *Amer.* 20
Hama | *Japanese* 23
Hostaria/Piccolo | *Italian* 24
James' | *Amer.* 20
Jody Maroni's | *Hot Dogs* 20
Joe's | *Cal./French* 26
Larry's | *Amer.* 23
Lemonade | *Cal.* 21
Maxwell's | *Diner* 19
Mosto | *Italian* 24
Piccolo | *Italian* 27
NEW Pichet | *French* -
Primitivo | *Med.* 22
Rose Cafe | *Cal.* 21
NEW Salt Air | *Seafood* -
Sunny Spot | *Caribb./Eclectic* 21
Superba | *Amer./Italian* 21
Tasting Kitchen | *Med.* 25
3 Square | *Sandwiches* 23
Tlapazola | *Mex.* 23
26 Beach | *Cal.* 23
Wabi-Sabi | *Japanese* 22
NEW Willie Jane | *Southern* -
Wurstküche | *Euro.* 23

WEST LA

All India | *Indian* 21
Apple Pan | *Amer.* 23
Aroma | *E Euro.* 20
Asahi | *Japanese* 20
Asakuma | *Japanese* 22
B.A.D. Sushi | *Japanese* 22
Bandera | *SW* 23
Bar Hayama | *Japanese* 24
Billingsley's | *Steak* 17
Bombay Cafe | *Indian* 22
Bossa Nova | *Brazilian* 22
Chan Dara | *Thai* 22
NEW Clusi Batusi | *Pizza* -
Daikokuya | *Japanese* 24
Echigo | *Japanese* 26
Enzo/Angela | *Italian* 21
Feast/East | *Asian* 22
NEW Flores | *Amer.* -
Freddy Smalls | *Amer.* 23
Gottsui | *Japanese* 21
Guido's | *Italian* 21
Gyu-Kaku | *Japanese* 20
Hamasaku | *Japanese* 28
Hide | *Japanese* 24
Hop Li | *Chinese/Seafood* 20
Il Grano | *Italian* 25
Il Moro | *Italian* 21
Jaipur | *Indian* 22

Javan | *Persian* 22
Kiriko | *Japanese* 26
La Bottega | *Italian* 21
La Serenata | *Mex.* 23
Lemon Moon | *Cal./Med.* 20
NEW Lenny's Deli | *Deli* -
Literati | *Cal./Eclectic* 18
Louise's | *Cal./Italian* 19
Maria's Italian | *Italian* 19
Matteo's | *Italian* 20
Mori Sushi | *Japanese* 27
Nanbankan | *Japanese* 27
Nong La | *Viet.* -
Nook | *Amer.* 24
Pastina | *Italian* 23
Pitfire | *Pizza* 22
Plan Check | *Amer.* 21
Poquito Más | *Mex.* 21
Ramen Hayatemaru | *Japanese* -
Ramenya | *Japanese* 20
Restaurant 2117 | *Asian/Euro.* 23
NEW ROC Star | *Chinese* -
Seoul House/Tofu | *Korean* -
Sushi Masu | *Japanese* 27
Sushi Sasabune | *Japanese* 26
Sushi Zo | *Japanese* 28
NEW Tapenade | *Cal./Med.* -
Tatsu Ramen | *Japanese* -
Tlapazola | *Mex.* 23
Tofu Ya | *Korean* 20
Torafuku | *Japanese* 21
Totoraku | *Japanese* -
Tsujita LA | *Japanese* 26
Upstairs 2 | *Med.* 24
U-Zen | *Japanese* 24
Westside Tav. | *Cal.* 22
Yabu | *Japanese* 23
Zankou | *Med.* 21

WESTWOOD

Ammo | *Cal.* 22
800 Degrees | *Pizza* 23
Fab Hot Dogs | *Hot Dogs* 22
Falafel King | *Mideast.* 18
Fundamental LA | *Sandwiches* 22
In-N-Out | *Burgers* 23
La Bruschetta | *Italian* 23
Lamonica's | *Pizza* 23
Le Pain Quotidien | *Bakery* 18
Napa Valley | *Cal.* 19
Native Foods | *Vegan* 22
Nine Thirty | *Amer.* 16
Palomino | *Amer.* 20
Panini Cafe | *Italian/Med.* 21
P'tit Soleil | *Québécois* -
Ramen Yamadaya | *Japanese* 23
Shaherzad | *Persian* 22
Shamshiri Grill | *Persian* 23
Soleil | *Canadian/French* 21
Sunnin | *Lebanese* 23
Tanino | *Italian* 22
Tender Greens | *Amer.* 23
Veggie Grill | *Vegan* 22

South Bay

CATALINA ISLAND

Bluewater | *Seafood* 21

DOWNEY

Porto's | *Bakery/Cuban* 25

EL SEGUNDO

B.A.D. Sushi | *Japanese* 22
Counter | *Burgers* 19
Farm Stand | *Eclectic* 22
Fleming's | *Steak* 23
NEW Jackson's Food/Drink | *Amer.* 17
Marmalade | *Amer.* 17
McCormick/Schmick | *Seafood* 18
Paul Martin's | *Amer.* 22
P.F. Chang's | *Chinese* 17
Rock & Brews | *Pub* 18
Salt Creek | *Steak* 19
Sammy's Pizza | *Pizza* 19
Valentino's | *Pizza* 22
Veggie Grill | *Vegan* 22

GARDENA

Eatalian | *Italian* 24
El Pollo Inka | *Peruvian* 21
El Rocoto | *Peruvian* 23
Hakata | *Japanese* 25
Pho So 1 | *Viet.* 25
Sea Empress | *Chinese* 21
Shin-Sen-Gumi Yakitori | *Japanese* 23

HERMOSA BEACH

Abigaile | *Amer.* 19
Akbar Cuisine | *Indian* 22
Bottle Inn | *Italian* 21
Chef Melba's | *Cal.* 26
Counter | *Burgers* 19
El Pollo Inka | *Peruvian* 21
Fritto Misto | *Italian* 22
Hot's Kitchen | *Eclectic* 25
NEW Kitchen/Perfecto | *Spanish* -
Martha's 22nd St. | *Amer.* 23
Mediterraneo | *Med.* 23
Palmilla | *Mex.* 18

Umami Burger | *Burgers* 23
Zane's | *Italian/Steak* 21

INGLEWOOD

Phillips BBQ | *BBQ* 24
Thai Dishes | *Thai* 20
Woody's BBQ | *BBQ* 24

LAX

Daily Grill | *Amer.* 19
Nate 'n Al | *Deli* 21
NEW Skewers/Morimoto | *Japanese* –
Thai Dishes | *Thai* 20

LONG BEACH

Alegria | *Nuevo Latino* 23
Beachwood BBQ | *BBQ* 23
Belmont Brewing | *Amer.* 20
Benley | *Viet.* 27
Café Piccolo | *Italian* 24
Congregation Ale | *Amer.* 18
Federal Bar | *Amer.* 19
555 East | *Steak* 25
Fuego/Maya | *Mex./Pan-Latin* 22
Gaucho | *Argent./Steak* 21
Gladstones | *Seafood* 17
Johnny Rebs' | *BBQ* 23
King's Fish | *Seafood* 21
La Crêperie | *French* 23
La Parolaccia | *Italian* 24
L'Opera | *Italian* 23
Lucille's | *BBQ* 22
McKenna's | *Seafood/Steak* 21
Michael's/Naples | *Italian* 27
Michael's Pizzeria | *Pizza* 27
Open Sesame | *Lebanese* 24
Parkers' Lighthouse | *Seafood* 22
P.F. Chang's | *Chinese* 17
Roscoe's | *Soul Food* 23
Simmzy's | *Amer.* 23
Sir Winston's | *Cal./Continental* 24
Sky Room | *Amer.* 23
Veggie Grill | *Vegan* 22
Wokcano | *Asian* 19
Yen | *Japanese* 22
Zephyr | *Veg.* 25

MANHATTAN BEACH

Beckers Bakery | *Bakery/Deli* 21
Brewco | *Amer.* 19
Café Pierre | *French* 24
NEW Chez Soi | *Cal.* –
NEW Circa | *Eclectic* –
Fishbar | *Seafood* 22
NEW Fishing/Dynamite | *Seafood* –
Hillstone/Houston's | *Amer.* 22
Il Fornaio | *Italian* 20
Izaka-ya/Katsu-ya | *Japanese* 25
Le Pain Quotidien | *Bakery* 18
NEW Little Sister | *Asian/Euro.* –
Mama D's | *Italian* 23
M.B. Post | *Amer.* 27
Open Sesame | *Lebanese* 24
Petros | *Greek* 24
Rock'n Fish | *Seafood* 20
Simmzy's | *Amer.* 23
Strand House | *Amer.* 20
Thai Dishes | *Thai* 20
Tin Roof | *Amer.* 23
Uncle Bill's | *Diner* 22
Valentino's | *Pizza* 22
Versailles | *Cuban* 22

REDONDO BEACH

Addi's | *Indian* 26
Asaka | *Japanese* 22
Bluewater | *Seafood* 21
Bouzy | *Amer.* 22
Cheesecake | *Amer.* 18
Chez Mélange | *Eclectic* 26
Coyote Cantina | *SW* 21
Gina Lee's | *Asian/Cal.* 24
Hudson Hse. | *Amer.* 21
Kincaid's | *Seafood/Steak* 22
Ocean Tava | *Indian* 25
Old Tony's | *Italian/Seafood* 20
Ortega 120 | *Mex.* 22
Pho Show | *Viet.* 19
Rock & Brews | *Pub* 18
W's China Bistro | *Chinese* 21
Zazou | *Med.* 25

SAN PEDRO

Limani Taverna | *Greek* 18
Think Café | *Amer./Eclectic* 23
22nd St. Landing | *Seafood* 22
Whale & Ale | *Pub* 19

TORRANCE

BCD Tofu | *Korean* 22
NEW Blaze | *Pizza* –
Buffalo Fire Dept. | *Amer.* 22
Christine | *Med./Pac. Rim* 27
Depot | *Eclectic* 25
El Pollo Inka | *Peruvian* 21
Five Guys | *Burgers* 16
Gonpachi | *Japanese* 19
Gyu-Kaku | *Japanese* 20
Lucille's | *BBQ* 22
Maruhide | *Japanese* –
Melting Pot | *Fondue* 15

Musha | *Japanese* 23
NEW Ocho 8 Taqueria | *Mex.* -
P.F. Chang's | *Chinese* 17
Ramen Hayatemaru | *Japanese* -
Ramen Yamadaya | *Japanese* 23
RA Sushi | *Japanese* 21
Santouka Ramen | *Japanese* 25
Veggie Grill | *Vegan* 22

WESTCHESTER

Alejo's/Eddie's italian | *Italian* 21
Ayara Thai | *Thai* 24
Buggy Whip | *Seafood/Steak* 19
Dinah's | *Diner* 18
In-N-Out | *Burgers* 23
Kabuki | *Japanese* 21
Paco's Tacos | *Mex.* 21
Truxton's | *Amer.* 20

Inland Empire

MORENO VALLEY

Portillo's | *Hot Dogs* 25

Pasadena & Environs

ARCADIA

Cheesecake | *Amer.* 18
Daikokuya | *Japanese* 24
Derby | *Steak* 23
Din Tai Fung | *Chinese* 26
101 Noodle | *Chinese* 23
Wood Ranch | *BBQ* 20
Zelo Pizzeria | *Pizza* 21

EAGLE ROCK

Auntie Em's | *Amer.* 22
Blue Hen | *Viet.* 21
CaCao | *Mex.* 24
Café Beaujolais | *French* 26
Casa Bianca | *Pizza* 23
NEW Little Beast | *Amer.* -
Oinkster | *Amer.* 21
Spitz | *Turkish* 22

LA CAÑADA FLINTRIDGE

Dish | *Amer.* 20
Taylor's | *Steak* 23

MONROVIA

Caffe Opera | *Amer./Eclectic* 21

PASADENA

Abricott | *Eclectic* 22
AKA Bistro | *Amer.* 23
Akbar Cuisine | *Indian* 22
All India | *Indian* 21
Arroyo | *Steak* 25
Azeen's | *Afghan* 26
B.A.D. Sushi | *Japanese* 22
Bistro 45 | *Cal.* 25
NEW Blaze | *Pizza* -
Burger Continental | *Mideast.* 18
Cafe Bizou | *French* 22
Café Santorini | *Med.* 21
Cafe Verde | *Cal./Pan-Latin* 23
Celestino | *Italian* 25
Cheesecake | *Amer.* 18
Cheval Bistro | *French* 23
Congregation Ale | *Amer.* 18
El Cholo | *Mex.* 19
Euro Pane | *Bakery* 25
Float | *Amer.* -
Gale's Restaurant | *Italian* 22
Gin Sushi | *Japanese* 22
Green St. | *Amer.* 21
Green St. Tavern | *Cal.* 23
Gyu-Kaku | *Japanese* 20
Hamburger Hamlet | *Diner* 18
Haven Gastropub | *Amer.* 19
Hillstone/Houston's | *Amer.* 22
Il Fornaio | *Italian* 20
Kabuki | *Japanese* 21
NEW Kal's Bistro | *Med.* -
La Grande Orange | *Cal.* 20
Le Pain Quotidien | *Bakery* 18
Louise's | *Cal./Italian* 19
Luggage Room | *Pizza* 23
Maison Akira | *French/Japanese* 26
Malbec | *Argent./Steak* 23
Maria's Italian | *Italian* 19
Marston's | *Amer.* 21
McCormick/Schmick | *Seafood* 18
Melting Pot | *Fondue* 15
Mijares | *Mex.* 18
Mi Piace | *Cal./Italian* 21
Original Tops | *Amer.* 22
NEW Osek Korean | *Korean* -
Panda Inn | *Chinese* 22
Parkway Grill | *Cal.* 26
P.F. Chang's | *Chinese* 17
Pie 'N Burger | *Diner* 20
Plate 38 | *Eclectic* 22
Racion | *Spanish* -
Raymond | *Cal.* 25
Real Food | *Vegan* 21
NEW Rice Thai | *Thai* -
Robin's BBQ | *BBQ* 22
Roscoe's | *Soul Food* 23
NEW Royce Wood-Fired | *Steak* 24

Roy's | *Hawaiian* 23
Ruth's Chris | *Steak* 25
Saladang | *Thai* 23
Settebello Pizzeria | *Pizza* 23
Slaw Dogs | *Hot Dogs* 22
Smitty's | *Amer.* 22
Stonefire | *BBQ* 21
Sushi Roku | *Japanese* 22
Tender Greens | *Amer.* 23
Twin Palms | *Amer.* -
Umami Burger | *Burgers* 23
Urth | *Amer.* 22
Vertical Wine | *Eclectic/Med.* 21
Wokcano | *Asian* 19
Yang Chow | *Chinese* 22
Zankou | *Med.* 21

SAN MARINO

Julienne | *Amer./French* 25

SOUTH PASADENA

Bistro/Gare | *French* 20
Firefly Bistro | *Amer.* 19
Gus's | *BBQ* 19
Mike & Anne's | *Amer.* 21
Shiro | *French/Japanese* 27

San Fernando Valley & Burbank

BURBANK

Bistro Provence | *French* 23
Chadaka | *Thai* 21
Daily Grill | *Amer.* 19
Gordon Biersch | *Pub* 18
Granville Cafe | *Amer.* 21
Kabuki | *Japanese* 21
Morton's | *Steak* 22
Mo's | *Amer.* 18
Olive/Thyme | *Eclectic* 22
P.F. Chang's | *Chinese* 17
Picanha | *Brazilian* 21
Poquito Más | *Mex.* 21
Porto's | *Bakery/Cuban* 25
Smoke Hse. | *Steak* 21
Wokcano | *Asian* 19
Zankou | *Med.* 21

CALABASAS

King's Fish | *Seafood* 21
Marmalade | *Amer.* 17
Rosti | *Italian* 17
Saddle Peak | *Amer.* 26
Sugarfish | *Japanese* 26
Toscanova | *Italian* 19

CANOGA PARK

Gyu-Kaku | *Japanese* 20
Yang Chow | *Chinese* 22

CHATSWORTH

Les Sisters | *Southern* 23
Poquito Más | *Mex.* 21
Stonefire | *BBQ* 21

ENCINO

Absolutely Pho | *Viet.* 20
Coral Tree | *Sandwiches* 19
Delmonico's | *Seafood* 23
Farfalla/Vinoteca | *Italian* 22
Hirosuke | *Japanese* 22
Itzik Hagadol | *Israeli* 20
Jerry's Deli | *Deli* 15
John O'Groats | *Amer.* 20
Katsu-ya | *Japanese* 27
Larsen's | *Steak* 24
Maria's Italian | *Italian* 19
More Than Waffles | *Amer.* 22
Mulberry St. Pizzeria | *Pizza* 23
Poquito Más | *Mex.* 21
Rosti | *Italian* 17
Stand | *Hot Dogs* 18
Veggie Grill | *Vegan* 22
Versailles | *Cuban* 22

GLENDALE

NEW Ara's Tacos | *Mex.* -
Carousel | *Mideast.* 25
Chi Dynasty | *Chinese* 20
Eat Well | *Amer.* 20
Farfalla/Vinoteca | *Italian* 22
Far Niente | *Italian* 24
Frida | *Mex.* 19
Granville Cafe | *Amer.* 21
Katsuya | *Japanese* 24
9021Pho | *Viet.* 21
Panda Inn | *Chinese* 22
Porto's | *Bakery/Cuban* 25
Raffi's Place | *Mideast.* 26
Trattoria Amici | *Italian* 21
Zankou | *Med.* 21

MONTROSE

Bashan | *Amer.* 27
Fat Dog | *Amer.* 20
Zeke's | *BBQ* 19

NORTH HOLLYWOOD

Bow & Truss | *Spanish* 18
Ca' del Sole | *Italian* 22
Counter | *Burgers* 19
Federal Bar | *Amer.* 19

Firenze | *Italian* 22
In-N-Out | *Burgers* 23
Pitfire | *Pizza* 22
Poquito Más | *Mex.* 21
Sanamluang Cafe | *Thai* 24
Umami Burger | *Burgers* 23
Zankou | *Med.* 21

NORTHRIDGE

Alessio/Bistro | *Italian* 21
Brent's Deli | *Deli* 26
Emle's | *Cal./Med.* 23
Falafel Palace | *Med./Mideast.* 22
Katsu-ya | *Japanese* 27
King's Burgers | *Burgers* 25
Maria's Italian | *Italian* 19
Musashi | *Japanese* 23
Wood Ranch | *BBQ* 20

RESEDA

BCD Tofu | *Korean* 22
Fab Hot Dogs | *Hot Dogs* 22
Pho So 1 | *Viet.* 25

SHERMAN OAKS

Bamboo Cuisine | *Chinese* 23
Barney's | *Burgers* 21
Blu Jam Café | *Amer./Euro.* 25
Boneyard | *BBQ* 22
Brats Brothers | *German* 22
Cafe Bizou | *French* 22
Carnival | *Lebanese* 25
Casa Vega | *Mex.* 19
Cheesecake | *Amer.* 18
Clay Oven | *Indian* 23
Great Greek | *Greek* 22
Gyu-Kaku | *Japanese* 20
Hamburger Hamlet | *Diner* 18
Il Tiramisù | *Italian* 22
In-N-Out | *Burgers* 23
Jinky's | *Diner* 20
Joe's Pizza | *Pizza* 23
La Pergola | *Italian* 25
Le Petit Rest. | *French* 23
Maria's Italian | *Italian* 19
Marmalade | *Amer.* 17
Mistral | *French* 26
Mulberry St. Pizzeria | *Pizza* 23
9021Pho | *Viet.* 21
Oliva | *Italian* 20
Panzanella | *Italian* 25
P.F. Chang's | *Chinese* 17
Poquito Más | *Mex.* 21
Ramen Yamadaya | *Japanese* 23
Sisley | *Italian* 19
Stanley's | *Cal.* 20

STUDIO CITY

Ahi | *Japanese* 23
Artisan | *Cheese/Sandwiches* 24
Art's | *Deli* 21
Asanebo | *Japanese* 29
Bistro Gdn. | *Continental* 21
Black Market | *Eclectic* 23
Bollywood | *Indian* 24
Caioti Pizza | *Pizza* 21
Chi Dynasty | *Chinese* 20
Chin Chin | *Asian* 19
Counter | *Burgers* 19
Daily Grill | *Amer.* 19
Du-par's | *Diner* 17
Firefly | *Amer.* 20
Five Guys | *Burgers* 16
NEW Girasol | *Amer.* -
Hugo's | *Cal.* 21
Il Tramezzino | *Italian* 22
In-N-Out | *Burgers* 23
Iroha | *Japanese* 24
Jinky's | *Diner* 20
Katsu-ya | *Japanese* 27
Kiwami | *Japanese* 27
Le Pain Quotidien | *Bakery* 18
Lotería! | *Mex.* 22
Marrakesh | *Moroccan* 21
Ombra | *Italian* 21
Poquito Más | *Mex.* 21
Ramen Jinya | *Japanese* 23
Raphael | *Amer.* 23
Sammy's Pizza | *Pizza* 19
Six | *Amer.* 19
Spark | *Amer.* 20
Sugarfish | *Japanese* 26
Take a Bao | *Asian* 19
Talésai | *Thai* 22
Teru Sushi | *Japanese* 21
Yen | *Japanese* 22

TARZANA

Absolutely Pho | *Viet.* 20
Hummus B&G | *Mideast.* 21
Il Tramezzino | *Italian* 22
Le Sanglier | *French* 24
Sol y Luna | *Mex.* 22
Zankou | *Med.* 21

TOLUCA LAKE

Malbec | *Argent./Steak* 23
Prosecco | *Italian* 25

UNIVERSAL CITY

Jody Maroni's | *Hot Dogs* 20
Miceli's | *Italian* 18

Panda Inn | *Chinese* 22

Wolfgang Puck Express/Bistro | *Cal.* 21

VAN NUYS

Dr. Hogly Wogly's | *BBQ* 22

In-N-Out | *Burgers* 23

Pho So 1 | *Viet.* 25

Sam Woo | *Chinese* 18

Smoke City | *BBQ* 22

Zankou | *Med.* 21

WEST HILLS

Alessio/Bistro | *Italian* 21

Stonefire | *BBQ* 21

WOODLAND HILLS

Adagio | *Italian* 22

Baker | *Bakery/Sandwiches* 24

Brandywine | *Continental* 27

Brother Sushi | *Japanese* 25

Cheesecake | *Amer.* 18

Fleming's | *Steak* 23

Giovanni Ristorante | *Italian* 21

In-N-Out | *Burgers* 23

Jerry's Deli | *Deli* 15

Kabuki | *Japanese* 21

Kate Mantilini | *Amer.* 20

Label's Table | *Sandwiches* 22

Maria's Italian | *Italian* 19

Morton's | *Steak* 22

Panini Cafe | *Italian/Med.* 21

P.F. Chang's | *Chinese* 17

Poquito Más | *Mex.* 21

Roy's | *Hawaiian* 23

Ruth's Chris | *Steak* 25

Slaw Dogs | *Hot Dogs* 22

Stand | *Hot Dogs* 18

San Gabriel Valley

ALHAMBRA

Boiling Crab | *Cajun/Seafood* 24

NEW Grill 'Em All | *Burgers* 19

101 Noodle | *Chinese* 23

Pho 79 | *Viet.* 23

Sam Woo | *Chinese* 18

Twohey's | *Amer.* 17

Wahib's | *Mideast.* 20

AZUSA

Congregation Ale | *Amer.* 18

CITY OF INDUSTRY

Honda-Ya | *Japanese* 21

CLAREMONT

La Parolaccia | *Italian* 24

Tutti Mangia | *Italian* 22

Walter's | *Eclectic* 20

DUARTE

Slaw Dogs | *Hot Dogs* 22

MONTEBELLO

Zankou | *Med.* 21

MONTEREY PARK

Cook's Tortas | *Mex.* 23

Daikokuya | *Japanese* 24

Duck Hse. | *Chinese* 22

Elite | *Chinese* 25

Ocean Star | *Chinese* 21

Shin-Sen-Gumi Yakitori | *Japanese* 23

PICO RIVERA

Dal Rae | *Continental* 25

ROSEMEAD

888 Seafood | *Chinese/Seafood* 23

Sea Harbour | *Chinese/Seafood* 25

ROWLAND HEIGHTS

BCD Tofu | *Korean* 22

Boiling Crab | *Cajun/Seafood* 24

Newport Seafood | *Chinese/Seafood* 26

SAN GABRIEL

Babita | *Mex.* 27

Golden Deli | *Viet.* 25

Newport Seafood | *Chinese/Seafood* 26

Sam Woo | *Chinese* 18

Conejo/Simi Valley/ Oxnard/Ventura & Environs

AGOURA HILLS/ OAK PARK

Café 14 | *Continental* 26

Grissini Ristorante | *Italian* 21

Hugo's | *Cal.* 21

Jinky's | *Diner* 20

Leila's | *Cal.* 27

Maria's Italian | *Italian* 19

Padri | *Italian* 22

Wood Ranch | *BBQ* 20

CAMARILLO

Lure Fish Hse. | *Seafood* 24

Safire | *Amer.* 25

Wood Ranch | *BBQ* 20

MOORPARK

Cafe Firenze | *Italian* 22

Wood Ranch | *BBQ* 20

OXNARD

Tierra Sur/Herzog | *Kosher/Med.* 28

SIMI VALLEY

Pho So 1 | *Viet.* 25

THOUSAND OAKS

Brats Brothers | *German* 22

Cheesecake | *Amer.* 18

Cholada | *Thai* 23

Grill on Alley | *Amer.* 24

Holdren's | *Seafood/Steak* 24

Jinky's | *Diner* 20

Mastro's | *Steak* 26

Mulberry St. Pizzeria | *Pizza* 23

P.F. Chang's | *Chinese* 17

NEW Public School 805 | *Amer.* -

Stonefire | *BBQ* 21

VENTURA

Bollywood | *Indian* 24

Brophy Bros. | *Seafood* 21

Cafe Fiore | *Italian* 22

71 Palm | *Amer./French* 24

Watermark on Main | *Amer.* 22

Wood Ranch | *BBQ* 20

WESTLAKE VILLAGE

Bollywood | *Indian* 24

Brent's Deli | *Deli* 26

Counter | *Burgers* 19

Farfalla/Vinoteca | *Italian* 22

Galletto | *Brazilian/Italian* 24

Lotería! | *Mex.* 22

Marmalade | *Amer.* 17

Mediterraneo | *Med.* 21

Melting Pot | *Fondue* 15

9021Pho | *Viet.* 21

Rustico | *Italian* 26

NEW Stonehaus | *Italian* -

Tuscany | *Italian* 26

Zin | *Amer.* 20

Santa Clarita Valley & Environs

SANTA CLARITA

Wokcano | *Asian* 19

SAUGUS/NEWHALL

Le Chêne | *French* 24

Wood Ranch | *BBQ* 20

VALENCIA

Marston's | *Amer.* 21

Salt Creek | *Steak* 19

Sisley | *Italian* 19

Stonefire | *BBQ* 21

Thai Dishes | *Thai* 20

Downtown/Koreatown

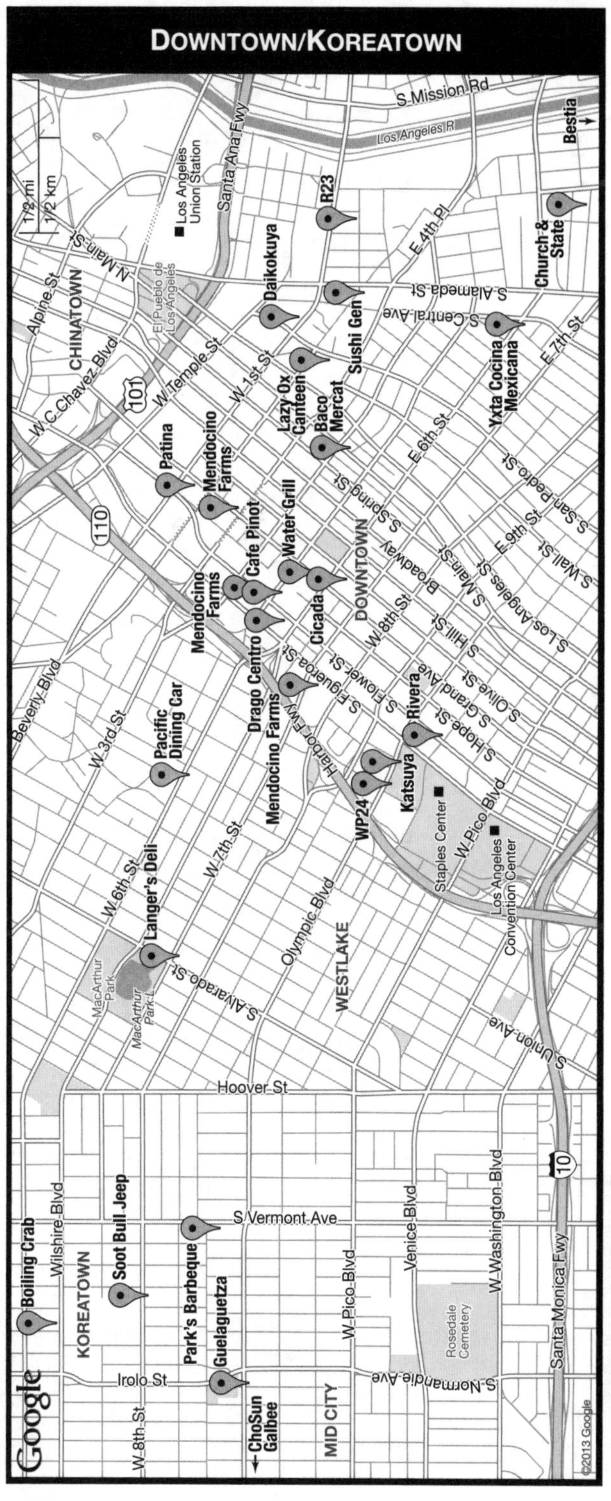

MAPS

Hollywood/West Hollywood

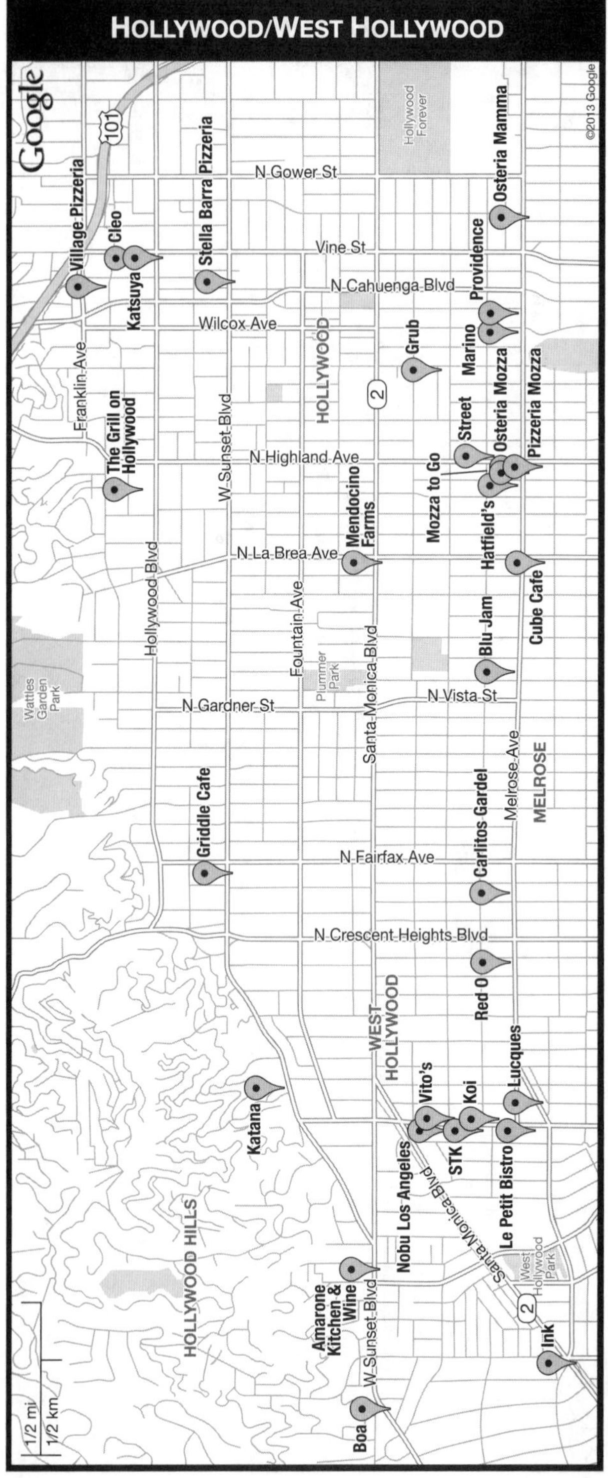

BEVERLY HILLS & ENVIRONS

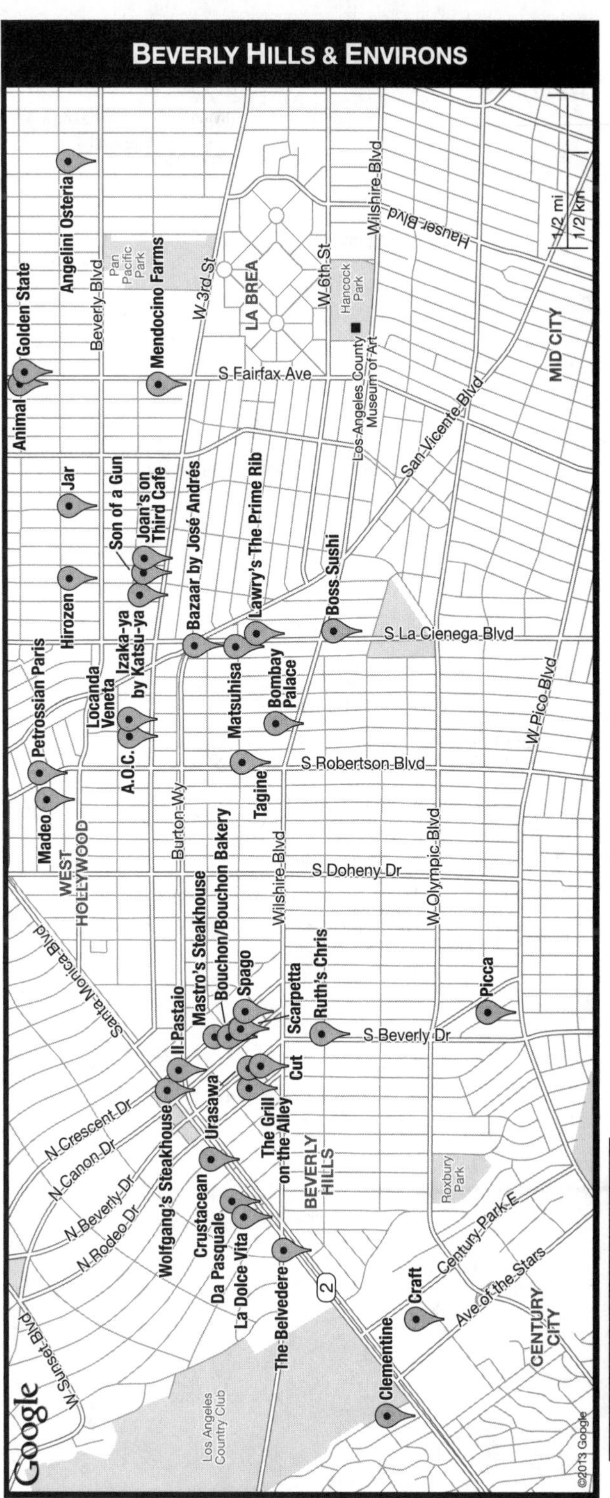

MAPS

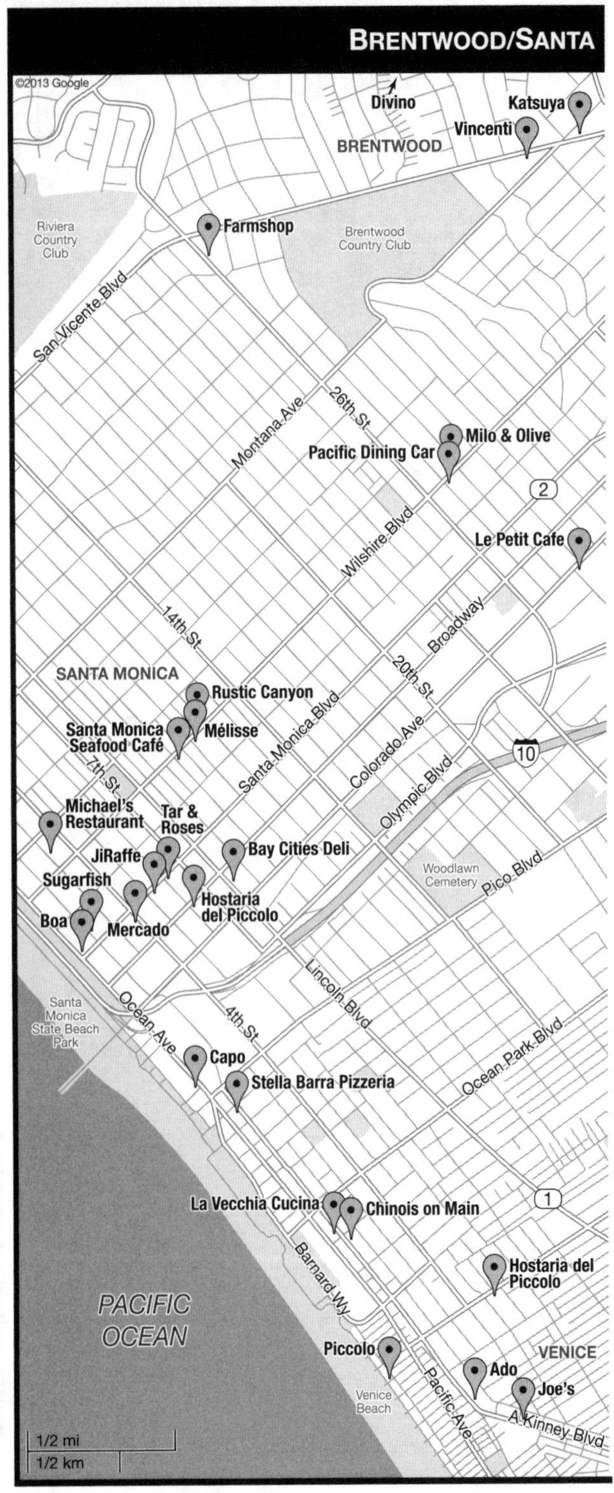
©2013 Google
Divino
Katsuya
Vincenti
BRENTWOOD
Riviera Country Club
Farmshop
Brentwood Country Club
San Vicente Blvd
Montana Ave
26th St
Milo & Olive
Pacific Dining Car
2
Wilshire Blvd
Le Petit Cafe
14th St
Broadway
20th St
SANTA MONICA
Rustic Canyon
Mélisse
Santa Monica Seafood Café
Santa Monica Blvd
Colorado Ave
10
7th St
Olympic Blvd
Michael's Restaurant
Tar & Roses
JiRaffe
Bay Cities Deli
Woodlawn Cemetery
Pico Blvd
Sugarfish
Boa
Mercado
Hostaria del Piccolo
Lincoln Blvd
Santa Monica State Beach Park
Ocean Ave
4th St
Capo
Stella Barra Pizzeria
Ocean Park Blvd
La Vecchia Cucina
Chinois on Main
1
Barnard Wy
Hostaria del Piccolo
PACIFIC OCEAN
Piccolo
VENICE
Ado
Joe's
Venice Beach
Pacific Ave
A Kinney Blvd
1/2 mi
1/2 km

ZAGAT
2014

Los Angeles Map

Most Popular Restaurants

Map coordinates follow each name. For multi-location restaurants, only flagship or central locations are plotted. Sections A-G show places in the city of Los Angeles and outlying regions (see adjacent map). Sections H-N show a detailed look at places in Beverly Hills (see reverse side of map).

1. Sugarfish by Sushi Nozawa† (C-7)
2. Angelini Osteria (K-8)
3. Mélisse (D-5)
4. Bazaar by José Andrés (M-5)
5. Spago (M-2)
6. Providence (C-6)
7. Osteria Mozza (C-6)
8. In-N-Out Burger† (E-6)
9. Lawry's The Prime Rib (M-5)
10. Mastro's Steakhouse (A-1, M-2)
11. Brent's Deli (A-4, B-1)
12. Pizzeria Mozza (C-6)
13. Cafe Bizou† (D-5)
14. Bouchon (M-2)
15. Lucques (K-5)
16. Ruth's Chris Steak House† (M-2)
17. The Palm (C-7, K-4)
18. Chinois on Main (D-5)
19. M.B. Post (F-6)
20. Din Tai Fung (B-9)
21. Bottega Louie (C-7)
22. Valentino* (D-5)
23. Bäco Mercat (C-7)
24. Drago Centro (C-7)
25. Umami Burger† (C-6)
26. A.O.C. (L-4)
27. Joe's (D-5)
28. JiRaffe (D-5)
29. Hatfield's (C-6)
30. Roy's† (C-7)
31. Ink (K-3)
32. Gjelina (C-7)
33. Morton's† (L-5)
34. Parkway Grill (B-8)
35. Boa (I-3, M-1)
36. Animal (K-7)
37. Father's Office* (C-5, D-6)
38. Water Grill (C-7, D-5)
39. Craft (C-5)
40. Michael's on Naples (G-9)
41. Piccolo* (D-5)
42. Daily Grill† (C-7)
43. Patina* (C-7)
44. Cut (M-2)
45. Philippe the Original (C-7)
46. Arroyo Chop House (B-8)
47. Border Grill (C-7, D-5)
48. Cheesecake Factory*† (B-8)
49. Crustacean (M-1)
50. The Grill on the Alley* (M-2
51. Il Fornaio† (M-2)
52. Saddle Peak Lodge* (C-3)
53. Apple Pan (C-5)
54. Tar & Roses* (D-5)
55. Fig & Olive (J-5)
56. Langer's Deli* (C-7)
57. Matsuhisa* (M-5)
58. Hillstone/Houston's† (D-5)
59. The Ivy (L-4)
60. Fleming's Prime (M-2)

*Indicates tie with above

†Indicates multiple branches

Hollywood
Park La Brea
Miracle Mile
CBS Television City
Pan Pacific Park
Hancock Park
Hillside Ave
Hollywood Blvd
Selma Ave
Sunset Blvd
De Longpre Ave
Fountain Ave
Lexington Ave
Norton Ave
Santa Monica Blvd
Romaine St
Willoughby Ave
Waring Ave
Melrose Ave
Clinton St
Rosewood Ave
Oakwood Ave
Beverly Blvd
W 1st St
W 2nd St
W 3rd St
Blackburn Ave
W 4th St
Colgate Ave
Drexel Ave
W 5th St
Maryland Dr
Lindenhurst Ave
W 6th St
Orange St
Warner Dr
Barrows Dr
W 8th St
W 9th St
Grove Ave
Alandele Ave
Fuller Ave
N Orange Grove Ave
Courtney Ave
N Stanley Ave
N Curson Ave
N Gardner St
N Fairfax Ave
Havenhurst Dr
N Crescent Heights Blvd
N Harper Ave
N Laurel Ave
N Ogden Dr
N Genesee Ave
N Vista St
N Martel Ave
N Fuller Ave
N Poinsettia Pl
Poinsettia Dr
Sierra Bonita Ave
N Edinburgh Ave
N Hayworth Ave
N Kilkea Dr
N Spaulding Ave
N Alta Vista Blvd
The Grove Dr
S Ogden Dr
S Gardner St
S Vista St
S Fuller Ave
S Poinsettia Pl
S Alta Vista Blvd
McCarthy Vista
San Vicente Blvd
S Fairfax Ave
S Orange Grove Ave
S Ogden Dr
S Benesee Ave
S Curson Ave
Courtyard Pl
Hauser Blvd
S Ridgeley Dr
S Burnside Ave
S Dunsmuir Ave
2
36
Map data ©2012 Google

ZAGAT